New Labour and the European Union

MANCHESTER
1824

Manchester University Press

New Labour and the European Union

Blair and Brown's logic of history

Oliver Daddow

Manchester University Press

Manchester and New York

distributed in the United States exclusively
by Palgrave Macmillan

Published by Manchester University Press
Oxford Road, Manchester M13 9NR, UK
and Room 400, 175 Fifth Avenue, New York, NY 10010, USA
www.manchesteruniversitypress.co.uk

Distributed in the United States exclusively by
Palgrave Macmillan, 175 Fifth Avenue, New York,
NY 10010, USA

Distributed in Canada exclusively by
UBC Press, University of British Columbia, 2029 West Mall,
Vancouver, BC, Canada V6T 1Z2

British Library Cataloguing-in-Publication Data
A catalogue record for this book is available from the British Library

Library of Congress Cataloging-in-Publication Data applied for

ISBN 978 0 7190 7640 4   *hardback*

ISBN 978 0 7190 7641 1   *paperback*

First published 2011

Typeset by R. J. Footring Ltd, Derby
Printed in Great Britain by Bell & Bain Ltd, Glasgow

For Elton, Justin, Tamsin, Joe and Freja

Contents

Images, figures, boxes and tables

Images

Figures

Boxes

Tables

Preface

To mark its Presidency of the Council of the European Union (EU) in 2009, the government of the Czech Republic commissioned artist David Černý to produce a sculpture put together by a team of twenty-seven artists, one from each member state, to celebrate diversity in the EU. When the huge installation, *Entropa*, was unveiled in the foyer of the Justus Lipsius building in Brussels in January 2009 it caused a furore in the political and art worlds alike. Controversy was initially sparked because it emerged that Černý had commissioned not twenty-seven people but just three assistants to build the piece, and had written fake artist profiles and spoof descriptions of the thinking behind their efforts in the accompanying brochure. Still more debate surrounded the nature of the stereotypes on offer. *Entropa* came in the form of a huge blue three-dimensional snap-out-and-build plastic modelling kit, containing striking static as well as multimedia and moving elements. Černý and his 'team' themed the work around 'the playful analysis of national stereotypes as well as individual characteristics of the original cultural identities' (Černý 2009). For example, Germany was represented by cars driving up and down autobahns laid out in a shape more than reminiscent of a Nazi Swastika, Sweden was portrayed as an Ikea-style piece of flat-packed furniture, Cyprus was sliced in half and the French were 'on strike'. The loudest public protest came from the Bulgarian ambassador to the EU, who was infuriated by his country's depiction as a series of Turkish squat toilets. He demanded that the sculpture be removed before it was even unveiled (Hines and Charter 2009). A compromise solution was found whereby the Bulgarian piece of the kit remained in place but was hidden from view under a black sheet.

Britain featured in the top left corner of *Entropa*, but to say it actually 'appeared' would be misleading because it was represented as an empty space. Twelve years on from Tony Blair's New Labour government coming to power exhorting Britain to engage constructively with the EU, and trying to help the British people feel at home in Europe, the impression persisted that Britain was both a member and non-member of the EU simultaneously. Britain, it could be argued, was in Europe geographically but not in spirit; in the EU diplomatically but not emotionally. Now, we could write off the Britain-as-empty-space idea as one artist's impression, a humorous yet mistaken understanding of where the New Labour government took British European policy after May 1997. Tony Blair would surely make this point. But if New Labour successfully turned Britain into a constructive European actor in policy terms, why, by the end of the party's term in office, did so many British people consistently still show themselves to be either apathetic about, or hostile to, the EU after all those years of being led by a Europhile Prime Minister? Or did the enthusiasm New Labour professed for the EU extend only as far as the Europeanized decision-making elites who worked with their EU counterparts on a day-to-day basis? What part did media coverage of the EU play in shaping the public's attitudes to the EU and what did New Labour do to try to effect change in the British approach to Europe? This book attempts to shed some fresh light on all these questions and in so doing answer one that has eluded academics and policy-makers for decades: why do the British people still seem psychologically distant from the EU?

I wrote this book to analyse the way the British (or is it the English?) *talk* about Europe, how they perpetually construct Europe as a hostile Other and how the images they hold about Europe are expressed culturally in the pages of the most popular tabloid and broadsheet newspapers. It is in these basic, everyday, but potent ways that the British have been kept in what I call a permanent state of discursive war with the continent of Europe. At its heart, the book explores the propaganda campaign New Labour undertook to undermine the appeal of this vision of Britain being separate from a dangerous and subversive Europe. It studies the various tactics the Prime Minister and Chancellor – taken to be the key progenitors of British foreign policy discourse – used in foreign policy speeches after 1997 to convince the country of the benefits of a European future. They did this first by challenging the British public to rethink the meaning of 'Britishness' and then by inviting them to reconsider memories of the national past. Tony Blair and Gordon Brown encouraged the public to see the 'Britain and Europe' story not as one of an eternal separateness from the continent but as an always-European one in which globalization and interdependence transcended the narrow nationalist take on Britain's past. The central argument in the book is that we can see in Blair and Brown's foreign and economic policy speeches their logic of history at work. It was always going to be difficult for the government to alter attitudes on an emotive question such as 'Europe' in a relatively short space of time and Blair and Brown were clearly up against it from the outset. However, through a close reading of their European discourses we come to a nuanced understanding of how it was they tried to project their own values and ideals onto the policies developed by the government and how they fought for them on the European and world stages. We find that New Labour was unsuccessful in trying to move the public towards its vision of Europe for reasons partly of their own making but partly beyond their control. So this book *is* about the 'Europe question' in British politics but about much more too. It is about the art of rhetoric, persuasion and the techniques of modern political communication; it is about Blair and Brown's leadership styles and management of the New Labour project; and, not least, it is about Britain's place in the world in the twenty-first century. But much more than all that, this book is about the clash between two logics of history: the nationalist and the globalist. We find that the former logic maintains the upper hand in Britain – for now at any rate.

Acknowledgements

In writing this book I have benefited enormously from testing out my arguments and evidence on willing victims at conferences and workshops in Berlin, Syracuse, London, Warwick, Austin, St Andrews, San Diego, Lodz, Cork, Portsmouth, Cambridge, Reading, Florence, Leicester and New Orleans. I have further benefited from presenting working papers at academic departments in Loughborough, Belfast, Leeds, Keele, Chichester, Liverpool, Aberystwyth, Plymouth and Connecticut. At these events, people too numerous to mention provided me with ideas, critique, inspiration and nuggets of information and I am grateful to them all, as I am to four generations of 'Euroscepticism in Britain' third-year students in the Department of Politics, History and International Relations at Loughborough University. Away from the conference circuit, I would like to thank the following for taking the time to discuss with me the subject matter of the book: Richard Aldrich, Dave Allen, Matthew Broad, Philip Catney, Andrew Chandler, Jamie Costulis, Helen Drake, Stephen Dyson, Patrick Finney, Maurice Fitzgerald, Robert Foley, Laura Ford, Hugo Frey, Jamie Gaskarth, Carine Germond, Peter Golding, Keith Jenkins, Piers Ludlow, David McCourt, Hilary McDermott, Anand Menon, Sue Morgan, Alun Munslow, Kai Opperman, Helen Parr, Viet-Hai Phung, Andrea Porter, Patrick Porter, Tapio Raunio, Oliver Reinert, John Richardson, Linda Risso, Pauline Schnapper, David Seawright, Jan Selby, Alistair Shepherd, Jennifer Sterling-Folker, Aleks Szczerbiak, William Wallace, Mark Webber, Dominic Wring and John Young. I would like to blame one, some or all of these people for any errors or omissions that appear in this book, but unfortunately I cannot; they are my responsibility alone and I am happy to correct them for future editions. Thanks are especially due to all those current and recently serving policy-makers who kindly gave their time in interview, to Lawrence Freedman for getting the ball rolling and to their staff for helping arrange the meetings. The proof-reading phase of the book coincided with a thoroughly enjoyable Visiting Fellowship at the University of California at Berkeley. I would like to thank everyone at the Center for British Studies, particularly Mark Bevir, Ethan Shagan and Candace Groskreutz, as well as the staff at International House, for helping me settle in and making me feel so welcome during my stay.

I am grateful to Steve Bell for permission to reproduce his cartoon on the book cover. Thanks also to John Jensen for permission to reproduce his cartoon in chapter 2 (image 3, p. 45) and to Jane Newton and the University of Kent's British Cartoon Archive for sending me the image, to Sinead Porter for tracking down and sending me the articles and cartoons from the *Sun* which appear in this volume (images 2, 5 and 6, pp. 6, 178 and 204), to the *Sun*/NI Syndication for copyright permission, and to David Scripps and Mel Knight for arranging to send me the *Daily Mirror* front page from 24 June 1996, reproduced in chapter 5 (image 4, p. 111). Thanks are also due to Stuart Notholt and the Campaign for an Independent Britain for permission to reproduce the material from its website in box 5 (chapter 6, p. 140). Anna Horolets kindly gave me permission to quote from her unpublished conference paper in chapter 5. Every effort has been made to secure necessary permissions to reproduce copyright material in this work, though in some cases it has proved impossible to trace copyright holders. If any omissions are brought to my notice, I will be happy to include appropriate acknowledgements in any subsequent edition.

Finally, and by no means least, a big thank you to my excellent editor, Tony Mason, for his support for this project and all the members of the MUP production team – especially Sarah Hunt and Ralph Footring – who have worked so professionally on it behind the scenes.

Abbreviations

BNP	British National Party
BSA	British Social Attitudes
CAP	Common Agricultural Policy
CBI	Confederation of British Industry
CIB	Campaign for an Independent Britain
DfID	Department for International Development
EC	European Communities
ECSC	European Coal and Steel Community
EEC	European Economic Community
EFTA	European Free Trade Association
EMU	Economic and Monetary Union
EPERN	European Parties, Elections and Referendums Research Network
EU	European Union
FCO	Foreign and Commonwealth Office
GDP	gross domestic product
IPPR	Institute for Public Policy Research
KWIC	keywords in context
MP	Member of Parliament
NAFTA	North American Free Trade Agreement
NATO	North Atlantic Treaty Organization
NHS	National Health Service
OERN	Opposing Europe Research Network
PLP	Parliamentary Labour Party
SCU	Strategic Communications Unit
SEA	Single European Act
SME	small and medium-size enterprise
TUC	Trades Union Congress
UKIP	United Kingdom Independence Party
UN	United Nations
WEU	Western European Union
WMD	weapons of mass destruction

Chapter 1

Introduction

Re-reading my speeches about Europe over the years, at the beginning, the task was to put Britain back at the centre of the European debate. We did so but it was never easy. There was always a feeling that at best, the British role was to be the pebble in the shoe; the thing that made others stop and think; but not the one that did the walking. (Blair 2006a)

But because of the intense pressures that arise from globalisation, Europe is now entering the second stage of its history as a union and is finding that the agenda relevant to its first phase – the era of a trade bloc – is quite different for its second stage – the Europe facing global competition. (Brown 2004d)

This book studies Tony Blair and Gordon Brown's combined attempt to sell the idea of a European future to the British people. It does so by analysing the propaganda offensive on which the Prime Minister and Chancellor of the Exchequer embarked after coming into office in May 1997 to convert a hesitant, broadly Eurosceptical public into a nation comfortable with the prospect of taking a full and active part in the life and work of the European Union (EU). Patchy at best in opposition, mainly to avoid opening itself up to attack on the thorny question of 'Europe', New Labour's thinking on foreign policy developed rapidly once in office. This book explores the lengths to which Blair and Brown were prepared to go to inform, persuade and cajole the British public into believing that being at the heart of European decision-making was in the country's best interests economically, politically, strategically and, crucially, emotionally and psychologically. It is, in essence, an account of New Labour's tricky encounter with pervasive and deeply rooted discourses about 'Europe' in Britain, as well as the tactics the government deployed to undermine them. When all is said and done, however, it shows how the government failed to make anything other than a faint impression on a nation deeply mired in its nationalist past. My aim in writing the book has been to cast some new and much-needed light on the ideas underpinning New Labour's propaganda in favour of a

European future. By considering the logic underpinning Blair and Brown's arguments about the British in Europe, I have tried to bring to centre stage an aspect of New Labour's foreign policy that has been strangely overlooked in the existing literature: political speeches.

Whatever the technological changes and challenges wrought by globalization and the twenty-four-hours-a-day, seven-days-a-week news media, political leaders still have to use the conventional tools of language, persuasion and image to try to shape the contours of national political debates, as well as those conducted in regional and global organizations. They have done this in increasingly creative ways, and New Labour invested as much time in office as any modern government in developing its strategic communications around media-friendly soundbites and messages. Maintaining consensus around existing norms, values and practices is one thing; generating a consensus around new sets of norms, values and practices can be extremely arduous given the nature of the environment into which a leader's targeted information missile is fired. Over the vexed question of Europe, however, this is exactly what Blair and Brown tried to do. The government's ambition was simple: to build a 'new consensus' (Brown 1997e) around the idea that Britain should play an active and wholehearted part in the EU through a policy described as 'constructive engagement with Europe' (Brown 1998f; Brown 1999d). To achieve this Blair, Brown and their teams set about rethinking the meaning of the national past in the present. By devising and espousing a new discourse they hoped to convey their approach pithily and as convincingly as possible. As New Labour saw it, British national history was overwhelmingly used by Eurosceptics to point up the differences between Britain and the British on the one hand and Europe and the Europeans on the other. The meaning of the past for Eurosceptics pointed the British *away* from Europe and therefore limited the legitimacy of any proactively Europeanist policy platform. Blair and Brown wanted to recast the British national past as part of European and, indeed, global history.

New Labour therefore acceded to power in 1997 on the back of a manifesto underscoring the party's modern left-of-centre credentials as well as its internationalist heritage. It set itself up, indeed, as 'the political arm of none other than the British people as a whole' (Labour Party 1997). However, while it pledged to represent the British people, New Labour wanted in fact to prompt those same people to reconsider the meaning of the nation's history, in order to help the party build a government-led consensus around a more positively inclined European dimension to British foreign policy. New Labour, it seems, wanted to represent a *different sort* of Britain, a *different kind* of British people. Far from Britain being

eternally cut off from the continent – or opposed to it – it was suggested, Britain had always and ever been a European country, and
the moment had arrived to recognize this. Economic, political and
cultural interdependence between countries, which Blair identified
as 'the characteristic of the modern world' (Blair 2006e), had, he explained, been accelerating for hundreds of years. Given modern mass
communication, the British simply noticed their interconnectedness
more now than in previous decades and should act accordingly.
In New Labour's rendering, therefore, British history could easily
be told as *part of* the European story rather than as the 'island
story' beloved by nationalist Eurosceptics. This book is about the
clash between those alternative visions of the British past, present
and future. As New Labour had it, British history pointed *towards*
Europe; in the Eurosceptics' logic, it pointed *away* from Europe.

To set the scene for what follows in the study, this introduction
is split into four main sections. The first argues that, in attempting
to devise a successful propaganda offensive, the New Labour government was on the back foot from the beginning, such was the appeal of
the Britain-as-separate-from-Europe conception of the national past.
The second details why I take the potentially controversial stance
that British European policy under New Labour is a case where the
government failed to achieve its objectives. This is certainly not the
line that Blair and Brown would take, so it is worth justifying the
basic premise of the study in detail. The third part surveys the literature which tries to explain the apparent failure by New Labour to
leave a positive, Europeanist legacy to British European policy. It
begins with a minority of writers who are kind to Blair and Brown
by arguing that they transformed Britain's relations with the EU
after 1997, until the Iraq invasion blew apart the EU–US bridge
New Labour had carefully constructed. It moves on to those writers
who are highly critical, seeing no real European strategy at all on
the government's part. It ends by studying the biggest group, that
is, of 'mid-range' commentators, critical of the ways in which the
supposedly principled question of Europe was subordinated to pragmatic electoral concerns and domestic party positioning. My book
sits most easily with the last group, albeit for quite different reasons
from those conventionally offered up by this school of interpretation.
The last main part of the chapter explains why this study tells the
story of New Labour's European policy through political speeches,
arguing that studying the language of policy allows us to see into
Blair and Brown's minds at work as they fought – sometimes with
each other – to develop a policy strategy that was simultaneously
'European' enough to satisfy their personal agendas and their
party's ambitions for Britain, but not so challenging that it might

risk alienating the 'middle England' voters who had been so helpful in bringing them to power in 1997. Uppermost in Blair and Brown's minds was the need to appease, or keep on side, a huge swathe of voters who might have voted for New Labour but who were not necessarily signed up to the idea of 'New Britain'. A final section of this introduction then outlines the argument and structure of the remainder of the study.

I. An ambiguous offensive

Between July and December 2008 France held the Presidency of the Council of the EU. Along with an ambitious work programme across the EU policy agenda (French Presidency 2008), the French government decided to mark the occasion very visibly and in glorious technicolour by lighting up the north side of the Eiffel Tower and adorning it with the yellow stars of the EU flag (image 1). Every evening for two months from 30 June 2008 this physical monument

Image 1. Eiffel Tower during the French Presidency of the EU, 2008.

to France and the French people proudly glowed blue, the circle of stars reflecting back at it off the river Seine. This was not the first time the Tower had been lit differently from its usual orange-gold to mark a big national occasion. The new millennium, the Chinese New Year in 2004 and the country's hosting of the Rugby World Cup in 2007 all saw the Tower coloured in celebration. Nor was it the first time the Tower had been used to give physical expression to France's Europeanism. On 9 May 2006 the Eiffel Tower was lit blue to mark the twentieth celebration of 'Europe Day', albeit without the innovation of the yellow stars included for the Presidency (Reuters 2008). It is instructive to compare the easy public embrace of the idea of Europe in France with the difficult, less accommodating approach to the EU prevalent in many areas of British political, media and public life. In Britain, the symbolism of the EU as represented in its flag and the mock 'national' anthem is routinely derided for hubristically portending the emergence of a 'superstate' that unstitches the fabric of life and traditions in sovereign member states (Adams 2008; Chapman 2009; National Policy Institute 2009).

One manifestation of this approach that sees a European identity as being antithetical or opposed to a notional British identity* is how the EU flag is transposed onto famous British national symbols of governance and statehood in press articles warning against the dangers of further British integration into the EU. For example, image 2 shows a mocked up photo of the House of Commons that appeared alongside an article from the popular British tabloid newspaper the *Sun* in September 2007 entitled 'No to a United States of Europe', in which its political editor, George Pascoe-Watson, judged that: 'The new European Constitution threatens to transform virtually every aspect of British life for ever' – none of it for the better.

---

* This book studies Euroscepticism in Britain, British policy towards the EU and British press attitudes to Europe. However, the expressions of opposition to the EU explored below are in many ways *English* expressions of angst; they rely crucially on English historical stories and on English symbolism and are, arguably, at their most common and most vitriolic in the English editions of the newspapers referred to in the study. My argument is that Tony Blair and Gordon Brown had in mind this variant of English nationalist scepticism when they came to try to alter opinions about 'Europe' in Britain. This is to deny neither the existence nor the import of opposition to the EU in Wales, Scotland and Northern Ireland; it is, rather, to suggest that detailed accounts of this opposition and its effect on New Labour policies and discourses are beyond the scope of this study. This confusion over terminology, Krishnan Kumar reminds us, is testament to the historically complex creation of a British identity, which goes back centuries and which manifests itself in the routine conflation of Britain with England. 'English – I mean British.' Does this confusion over nationality so often arise in the minds of the Scots, Welsh and Northern Irish? (Kumar 2003: 1. See also Gamble 2003: 18–22; Robbins 1998.)

WE TOLD EU SO..
EU flags flutter outside the Houses of
Parliament in our mocked-up picture
symbolising the massive impact the
Constitution would have on Britain's
treasured freedom to govern itself

Image 2. 'We told EU so', *Sun*, 23 September 2007, p. 4.

The accompanying image of EU flags fluttering over the Palace of
Westminster, the seat of Parliament, graphically illustrated his
contention that 'Brussels is relentlessly bolstering its control over
Britain and the rest of Europe'. Any such European entanglement
would detract from Britain's parliamentary and judicial sovereignty
because power under the Lisbon Treaty would flow *from* Britain *to*
the EU institutions in Belgium (Pascoe-Watson 2007). The picture
could just as easily have shown the EU flag flying over the Queen's
official residence down the Mall at Buckingham Palace or twelve
yellow stars circling the face of Big Ben and the point about the
British in Europe would have been the same. Where French national
identity seems indissoluble from its identity as a European country,
Britain's status as a European country is hotly contested. In France
as in Britain there is opposition to the EU across the political
spectrum and in the country at large (Flood 1995). This resistance

reached new levels during the 1990s, when it crystallized around the debates surrounding the Treaty of Maastricht in the early to middle years of the decade (Benoit 1997) and culminated in the *'non'* in the referendum on the Constitutional Treaty in 2005. Britain appears, however, to suffer many more agonized contortions than France about its status as part of the European family of nations, where zero-sum identity constructions take 'more Europe' to mean 'less Britain'. The juxtaposition of images 1 and 2 makes this abundantly clear. In France there is a broad consensus that the country is already and inextricably *in* Europe, *is* European – the yellow stars on the blue Eiffel Tower are a reality – whereas there is less than total assent in Britain that it is a European country by virtue of either its geography or its history. Pictures of EU flags hovering over the Houses of Parliament seem to imply that Britain is not European yet; it will become so only if the government connives to sign up to integrationist measures such as the Lisbon Treaty. The message is a simple one: Britain is not European.

Pascoe-Watson's visceral opposition to the EU was never welcomed by Tony Blair, who resigned from office in June 2007 having spent a decade trying to improve the image of the EU in the eyes of the British media and public. Supposedly the most Europhile Prime Minister Britain had had since Edward Heath, the Prime Minister responsible for taking the country into the European Economic Community (EEC) in 1973, Blair was explicit about the place Europe occupied in his foreign policy strategy from the moment he took office. He had already sketched the contours of his approach two years before, in a speech on 'Britain in Europe' at the London think-tank Chatham House (covered in Scott 2004: 207–12; and reprinted in Blair 1996: 280–7). The ideas set out in this speech crucially moulded his European thought and pronouncements in office, particularly as far as his concepts of patriotism, self-confidence and 'constructive engagement' went, as well as his understanding of the meaning of the national past. During his victory speech outside Downing Street on 2 May 1997, the newly elected Prime Minister began by talking about the improvements he wanted to make to the country's education system, its National Health Service (NHS) and its overall economic performance, all staples of the preceding election campaign. Foreign policy received only cursory, yet telling, attention: 'it shall be a government, too, that gives this country strength and confidence in leadership both at home and abroad, particularly in respect of Europe' (Blair 1997b). This was a classic statement of Blair's foreign policy agenda, for two reasons. First, he sought to demonstrate that the national interest would be safe in Labour's hands through his stress on continuity with past approaches.

Incoming Prime Ministers always pledge to strengthen Britain's standing and status in the world and the majority of Blair's words were given over to reinforcing that agenda. Second, however, we see some distinctive Blair in the last phrase, 'particularly in respect of Europe', which need not have been included to help that sentence resonate with the public. Blair's refrain from first to last was that he wanted to build a 'young country' in his own image and, maybe influenced by some fond early memories of growing up in Australia, he clearly valued the participation of 'confident, outward bound, and "up for it"' types of people to help him achieve this (Blair 2006c). Becoming closer to Europe was the means by which he sought to modernize Britain. Why did he not go down the easier route of saying he would enhance the 'special relationship', or strengthen the United Nations (UN), or pledge to tackle global poverty, or bring about peace in the Middle East? Those final words on foreign policy, 'particularly in respect of Europe', were no doubt pored over and then included for a reason. They reflected Blair's desire to make lasting and positive changes not just to British policy in Europe but also to the way the country as a whole – not just an already Europeanized diplomatic elite – *related* to Europe. As Sally Morgan, a close adviser to Blair, has reflected, in 1997, before Blair had developed any ideas about liberal interventionism or confronting terrorists, dictators or poverty around the globe, 'a commitment to the EU was a strong tenet of New Labour, in the formation of it; it was one of the pillars ... that was there from the beginning' (interview with Morgan).

This unequivocal opening gambit masked a sobering reality for the Europeanists who might have been tempted to construe Blair's time in Number 10 as heralding a new dawn in British European policy, for two reasons. The first harbinger of doom was that Blair's thinking on Europe was not yet fully formed or particularly substantive at this stage, if it ever became so. As one Blair biographer has put it, 'Blair's thinking about the EU ... lacked the long pedigree of visceral commitment of the true Europhile. His position was pragmatic and opportunistic – as was much of his thinking' (Seldon 2005: 316). According to this interpretation it is too simplistic to read 'Blair' for 'Heath', whatever the apparent similarities in their European rhetoric or professed ambitions. On general election day Blair put Europe at the centre of his project for national renewal, but he had spent the previous month making more than the odd comment that resonated with the opinion of the very sceptics he would have to confront once in government. Casting doubt on whether the single currency would even work, cautioning that it might not be in British interests to join and affecting sentiment for the image of the Queen's head on the pound, Blair's electoral strategy culminated in him declaring in the *Sun* on 22 April 1997, 'I will have no truck with a European superstate. If there are moves to create that dragon I will slay it' (Blair 1997a). We return to Blair's pre-election Euroscepticism in chapter 7 but a few remarks on it are in order here. Summing up on Blair's apparently 'jingoistic' stance before polling day (Seldon 2005: 317), Andrew Rawnsley has pointed out that he was 'talking the language of Europhobia to win an election, but nothing had been surrendered in policy' (Rawnsley 2001: 73). Rawnsley's argument is that we can ignore the language and judge Blair by the substance of his policy on Europe, which was more positive than his naked electioneering rhetoric would suggest. That may be so, but it rather depends on how we judge the policy and it was far from clear even in 1997 what that policy would be, who would be leading it and what impact it would or could have on British public opinion.

This feeds into the second reason why Europhiles might justifiably have been wary of Blair's Europeanism on the steps of Downing Street in 1997. As central as he was, Blair was by no means the only player in the making or execution of New Labour's European policy. When Rawnsley argued that nothing had been surrendered in policy terms, he overlooked some critical countervailing forces working against Blair being able to put a Europe-centred foreign policy into action after 1997. Mostly, these forces coalesced around the figure of Gordon Brown. The Chancellor of the Exchequer throughout Blair's time as Prime Minister looms large in any discussion of Blair's policies, character, opinions, leadership style and manner of taking decisions. If that is true of the New Labour years in general then it is most acutely seen in the conduct of its European policy. It is open to question whether Brown had the same level of passion as Blair did for Britain playing a greater part in the EU – not least economically – yet it is too simplistic to say that the Prime Minister was 'pro' while the Chancellor was 'anti' (following Seldon 2005: 666). It is perhaps fairer to suggest that neither the Chancellor, his close advisers such as Ed Balls and Charlie Whelan nor large swathes of the Treasury team they headed were convinced about the economic merits of Britain joining the single currency. In fact, as Robert Peston, a close observer of Brown, has remarked, 'innate mistrust of our friends in Europe ... has been a characteristic of the Treasury for decades' (Peston 2005: 179). Establishment Britain still shuddered at the memory of the damage done to the reputation and image of John Major's Conservative government when sterling was forced unceremoniously out of the Exchange Rate Mechanism during 'Black Wednesday' in September 1992 (detailed in Stephens 1997: 226–62). After that episode, notes Simon Jenkins, 'Division over Europe, magnified in the press, dogged [Major's] every step' (Jenkins

2007: 162; for a quantitative study of the extent of the Conservative Party's 'rebellion' over Europe see Berrington and Hague 1998). The Treasury (and many a British politician) learnt a harsh lesson that day about the potential dangers of British entanglement in the EU's schemes for closer economic integration. It is also noteworthy that, as shadow Chancellor at the time, Brown had supported the government's decision to join the Exchange Rate Mechanism (Bower 2007: 74–5, 77, 96; O'Donnell and Whitman 2007: 268). While the single currency might not have been 'real' in 1997 it was the most pressing concern facing policy-makers in Britain and on the continent. Its name had been agreed upon in 1995, the conditions of the Stability and Growth Pact were in place, and Brussels institutions were legislating on its introduction and deliberating how the economics of the new currency would be managed by the European Central Bank. By May 1998 – exactly one year after New Labour came to power – decisions had to be taken on which countries would join in the first wave of euro entrants in January 1999 (BBC 1997). An economic move with clear political implications, the euro was to dog New Labour's early attempts to generate a Europeanist consensus within Whitehall, let alone in the country at large. While Blair was convinced of the political case for joining the euro, but not so much so that he would risk a major split within government over the issue, Brown and his Treasury team were firmly of the opposite mind. The Treasury worried that the British economy could be unduly harmed by another false move in economic integration, while Brown calculated that it was a risk to the credibility of the government to be involved in a potentially damaging economic adventure in Europe. Effectively handing control over the economic agenda to Brown and the Treasury meant Blair was always going to be on the back foot over the creation of a positive European policy in which British membership of the single currency was the central plank.

It would always be difficult for Blair or Brown to put Britain at the 'heart' of Europe (still the refrain in Brown 2009b) when at the heart of New Labour there was no clear thinking on how best to approach the Europe question. This played out in New Labour's 1997 election manifesto, 'Because Britain deserves better'. There were the odd elements of novelty but these tended to be in areas such as human rights, global poverty and the environment (for a good discussion of the overall foreign policy agenda in the manifesto see Williams 2005: 15–17). It predictably featured lots of partisan point-scoring against the 'shambles of the last six years' and Conservative policy towards the EU under Major, which was 'riven by faction', and Labour's tenth election promise of ten was to 'give Britain the leadership in Europe which Britain and Europe need' (Labour Party 1997). Brown's mark was made via the commitment to hold a referendum on membership of the single currency and the six-point agenda for reforming the EU, which brought British interests persistently to the fore: 'Europe isn't working in the way this country and Europe need. But to lead means to be involved, to be constructive, to be capable of getting our own way.' Even the commitment to signing the Social Chapter at the end of the manifesto's proposed reform agenda was hedged with qualifications and the need to channel the EU's 'social agenda' into realms, and in ways, that would suit British national interests and promote the Anglo-Saxon neoliberal economic model (Labour Party 1997). What there was in the manifesto on foreign and defence policy centred on Britain's relations with Europe but underscored the party's commitment to the North Atlantic Treaty Organization (NATO) and to the Trident nuclear capability, both of which were uncontentious areas of bipartisan agreement. Where Europe featured, it did so in a manner that spoke more of the Brown agenda than the Blair one, bringing seriously into doubt Rawnsley's argument that 'Of all [Blair's] strategic objectives few were so central to his project as the European Question' (Rawnsley 2001: 73). The wording of the 1997 manifesto seems to suggest either that Blair's own Europeanism has to be called into question, or that he had already been outflanked by Brown before New Labour took power. Perhaps the most likely explanation combines the two: Blair was a convinced Europeanist only until it threatened New Labour's electoral prospects, its relations with the key sectors of the press or the internal harmony of the government.

From the above we can start to pull out some of the key themes running through this book. First, Britain's awkward relationship with the EU stems in no small measure from conceptions of the national interest and national identity which are antithetical to the idea of a concentric circle, or multi-level, approach to identity in which the 'British' component sits inside or below a 'European' identity (Schnapper 2011: 8). The zero-sum conception of British–European relations causes suspicion and hostility not only towards the EU but also in some quarters towards the entire idea of 'Europe' that underpins the project. Second, we see the malleability of the linguistic construction of the British debates about Europe. I have been intentionally loose in not defining key terms so far, in order to raise awareness of the very real problems of studying representations of 'Europe' in 'Britain' with reference to the 'media', the 'press', the 'public' and 'politicians'. It is equally difficult to deal effectively with such slippery terms as 'pro-European', 'Europhile', 'Europhobe' and 'Eurosceptic', such classifications inevitably saying as much about the agent doing the classifying as the person, organization or political party being classified. The third issue pertains to the structural constraints facing New Labour in assuming the guise of a 'pro-European' government actively seeking to challenge what it saw as a Eurosceptical consensus in Britain. The book unashamedly centres on the words of Blair and Brown, who argued the case for Europe on the grounds of a fresh idea of Europe, a new understanding of Britishness, 'enlightened patriotism', the EU as international actor and a re-rendering of British and European history. This focus on agents is not, I hope, to downplay the significance of structural constraints militating against the development of a more positive EU policy on the part of the New Labour governments after 1997. Where this book diverges from previous studies is that, in seeking explanations for the failings of New Labour's European policy, it looks beyond both the structural constraints and the personal politicking and policy disagreements over the EU. It instead leans more towards the European discourses Blair and Brown put about in order to try to convince their party, the media and the public – perhaps even each other – of the merits of European integration. Take away the structural constraints, I suggest, and we still find discourses riven with inconsistencies, mired in the past and therefore lacking in the narrative power to persuade *at the level of language itself*, which is where any strategic communications initiative has to be pitched in order to be successful. In terms of putting a consistently positive case for Europe, Blair might usefully have heeded the advice of the novelist John Updike: 'The world is quick-sand. Find the straight path and stick to it' (Updike 1991a: 198). On the evidence presented in this book, Blair and Brown did not necessarily know what path they wanted to take with regard to European policy and they were too often sucked back into rehashing the very ideas about British foreign policy they told the public they were trying to escape. The next part of the introduction explains why I am so critical of European policy during the Blair–Brown years, going so far as to label it a case of policy failure.

II. Policy failure?

We achieved enlargement. We took over, with France, the shaping of European defence. We formulated the economic reform programme from Lisbon onwards. Even where we divided from others, we did so with allies. Finally, we put through a budget deal that most thought couldn't be done. (Blair 2006a)

I think it's one of the things he would leave office feeling most unhappy about really, that he hadn't managed to change things. (Interview with Morgan)

By the time of his valedictory lecture tour that began in 2006, Blair believed he could look back with pride on his government's record on Europe, citing enlargement, defence cooperation and consensus on the Lisbon reform agenda as his lasting achievements. The Prime Minister began to mould his legacy by playing down the divisions that opened within the EU over the decision to join the US-led coalition that invaded Iraq in 2003 by noting that the British were not alone at least in joining the US. Not being isolated over such a controversial foreign policy venture seems to have counted in Blair's mind as something of a success, though it does beg the question, what would a failure have looked like? Blair would not, therefore, agree with the starting premise of this book, that New Labour failed to live up to its European aspirations over 1997–2010. In his final foreign policy speech, at the Lord Mayor's Banquet in 2006, Blair argued, in fact, the reverse: 'I have put Britain at the centre of Europe because I am proud that we are part of the largest political union and biggest economic market in the world' (Blair 2006h). Commentators such as Timothy Garton Ash have echoed Blair in suggesting that 'Britain's relations both with the US and our partners in the European Union are better than they were in 1997' (Garton Ash 2007). Blairite David Miliband, whom Brown appointed Foreign Secretary in June 2007, was equally persuaded that New Labour had managed to pull off a difficult juggling act. For example, in a 2009 speech he argued that the government had made the 'correct decision not to join the Euro when the five tests were applied', celebrating the fact that, contrary to the predictions of the Europhiles, the government's actions had 'not left Britain at the margins of Europe' (Miliband 2009a; Brown had put this view some three years earlier – see Brown 2006c). It should be noted, however, that the academic evidence to support this view is less than convincing, certainly as far as the microeconomic benefits to Britain can be judged. It is, further, difficult to make any macroeconomic judgements about the future given the structure of the British housing market, which 'finds no direct parallel anywhere else in the EU', and when it is empirically impossible to disentangle the 'Eurozone' effects on specific economies from wider global forces at work (Hay *et al.* 2006: this quotation from 102). Yet, if the evidence for a successful New Labour European policy is, at best, mixed, is it appropriate to declare it a failure?

There is no agreed method for isolating a policy sector – in this case European policy – for the purposes of measuring and coming to an evaluation of the extent to which it was successfully implemented (see for instance Sowemimo 1999; Menon 2003: 963). However, try we must, and there are three good grounds on which we might argue that New Labour's European policy was a success. The first is to follow the official wisdom of Blair, Brown and Miliband, by arguing that after 1997 they managed to locate Britain nearer, or directly at, the epicentre of decision-making in the EU. This positioning at the heart of Europe could be defined either in policy terms or in terms of the British being involved earlier and more constructively in agenda-setting for the organization. Thus we could follow Matthew Sowemimo in suggesting that Blair successfully 'normalized' Britain's relations with the EU during the Amsterdam Intergovernmental Conference of 1997 and notch that up as a positive, along with the Labour government's record on promoting successful European defence initiatives, such as the December 1998 St Malo agreement with France. Drawing up a simple balance sheet is difficult, however, because not all policy issues are weighted the same, either for the government, the national public and media, or in the eyes of Britain's EU partners. As Sowemimo points out, higher-profile and more contentious policy sectors, such as the issue of whether or not to join the single currency, saw the government if not in disarray then certainly paralysed into obfuscation and delay (Sowemimo 1999). Success at taking Britain into the eurozone might ultimately have outweighed 'failures' in any or all of the sectors on which Blair and his sympathisers now alight to make their claims for their record on the EU when in office.

A second argument for the success of New Labour's European policy involves looking at how the government managed the poten-tially explosive Europe question as part of its national electoral successes between 1997 and 2007. Success here would be defined in party political terms, as about gaining and keeping hold of power. Reconstructing the Labour Party at a time when the issue of Europe had torn the Conservatives apart under the Major governments of 1990–97, the architects of New Labour were well aware of the power of the European issue to damage a mainstream party's credibility and ability to govern and legislate effectively. Black Wednesday, Conservative backbench rebellions over the Maastricht Treaty and public sniping and back-biting within the Tory Party were for New Labour highly instructive lessons in the destructive power of Europe, especially given the party's own historically troubled policy U-turns on the question of EEC membership in the 1980s. That New Labour managed to neutralize the issue in its manifestos and keep discussion of European policy down to a bare minimum during its election campaigns was surely some sort of success for Blair and Brown. The other leading parties were complicit for the most part. With the exception of William Hague's doomed effort to play the 'Keep the Pound' card in the closing stages of the 2001 election, the main parties were aware that Europe was hardly a vote-winner but had the strong potential to be the reverse because the public had such 'strong reservations', particularly about the single currency (Schnapper 2011: 20). Thus, in 1997 New Labour achieved a working majority of 178 seats, winning 418 of 659 seats in the House of Commons, compared with the Conservatives' 165 seats and the Liberal Democrats' 46 seats (Kimber 2008a). This majority far outstripped even that of the 150 achieved by the reforming Clement Attlee governments after 1945 (Kimber 2008d). On 7 July 2001 Blair was re-elected on a slightly smaller but no less wholesome majority of 166 seats. New Labour won 412 seats, the Conservative Party held its ground at 166 seats and the Liberal Democrats received even more support with 52 seats (Kimber 2008b). The 2005 election saw a sharp turnaround in electoral fortunes, but nowhere near enough to take New Labour out of office. Blair's party won a majority of 65, or 70 if the five Sinn Féin parliamentarians who did not take up their seats are excluded. New Labour won 355 seats, the Conservatives picked up to 198 and the Liberal Democrats rose to 62 seats (Kimber 2008c). These figures indicate first the scale of the swing to New Labour in 1997 and second the party's maintenance of its popular appeal at least through to 2001, although some dissatisfaction with Labour became evident from 2005, a trend that continued under Gordon Brown after he became Prime Minister in June 2007.

The third and final argument in favour of seeing Blair's European policy as a success involves moving from a consideration of national opinion on New Labour to Blair's own position within the Cabinet and party. Success in this context is even more narrowly defined as success for the Prime Minister personally or politically. Some previous Prime Ministers, even hugely influential leaders such as Margaret Thatcher, have been hounded over the question of Europe, sometimes out of office altogether. Blair wanted to establish his reputation by securing Britain's place in Europe but, should he fail, he did not want to lose his authority in Cabinet or his popularity with the electorate over European affairs. We could say that by hiving off control over policy on the single currency Blair successfully neutralized the impact on him personally of statements about the single currency on the part of Brown, his Chancellor and rival for the premiership. While this resulted in something of a Cold War between Number 10 and Number 11 Downing Street, which spread to other policy sectors across Whitehall, this could be seen as a triumph for Blair, and the same might be said for the relative level of Cabinet and backbench support (also known as silence) on the issue of Europe under Blair and Brown. Certainly the questions of the single currency and the Constitutional Treaty never kindled the same levels of party rebellion or threats of resignation as happened over university tuition fees or the decision to invade Iraq in spring

2003. Over Iraq, for instance, both former Foreign Secretary and then Leader of the House Robin Cook, and a little later Clare Short, the International Development Secretary, chose to stand down. However, there were clear differences of opinion over European policy within Cabinet and these 'formed part of the running tension that was to characterize the Blair–Brown relationship' (Smith 2005: 708). Managing to keep a united Cabinet could itself be seen as an achievement for Blair, who was at pains not to repeat the scenes that characterized the later Major years. Added to the other two arguments about the policy record and the electoral politics of the Europe question, these are the three principal grounds on which we could build a case that New Labour's European policy was a success.

Against this, we can set three arguments. The first looks behind the election statistics to question the idea that New Labour's victory at the polls was as decisive as the bald figures on numbers of parliamentary seats won might suggest. It could be argued, for instance, that they revealed as much dissatisfaction with the Conservative Party as they did support for the Labour Party. The voter turnouts were suggestive: from 77.7% in 1992, voter turnout fell to 71.3% in 1997; more dramatic was the next fall, to a record post-Second World War low of 59.4% in 2001, with only a moderate increase, to 61.4%, in 2005 (Kimber 2008e). Britain has not been immune to the malaise afflicting political interest and participation in Western Europe over the past two decades and has been further damaged by the issue of 'trust' in politicians following revelations about fraudulent expenses claims by Members of Parliament (MPs) that hit the headlines in May 2009. The British first-past-the-post electoral system gave New Labour big working majorities, but in terms of the actual number of people turning out to vote for the government, the mandate was less than convincing and weakened with every election. Polls from as early as 2008 were pointing to Labour's defeat at the 2010 general election (Ipsos-MORI 2008) and the early predictions came to prove accurate, with Brown's government ousted in favour of a Conservative–Liberal coalition in June 2010. The New Labour years were brought to a close with the party obtaining a total of only 258 seats in the House of Commons, the Conservatives winning 307 seats and the Liberal Democrats 57 (Kimber 2010).

The second retort we might make is that Europe possesses 'relatively low salience as an issue in the UK' (Sherrington 2006: 69). Voters have traditionally chosen their political party based on their relative perception of a party's achievements and proposed policies in the domestic arena more than the international. In comparative work on Euroscepticism Britain has been found to be no different from any other member or candidate state in this regard:

one of the most striking features of the issue of European integration
is how little salience it has among voters in any country. It is difficult
to think of any parliamentary or presidential election were [sic] European integration has played a major role in determining its outcome.
(Taggart and Szczerbiak 2002: 31)

Even though New Labour superficially received a succession of
ringing endorsements from the electorate, this was achieved despite
rather than because of any stance it might or might not have taken on
the Europe question. It is all the more telling that an electorate positively switched off from the idea of European integration consistently
voted in a government committed to taking steps, however cautious,
to improve the country's relationship with the EU. Such election
successes as there have been for fringe parties openly opposed to
Britain's EU membership, such as the Referendum Party in the 1990s
(see McAllister and Studlar 2000) and latterly the United Kingdom
Independence Party (UKIP) and the British National Party (BNP),
have tended to come at second-order European and local council
elections, where sitting governments do relatively poorly anyway. For
example, between delivering Labour two historic domestic majorities
in 1997 and 2001, voters at the European Parliament elections in
June 1999 gave the Conservatives 34.6% of the vote, compared with
Labour's 29.4% (figures calculated from Kimber 2008f), a pattern
repeated in the 2009 European elections (Daddow 2010). There is no
automatic association between a voter's attitudes to Europe and his
or her vote at national and mid-term elections and this makes it all
the more necessary to try to isolate attitudes to the EU from wider
sentiments towards a particular political party.

This leads to the third and most convincing riposte to the argument that Blair's European policy could be judged a success because
of its non-impact at national elections: it casts unnecessary doubt
on the sincerity of Blair and Brown's oft-stated commitment to reforming British public opinion about Europe. It is tempting but not,
to my mind, intellectually convincing to write off the government's
rhetoric about Europe as just that – rhetoric or, to use the popular
word, 'spin'. Blair may not have been a Europhile in the mould of
Heath, it might not always have been clear what he stood for on
Europe and he may not have been as prepared as one of his Labour
predecessors, Harold Wilson, was to stand up to the US (by not
sending British troops to participate in the Vietnam War). However,
as we will see from the time and attention he gave European affairs
in his foreign policy speeches after 1997, he was not merely using
these speeches for window-dressing. Along with Brown, Blair seems
to have believed that he could and would alter public opinion; it was
just that he was not willing to sacrifice the New Labour project at

the altar of his European convictions. New Labour came to office on the back of a 22% fall in the British public's support for EU membership after Major's Conservative government instigated a policy of 'non-cooperation' with the EU over its handling of the British beef crisis in May 1996 (James and Opperman 2009: 286). Diplomatically things were at a low ebb; the Eurosceptical press was hostile and anti-European sentiment was on the march (Castle 1996); the only way appeared to be up after the beef crisis, which was widely judged to have been 'one of the most damaging British foreign policy episodes in recent history' (Hughes and Smith 1998: 94). The scale of the public opinion deficit Blair left behind is therefore telling. 'The whole question of Britain's role in the EU remained unresolved after more than eight years in office', Peter Riddell observed, 'and the British public was, if anything, more sceptical than it had been in 1997' (Riddell 2005: 199). No small cause of this sorry state of affairs was that Blair was reluctant to push the issue of the single currency against Brown's cautious scepticism, and this set the tone for the crucial first term of New Labour. Blair, moreover, 'despite favouring entry, ... was reluctant to challenge popular opinion head-on' (Fielding 2003: 157). We can look to two authoritative polling sources to help us here, and they tell exactly the same story.

The European Commission's Eurobarometer polling team has been measuring public attitudes to European affairs in the member states since 1973, publishing twice-yearly reports as well as 'Flash' or one-off surveys about specific issues such as enlargement and the environment (Eurobarometer 2009). Of the forty-three questions it asks in its regular poll, the one that interests us here is question number 4: 'Generally speaking, do you think your country's membership of the European Community (Common Market) is: 1. A good thing; 2. A bad thing; 3. Neither good nor bad; 4. Don't know'. The archive data on Blair's first seven years in office reveals that the number of British citizens considering membership of the EU to be a 'good thing' was consistently higher than the number considering it a 'bad thing', although the former steadily declined after 1999, so that by April 2004 the percentage was exactly the same. My own research has found that well into Blair's period in office Britain was showing up as one of the most 'sceptical' members of the EU according to both regional polling and analyses provided by a range of scholars (Daddow 2006), a pattern that extends back many years (Schnapper 2011: 7). Nothing I have seen from recent polling (see for instance Bulmer 2008: 617) makes me want to revise this conclusion. In the spring of 2007 Eurobarometer found 39% of the polled population in Britain considered EU membership a 'good thing', while those responding 'bad thing' remained at its 2004 level

of 30%, with 31% neutral (Eurobarometer 2007a: 2). By the autumn
of 2007 the percentage of UK respondents considering membership
to be 'good' had fallen to 34%, with the percentage considering it bad
also down, but by less, at 28%; 38% were neutral. These figures can
be compared with an average across all twenty-seven EU member
states (EU-27) for autumn 2007 of 58% considering their nation's
membership of the EU a 'good thing', 13% a 'bad thing' and 25%
neutral (Eurobarometer 2007b). In later 2007, therefore, British
support for the EU was running at not much more than half the EU
average, while openly critical attitudes were over twice as high in
Britain compared with the EU-27 as a whole. If one were to make
the case that, if pushed, the 'neutrals' might swing more to negative
than positive evaluations of the EU then the picture would look even
gloomier. A one-off Eurobarometer poll of British attitudes in early
2007 found the same levels of apathy about EU membership and
low levels of knowledge and interest in EU affairs as it discovered
in a similar investigation from 2002. Its blunt conclusion was that,
in the five-year period, there had been 'no real improvement in the
UK's attitude towards the EU' (Eurobarometer 2007c: 4). To put
these isolated statistics in comparative perspective we can note that,
shortly before Blair left office, Eurobarometer's finding that the 39%
of the British public considering membership a 'good thing' 'shows
a higher level of support than exists in Austria (36%), Hungary and
Latvia (37%) but all are well below the EU-27 average figure of 57%.
This compares with figures as high as 77% in the Netherlands and
76% in Ireland' (Eurobarometer 2007a: 5). Exactly one year later, in
June 2008, the Irish people rejected the proposed Lisbon Treaty in
the first of its two national referendums on the subject.

Domestic opinion polling shows the same patterns of suspicion,
hostility and low level of information and interest about the EU in
Britain. The annual British Social Attitudes (BSA) survey has a
range of questions relating to the EU, one being about what respondents think Britain's long-term policy towards the organization should
be. In 1997, 17.5% of respondents thought Britain should withdraw
from the EU; this had fallen to 14.5% in 2001 and was up to 15.6% in
2006. Unless success is accorded to a drop of two percentage points
in the proportion of citizens wanting to leave the EU, it appears New
Labour's push for Europe hardly had radical effects on public attitudes. The highest-scoring response to this BSA question was 'stay
in but try to reduce powers' (and arguably describing the government's preferred policy), which rose from 28.7% in 1997 to 37.7% in
2001 and 35.8% in 2006. This was hardly a ringing endorsement of
membership of the EU, especially given that support for the option
of remaining in and trying to increase the EU's powers was almost

always in single figures (BSA 2007). These figures confirm what Eurobarometer opinion polling discovered over the same period: that Britain is usually at, or very near, the bottom of the EU league in terms of national support and enthusiasm for European integration.

To argue that New Labour's European policy was a success, or not a failure at any rate, we thus have to do one of two things. Either we have to doubt the sincerity of Blair and Brown's commitment to changing British attitudes and helping Britain play a leading role in the EU, spelled out in election manifestos, speeches and statements over a prolonged period. Or we have to envelop the study of European policy within a wider study of New Labour as an election-winning machine, in effect arguing that the success of any one policy sector can be judged by looking at the overall 'New Labour effect' on the outcome of general elections. Success at the polls, according to this line of thinking, can mean as much or as little as we want it to mean for the various components of a party's domestic or external policy agenda. In both cases different ontologies are at work and both ignore the public-opinion aspects of British foreign policy. In the first case our underlying ontology works to the popular refrain that we cannot trust politicians to do what they say, even if we want to believe in what they say. In the second case our underlying ontology is a world in which only grabbing power and election results matter – everything else can be used to explain those results but has little or no intrinsic value beyond seeing policy stances as causal determinants of election outcomes. The first smacks of an unhealthy and overbearing cynicism about politics and politicians; the second seems to be the worst form of explanatory theory, where we seek only to explain outcomes rather than to understand the various practices and processes by which they were achieved. This book takes a more nuanced approach. I assume that Blair and Brown genuinely wanted to reform British public attitudes to Europe *and* that they set great store by winning successive elections. These election victories were not ends in themselves but the means of giving them the time to enact the reform agenda they set out, principally in the domestic arena but also regarding external relations. Where they failed on Europe was that they gave it neither the time nor the attention it deserved and they made a particularly damaging move early on to close off any decisive moves towards joining the single currency in the first wave. Blair and Brown failed to deliver on the promises for New Labour's European policy by preventing Britain assuming the leadership role they had marked out for it. More importantly, though, they failed to shift public opinion in the country at large (Blair now *almost* admits as much – see Blair 2010: 501) and that, surely, has to be the benchmark by which we judge the actions of avowed Europeanist public servants such has these. Jonathan Powell, Blair's highly influential Downing Street chief of staff, summed up the position in interview by agreeing with Blair that 'What we managed to do was shift Britain's position in Europe', but he then added: 'What we failed to do was change British public opinion about it' (interview with Powell). Philip Collins, another person close to Blair, in his role as chief speech-writer 2005–7, confirms that by the end of his tenure the Prime Minister 'felt that, generally speaking, the agenda that Europe had set itself was a much better one and the result of a lot of British pressure. However, I don't think he felt the relationship the British people had with the European Union had altered at all; not very much anyway' (interview with Collins). The chasm that opened up between the sometimes impressive momentum the New Labour governments achieved in European policy terms and the negative trend in public opinion towards the EU over the same period was one Blair and Brown were never able to bridge. If anything, the gap between establishment Europeanism and public scepticism became more evident under their stewardship. The next section will consider how the existing literature explains this failure and explain how this book adds a novel dimension to this corpus.

III. New Labour's European policy: the verdict

Our slogan is Britain is ready for the euro and we will be. (Brown 1998a)

There is a substantial collection of works which together make up the New Labour industry. Witness diaries, memoirs, biographies, autobiographies and secondary accounts all put forward three distinct interpretations of Britain's relations with Europe after 1997, which I label as follows: the 'blown off course' interpretation; the 'no strategy' interpretation; and the 'electoral considerations' interpretation. We shall examine each school in turn with a view to placing the arguments put forward in this book in the last category, if not for the reasons writers in that tradition usually offer up.

The most sympathetic but least fashionable is the 'blown off course' interpretation. This is found in the positive evaluations of British European policy put about by Blair in his speeches, covered above. Robin Cook, Foreign Secretary throughout Blair's first term in office, was sympathetic to Blair in his memoirs, indicating that this is the official history of New Labour and the EU as its creators would have us remember it. Cook was replaced by Jack Straw after the general election in June 2001 and resigned from government in March 2003 in protest at Britain's Iraq policy. He published extracts from his diaries shortly before his death in August 2005 but, unfortunately, only back to 2001. When the Europe question did get a mention he tried to persuade us that Blair deserves credit for 'achieving more than any previous Prime Minister in promoting Britain's place in Europe, until the hurricane over his support for the war in Iraq blew him off course' (Cook 2003: 1). He lauded Blair's achievements during his first term in office, when, apparently, 'he transformed Britain's relations with Europe', presumably wanting to take some of the credit for himself (Cook 2003: 131). For Cook, Blair's failure was not one related to the conduct or content of European policy per se through to 2001, but only came about when European policy fell off Downing Street's foreign policy agenda with the ill-conceived build-up to the invasion of Iraq from 2002 onwards. Moreover, all was well, Cook suggested, had not the Prime Minister's judgement failed him over the conduct of the 'war on terror', which irreparably damaged his European dreams by subjugating British foreign policy to the imperialist ambitions of the neo-cons in the White House, State Department and, particularly, the Pentagon. Another ex-Cabinet minister under Blair, Clare Short, head of the Department for International Development (DfID) from May 1997 to May 2003, judges in her memoirs that whatever we make of the extent of Blair's Europeanism before the terrorist attacks in the US on 11 September 2001 ('9/11'), his actions after that date made Britain little more 'a mouthpiece of the US' (Short 2005: 296).

There is half-hearted backing for the official wisdom in the scholarly literature. Paul Williams, for example, highlights the positive aspects of Blair's European policy, which persisted even after the inception of the war on terror, especially in the security arena: 'although Blair's government remained supportive of ESDP [European Security and Defence Policy], the post-9/11 broadening of its foreign policy horizons beyond Europe meant that it slipped down the list of priorities' (Williams 2005: 71; a similar view is to be found in Jenkins 2007: 251). Anthony Seldon also offers qualified support by noting that Blair managed to make Britain as influential in the EU as France and Germany; however (and opening up the space within which this book operates), 'he failed to convince the British voters of the case for the EU' (Seldon 2007: 572). All these writers share one thing in common: they take seriously Blair's efforts prior to 9/11 to engage more with the EU, whether in the realm of security (Williams), the single currency (Short 2005: 108), or normalizing relations across the board (Cook). Where they differ is in their reading of the seriousness of this engagement. Of the three, only the well known horse-racing enthusiast Cook was willing to bet that things would have turned out differently had 9/11 and Iraq not materialized. Such are the writers who belong to the loose but nonetheless identifiable grouping that constitutes the 'blown off course' school of writing about Blair's European policy.

At the opposite end of the spectrum, and as its name implies, the 'no strategy' school is markedly different in tone and substance from the 'blown off course' school. Where 'blown off course' writers concentrate on Blair's efforts to generate enthusiasm for Europe at home through an active and wholehearted engagement with the EU, the 'no strategy' school is doubtful that Downing Street had anything approaching a coherent strategy. It sees instead a series of short-term tactical, reactionary moves which it is kind in the extreme to label a 'policy'. This school concentrates on the big picture of British European policy under New Labour and suggests that, with or without the Prime Minister taking his eyes off the ball over Iraq, Britain's European policy was doomed to fall short of the ambitions New Labour had for it, by virtue of the government never managing the policy in a consistent or organized manner. The key exponent of this view is one of the most prominent insider diarists from the New Labour years: Lance Price. A former BBC journalist, Price was press adviser to Tony Blair between June 1998 and June 2000 and then spent a year as the party's director of communications, up to and including the 2001 general election, after which he moved on to become a freelance writer, broadcaster and commentator (Price 2007–8). His diaries give telling on-the-ground insights into Blair's European policy as it unfolded over New Labour's first four years governing Britain. In June 1998, at a Policy Unit lunch at which Europe was discussed, he noted: 'Quite clear there is no coherent strategy'. Things had not improved almost a year later when he asked himself: 'What are the actual objectives of our foreign policy?' (Price 2005: 14 and 88). The main impression one has reading Price's diaries is of policy 'drift' (Price 2005: 114) combined, paradoxically, with supreme confidence on Blair's part that at a moment of his choosing he could oversee a successful referendum campaign on the single currency (Price 2005: 123; see also Blair 2010: 314; the public opinion data would not have given him much confidence, however – see Opperman 2008: 191). Another insider, Jonathan Powell, suggested in interview that Blair believed he could win a referendum – but only on the question of membership of the EU, not on a specific policy measure such as the euro or the Lisbon Treaty (interview with Powell; confirmed in Blair 2010: 530). But, notes Riddell: 'It was always a case of tomorrow. There has been an occasional speech and then nothing' (Riddell 2005: 151). That a referendum campaign was never launched meant, Price reflected, that 'By the end of 2005 Britain was no closer to joining the euro than it had been in 2001, and arguably further away than in 1997' (Price 2005: 366).

Price's eyewitness account constitutes the definitive work in the 'no strategy' school, but he is by no means alone. In his first survey of the New Labour years, relying on interviews with serving politicians and civil servants, Andrew Rawnsley identified a supposition within the top echelons of the party prior to 1997 that a proactive European agenda would pose problems to any incoming government that had spent its final years in opposition wooing right-wing newspapers over the Europe question. Two factors were of special concern to the Blair team: first, Philip Gould's focus groups 'showed deep hostility to the euro' (Rawnsley 2001: 75); and second, the Treasury had done little serious preparatory work to make British entry to the single currency either feasible or practical (Rawnsley 2001: 81). On coming to power New Labour's key Cabinet decision-makers and special advisers continued to discuss the issue without arriving at a consensus, so that 'by the end of 1997 these arguments within New Labour's high command had still not produced an actual policy' (Rawnsley 2001: 76). Thus, when a story broke in *The Times* that, as the headline had it on 18 October 1997, 'Brown rules out single currency for lifetime of this Parliament', the government was in a quandary because the Treasury had effectively put a sceptical twist on a U-turn on a manifesto commitment to hold a referendum – without consulting the Prime Minister. The next few days were spent trying to 'dress up the chaos as a well-ordered decision' through briefings suggesting that the detail of the policy had been 'meticulously agreed the previous week' between Prime Minister and Chancellor, when in fact 'the farrago had flowed from a five-minute phone call' (Rawnsley 2001: 83). We return to this fascinating episode in chapter 2 because it did more than any other to succour the 'no strategy' interpretation of Blair's European policy. As one anonymous official recalled of the Treasury discussions that led to Brown's statement to Parliament on British policy towards the single currency nine days later (Brown 1997d), they revolved around 'how to make it look as if Gordon Brown's statement was part of a planned, properly thought-out process rather than the reality, which is that we were jumped, and had to act in a panic to sort out exactly what our position was' (quoted in Seldon 2005: 325). In summary, we can see that where the 'blown off course' school implies that all was well, or more or less well, with British European policy prior to 9/11, the 'no strategy' school alights on the disagreements over European policy at the heart of the New Labour governments. This led to divisions opening between Downing Street on the one hand and the Treasury on the other, these in turn being gleefully levered apart by a media quick to pounce on any sign of tension between the 'big beasts' running the New Labour project. For 'no strategy' writers, policy spats, no master plan and policies made on the hoof were the order of the day.

In the middle of these polar interpretations of Blair's European policy we find the largest number of writers, who together form the 'electoral considerations' school. These writers are partly interested, like the 'no strategy' school, in the to-ing and fro-ing and intra-government quarrels over the appropriate course for British European policy. They also overlap with the 'blown off course' school in their consideration of the position the European issue occupied on the New Labour foreign policy agenda. However, writers in the third school break with both the other schools in foregrounding the party political considerations and domestic party politicking that shaped British European policy under Blair and Brown. Julie Smith encapsulates this school's approach by arguing that the reason why New Labour made only limited headway in selling 'Europe' to the British people was that 'however deeply committed the Prime Minister and his colleagues were to the European Union, they were ultimately more committed to ensuring that the Labour Party remained in power nationally' (Smith 2005: 704). Hence, in 2005 the Director of the pro-European pressure group the Federal Trust, Brendan Donnelly, claimed that the best we could say of New Labour, two terms into office, was that it had positioned itself as an 'anti-anti-European' party. To appreciate the seriousness of his charge in applying that label we can rewrite it as 'anti-[anti-European]', bringing home Donnelly's point that New Labour was more interested in stealing the electoral clothes of the Conservatives and Liberal Democrats than in developing a distinctive policy of principled support for the European idea (Donnelly 2005: 2). The label further suggests that rather than marking a break with past practices, Blair instead prolonged a historic trend in British European policy since 1945 by opportunistically using the issue of 'Europe' to settle scores against opponents from within his party and against other parties. As Nicholas Crowson has put it, 'Domestic considerations have nearly always informed the stance of the British government's European policy' (Crowson 2007: 2; see also Kaiser 1996; Daniels 1998: 74). Robert Worcester and Roger Mortimore found in their statistical analysis of the 1997 election that Labour's European stance was hardly a vote winner, but at least it was not a vote *loser*. Manifest public divisions within the parliamentary party helped lose the Conservatives crucial votes in the 1997 general election and settling the matter once and for all in a referendum would have removed a key impediment to the Conservatives mounting a serious challenge to Labour's electoral dominance (Worcester and Mortimore 1999: 113). Hence, the perpetually delayed euro referendum could, to a cynic, be seen as a partisan ploy to keep the Conservatives on the back foot over Europe. Most critically, however, Blair wanted to defuse Europe as a political issue and this he successfully did by lowering its voter salience year on year after 1997: he transformed the British public's attention to Europe as a factor in its voting decisions from 'a decidedly high salience issue at the beginning of the Blair government's tenure into a downright low-salience issue at the end' (James and Opperman 2009: 295).

This strategy, 'electoral considerations' writers suggest, was the result of two interlocking problems afflicting New Labour's European decision-making. First of all, they pick up the 'no strategy' view that Europe was kicked around as a political football between Blair and Downing Street on the one hand and Brown and the Treasury on the other (Sowemimo 1999: 357–61). Second, there was a failure of leadership brought about by a loss of nerve on the part of the Prime Minister about holding a referendum on the single currency. On the Blair–Brown factor, Donnelly suggests that British European policy became intimately woven into the fabric of an increasingly fraught relationship between the Prime Minister and the Chancellor after 1997. Their personal wrangling, he suggests, fatally ossified a policy already paralysed by sceptical media and public opinion. On the issue of the euro, Donnelly judged: 'The need to preserve the internal and external political equilibrium of New Labour has clearly taken precedence in his calculations over any personal inclination [Blair] may have, or have had, to move to quick resolution of the single currency issue' (Donnelly 2005: 4). Meanwhile, in his preparedness to take a tough, pragmatic stance on European policy, Brown was echoing a well established Treasury position. In comparison with, say, the Foreign Office, which was more inclined to 'think European' by virtue of its entanglement in routine European-level policy-making debates in Brussels, the Treasury seems to have been perennially cool on the question of the British in Europe:

> Outside a small group of European specialists it still tends not to 'think European', or engage very much in Europe. This situation is partly a matter of Brown's political preferences, partly an organizational matter, and partly a prioritization given to global economic institutions within the department. (Bulmer and Burch 2006: 46)

The government fell into disarray over the single-currency issue in October 1997 and this apparent partitioning of European policy-making between Blair and Brown has discomfited writers who see personal machinations between the two men damaging what should have been an issue driven by principle rather than personal rivalry. It even, apparently, impacted on the choice of the first Minister for Europe under New Labour. Having rejected all of Robin Cook's nominees, Blair chose Doug Henderson, an odd but revealing choice. 'With no experience of European issues, his principal qualification for the post was that he was pushed by Gordon Brown' – an early example, Rawnsley concludes, of Blair's deference to his Chancellor in the realm of European affairs (Rawnsley 2001: 22).

If Brown and the Treasury's domination hampered the Prime Minister's power even to appoint his preferred candidate as Minister for Europe, nowhere was it more obvious than over the Treasury's 'five economic tests' on British membership of the single currency. These were devised as the cornerstone of Brown's statement to Parliament in October 1997 (Brown 1997d), the abrupt genesis of which was explored above. First, can there be sustainable convergence between Britain and the eurozone? Second, is there sufficient flexibility to cope with economic change? Third, what will be the effect on investment? Fourth, what will be the impact on the national financial services industry? And finally, would eurozone membership be good for employment? Writers in the 'electoral considerations' school really come into their own on these conditions, arguing that they were nothing more than a delaying tactic designed to give the Treasury control, via British euro policy, over both the timing and the pace of any British moves towards the EU more generally. Rawnsley states that 'There was nothing scientific about these tests, not the number of them. It could have been three, it might have been seven.' Originally taken to be 'conveniently elastic', he continues, they 'would ironically come to be seen as serious hurdles' (Rawnsley 2001: 86). Bulmer agrees, seeing the announcement of the tests as an 'attempt to de-politicise the issue through a rules-based approach, thereby reducing its electoral salience' (Bulmer 2008: 601). Mark Aspinwall remarks that 'the most common British technique of party management is to delay making a decision' and New Labour was treading the path of many a predecessor in fudging a euro referendum (Aspinwall 2004: 170). Even if we were to take the tests as a rational effort to calculate Britain's economic readiness to join the single currency, economist Paul Temperton has argued that they were so vague as to have been as passable or failable as the Treasury wished. It would have made more sense in the interests of scientific objectivity, he argues, for the government to have used the European Commission's Maastricht criteria as the benchmark for economic readiness, which every other country wishing to join has had to do (detailed in Lipinska 2008). By Temperton's reckoning in 2001: 'The UK easily meets four out of five of the Maastricht requirements for euro membership', the exception being the assessment of sterling's exchange rate stability vis-à-vis the euro (Temperton 2001: 67–78). By the time the Treasury verdict was announced ('not ready yet'), mid-way through the second term, on 9 June 2003 (Brown 2003c), the Blair–Brown split was public knowledge and the source of much journalistic intrigue. According to Seldon, in relation to the announcement, 'Blair was determined to keep the door open, above all to show pro-Europeans, at home and abroad, that in principle he was still keen on joining the single currency; Brown was equally determined to stress the economic perils of joining in the near future, and the damage that would be caused by continual uncertainty'. With it, Seldon concludes: 'All remaining hopes for the Euro in Blair's premiership were effectively at an end' (Seldon 2005: 639 and 640; see also Seldon 2007: 213).

The key to understanding the place of the Treasury tests for writers in the 'electoral considerations' school is to see them, in Ian Bache and Andrew Jordan's words, as 'in some respects a camouflage to disguise the real test: whether the government could win a referendum on entry' (Bache and Jordan 2006: 9; see also Wall 2008: 170). The absence of a referendum on the single currency and later the Lisbon Treaty has fed the second strand of writing in the 'electoral considerations' school: Blair's loss of nerve over taking on the press and public over the Europe question, or what Price described in his diary in January 2000 as an unofficial 'sixth condition' on top of the official five economic tests (Price 2005: 188). If the policy really amounted to 'prepare and then decide' (Brown 1997e; Brown 1998a), then surely part of the preparations had to involve a targeted promotion to win the public over? Unfortunately, reflected Polly Toynbee and David Walker in 2001, such an information campaign was never even launched:

> The people were not prepared, quite the contrary. If entry [to the euro] had been Blair's clear intent, Labour surely needed to make a continuous and convincing public case. Labour would have had to set its face against the howling gales of anti-Europeanism swirling through the pages owned and written by Tories, Little Englanders and North Americans. (Toynbee and Walker 2001: 145)

Likewise for former ambassador to the US Christopher Meyer, Blair's entire European policy 'masked a failure of political will' (Meyer 2006: 32); similarly, Jonathan Tonge sees the 'fear of a referendum defeat', not the economic tests, as being the real driver of New Labour's policy on the single currency (Tonge 2009: 303). William Wallace gets to the heart of the matter by arguing that 'The absence of any attempt by the Labour government to persuade its public that Britain's commitment to the European Union is in the national interest has allowed the Eurosceptical press to entrench a sullen resistance to closer integration' (Wallace 2005: 56).

Here we see the subtle but significant difference between the 'no strategy' school and the 'electoral considerations' school. The former has been driven by the worm's-eye view of the daily comings and goings of policy-making we tend to get from political diaries and insider interviews. The latter has the benefit of hindsight, taking stock of the overall policy flow over a longer period, enabling more dots to be joined up in the search for the causes of New Labour's policy failure on Europe. This distinction is critical in terms of each school's appreciation of the drivers of Blair and Brown's thinking on Europe. Where 'no strategy' writers cannot conceive of any direction to European policy other than drifting with the tides of media prejudice, 'electoral considerations' writers see all too clearly a strategy of carving up European policy between Blair and Brown, which led to a loss of the very purpose they were trying to inject into it. This came to be the preferred strategy, we could surmise, for one or several of five reasons. First, Blair did not see it as electorally important enough to make the case for Europe, when domestic issues were his top priority and the bulk of his much publicized election 'pledges' to the British people. Second, Europe was a contentious issue within the Cabinet and Parliamentary Labour Party (PLP) and it would have been problematic to try to settle the matter, even on the back of a huge majority in the House of Commons. Third, it gave Brown a slice of the foreign policy action, leaving Blair to concentrate on personal diplomacy, especially relations with the US and other prime facets of his global agenda that developed through his time in power. Fourth, keeping the issue open helped keep the Conservative opposition on the back foot. Finally, Blair seems to have believed that at a moment of his choosing he could put the issue to a referendum and win it by turning it into a debate on EU membership per se. For all these reasons the 'electoral considerations' school takes the view *not* that New Labour lacked a European strategy, but that the strategy was all too apparent. It was simply the wrong one for a supposedly pro-European Prime Minister to have pursued. For these writers, lauding 'policy successes' where Blair was proactive, such as over European defence initiatives, misses the point that not all policy sectors were of equal salience to British voters or to the Europeans, and on issues such as the single currency Blair consistently pulled back from making the hard decisions that could have decisively helped him start to fashion a pro-European consensus in Britain and helped him 'play the leading role in Europe that [the country's] weight and status deserves' (James and Opperman 2009: 298). Low-salience policy successes were never going to be the real test for Blair; winning the battle for hearts and minds was, and this is why the propaganda campaign is foregrounded in this study.

IV. Putting speeches in the spotlight

The previous section identified three interpretations of Britain's European policy under New Labour. From the self-congratulatory official wisdom of the 'blown off course' school to the highly critical 'no strategy' school we arrived at the 'electoral considerations' school in the middle. There are clear if sometimes delicate differences between their respective interpretations of British European policy after 1997. What they share, however, is an almost total dearth of attention to the component parts of New Labour's information campaign when the Blair–Brown governments *did* try to build a national consensus around the idea of Britain being a 'European' country. The 'blown off course' school says the least about the mechanics of Blair's attempt to make the case for Europe, resting on the rather questionable assumptions first of all that Blair was an undoubted Europhile and secondly that only diplomatic ructions and the slippage of Europe down the foreign policy agenda after 9/11 caused it to become the disaster area it did. The 'no strategy' school – the insiders looking out – could not see far enough beyond the hurly-burly of day-to-day policy-making on Europe to enable them to weave a narrative out of the apparently disjointed, short-term steps Blair took over Europe. The 'electoral considerations' school goes the furthest in actually assessing the component parts of British European policy under New Labour. Even there, though, we find a tendency to want to explain failure rather than identify the nature of the policy that is said to have come up short. The ontology of each school (the social reality each sees) shapes the story each tells about British European policy, and as such leads them to miss critical components of the policy process itself (table 1).

The ontological suppositions of this book are at odds with all the above approaches, even if the spirit in which it has been written has more than a little in common with the assumption of the second and third schools, that here we have a case of policy failure. I have tried to empathize with the position Blair and Brown found themselves in and to take seriously such efforts as *were* made to put together a campaign for Europe. Each of the existing schools privileges structure over agency by portraying Blair fighting against Brown and the Treasury's opposition to the single currency, Blair labouring to convince the editors and owners of key press outlets that closer integration with the EU would be beneficial for Britain, or Blair being swept along in the slipstream of US foreign policy in the war on terror. What each school misses is detailed attention to the agents themselves: the lengths to which Blair and Brown went, as people with real power to form opinions, to try to sell the European ideal.

Table I. Ontological positioning of the schools of writing about Blair and Europe

'Blown off course'	'Electoral considerations'	'No strategy'
Policy failure over Iraq	Neutralization of issue	Reactive policy
Obsession with 'special relationship'	Brown–Blair feuding	Limited planning prior to 1997
'Everything changed' after 9/11	Labour Party and Cabinet divisions (potential for)	No medium- or long-term planning after 1997
	Treasury opposition	
Inattentiveness to European politics	Failure of leadership	Obsession with media, especially press, cover-age of policy
Diplomatic ructions, especially with France and Germany	Issue avoidance	
	Reliance on sceptical press for support	Murdoch opposition limited room for manoeuvre
	Europe not a salient issue for voters	

They might in the end have been insufficient to rouse the British public from its hostility to the EU, but some key steps were taken to this end and in overlooking them we oversimplify the narratives we can tell about New Labour's European policy.

This book elevates the profile of Blair and Brown's agency through analysis of four interlinked sets of speeches: first, speeches on foreign affairs generally; second, speeches specifically on the EU; third, those on other topics but that made reference to the government's European policy; and finally, speeches that revealed the New Labour take on the meaning of the national past in the present. Chapter 3, on discourse and norm entrepreneurship, explains in depth the rationale for concentrating on political language as the prime focus for analysis, so a few preparatory remarks will suffice now. My prime reason for wanting to concentrate on policy presentation is that, whatever faltering or clumsy steps the British government might have taken in the direction of Europe after 1997, what matters is not what those moves *were* but how they were *perceived* by the various audiences the government was playing to. As Worcester and Mortimore presciently remark, 'the reality of the world of public policy as well as the media and industry, is that it is perception, not facts, that determines public opinion' (Worcester and Mortimore 1999: 23). Policy presentation is not something that occurs chronologically after the development of policy; it is an essential part *of* policy development, can in some cases

actually *precede* policy development and relies on an astute understanding of how to handle both language and the media. As journalist
Nicholas Jones has written: 'Effective political communication has
always relied on easily understood slogans and phrases aimed at
promoting and justifying the policy decisions of governments and
their opponents' (Jones 1996: 27). This is especially pertinent in
the case of a New Labour government that was famously wedded to
modern techniques of 'strategic communication' (Bird 2008) to help
get its 'messages' across to the public (Hyman 2005: 254–7). The
second reason for privileging the study of discourses is that we see
in them an array of behind-the-scenes tensions, disagreements and
personal infighting playing out in New Labour's pronouncements on
Europe. In studying the language through which Blair and Brown
spoke 'Europe' we see the difficulties they encountered in shifting
the terms of the debate in the directions they wished. It was a constant struggle, it seems, to escape the past and modernize attitudes
to Europe when the domestic audience (elite decision-makers, media
and public alike) was not ready to transcend the history of separateness that had come to characterize the received construction of
Britain's relations with the continent.

The government's ability to convince the British people that
Europe was not a foreboding Other across the English Channel
consistently came up against its desire not to risk losing votes or
the support of the press by dismissing 'one thousand years' of the
nation's history. This concern had been emotively expressed by
Labour leader Hugh Gaitskell in 1962 (and was also known to be used
by Churchill – see Charteris-Black 2006: 55), as the Conservative
government of the day was putting together the first of three British
applications to what was then the EEC. For Gaitskell, participation
in a continental federation would have meant 'the end of Britain
as an independent European state ... the end of a thousand years
of history'. His concerns have resonated well with a public steeped
in patriotic sentimentality (Wall 2008: 3) and Gaitskell's words
that year have become a staple of the discourses against European
integration put about by sceptics of all political hues in Britain (for
a reassessment of the meaning of the Gaitskell prophecy see Broad
and Daddow 2010). Tony Blair would have been only too aware of an
article in the *Daily Mail* just prior to the May 1997 election in which,
overlaying a picture of the Union Jack, was the warning: 'There is a
terrible danger that the British people, drugged with the seductive
mantra "It's time for change" are stumbling, eyes glazed, into an
election that could undo 1,000 years of our nation's history' (quoted
in Worcester and Mortimore 1999: 142). Cautionary tales such as
this are more than frivolous verbiage. They mean real things to real

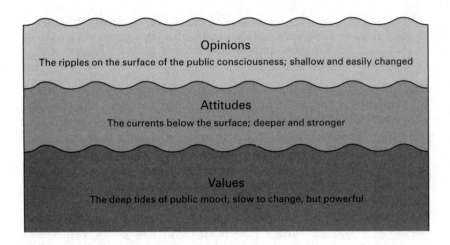

Figure 1. Opinions–attitudes–values. Source: Worcester and Mortimore (1999: 16).

people, are invested with political capital and emotional effect and can therefore alter not just short-term opinions but longer-term attitudes and the deeply held values of individuals (figure 1).

To go back to that earlier era, why did many in Britain in the 1960s insist on talking about the European 'Common Market' as opposed to 'Community' as they did, say, in Germany (Diez 1999: 602)? Why did Margaret Thatcher – who headed a government returned ten days previously with a parliamentary majority of 144 – prevent the 19 June 1983 Solemn Declaration on European Union (European Council 1983) being called an 'Act'? Because she was 'showing sensitivity to the impact of words on British parliamentary and public opinion' (Wall 2008: 22) and to the special troubles that issues in European integration can cause even popular and cohesive political parties in Britain governing with large mandates. Why, more recently, was there such uproar over the possibility of updating the EU through a 'Constitution' as opposed to a 'Treaty' (Wall 2008: 207)? Because words like these are of symbolic significance to their receivers and reflect real political divisions over what the eternally moving target of 'Europe' is and where it is heading. As Paul Taggart and Aleks Szczerbiak have observed:

> 'The' EU is a changing set of institutions with ever new competencies, new treaties, new coalitions and, of course, an expanding acquis. This means that employing Euroscepticism allows parties to adopt

> positions that can relatively easily be moderated over time. Whereas the values of democracy, nation or capitalism are portrayed as unchanging, the European project is inherently in flux. (Taggart and Szczerbiak 2001: 30)

The inherent malleability of the terms 'Europe' and 'EU' opens up avenues for debate and opposition to the EU given the slippery, essentially contested nature of these deceptively simple terms.

Using the distinctions set down in figure 1, at a bare minimum the New Labour government would have needed to shift public *opinion* about the EU in a positive direction in order to win one of its promised-but-never-held referendums on the single currency or the Lisbon Treaty. Ideally this ephemeral, short-term alteration in opinion would have been accompanied by a swing in public *attitude* to the EU and all things European, with the public expressing not only short-term support for a specific move in British policy but also positive sentiment about the country's membership of the EU. This might have been seen, for example, by the British slowly moving off the bottom of the Eurobarometer polling on whether people think their country's membership of the EU is a 'good' or 'bad' thing. Deeper still, and to set in motion a sea-change in the British approach to the EU (and maybe even bring about the longed for 'European consensus'), Blair and Brown would have wanted the British to undergo a *value* shift. Adopting positive European values would have meant currently apathetic or sceptical members of the public becoming comfortable with the idea of multi-level identities as British *and* European, and beginning to think 'European' instinctively, instead of being bribed to do so by an exposition of the vital economic interests at stake and the damage that would be incurred by withdrawing from the organization. In the Blair and Brown speeches examined in this study we see a combination of tactics designed to shift everything from opinions down to values and attitudes in between. Their rhetorical strategies worked at many levels simultaneously, targeting short-term attitudes, medium-term opinions and longer-term values.

This book therefore takes the complex character of political discourses and opens them up for critical scrutiny, suggesting in the process that it is never easy to write off the linguistic framing of policy as political 'spin'. This word has come to be inserted into many a study of New Labour and means a form of verbal deception (Charteris-Black 2006: 206–7) or 'feeding false information to the gullible' (Bower 2007: 144). It implies that some words, especially when used by New Labour ministers and directors of communication ('spin doctors'), are mere froth, lacking any foundation in the supposed 'reality' of a situation: 'the cynical and disingenuous manipulation of the truth by untrustworthy politicians' (Wodak 2009: 2). My view is that we need to take New Labour language critically yet seriously, neither as intending to deceive nor as mere window-dressing. Paul Chilton's view is most apt here, that strategic communication as practised by New Labour aimed to achieve two things: to manage information flows and to actively shape opinion through the careful 'design and monitor' of words and phrasings. In effect, the media operation run by New Labour was intrinsically about 'discourse management by hired rhetoricians' (Chilton 2004: 8). Language is as much a part of the policy as the money spent, the targets set and the treaties signed. If we write off policy discourses as sources of information about policy formation, we are ignoring a valuable archive containing actual traces of these 'realities' of policy discussion which were played out in a very public fashion. As a former chief speech-writer for Blair and head of the Strategic Communications Unit (SCU) in Downing Street 2001–3, Peter Hyman is well placed to summarize this argument: 'Politics to an extraordinary extent, is about words. What is reported are the speeches of politicians, the articles they write, the interviews they give, the statements they make in the House of Commons' (Hyman 2005: 5; on the composition and aims of the SCU see Jones 2000: 131–2). In bringing New Labour's words to the fore, I hope to make a novel contribution both to the study of British European policy after 1997 and to the study of New Labour's political project. The next section will explain the core arguments made in the book and how it has been arranged to advance them systematically.

V. Argument and structure of the book

In studying the neglected narratives Blair and Brown tried to construct about Europe, I will argue firstly in this book that in this corpus of speeches we can see New Labour's distinctive logic of history at work. The government's view was that the British had always been European and that it was a denial of the tide of history to suggest otherwise, or to fight against it. Secondly, however, I will claim that this logic was premised upon the development of a more proactive European policy than the government could actually deliver, rhetorically or otherwise. Put another way, Blair and Brown's Britain-as-European logic worked well all the time they presented constructive engagement with the EU as a modest but achievable end for British European policy. However, the Blair–Brown vision extended far beyond what they saw as the confines of a regional role for Britain. Their vision actually spoke to timeless aspirations of British global power and leadership, the stock in trade of many a previous Prime Minister over the past century and more. For New Labour, success in Europe came to mean using Europe as the means by which Britain could act out its pre-ordained leadership role on the world stage. The misreading of history they attributed to their Eurosceptic opponents was not, they implied, so much rooted in a misunderstanding of the British national project; rather, it was strategically well meaning but naive and therefore tactically flawed. Blair, Brown and their notional Eurosceptic opponents all wanted Britain to 'regain' its status as an influential global actor. (Blair remains convinced that the British public crave a leader who is 'a world and not just a national leader' – see Blair 2010: 310.) It was just that New Labour wanted to use Europe to achieve this goal rather than rely on outmoded conceptions of Empire or the jaded concept of the 'special relationship' as the method of doing so. In taking this position I concur with writers such as Anne Deighton (2002), who has argued that New Labour presented its discourses on Europe as progressive, forward-thinking efforts to reinterpret British history. On closer inspection, however, its discourses were as stuck in the past as were the discourses put about by the opponents of closer British involvement with the EU. Gordon Brown, it appears, was even more of this mind than Tony Blair, and the New Labour project ended up becoming a reworking of Winston Churchill's 'three circles' model of British foreign policy (see figure 9, p. 223) instead of the radical modification of it which a Europeanist foreign policy agenda would surely have required in order to succeed. After 1997 New Labour made precious little headway in developing and publicizing a distinctive alternative narrative about Britain's place in the world to challenge the hegemonic narrative about Britain's isolation from Europe. The government sought, at best, to 'manage' the European issue and lessen its salience within domestic politics and I therefore also follow Simon Bulmer in arguing that, despite more constructive diplomacy after 1997, 'little progress was achieved domestically in establishing public support' for such policy imprints it did manage to leave on the EU. Schizophrenically, New Labour combined electoral defensiveness at home with policy offensiveness abroad (Bulmer 2008: 598–9). In suffocating rather than breathing life into the domestic debate, Blair and Brown opened the door for their adversaries, notably but not only confined to the Eurosceptical press, to keep the country in a permanent state of discursive war with the continent (see chapter 5) and preserve the frosty public attitude in Britain to things 'European'.

To advance the case that New Labour struggled to exorcise the ghosts of the past in British European policy the book is divided into nine main chapters, a conclusion and then an epilogue on trends in foreign policy discourse in the Brown years which takes the story to the spring of 2009, shortly before the June European and local council elections in Britain. The cut-off point comes approximately one year before the end of the New Labour era, but there is nothing to suggest that there would be (nor indeed were there) any ruptures in foreign policy thinking in the course of the government's death throes in office, for all the reasons set out in the epilogue. In deciding how to structure the book I faced a difficult choice. Initially I planned to write a series of background chapters on various aspects of the politics, language and decision-making style of New Labour (a Part I); this would have been followed by the empirical evidence from the speeches in Part II. I reworked this format halfway through the research (in 2007) because I wanted to choose a form for the book that spoke directly to the content. That is, the discourses on Europe New Labour developed were firmly shaped (fixed, to a degree) by both the legacy of past discourses and wider currents in public–media discourses on Europe in Britain after 1997. There are some things it is just not feasible to say about Europe for a politician wanting to maintain the support of voters of the centre ground (a term I use interchangeably with 'middle England'). The government might have wanted to project an image of freshness, originality and departure from conventional practices, but in fact it was consistently running up against the limits of what it is (electorally) possible to say about Europe in Britain. Blair and Brown were taking on the role of norm entrepreneurs in the knowledge that there were certain things it was necessary to say to keep the voting public onside. Their discourses were simultaneously reflective of internal government policy development *and* highly structured or fixed, as it were, by the conditions of their existence. To try to get this point across I have structured the book around a series of 'context' chapters which precede the relevant empirical chapters and set the scene for them by spelling out how, in their speeches, Blair and Brown were looking to respond to key aspects of the 'reality' of the British in Europe as they saw it. As the reader progresses through the book, bounced between the speeches and the context, I hope to convey some of the complexity of the discursive webs woven about Britain and Europe which must have made writing a successful speech on the subject arduous in the extreme.

Chapter 2 contextualizes the New Labour project by studying two issues: first, how New Labour presented itself for public consumption and how it defined itself against other parties in British politics in the 1990s; and second, the powerful Blair–Brown axis at the heart of the 'project', which drove my choice of sources for the study. Chapter 3, another context chapter, is theoretical. It first explains the idea of 'norm entrepreneurship' and how it can be adapted to help us think through New Labour's handling of British European policy. It then considers the rationale for treating these texts as 'discourses' and sets out the method used to process the data in the speeches. Chapter 4 is the first empirical chapter, on the national interests deemed to be at stake over European policy: in economic, security and influence terms. It is almost a stand-alone chapter because it sets out what Blair called the 'crude appeal' of Europe: the most openly propagandist elements of the case he and Brown made to change public opinion on the EU. Chapter 5, another context chapter, sketches the backdrop to New Labour's encounter with Euroscepticism. It does this not by telling the salient 'facts' of British and European history, but instead by staking out some of the main features of the discursive field about 'Europe' in Britain that Blair and Brown manifestly wanted to undermine or develop in their speeches. This chapter centres on the idea that the British *talk* of Europe and European affairs as an Other and Others 'over there', and this sense of foreboding about the future has come to characterize Eurosceptical discourses about the EU in Britain. Blair and Brown felt it necessary to tear the heart out of this construction of Europe as Other by rethinking British and European history and identity as a means of helping the British be more at ease with their multilayered British-national and Europe-regional identities.

Chapter 6 applies theoretical approaches to Euroscepticism to help us understand – through the empirical data in the speeches – how Blair and Brown constructed their identity as 'Europeans' against their perceived 'sceptical' opponents. It shows some interplay between the terms used by academics and politicians, suggesting scope for mutually beneficial debate between the two communities. Chapter 7 is a final context chapter, this time on the ambiguous roles that history and memories of the past played in the New Labour project. It shows that the architects of New Labour initially wanted to position the party as an entity distinct from 'Old' Labour and then in government wanted to assume the role of heir to traditions in British politics they saw as 'great'. Professing that Britain should get over its past and move on, New Labour in fact became a history-producing and history-consuming machine that suffered from an acute identity crisis as a result. Chapter 8 studies the empirical evidence on how New Labour rendered and rethought history in its widest senses. It suggests that there was lots of 'history' in Blair and Brown's speeches but less in the way of a critical appreciation of the difficulties of applying analogies from the past in the present – by Blair the non-historian (a claim Blair unconvincingly disputes in his memoirs – see Blair 2010) and the historically minded Brown alike. Chapter 9 takes the empirical data a stage further in terms of critique by nailing down the New Labour will to 'lead' through its European policy by portraying Britain as a 'bridge' between the EU and the US. It then studies how we can use these foreign policy speeches to see New Labour's thinking on the qualities that make for a successful leader and a successful country in the 'modern' world. Unsurprisingly for a Prime Minister and Chancellor who, in their distinctive ways, wanted to be seen as personifications of the Labour Party, we find evidence that, in talking about Britain and Europe, Blair and Brown were actually writing elements of their *own* personalities, characteristics, self-identities and life-worlds into their European policy discourses. I want to suggest in the final chapter that seeking out the 'Britain and Europe' story during the New Labour years in fact necessitates an understanding of the Blair–Brown story and this spins us full circle back to chapter 2. The conclusion reflects on two prominent issues to emerge from the book by asking two general questions. First, what were the causes and consequences of New Labour's European policy failure? Second, how far can we understand and explain the phenomenon of Euro-scepticism in Britain today? It wraps up by considering how we might take forward research into British foreign policy discourses.

Chapter 2

Context I. The New Labour project

> Controlling the presentation and perception of policy is no longer a secondary matter, it is virtually inseparable from policy making, and advisers like [Alastair] Campbell seem now to be inside the process of policy making. (Fairclough 2000: 122)

> Blair was starting to invent a New Labour language. (Naughtie 2002: 88)

Aristotle said that the art of political persuasion relies fundamentally on a leader's mastery of language, skilful rhetoric and the ability to create empathy between speaker and listener (Kennedy 1991). The nature of the trade compels politicians to think about how they present themselves, their policies and their aspirations in the best possible light to convince their multiple audiences of the rectitude and moral force of their arguments. Paul Chilton is just one of a number commentators coming at politics from a linguistic direction to make this case: 'However politics is defined, there is a linguistic, discursive and communicative dimension, generally only partly acknowledged, if at all, by practitioners and theorists' (Chilton 2004: 4). Politicians deliver set-piece speeches, debate with each other in national parliaments, are grilled by interviewers in television and radio studios and get door-stopped by journalists. On each and every occasion they are invited, variously, to present their arguments, defend their positions, explain their policies and justify their decisions to the public via press and broadcast outlets which, literally, mediate their words and ideas to their respective readers, listeners and viewers. More than ever in a fast-paced twenty-four-hour news environment, politicians have to achieve three things simultaneously. First, they have to communicate a vision. Second, they have to establish their authority to speak on a given topic. Third, they have to assume a leadership role in generating legitimacy for their policy agenda. As Jonathan Charteris-Black has put it, 'the most important type of behaviour by which leaders mobilise their followers is their linguistic performance. In democratic frameworks

40

it is primarily through language that leaders legitimise their leadership' (Charteris-Black 2006: 1).

The central claim advanced in this chapter is that establishing New Labour as a successful national political movement entailed the reinvention of the language of the party's politics for public consumption. It opens by considering the connections between language on the one hand and policy on the other, and shows how New Labour took the collapse of an already fragile distinction between the two to new levels. It moves on to study the Blair–Brown axis around which the language of New Labour was developed and used to try, if not to control events, then certainly to manage their production and representation in ways that would keep the government at the forefront of people's minds and on top of political debates and crises as they arose.

I. Language and policy

> We often made policy in speeches. It's one of the vehicles you've got. As Prime Minister, people pay an incredible amount of attention to what you say and ... if you want to push a policy that is being stymied somewhere in the system ... a speech is a very good way of doing that. Words are deeds. (Interview with Collins)

One of the most pressing tasks facing modern governments is to market their suite of domestic and foreign policies by shaping perceptions of what is being achieved, and why, and how rapidly the government is advancing towards its stated objectives. Domestically, a national public can often *see* how far and how fast a government makes an impact because domestic policy outputs are a tangible part of the lives and experiences of members of that national public. Being stuck on a hospital waiting list, filling out self-assessment tax forms, trying to get your offspring into an oversubscribed local school, or waiting in another traffic jam on the M1 motorway: these are the events that ground political debates in the realm of public 'reality' and everyday life. Even domestically, however, media debates rage about how far an increase in investment in the NHS, for example, has led to real improvement on the ground in the quality of hospital facilities, the length of operation waiting lists and so on, and these in turn mould public perceptions of the state of affairs nationally, away from individuals' personal experiences. Peter Riddell made a telling point about the possibility for a 'spin gap' to open between politicians' claims about the impact of their policies and public perceptions of those policies when he reviewed Populus polling carried out for *The Times* after 1997. The results showed 'a consistent and marked difference between voters' personal experience of various services and their impression of how the service was performing nationally' (Riddell 2005: 54), the former being more favourable than the latter. Even the sums of money pledged by governments can be a source of dispute: is a promised rise in expenditure as big as the government makes out or does it include in the small print previously announced funding increases? The bare statistics can cause as much controversy as the qualitative change such fiscal stimuli are intended to bring about. The first decade of New Labour, argues Terence Casey, presented some paradoxical findings:

> By many of the objective measures of political performance – economic growth, low unemployment, and improved public service – the Blair government was a success. But the public was having none of it…. Only 27 percent thought the country a more successful place [in 2007] than in 1997; only 26 percent gave the government a positive overall rating. (Casey 2009: 1)

If a spin gap can open domestically, it is even more likely to do so in the realm of foreign policy, where the state (the national Self) is devising and enacting policies towards peoples, governments and states (national/international Others) the vast majority of which the domestic electorate will never see or experience at first hand. Take a conventional definition of New Labour's foreign policy from Paul Williams: 'the sum of the UK's official external relations between May 1997 and May 2005, especially those actions undertaken to effect certain stated objectives, conditions and actors that lie beyond its territorial legitimacy' (Williams 2005: 5). Foreign policy in this view is about the use of national instruments to stimulate change(s) at the international level which will be of benefit to the nation domestically, in economic, political or security terms. It is about meeting 'objectives' and altering 'conditions' and the behaviour of various 'actors' in the international system, whether these actors be other states, sub-state actors, non-state actors, trans-state actors or individuals – Osama bin Laden for example – who have the capacity to influence the perceived British national interest.

Managing the representation of Britain's European policy was one critical task for New Labour. As we saw in the previous chapter, the official line Blair took as he approached the end of his premiership was that his European policy *on the ground* had been a success. To support his version of events we could follow Riddell and Seldon in totting up the balance sheet of the positives in British European policy under New Labour. Riddell's list reads: a more effective Common Foreign and Security Policy; a more coherent European defence policy and capability; increasing participation in the EU's Justice and Home Affairs pillar; EU enlargement in May 2004; and giving impetus to the EU's economic reform and liberalization agenda (Riddell 2005:

150). Seldon (echoing Blair 2010: 536–7) lists: enlargement, 'for which he received little recognition during his premiership' (Seldon 2007: 408 and 572); helping the free-marketeer José Manuel Barroso secure the Commission Presidency ahead of Guy Verhofstadt, also in 2004; and devising and pushing the Hampton Court Agenda, 2005–7. Against these we could set Richard Whitman's negatives: 'remaining outside the euro and not being a member of the Schengen zone'. Fewer in number, admittedly, but arguably of greater political weight and certainly 'hindrances to British pretensions to leadership' (Whitman 2005: 684). However, even if we take the policy positives to have outweighed the negatives there is a worrying fact that despite all these 'factual' advances in British European policy there was still an evident spin gap: 'The whole question of Britain's role in the EU remained unresolved after more than eight years in office' (Riddell 2005: 199), implying that the improved diplomatic climate between Britain and the EU under New Labour was not accompanied by a waning of the British public's exceptional levels of Euroscepticism. In other words, elite-level achievements, in this case the normalization of British–European relations after the turmoil of the Conservative years, meant nothing if the sense and meaning of these achievements were not, for whatever reason, communicated effectively to the public – or if that public chose not to listen. Following Riddell, we could argue that, at the level of political discourse, New Labour failed to plug the spin gap because it was unable to shift public opinion on the EU to anywhere near the extent it was able to normalize Britain's diplomatic and political relations with the country's EU partners. If we take together the once-removed-from-everyday-experience argument about foreign policy with the idea of the spin gap, then arguably foreign policy debates are driven to a greater extent than domestic debates by *perceptions* of occurrences in the 'external' world, the meaning of which is perpetually beyond our grasp as fallible interpreters of a complex world 'out there'. The closest contact with the 'reality' of foreign policy for the average citizen is to watch a national foreign policy strategy being acted out through media reporting and broadcasting, whether as passive 'spectators' on a war (McInnes 2002) or as active contributors to a televised famine relief charity extravaganza. That 'reality' is in turn shaped fundamentally by the language used to call it to mind – the way the realm of the 'foreign' is construed and represented in discourse.

The point that language shapes policy, rather than putting the gloss on it *post hoc* for public consumption, is relevant to the study of New Labour because of the close attention its architects paid to the performative aspects of language (on the performativity of language see Austin 1975 and on its practical application see Diez 1999: 600–2).

The party devoted particular attention to branding, representing and selling its policy ideas to a British public who during the 1980s had come to be hugely turned off by many of the key planks of the Labour Party's policy platform. Its 'anti-Europeanism' was one such source of public antipathy to Labour and this features in chapter 7. Language has a performative element that marks it out as one of, if not *the*, vital dimension of any successful policy strategy at home or abroad. Language is more than a means of communication because it has an intrinsic meaning-making function. Language helps us communicate and talk the world into existence because our words necessarily have to stand in for the objects, people, events and actions we talk about. This performative notion of language is 'one in which language does not just transmit thoughts or reflect the meanings of social context but actually takes part in the constitution of both' (Cabrera 2005: 27). It is not as simple as saying there is 'policy' on the one hand and 'language used to describe that policy' on the other. The two co-constitute each other and it has long been a New Labour mantra that: 'communication is only truly successful when it works together with other elements in pursuit of a common objective' (Bird 2008).

Strategic communication lay at the very heart of the New Labour project, which was advanced by Tony Blair, former tabloid journalist Alastair Campbell and Peter Mandelson and Gordon Brown. Significantly, the last two figures both had a background in television and it is reported that in opposition during the early 1980s Brown coached Blair in the art of writing pithy press releases (Sopel 1995: 76). New

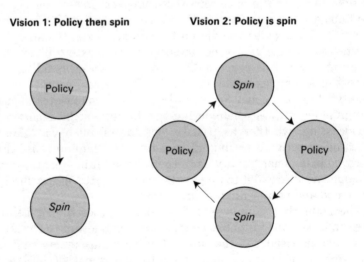

Figure 2. Two visions of policy and spin.

Labour operated its strategic communications with a perspective on the policy–spin relationship that is closer to vision 2 than vision 1 in figure 2. The party leadership's starting premise was that it was operating in a dynamic twenty-four-hour-a-day media environment in which the government should try to control or manage as many of the political messages 'out there' for public consumption as it could. It should also have the capacity to be able to react purposefully to unforeseen crises or to respond when, in the government's view, its messages were wilfully misinterpreted and thrown back at it by media outlets. The government's near obsessive attention to language and communication strategies naturally attracted opprobrium from those who felt that what came to be known as New Labour 'spin' was somehow pernicious and untrustworthy, and inherently privileged deception over honesty. The cartoon from the *Mail on Sunday* in 2001 (image 3) sums it up nicely. Here, the much maligned Campbell (on the left) is puzzled as to why his 'spin' telescope does not appear to be illuminating the 'facts' for him. He has not realized he is looking

Image 3. John Jensen, no title, *Mail on Sunday*, 4 March 2001.

at the world through the wrong end of his telescope. On the right, what appear to be members of the public (and journalists, perhaps) are seeing the facts through their telescope, implying that they can see the truth of this world more clearly and distinctly than can spin doctors and politicians who get tangled up in linguistic webs of their own weaving. One critic who juxtaposes spin against truth is the journalist Peter Oborne, who, early on in the Blair years, expressed unease that David Miliband, then head of Blair's Number 10 Policy Unit, all too easily elided presentation and substance:

> It is noticeable, listening to David Miliband, that he does not talk about issues, he talks about 'stories'.... In Tony Blair's Downing Street, the policy man even speaks and thinks like a spin doctor. This is no coincidence. New Labour does not believe that policy and presentation are two separate functions, but indivisible parts of the same seamless process. (Oborne 1999: 5)

Oborne's judgement is that Miliband was there to talk 'policy' but in fact thought 'spin'. The policy substance was the 'good' or construc-tive facet that Miliband should have been concentrating on. The 'spin' was the 'bad' or potentially distortive aspect that should have featured less in Miliband's day-to-day decision- and policy-making. Only if we accept an arbitrary dualism between spin on the one hand and policy on the other can we make sense of all the ink that has been spilt on spin's purportedly destructive impact on democracy in contemporary Britain. A subtler appreciation of the nature of knowl-edge and information as inevitably positioned brings us to empathize more with the New Labour position. The very allegation that 'spin' was a pernicious or corruptible element of New Labour's governance of Britain was itself a piece of spin premised on a false dichotomy between 'fact' and 'representation'. Critics of spin sought to under-mine the narrative power of the New Labour message by portraying the New Labour project as shallow and lacking in substance. Con-trary to this, David Hill, Labour Party director of communications 1991–97 and 2003–7, has observed that: 'The answer is that these were not black arts. The answer is that you can't deliver unless you have got something *to* deliver.' Empty bluster, says Hill, will always be exposed if it does not match the direction and intent of 'core policies' (interview with Hill). It is also important to note the reason *why* New Labour's progenitors took this approach to political communication. They had seen the damage the press caused to the electoral fortunes of the Labour Party under Michael Foot and Neil Kinnock in the 1980s and early 1990s and were set firmly against a repeat performance in the later 1990s. They remoulded the party around the concept of 'modernity', an 'overall picture of images, of words and of policies, all of which have this vital underlying purpose of saying "we are not the party you used to think we were"' (interview with Hill). Obsessing about 'spin' is, therefore, wasted energy on two levels. As a theory about New Labour's media management it overplays a far more complex relationship between knowledge and prejudice. Moreover, it is ahistorical in overlooking the genesis of New Labour as a media-savvy election-winning machine.

To illustrate the point that policy and the language of policy are two sides of the same coin let us take two examples: Blair's Labour Party conference speech of 1 October 2002 and an episode from five years earlier that helped define Britain's stance on membership of the single European currency throughout the New Labour years. Blair's 'At our best when at our boldest' conference speech contained more than the usual amount of foreign policy discussion because of the post-9/11 focus on the invasion of Afghanistan and what were then ongoing discussions between the US, Britain and potential coalition partners over Saddam Hussein's continuing non-compliance with UN resolutions on Iraq's alleged weapons of mass destruction (WMD) programme. As Blair saw it, New Labour had 'made a good start but we've not been bold enough', and he went on to think through the causes and consequences of the interdependence that was 'obliterating the distinction between foreign and domestic policy' (Blair 2002b). When talking about national security, Blair would persistently warn about 'the fact of a crisis somewhere becoming a crisis everywhere' (Blair 2006e). Having reviewed his preferred vision for Britain's role in the world, Blair considered the Iraq issue and set out his rationale for choosing to ally London so closely with Washington in the emerging rounds of UN diplomacy on Iraq's WMD programme (Blair 2002b). John Kampfner's sources told him that the key Iraq segments of the speech were inserted by Blair after last-minute discussions with his Number 10 chief of staff Jonathan Powell. 'They did it to head off dissent within the party – or in the words of one who was involved in the speech "to sweeten the pill of Iraq"' (Kampfner 2004: 213). Here, then, was Blair using a set-piece speech to confront head on waverers and dissenters within his party and the country at large. In a rapidly changing international environment there can never be such thing as a 'completed' policy as vision 1 in figure 2 implies. Blair was working instead to vision 2 and seeking through his words to alter the terms of the debate within his party and the government machine in Whitehall. One disgruntled Foreign Office figure later complained to Kampfner: 'Nobody in this building knew. It might have turned out for the best, but it's not the best way of conducting foreign policy' (quoted in Kampfner 2004: 213). We will return to Blair's preferred way of reaching policy decisions later in the chapter but on the back of this quote it is worth asking whether the Foreign Office mandarin, like Oborne and other critics of 'spin', was working to a vision 1 agenda when Blair and his team were working to the vision 2 approach to policy-making. If that is the case, it might explain much of the civil service unease at Blair's style of leadership and foreign policy decision-making.

The second example is better known and relates to the evolution of Labour's policy on the single currency in October 1997. Paul Routledge has colourfully described this episode as 'a Whitehall farce of "government by spin", with nobody really knowing the chancellor's precise intentions' (Routledge 1998: 325; see also Hughes and Smith 1998: 97). If there was one issue that drew attention to the behind-the-scenes activities of New Labour's spin doctors, this was it.

Box 1 chronicles the series of events leading up to the Chancellor's statement to the House of Commons on 27 October 1997, when he announced that the British economy would have to pass 'five tests' before the New Labour government would consider it timely or appropriate to put the decision on euro membership to the British people in a referendum (all quotes below from Brown 1997d). Wanting to move on from the 'indecision' that had characterized previous British policy on the Europe question, Brown said he hoped the statement would initiate a 'new national purpose'. His statement was divided into three parts. In the first part he argued against rejecting membership of the single currency on principle: 'if it works economically, it is, in our view, worth doing'; if it can be shown to work and to be in the British national interest 'then the Government believes Britain should be part of it'. The second part of the statement set out the five tests for membership: on economic cycles, on flexibility, on investment, on financial services and on employment. The Treasury had run the tests and found, he declared, that 'British membership of a single currency in 1999 could not meet the tests and therefore [it] is not in the country's economic interests' to join in the first wave. Hence, 'barring some fundamental and unforeseen change in economic circumstances, making a decision, during this Parliament, to join is not realistic'. However, this apparently hard-line stance was softened in the next part of the speech, on preparations for entry should the euro prove to be a success and the tests be met. 'We should therefore begin now to prepare ourselves so that, should we meet the economic tests, we can make a decision to join a successful single currency early in the next Parliament.' These preparations were to be made on three levels: by individual businesses; nationally through a 'changeover plan' and the government's introduction of greater flexibility into the British economy; and at EU level via completion of the single market, improved market competition and labour market reforms. Summing up, Brown said: 'On

---

Box I. Whelan, Brown and the euro, October 1997

16 October. Brown telephones Blair to say he wants to clarify the government's position on the single currency; Blair agrees to Brown giving a newspaper interview on the single currency.

18 October. Publication of Brown interview in *The Times*, 'Brown rules out single currency for lifetime of this Parliament'. In the *Sun* the story was headlined 'Brown Says No to the Euro'.

18 October. Charlie Whelan is overheard 'clarifying' Brown's position over the telephone outside the Red Lion pub in Westminster: 'No, it doesn't say it in the interview, but Gordon is effectively ruling out joining in this Parliament'.

18 October. Mandelson alerts Blair to the apparent reversal in the government's open-door policy on the euro. Brown and Campbell are non-contactable.

18 October. Blair calls Whelan: 'it's far too hard. You've got to row back'. 'It's too late', Whelan tells Blair.

19 October. Sunday papers carry stories of Blair and Brown 'meticulously' agreeing the policy during the previous week.

20 October. Accusations of a government being 'in a spin' over its euro policy; £20 billion wiped off share values on 'Brown Monday'.

21 October. Meeting of key protagonists in Downing Street.

c.23–24 October. Policy statement drafted amid much disagreement; 'Each time Blair put words in, Brown struck them out'.

c.23–24 October. 'Five tests' of economic convergence are set in stone by Brown and Ed Balls.

24 October. Treasury announces that Brown is to make a statement to Parliament.

27 October. Chancellor's Commons statement on the single currency: 'prepare and decide'.

Based on Rawnsley (2001: 72–88); see also Jones (2000: 83–97) and Bower (2007: 247–53).

Europe, Madam Speaker, the time of indecision is over. The period for practical preparation has begun.'

The rationale of political discourse is that it creates an aura of certainty and direction where in practice things can be less clear cut. Comparing the chronicle of events leading up to the statement with the timing and nature of the statement itself, we can see that Brown was acting to close down debates about the government's European policy as well as shoring up his relationship with Blair, which Whelan's untimely intervention had soured (not for the first time, notably over the leadership of the Labour Party after John Smith's death in 1994 – see Sopel 1995: 186–7). As Scott James and Kai Opperman have written, this was not part of a strategic plan but a 'hastily formulated policy' (James and Opperman 2009: 289). The question is the extent to which Whelan's spin pushed New Labour further than it felt able to go in policy terms just five months into office. To use Riddell's idea of the spin gap: what was the size of the lacuna between Whelan saying 'Gordon is effectively ruling out joining in this Parliament' and Brown in his Commons statement saying 'We should therefore begin now to prepare ourselves so that, should we meet the economic tests, we can make a decision to join a successful single currency early in the next Parliament'? Put like that, not much, which takes us back to the alleged spin/substance dichotomy. Whelan attracted so much attention not on policy grounds but on policy-*making* grounds. As Derek Scott, Blair's economics adviser, later wrote: 'when Tony Blair arrived at No. 10 it was ... the manner of the policy announcement that irked those within the civil service' (as well as some among the top echelons of New Labour), as they 'felt the power to deliver government announcements should be in the grip of elected government ministers' (Scott 2004: 207). From the accounts available to us, the apparent truth in this case was that there was a European 'policy vacuum' in 1997 (Peston 2005: 201). New Labour was loathe to spend time filling it, having come to power trumpeting domestic issues above all else, and had not spent much time devising a coherent set of foreign policy ideas and ambitions. Blair himself had a certain 'innocence', coming from a relatively limited set of travelling experiences globally or in Europe and an 'inexperience' that flowed from that (Stephens 2004: 107–8). The testimony of a key Blair adviser on foreign policy backs this up: 'Blair's foreign policy record developed as time passed. I don't think he came in with a clear set of ideas that he then delivered' (interview with Sawers). Outside of government Whelan's intervention alerted journalists and commentators to a certain New Labour 'style' which, in their view, was over-reliant on an extended court of unelected advisers that damaged democratic government decision-making and the idea of collective Cabinet responsibility.

In sum, the Whelan episode was more remarkable for what it unleashed in terms of commentary on New Labour than it was for any spin gap it created in terms of British European policy. 'Spin' in this sense was never much more than another ideological weapon used by New Labour's critics to attack the government, conveniently overlooking its own genesis as a form of 'spin'. Crucially, it overlooked the subtleties of the discursive modes by which New Labour tried to keep its options open as long as possible on difficult questions such as the single currency. If there was a spin gap it was often in the eye of the beholder and a euphemism for some other charge about the existence of a democratic deficit at the heart of New Labour policy-making. It has therefore been instructive to revisit these two examples of when spin supposedly took precedence over substance as a way of highlighting the complex nature of political communication and how discourse domains are always imbricated with complex sets of power relations, within government and between government and the public and government and commentators.

In this section I have tried to collapse the supposed distinction between policy substance on the one hand and language as the descriptor or representation of that policy on the other. Perhaps the distinction has never been as clear cut as I have presented it, but during the rule of New Labour we were bombarded with articles labelling 'spin' as pernicious because it distorted the 'facts' or the 'truth' of the world as we apprehended it. It is hard not to conclude from this that some sort of 'spin versus reality' binary shaped the analysis of New Labour as a communications and message-making machine. Looked at theoretically, the word 'spin' came to form part of a discourse that accepted a rather shaky positivist distinction between knower and known, subject and object (Cabrera 2005: 9) and which therefore permitted its proponents to gauge truth claims with reference to a reality that was external to them and easily accessible through sensory experience. Looked at practically, the moniker 'spin' became a useful stick with which to beat a party that, argu-ably in its later opposition years and early years in power, was one step ahead of media organizations in its message-management tech-niques. I have argued the case for a quite different view of spin, that it was neither illegitimate nor a distortion of a reality whose essence was always a source of dispute. Indeed, it could be argued that the essence of spin was as much in dispute as was the essence of the reality that spin supposedly corroded. We now need to move from strategic communication as political discourse to make the case for concentrating so heavily in what follows in the rest of the book on Blair and Brown as the main progenitors of the way New Labour 'talked Europe' after 1997.

II. Blair and Brown as figureheads

The debate was driven by Number 10 and Number 11 and the decision had been made to let it idle in neutral. Until that changed, no-one would move. They were definite. Maybe. (Naughtie 2002: 155)

Rivals they might have been, but when Blair and Brown worked together to present a united front it was impossible for anyone in government to challenge their authority. As Adam Boulton has remarked: 'In many ways, it could be said that the Blair–Brown relationship provided the creative tension which helped drive New Labour' (Boulton 2008: 271). Moving on from the language–policy debate, the next step we need to take is to refine who it is that stands both for 'Britain' and for 'New Labour' in this book. My focus is predominantly on the words of Tony Blair and Gordon Brown, who as British Prime Minister and Chancellor (later Prime Minister) respectively are obvious choices. But let us problematize this in two ways, first by noting that Blair and Brown by definition did not have total control over British foreign policy (what about the Foreign Office?) and second by working the point Philip Stephens made above, about Blair's relative inexperience, uninterest even, in foreign affairs prior to assuming power.

Investigations into how British foreign policy is put together tell us that Prime Ministers may assume the mantle of unofficial foreign policy figureheads but that they are not the only or even the most important actors to account for when explaining trends in policy (Frankel 1968; Vital 1971; Wallace 1977; Forster and Blair 2002). Foreign policy seeks to advance a broadly conceived 'national interest' and it is therefore to be expected that Cabinet colleagues, not least those representing the Foreign Office, Treasury and Ministry of Defence, will have inputs, as, under New Labour, did the head of the newly named DfID, successor to the Overseas Development Agency. Civil servants in Whitehall and diplomats in embassies around the world all feed in information, memoranda, advice and recommendations on a day-to-day basis. Non-governmental organizations and interest groups will have their say, and of course public debates in the print and broadcast media will impinge on the government's perception of what it might be able to achieve and how far it might legitimately be able to act on a given policy sector or international crisis. However, this book concentrates on Blair and Brown for the simple reason that, from the evidence I have seen, they were the driving force behind New Labour's policy and language on Europe. Blair and his Downing Street team were also the driving force behind the broader trends in British foreign policy over this period, whatever claims we might want to make for his successive Foreign Secretaries, Robin Cook, Jack Straw and Margaret Beckett. The Brown–Miliband nexus (with David Miliband as Foreign Secretary) was slightly different and this will be explored in the epilogue. Let us start with Blair.

The phrase (it could be a command or a plea, depending on circumstance) 'Tony wants' was routinely heard in Whitehall right down to the lowest echelons of the ministerial elites and civil servants. Although it has been mimicked to the point of parody it does indicate the extent to which Blair, aided and abetted by his small team of advisers, was both the personification and the 'face' of the New Labour project after 1994. Now, Blair is not alone among British Prime Ministers in being accused of running a 'kitchen cabinet', an unofficial band of colleagues and/or advisers which sidelines the elected Cabinet as a strategic policy-making and agenda-setting unit. Looking at the literature on one of Blair's Labour predecessors, Harold Wilson, Prime Minister 1964–70 and 1974–76, helps us appreciate the essence of the critique of this closed policy-making style. Kevin Jefferys notes that Wilson's 'inner cabinet' advised him chiefly but not only on foreign affairs. It consisted of 'a shifting group of up to ten senior ministers who met informally in order to take a broad view of government policy and to suggest new initiatives' (Jefferys 1999: 132). Particularly galling for Wilson's Cabinet colleagues was the presence in the premier's cabal of unelected advisers such as his security adviser, George Wigg, and his private secretary, Marcia Williams (see Wigg 1972; Williams 1972). Wilson's press secretary, Joe Haines, and Douglas Jay, President of the Board of Trade 1964–67, both testify to the existence and genuine behind-the-scenes influence of this kitchen cabinet (Haines 1977: 157; Jay 1980: 378). The expansion of the Prime Minister's private office is a theme that runs through the prolific commentaries on the Wilson years. The diaries of Tony Benn (1987), Richard Crossman (1976, 1977) and Barbara Castle (1984) all contributed to the idea that 'something changed' in British politics and policy-making in the 1960s. This view has died hard, not least because it found its way into influential histories of the period (for example Morgan 1989: 256), and into school and university politics programmes covering the nature of Prime Ministerial power and influence in post-war Britain. For example, in the chapter on the Cabinet and core executive in one contemporary textbook on British politics, the 'kitchen cabinet' gets a mention and a definition all of its own, together with the obligatory reference to Crossman on the 'presidentialization' of the premiership (Budge *et al.* 2007: 104, 112; see also Jones *et al.* 2007: 638–9).

Summoning up the Wilson years is valuable because they helped give rise to a powerful discourse about the beginning of the end of Cabinet government in Britain. As Hugh Heclo and Aaron Wildavsky surmised: 'By the end of the 1960s few insiders were particularly happy with the way their machine was working' (Heclo and Wildavsky 1974: 266). Once framed and having entered the popular consciousness, it has been difficult for commentators to talk about British policy-making *without* mentioning the actuality or the possibility of anti-democratic policy-making practices at the heart of government. In the place of Wilson's kitchen cabinet, therefore, we find Blair's 'presidential style of decision-making' (Whitman 2005: 677) or 'denocracy', to coin Anthony Seldon's term. 'Denocracy' describes Blair's preferred mode of decision-making, mulling over issues with his aides, sat on the sofa in his 'den' at the rear of Downing Street (Seldon 2005: 112, 261, 281), a style he seems to have transplanted straight from his time in opposition to his time in government. Blair's predilection was for a smaller group of people than the reported ten or so who surrounded Wilson. In terms of personnel it was less an 'inner cabinet' (a cabinet-within-a-Cabinet) than a group of close confidantes hardly drawn from the Cabinet at all. Its members were Peter Mandelson, Jonathan Powell, Alastair Campbell, Philip Gould, Anji Hunter and Sally Morgan. Mandelson was initially Minister of State Without Portfolio, located in the Cabinet Office from May 1997 to July 1998. He then served in government as Secretary of State for Trade and Industry from July to December 1998 and Secretary of State for Northern Ireland between October 1999 and January 2001. Powell, a former diplomat *au fait* with the US from his days at the Washington embassy, had a wide policy remit as Blair's Downing Street chief of staff, including – but not limited to – the peace process in Northern Ireland (Powell 2008). Campbell was Blair's press secretary from 1997 to 2003. Gould was Blair's focus group rapporteur and 'court strategist of New Labour' (Seldon 2005: 137; Savigny 2007: 129–31). Hunter – long a personal acquaintance of Blair – was director of political and government relations and was succeeded by Sally Morgan in 2001, who for the four years previously had been political secretary to the Prime Minister. Presidential policy-making seems to have been New Labour's style, suggests Seldon, because Brown ran the Treasury in the same fashion: 'all power was centralized in the Chancellor's Office, which effectively meant Brown, [adviser Ed] Balls and [press secretary Charlie] Whelan. Some officials, who had worked in the Treasury all their lives, found themselves out in the cold' (Seldon 2005: 688; see also Beckett 2007: 126; Bower 2007: 204; Tonge 2009: 308–9). To summarize, we can turn to Robin Butler, who as Cabinet Secretary 1988–98 had direct experience of New Labour's decision-making style in its formative years in power: 'Tony Blair and Gordon Brown were the inner cell of New Labour ... they weren't much in the business of consulting their colleagues in order to determine policies' (BBC 2007). British foreign policy was under the watchful gaze of Downing Street, even if Blair and his team did not always know where they wanted to take it.

Brown is the other focal point in the study because of his sustained public efforts to think through the meaning of Britishness in the twenty-first century. This 'big Brown idea' (Tonge 2009: 309) was inspired by George Orwell's wartime essay on the 'English genius' (Routledge 1998: 3–4, 232), which Brown cunningly reframed as the 'British genius'. He used it to describe the values and outward-looking globalism that characterize the people living on this small island off the north-west of mainland Europe. The British, said Brown in May 1997, possess all the qualities a country needs to succeed in the twenty-first century: 'inventiveness and creativity; a capacity for hard work alongside ... adaptability...; a culture of learning and a belief in fair play and opportunity for all; and an ability to look outwards. These are the qualities that make up the British genius' (Brown 1997a). These were not just *characteristics* Brown ascribed to the British but were actually *values* he believed the British hold dear. The nation's 'great historic qualities' (Brown 2001c) had been 'impor-tant to success in the years of the first British industrial revolution' (Brown 2001d; see also Brown 2006c) and he clearly believed they had been quashed or repressed by irresponsible governments after the Second World War. Brown pledged that through its economic and education policies, New Labour would help the people discover 'new ways of harnessing' (Brown 2000a; Brown 2000b) these apparently genetic 'great British assets and advantages' (Brown 2004f) in the post-industrial age, as part of the project of renewing Britain for the twenty-first century (Brown 1999a; Brown 2004e) around 'a thriving modern civic society' (Brown 2000f). Furthering the biological take on things, Brown said in November 2006 that 'in the DNA' of all the best British companies were precisely those qualities that made the British people and nation great (Brown 2006d). The 'British genius' was a staple of Brownite foreign and economic policy discourse throughout his time at the Treasury (see Brown 1997b; Brown 1997c; Brown 1997e; Brown 1998b; Brown 1998f; Brown 1999c; Brown 2000c; Brown 2002c; Brown 2005e; Brown 2005g). As the Blair years progressed, the Chancellor became firmer in his conviction that these values could help lead to a 'changed Europe' (Brown 2003c) and help Britain compete more effectively in the global economy (Brown 2004g; Brown 2005c). Brown's stress on the 'outward looking' British underscored the message Blair wanted to send out over the most appropriate course for British foreign policy, framed in terms of a debate 'about how the British national interest is defined and what we should stand for as a country' (Brown 2004g).

Given the above, it is an axiom of this book that to get to grips with the construction of New Labour as a progressive political move-ment it is imperative to appreciate the characteristics and working habits of its two central characters. Blair and Brown's proclivity for personalized and highly centralized decision-making issued a stark

challenge to conventional diplomatic practices, especially when it
came to foreign and defence policy-making. As one official put it of
Blair (quoted in Seldon 2005: 329): 'He ran the European defence
policy out of Number 10, not the Foreign Office. It was typical Blair,
dazzled by the bright lights but short on detail, on planning ahead
and on substance.' If this was true of policies such as European
defence cooperation, it was at its most obvious during times of crisis
decision-making. In a previous article I have examined one notable
occasion – the decision to involve Britain in NATO's humanitar-
ian intervention in Kosovo during the spring of 1999 – when Blair
instinctively turned to his denocracy to help him put together his
famous 'doctrine of the international community' speech in Chicago
in April 1999, almost totally ignoring input from the Foreign Office
mandarins (Daddow 2009). This was becoming part of a pattern,
John Kampfner concluded from this episode, 'in which Blair and his
people often did not bother to consult the organisation supposedly
in charge of British diplomacy' (Kampfner 2004: 51, 53; see also
Phythian 2008: 217). Blair sympathizers (and now Blair himself – see
Blair 2010: 338, 428) might argue that he was scrupulous in working
through the Cabinet's Defence and Overseas Policy Committee
during the bombing of Iraq with the US in Operation Desert Fox in
December 1998, and again during Operation Allied Force in Kosovo
in early 1999 (see for instance Riddell 2001: 32). Other commentators,
however, saw this as a tactical manoeuvre to outflank criticisms that
the Prime Minister was acting more like a president than out of any
real interest in what the members of that committee had to contribute
(Williams 2004: 917). In any case, using Cabinet committees during
military operations is not the same as debating the principle of using
military force outside of crisis periods. As one Cabinet member from
the time has complained: 'At no stage over those first four years did
we have a single Cabinet discussion about the principles, or conduct,
of foreign policy' (quoted in Kampfner 2004: 14).

Taking this into account, one research design option for this study,
rejected early on, was to analyse the language of successive Foreign
Secretaries and Ministers for Europe in the Foreign Office, both
of whom were, nominally speaking, tasked with implementing and
presenting British European policy. The problems of theming a study
around Foreign Office activity was that the thrust of foreign policy
was determined in Downing Street not King Charles Street. Even
relatively long-serving Foreign Secretaries such as Cook or Straw
were, over the Europe question perhaps more than any other foreign
affairs issue, working to an agenda that was tightly controlled by the
Prime Minister and usually by the Chancellor too. Studying the Ministers for Europe would have posed even more insuperable obstacles.

Table 2. New Labour Ministers for Europe (May 1997–May 2010)

Minister for Europe	Dates in office
Doug Henderson	May 1997 to July 1998
Joyce Quin	July 1998 to July 1999
Geoff Hoon	July 1999 to October 1999
Keith Vaz	October 1999 to June 2001
Peter Hain	June 2001 to October 2002
Denis MacShane	October 2002 to May 2005
Douglas Alexander	May 2005 to May 2006
Geoff Hoon	May 2006 to June 2007
Jim Murphy	June 2007 to October 2008
Caroline Flint	October 2008 to June 2009
Glenys Kinnock	June 2009 to October 2009
Chris Bryant	October 2009 to May 2010

The first is that Europe Ministers are little known publicly and do not last particularly long in office, giving them an insufficient platform or time to leave a real imprint on Britain's Europe debates. From table 2 we can see that they have lasted, on average, just over one year in the post. Geoff Hoon served two stints, making him and Denis MacShane the two longest-serving Europe Ministers, at around two years each. But generally, holding the title Minister for Europe in the New Labour years seems either to have been preparation for more prominent positions within the government, or to have led nowhere at all in career terms. In theory, therefore, we could design a research programme into the part Ministers for Europe played in devising, selling and executing British European policy and it would no doubt add to our stock of knowledge about the workings of British central government. However, the relative brevity of their tenure in post, even by British government standards, and their rather obscure public profile (not necessarily their fault of course) would make such a programme self-defeating if it was intended to uncover the rhetorical tactics New Labour used to push the case for Europe.

The second and much more significant obstacle, however, is that to theme a study around Ministers for Europe or even the Foreign Secretary would be to overlook the control over European policy Blair and later Brown were able to exert from Downing Street. For example, the former's grip steadily increased after 1997 to the point where James and Opperman argue, quoting an anonymous official in the process:

the strategic role of the Cabinet Office was greatly enhanced, with around two-thirds of its workload devoted to driving forward the

prime minister's priorities on Europe. Its European expertise was
such that by the time of Blair's departure, No. 10 was 'pretty close'
to the point at which it could bypass the FCO [Foreign and Commonwealth Office] altogether for policy advice and strategic thinking on
Europe. (James and Opperman 2009: 293)

Europe Ministers were involved, among other things, in chair-
ing the committee charged with putting into practice eye-catching
initiatives such as the 'step change' policy after 1997 which led to
'a significant thickening of the relationship' between London and
various EU member states (for details see Smith 2005: 709–10). But
such initiatives were influential in the short term rather than long
term and still directed overall from Downing Street. One Europe
adviser retrospectively judged that 'step change' did not deliver
'dramatic results' (Wall 2008: 176). When we add to the mix Brown's
control over the timing of any decision to hold a referendum on the
euro, it seems highly unlikely that a Europe Minister in post for a
few short months could have been 'in control' of British European
policy, any more than the Foreign Secretary could have been. As
Simon Jenkins has written of Blair: 'Whereas he had to defer to
Brown in matters of domestic policy, he felt no such deference to his
foreign secretaries, Robin Cook, Jack Straw and Margaret Beckett.
He led from the start' (Jenkins 2007: 243). Nowhere better was
Downing Street's ability to command New Labour language seen
than in the words of a document it produced in 1997 called 'Questions of Procedure for Ministers', quoted by James Naughtie:

> all major interviews and media appearances, both in print and
> broadcast, should be agreed with the Number 10 Press Office before
> any commitments are entered into. The policy content of all major
> speeches, press releases and new policy initiatives should be cleared
> in good time with the Number 10 Private Office; the timings and
> forms of announcements should be cleared with the Number 10 Press
> Office. (Naughtie 2002: 100)

The formidable Alastair Campbell was not an operator a minister wanted to be on the wrong side of, so at a basic personal level
it was in their interests to remain 'on message' – and in any case
many senior New Labour ministers had bought into this way of
doing their political business (for details see Wring 2005: 147–50). In
substantive terms, furthermore, it was politically dangerous for any
minister to speak out on sensitive subjects like the EU 'for fear of
offending either the Prime Minister or the Chancellor' (Wall 2008:
180). A memorable quote from Doug Henderson, Blair's first Europe
Minister, vividly makes this point:

> I was propelled into this job just a few days after the election. I was
> summoned to London by the Prime Minister for a quick briefing on

the [Amsterdam] Intergovernmental Conference. *Then I was handed a speech to learn* and told to be in Brussels at 9 o'clock the following morning. (Henderson 1998: 4, emphasis added)

Maybe this was not always the way of things and time was admittedly tight, but the idea that the Prime Minister 'summoned' Henderson and gave him a pre-prepared speech speaks volumes about how after 1997 Blair ran a *West Wing*-style government personalized around him and his inner cell of advisers, sometimes working with Brown, sometimes against. The pattern recurred under Gordon Brown as Prime Minister, it seems. Resigning from the government in June 2009, Minister for Europe Caroline Flint complained that, as both a woman and a lowly junior minister, she operated in the bottom tier of a two-tier government: 'Your inner circle and then the remainder of the Cabinet'. On policy she felt the Europe Minister had no sway over its direction or content. 'In my current role, you advised that I would attend Cabinet when Europe was on the agenda. I have only been invited once since October and not to a single political Cabinet – not even the one held a few weeks before the European elections' (Flint 2009).

To suggest that the Foreign Secretary, let alone a Minister for Europe, could go against the agreed line of Blair and Brown, either individually or especially when the two of them formed a united front, would seem to do violence to the record of how foreign policy was made under New Labour. To test the hypothesis that Downing Street crucially shaped both policy and language on the question of the British in Europe, I studied four speeches on the EU given by Peter Hain, Europe Minister from June 2001 to October 2002, who went on to work in the Wales Office and simultaneously as Leader of the House from 2003. The corpus was made up of two speeches at the 2002 annual party conference, one at the Institute for Public Policy Research (IPPR) in 2003 and one at the Trades Union Congress (TUC) annual conference in 2003. I coded the speeches as I did Blair and Brown's (see the following chapter for the coding method used), looking for the keywords that signified aspects of New Labour's thinking on the Europe question under three headings: interests, identity and approach to history. The recurring use of Blair–Brown key terms is fascinating and points up the fact that Hain, like all government ministers charged with speaking about British European policy, was working to a certain script that was helped into existence and cleared by the central Downing Street press operation (see chapters 4, 6 and 8 for the full rendition of New Labour key terms as they appear in the Blair and Brown speeches). In terms of framing the push for Europe as beneficial to the national interest, Hain consistently put the economic case that 'two thirds of British trade' and over '3 million British jobs' depended on Britain's trade with Europe (Hain 2002a; Hain 2003a; Hain 2003b), the same message Blair and Brown stuck to – with subtle variations – throughout the period. The security case was made by playing up 'Europe's success story' (Hain 2003b) as states progressively came together to remove the scourge of war from the continent after 1945 (Hain 2002a; Hain 2003a). In privileging the interests of the nation state Hain in his speech at the IPPR echoed Brown and Blair by suggesting that 'The nation state will always remain the bedrock of the EU' (Hain 2003a), and reiterating to the TUC that 'Our vision is of a Europe of sovereign nation-states ... not a federal super state' (Hain 2003b). (This British position was staunchly defended during the negotiations on the Constitutional Treaty – see Menon 2003: 966.) In terms of the identity construction aspects of the speeches, and as we might expect of a party conference speech in particular, the partisan point-scoring occurred when Hain called the Conservatives 'extremists', as would Brown, and 'rabid right wing anti-Europeans' who oppose Europe because 'Europe's values ... are our values' (Hain 2002a). Hain reached out to the sceptical elements of his audience with references to 'the much maligned bureaucrats of Brussels' but couched it in a wider narrative that said all the sceptics did was spread 'myths', helped by 'their friends in the British media' (Hain 2003b).

Dealing in retrograde 'myths' set the sceptics firmly against Labour's policy of leaning towards Europe by staying 'engaged' rather than 'whinging from the fringe' like the Conservatives (Hain 2002a; Hain 2002b). Like Blair, Hain diagnosed that anti-Europeans suffered from an 'inferiority complex' fuelled by 'prejudice and paranoia that Europe is about that [sic] fiendish foreigners doing us over' (Hain 2003b). The basic juxtaposition as he saw it was between a 'positive' Labour approach and a 'negative' Conservative one (Hain 2002a). He took a Third Way approach by arguing that, 'like most people, I'm not fanatically pro or anti the Euro: for me it's a practical issue about Britain's interests'. Hain's identity was constructed, like Blair's and Brown's, around the idea that he was a fair-minded, reasonable, rational person seeking first and foremost to safeguard the national interest (Hain 2002b; see also Blair 2010: 502). Hain supported the case for Brown's 'prepare and decide' policy on the single currency (Hain 2002a; Hain 2003b) and used a Brown favourite, 'rigorous and hard-headed', to describe the five tests (Hain 2002b). In terms of the recent past, Hain saw a litany of 'missed opportunities and wrong policies' in earlier British European policy – not just on the Conservative side but on Labour's too – that the government was seeking to correct (Hain 2002b). He was quick to distance the 'pro-European leadership' of Blair from the 'euro sceptic rhetoric' that 'dominated Labour' until Neil Kinnock became leader (Hain 2002b), which helped to put a chronological boundary between 'New' and 'Old' Labour (see chapter 7).

In the four speeches, Hain did take some distinctive positions when he set out the benefits of the EU and the case for reform of its institutions, but these were couched in an argument which was clearly constructed around a series of Downing Street and Treasury keywords. The discourse Hain put out was held together by defining features of the language New Labour used to construct its European policy in terms of safeguarding the national interest, in terms of what it stood for – and what its opponents stood for – identity-wise, and in terms of how the government positioned itself in the stream of what it saw as a series of failures in Europe by the Conservative Party and the Old Labour Party. Hain usually ended by repeating one or other of the typical Blair–Brown soundbites, for example that under Labour the country had become 'what Britain should always have been: a confident, leading European power' (Hain 2002a). He also underscored the idea that the British could help the EU to reform, to become an 'outward' not 'protectionist' actor in the global political economy, not by Britain being 'isolated' but by positioning itself 'at Europe's heart' (Hain 2003a). In his TUC speech the Blairite keyword 'confident' appeared seven times in the closing paragraph, on average once every fourteen words. New Labour's penchant for transcending binaries lent itself to presenting not necessarily reconcilable conceptual opposites and Hain was reflecting this not just in his choice of words in these speeches but also in how he paired them to make sense of the New Labour project at home and abroad (other examples include the four binaries early on in MacShane 2006; four at the end of Brown 2006c; and a set of four at the end of Brown 2008c). The Hain case study first of all gives us a taster of the textual signifiers around which Blair, Brown and their speech-writers fashioned their response to the European dilemmas facing the government after 1997. Second, it shows how these signifiers fixed New Labour's European discourses to such a degree that to understand New Labour is, to my mind, to study the Blair–Brown axis and how, through a sophisticated media operation run out of 10 Downing Street, the two men led the discursive construction of the government's foreign policy.

Summary

In this chapter we have explored New Labour as a producer of language and the places Tony Blair and Gordon Brown occupied at the pinnacle of New Labour government decision-making from May

1997. It could be argued that to concentrate mainly on Blair and Brown is to ignore or at the very least downplay the policy input and advice about the EU coming from established decision-making channels such as the Foreign Office and Britain's embassies abroad. This argument carries some water, in that the vision of a highly centralized system could be seen to be pandering to the views of the New Labour critics who slotted neatly into the British establishment tradition of criticizing the existence of 'kitchen cabinets'. Seen in this light, the baton has been handed on from the likes of Benn, Crossman and Castle in the 1960s to contemporary critics such as the former head of DfID and member of the New Labour Cabinet Clare Short. The running theme of her analysis of Blair's *folie de grandeur* over Iraq was precisely the breakdown of collective Cabinet responsibility for foreign policy under Blair that allowed 'groupthink' to damage clear and foresighted policy after 9/11 (Short 2005: 70, 73, 102, 125, 134, 146–7, 150, 151, 160, 187, 236, 272, 278–9). The aim of this book is not to take a normative position by arguing, for example, that Blair was somehow 'wrong' or that he was 'misusing power' in gathering around him a team of close advisers to set down and help push through New Labour's strategy. My position is both less and more than that: less, in that the book is not trying to judge the quality of New Labour's decision-making style; more, in that spotlighting Blair and Brown throws up the possibility of exaggerating the extent to which they were the architects of the discourse.

The British foreign policy process is undoubtedly more complex and multifaceted than I can portray here, particularly when the input from specialist speech-writers and press and policy advisers is taken into account. However, on the evidence I have seen from ex-ministers and close observers alike, they may not have been unique but Blair and Brown certainly continued a trend towards the centralization of foreign policy decision-making in the private office in Downing Street that was begun in earnest by many of their predecessors. It was Blair in Downing Street, Brown at the Treasury and Campbell in the media strategy team who controlled the language of policy. As I see it, therefore, it is fair to study New Labour discourses in the first place by concentrating on the figures, not to say figureheads, of Tony Blair and Gordon Brown. Analysing discursive inputs from the other organs of state would no doubt add something to our understanding, but this was a web mainly spun by Blair, Brown and the Number 10 press operation. The next chapter explains the theoretical backdrop to the study and the qualitative method of discourse analysis used to generate data on the ideas and the logic of history underpinning Blair and Brown's European policy thinking.

Chapter 3

Context II. Discourse and norm entrepreneurship

He may not have had an ideology, but he sure as hell had an agenda.
(Harris 2007: 250)

Discourse analysis worked its way into the discipline of political science through the 1990s. Its gradual incorporation has been a by-product of the rise of the interpretivist turn in the social sciences more generally, leading to heightened awareness in foreign policy analysis of the ideational aspects of decision-making on external issues. It did not take post-structuralists to alert scholars to the significance of language or rhetoric for political practice (see for example Weldon 1953) but recent developments in philosophy and linguistic theory have sharpened our ability to deconstruct the language–reality dichotomy. Scholars from myriad theoretical traditions have sharpened the intellectual tools we use to evaluate the functions of language in politics and political communications, particularly as far as the gathering and exercise of power go. This chapter provides the theoretical backdrop to the study by marrying discourse theory to an adapted version of Martha Finnemore and Kathryn Sikkink's theory of 'norm entrepreneurship' to explain what it was Blair and Brown tried to achieve in the realm of European policy *at the level of language*. In relation to their attempt to build a pro-European consensus in Britain, I first argue that we can use the norms literature both to empathize with New Labour's approach and to contextualize it, by highlighting the ideational and material obstacles the government encountered in getting its pro-European message across to the public. The chapter then focuses on the method of discourse analysis used to study the strategies Blair and Brown put in place to realize their goals. It sets out the main research questions asked and explains the data gathering and analysis techniques employed. By the end of the chapter we should have a good understanding of how the Prime Minister and Chancellor wanted to act as norm entrepreneurs in this debate, as well as the structural problems they encountered. As later chapters will show, however, there was more going on in their speeches than is obvious on first sighting. A discourse approach helps us get to grips with problems in the strategy *internal* to the texts themselves – *in* the messages the government was emitting on Europe – and these will become clear in the empirical chapters, 4, 6 and 8.

I. Blair and Brown: norm entrepreneurs

And I believe we can build a consensus in Britain about Britain's future in Europe as we also build a consensus in Europe about how, together, we equip ourselves to succeed in the global economy. (Brown 2003c)

In assuming the mantle of norm entrepreneurs, Tony Blair and Gordon Brown were seeking to alter the way the British thought about, and related to, Europe and the EU by devising and marketing new ways of thinking about Britain's role in the world. Their repackaging of British national identity involved challenging what they saw as widespread 'anti-European' modes of thinking and talking about the British in Europe (for a restatement see Blair 2010: 533–4). The paradox as they saw it was that anti-Europeanism denied the British a role in Europe at all. Combining insights from the literatures on discourse theory and norms, this section helps us appreciate what Blair and Brown were trying to achieve from a theoretical vantage point. The cue from the discourse literature comes from the work of Ruth Wodak, Rudolf de Cilia, Martin Reisigl and Karen Liebhart, who, in answering the question 'why study discourse?', discuss the uses of discourse in perpetuating or challenging the status quo construction of a given subject or political issue (Wodak *et al.* 2003). Their reasoning is that: 'Through discourses, social actors constitute objects of knowledge, situations and social roles as well as identities and interpersonal relations, between different social groups and those who interact with them' (Wodak *et al.* 2003: 33). They privilege ideas and the ideational component of constructions of Self, Other and the world around us, with language (through discourse) playing a vital role in these creative processes of constituting reality.

Wodak *et al.* point out that discourse acts: are largely responsible for the genesis, production and construction of particular social conditions; can contribute to the restoration, legitimation or relativization of a status quo; can be employed to maintain and reproduce a prevailing status quo; but conversely may be effective in transforming, dismantling and/or destroying a status quo. Here we see the emancipatory as well as the paralysing potential of discourses that renders them so fertile for academic analysis. They conclude the relevant section of their work by identifying two contrasting types of discourse, based around the uses to which a discourse can be put. On the one hand we have constructive, perpetuating and justifying discursive strategies. On the other we have transforming, dismantling and disparaging discursive strategies. The former strategies maintain and uphold a status quo while the latter work to alter or transform a status quo (Wodak *et al.* 2003: 33). From the work of Wodak *et al.* we can start to move towards the norms literature by noting Siegfried Jäger's point that discourses serve either to prolong or to destabilize 'assumed truths', these being 'presented as being rational, sensible and beyond all doubt' (Jäger 2006: 34). One way discourses prolong and maintain a status quo is via the proliferation of 'topoi' or collective symbols: 'cultural stereotypes ... which are handed down and used collectively' (Ricento 2003: 613). Describing these topoi Jäger writes:

> In the store of the collective symbols that all the members of a society know, a repertoire of images is available with which we visualize a complete picture of social reality and/or the political landscape of society, and through which we then interpret these and are provided with interpretations – in particular by the media. (Jäger 2006: 35)

On coming to power, Blair and Brown were well aware, or made well aware by their advisers and Blair's unofficial history teacher Roy Jenkins (Naughtie 2002: 74), of the collective symbols and stereotypes that made British discourses about Europe function to preserve a certain status quo in the country's hesitant approach to the EU. They identified that the British were being kept in a permanent state of discursive war with the continent, in which a hegemonic Eurosceptical discourse acted as both frame and limit on the way the British people called Europe to mind by speaking about it and acting towards it (see chapter 5). There is no space in this book to study the theoretically pregnant idea of 'framing' from a communications perspective. I take it to be linked to, but separate from, techniques of 'persuasion' or 'belief change'. To quote from William Gamson and Andre Modigliani: 'A frame is a central organizing idea for making sense of relevant events and suggesting what is at issue' (cited in Nelson *et al.* 1997: 222), including the most preferable policy outcome. The frame–discourse overlap is potentially confusing and, as far as this study goes, has not been unravelled as much as perhaps it might. Having said that, the two concepts tend to be equated in much influential literature (for example Wodak 2009: 42). I tend, therefore, to talk in terms of discourses rather than frames. Elite Eurosceptical discourses do a lot of ideological work for their reader/listener by refracting EU legislation, EU summits and EU debates through the lenses of Britain's martial past. By discursively constructing

Europe as a hostile Other, 'over there', across the English Channel, the media and related organs of cultural transmission were complicit in reinforcing the domination of the past over the present as far as coverage of British European policy was concerned.

Into this sclerotic discursive and policy environment stepped Blair and Brown, seeking to play the part of what Finnemore and Sikkink (1998) would call 'norm entrepreneurs'. Analysing why and how the Prime Minister and Chancellor took on this role will clarify the link between discourse theory and norms. This will prepare the way for a consideration in the following chapters of how they tried to transform, dismantle and disparage the hegemonic stories about Britain's relations with Europe. The focus in the first half of Finnemore and Sikkink's article is on what norms are, how they change and the ways in which norm changes can have real and lasting effects on other features of the political landscape (Finnemore and Sikkink 1998: 888). Finnemore and Sikkink define a norm as 'a standard of appropriate behaviour for actors with a given identity', noting, à la the discourse analysts mentioned above, that norms can be both regulative (or constraining) and constitutive (or enabling) (Finnemore and Sikkink 1998: 891). We shall see, both in this chapter and in the remainder of the book, how discourse analysis delivers on this promise by allying it to the theoretical work on the resistance of inbuilt norms to rapid or abrupt change. The rest of the first section of Finnemore and Sikkink's article explores how we can identify a norm methodologically speaking and how far we can measure when a norm has changed as opposed to remaining stable over a set period of time (Finnemore and Sikkink 1998: 892–4). Their point is that it is simpler to explain why norms prevail than to explain how they are transformed. Indeed, as Ole Wæver has argued, discourse analysis is in fact all *about* the search for structural constraints at the level of language on the making of foreign policy (Wæver 1996: 5).

In the second part of the article Finnemore and Sikkink set out their concept of an ideal-type 'norm life cycle' (see figure 3). In this three-phase cycle the first phase is 'norm emergence', a process that requires two elements. The first is the existence of norm entrepreneurs, because 'Norms do not appear out of thin air; they are actively built by agents having strong notions about appropriate or desirable behaviour in their community' (Finnemore and Sikkink 1998: 896). Norm entrepreneurs call attention to issues but just as importantly they 'create' issues by inventing language that names, interprets and dramatizes them. In other words, norm entrepreneurs thrust new issues onto the political agenda by challenging existing ways of representing the world, and they have to take account of 'prior norms' in the framing of new ones, risking being labelled

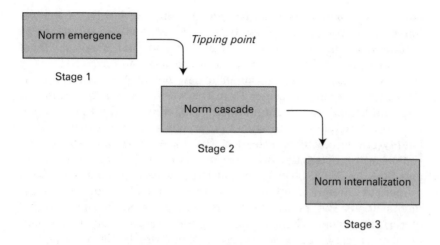

Figure 3. Finnemore and Sikkink's norm life cycle (Finnemore and Sikkink 1998: 896).

'inappropriate' in the process (Finnemore and Sikkink 1998: 897). Blair and Brown could be said to have acted as norm entrepreneurs because they wanted to reframe Britain's debates about Europe and the EU through a systematic re-visioning of the language, imagery and points of historical reference around which Britain's Europe debates occurred in the political, public and media worlds. The second element required for the emergence of a norm is an organizational platform on which to build a consensus around the proposed new norm. Such a platform can be constructed specifically for norm promotion, for example non-governmental organizations or transnational advocacy networks. Alternatively, existing organizations and networks can be used. Although it is not a focus for this book per se, it is noteworthy that Blair and Brown actively used a variety of existing platforms, such as the re-activation of the cross-party pressure group Britain in Europe, to make their pro-European case. They also used public platforms such as set-piece speeches at universities, business organizations, think-tanks and institutions of the EU such as the European Parliament to spread their Europeanist messages.

In the transition between stages 1 and 2 of the norm life cycle we have what is known as a 'tipping point'. Bearing in mind that Finnemore and Sikkink's article was written about the evolution and spread of norms around the international system, the tipping or 'threshold' point is the point at which norm entrepreneurs 'have persuaded a critical mass of states to become norm leaders and adopt new norms' (Finnemore and Sikkink 1998: 901). A 'critical mass' eludes precise definition but could be one of two things. From a numerical perspective it has been argued that a critical mass has been achieved when one-third of the total number of states in the system have chosen to adopt a new norm. An example of the quantitative approach comes from the work of Francisco Ramirez, Yasemin Soysal and Suzanne Shanahan, who found a tipping point in the evolution of the movement on women's suffrage in 1930, when twenty states (about one-third of the states in the system at that time) had accepted the principle of women's suffrage (Finnemore and Sikkink 1998: 901). A second hypothesis moves us away from numerical measurement and into the realm of normative judgements about the relative significance of states to the adoption of certain norms. Then, a tipping point occurs when a sufficient number of 'critical states' – those without which 'the achievement of the substantive norm goal is compromised' – adopt a new norm, such that the adoption by these states make the onward adoption of the norm more likely. States are deemed to be critical either because they are influential actors in a policy area shaped by, and shaping, a norm, or because they have a certain 'moral stature' or leadership role in a given area. Translating all this to the intra-state issue of New Labour's projection of the European ideal in Britain we can use the concept of a tipping point in two ways. One would be to suggest that a tipping point would be reached if a majority of the British population polled, say, by Eurobarometer or BSA came to hold the opinion that Britain's membership of the EU was a 'good thing', as opposed to the paltry figure of one in four who currently believe this. A second way of identifying a tipping point might be to count the number of leading national newspapers that are broadly supportive (or at least not critical) of the EU, and this could be done using readership figures to identify 'critical' outlets rather than weighting all newspapers equally. We might, for instance, categorize the *Sun, The Times* and *Daily Mail* as critical newspapers, given their readership numbers and sceptical attitudes to Europe. Without their backing, we could suggest that Britain would stand little chance of making the transition from stage 1 to stage 2 of a pro-European norm life cycle. Even if every other regional and national newspaper in Britain adopted supportive attitudes towards the EU, a government would not be able to spread the new norm of being supportive of the European idea and the EU without the support or at least silent acquiescence of these critical press outlets.

That Blair and Brown did not succeed in creating a tipping point during New Labour's period in office makes it helpful to look to an earlier tipping point in the history of Britain's relations with Europe, one which offers up some clues as to what a tipping point in the direction of a 'pro-European' norm might look like. The tipping point chosen is Margaret Thatcher's speech to the College of Europe on 20 September 1988, commonly known as the 'Bruges speech' (all quotes in the next two paragraphs are from Thatcher 1988). After the usual diplomatic opening remarks Thatcher began by asserting: 'We British are as much heirs to the legacy of European culture as any other nation. Our links to the rest of Europe, the continent of Europe, have been the dominant factor in our history.' Her argument about the essential indivisibility of British and European history and the 'common experience' shared by the British and continental European nations would be picked up by Blair and especially by Brown a decade later. In the latter part of the opening section she went on to identify the ways in which Britain has contributed to Europe's liberty, particularly in times of global war, remarking that 'Europe' as an idea extends far beyond the borders of what was then the EEC, through the Iron Curtain to Warsaw, Prague and Budapest. Lest anyone be in any doubt, Thatcher's opinion set out in the following section, entitled 'Europe's future', was that: 'Our destiny is in Europe, as part of the Community', even if the British, like many partner states, had horizons that went far beyond the borders of the EEC itself, the 'special relationship' being the ghost at the banquet here.

Having established the backdrop, Thatcher went on to elaborate on the 'guiding principles' she believed would help Europe succeed in the future. The first was that the best way to build the EEC would be via 'willing and active cooperation between independent sovereign states' rather than through the creation of some centrally controlled 'identikit European personality'. Her bogey man here was the Commission, with its decisions 'taken by an appointed bureaucracy'. In the best-remembered portion of the speech Thatcher said: 'We have not successfully rolled back the frontiers of the state in Britain, only to see them re-imposed at a European level with a European super-state exercising a new dominance from Brussels'. More common purpose between states should go hand in hand with the preservation of different traditions around Europe, not their eradication. Her second guiding principle was that the Community ought to tackle problems in a practical way so as to keep public levels of support for the EEC high. She spoke of promoting further reform of the Common Agricultural Policy (CAP), about budgetary discipline and the establishment of sound financial foundations for the Community. Thatcher's third guiding principle was that the EEC should do more to encourage enterprise by breaking down barriers to trade and by lightening the load of interventionist regulations on businesses: 'action to *free* markets, action to *widen* choice, action to *reduce* government intervention' (her emphasis). She set out the ways in which Britain had been leading the way as a beacon of economic liberalization through the 1980s and identified how the Community could travel the same enlightened path. This would also be a staple of New Labour's discourse after 1997. Her fourth and related guiding principle was that 'Europe should not be protectionist' towards the outside world. Thatcher's fifth and final guiding principle was that Europeans must continue to see NATO as the bedrock of their efforts at defence cooperation, but that each member of the Alliance must shoulder a fair portion of the burden, military and economic. There was to be a role for the Western European Union (WEU), not as an 'alternative' to NATO but as a means of enhancing the credibility of the European 'contribution to the common defence of the West'. Thatcher wrapped the speech up by contrasting her pragmatic, practical agenda with the 'utopian' goals she too often saw driving the EEC forward. She warned her audience that holding on to utopian dreams will always end in disappointment, not just because they are unobtainable but because they are intrinsically flawed, using the circular argument that: 'Utopia never comes, because we know we should not like it if it did'.

The impact of Thatcher's Bruges speech on Britain's Europe debates can barely be overstated. Its 'explicit Eurosceptical message' (Daniels 1998: 80) popularized a certain set of critical attitudes towards the EEC by infusing them with real discursive force and legitimacy. First, she had the authority built up as a serving British Prime Minister with experience of nearly ten years in office. Second, she gave the speech close to the institutional heart of Europe. Finally, this was a long, comprehensive and heavily briefed speech which set out an ambitious and controversial reform agenda for the EEC, and was widely reported as such in Britain and Europe. In terms of the ideational impact of the Bruges speech we can look to Martin Holmes for a description of the shot in the arm it gave the sceptic cause:

> The 'great debate' of the 1970s was seemingly ended with the decisive two-to-one majority of the 1975 referendum; indeed Euroscepticism was dormant, subdued or outside the political mainstream for the next decade. Its rebirth was a slow process until Mrs Thatcher's Bruges speech in 1988 which transformed the issue from sideshow to centre stage…. the long-term consequences have been positive for Eurosceptics. Euroscepticism has become a permanent feature of the political landscape…. (Holmes 2002: 1)

Holmes's narrative is themed around the decline and rise of Euroscepticism – decline in and around the burst of elite and media campaigning for EEC entry in the 1960s and 1970s followed by a 'rebirth' in the later 1980s, when Thatcher brought it back 'centre stage'. The speech's ideational impact was matched by material developments such as the establishment of the Bruges Group, an independent all-party think-tank set up in February 1989, not six months after the Bruges speech, 'to promote the idea of a less centralised European structure than that emerging in Brussels'. Its inspiration was the quote from Thatcher identified above – 'We have not successfully rolled back the frontiers of the state in Britain, only to see them re-imposed at a European level' – and its ambition is nothing less than 'a complete restructuring of Britain's relationship with other European countries' (Bruges Group undated a). In 2008 the Bruges Group held a twentieth anniversary dinner in London to celebrate the Bruges speech, in the presence of Baroness Thatcher, followed by talks against 'EU centralisation' (Bruges Group undated b). The Bruges speech stands out as a clear tipping point in the history of Britain's discursive construction of 'Europe' because of its ideational and material consequences for Britain's debates about Europe. It helped shape Conservative policy during the Maastricht negotiations and after, a period which saw 'an intensification of anti-European activity in Britain' in and outside Parliament (Sowemimo 1999: 347). Returning to the Finnemore and Sikkink article we can now trace what tipping points such as this lead to in the norm life cycle.

A tipping point helps moves us to stage 2 in the life cycle: the 'norm cascade', a dynamic process of 'international socialization intended to induce norm breakers to become norm followers' (Finnemore and Sikkink 1998: 902). Before a tipping point occurs, a new norm may not take a grip on the international system despite domestic pressure from within states for change to occur. After passing that threshold more and more countries adopt a new norm even without domestic pressure to do so. Kenneth Waltz's idea of socialization is the inspiration here. Socialization occurs because of emulation (of heroes), praise (for behaviour that conforms to the new norm) or ridicule/shame (for deviation from the norm) (Waltz summarized in Finnemore and Sikkink 1998: 902). It builds 'peer pressure' among states which encourages the adoption of the new norm and states adapt their behaviour for a variety of reasons. For example, states might not want to be seen to be 'rogue states' and therefore accept the norm as a means of legitimating their behaviour; states may act out of conformity or a sense of 'belonging'; or they may do so to gain esteem from other states in the system – wanting to think well of themselves and be well thought of by others. Jumping to Britain's Europe debates, we could argue that similar processes of socialization around norms and expectations occur within states as they do at the level of inter-state relations. After all, in Waltz's neorealist theory of international relations states are treated as unopened 'black boxes', as units within a larger system (Waltz 1979). Just as classic international relations theory ascribes human qualities to individual states, we could see the various individuals in a domestic political environment (who really *are* human) being even more susceptible to these types of socializing peer pressures. Thus, where the hegemonic norm encompassing everything about the way the British think, talk and act towards Europe has explicit and implicit support from such fundamental cultural transmitters as the education system, key segments of the media, politicians and pressure groups, and even infiltrating basic figures of speech, a new norm would have to cascade from a variety of locations to take effect. It would involve new ways of thinking about Britain's history, Britain's role in the world, British national identity and the part the EU plays in the domestic politics and day-to-day functioning of Britain as a nation and civic society. This would be no mean feat, might take decades and would depend critically on the extent to which the emergence of the new norm was institutionalized and internalized by governing elites, mainstream political parties, campaigning organizations and organs of the press and broadcast media during stage 1 of the life cycle. Without serious alterations to political thinking and linguistic practice we would never even reach a tipping point, let alone witness a norm cascade on this issue. Blair and Brown signally failed to set out a credible alternative vision to match that of Thatcher in Bruges – but then conditions were not as favourable in the later 1990s as they were in the later 1980s.

In the third and final stage of the norm life cycle, 'norms may become so widely accepted that they are internalized by actors and achieve a "taken-for-granted" quality that makes conformance with the norm almost automatic' (Finnemore and Sikkink 1998: 904). For this reason internalized norms are both powerful and hard to discern, barely forming points of political contestation or public debate. Finnemore and Sikkink suggest that many of the norms we take for granted in the industrialized West, such as about market exchange, sovereignty and individualism, have become a focus for sociological institutionalists wanting to 'denaturalize' and problematize these fundamental concepts we accept as real and natural without debating their meaning (Finnemore and Sikkink 1998: 904–5). This is where the study of norms feeds synergistic-ally into the work of critical discourse analysts such as Norman Fairclough (for example Fairclough 2009), who denaturalize the taken-for-granted ways of viewing the world by elevating the profile of deeply submerged ideologies that mould how we talk the world into existence. In stage 3 of the norm life cycle, ways of speaking, seeing – *representing* the world – have become internalized to such an extent that even to set about investigating them poses huge conceptual problems and methodological challenges.

Finnemore and Sikkink's norm life cycle is valuable to this study in two ways. First, it helps us appreciate the processes and institutional mechanisms through which norms emerge, become accepted and finally internalized as the 'normal' or perhaps hegemonic or dominant way of constructing a particular issue or interpreting a particular series of events. Second, it draws attention to the subtle, coercive power of norms to set agendas and thus points up the role methods such as discourse analysis have in identifying and unpicking these seemingly instinctive or accepted-as-given modes of interpreting politics and public policy. In this final segment on norms I will adapt the original Finnemore and Sikkink norm life cycle model to account for the emergence of what has become the dominant norm about 'Europe' in Britain. This will contextualize what I am going to argue in the rest of the book about New Labour's attempt to generate a new understanding of Britain's relations with Europe through the establishment of a quite different rhetorical norm about this relationship. In figure 4 we can see the adapted model, so let us consider its key features and its implications for the New Labour years.

It is impossible to date with any exactitude the emergence of today's ways of talking about Europe and the EU in Britain because it is so dependent on one's take on the origins of the contemporary debates about the British national identity and Britain's role in the world

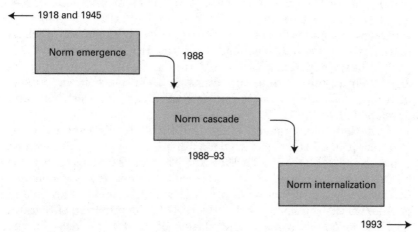

Figure 4. Norm life cycle: Britain and the EU.

with regard not just to Europe but to the Empire/Commonwealth, the US and so on. In figure 4 I have circumvented this problem by 'opening up' each end of the cycle, to show that the set of dominant attitudes associated with Euroscepticism in this book (see chapter 5) come from (and are *about*) a hazily remembered, not to say nostalgic-ally patriotic sense of the past, and are likely to endure indefinitely into the future. I have, however, identified both 1918 and 1945 as key markers because of the amount of time national and European-level politicians spend justifying European integration with reference to the eradication of the scourge of war. Integration initially occurred through the creation after the Second World War of a network of economic–political–security interdependences between France and Germany, but in the post-Cold War era (and since) has encompassed the eastward expansion of 'Europe' to take in former Warsaw Pact countries and beyond. Thatcher used these key events in her Bruges speech when she spoke of the '120,000 British soldiers who died in the First World War' in Belgium and, tellingly, of the fact that 'it was from our island fortress that the liberation of Europe itself was mounted' in the Second World War (Thatcher 1988). Blair echoed Thatcher ten years on when he argued that:

> The European Union was, and remains, the prize of peace. The heart-felt cry of 'the war to end all wars' has gone up twice on our continent this century. The genius of [Jean] Monnet, [Paul-Henri] Spaak and [Robert] Schuman was to take that heartfelt cry and mobilise it into an organisation based on the principle of democratic consent and the practical foundation of increasingly close co-operation. (Blair 1998b)

Marking the period in and around the two global wars of the twentieth century is not so much an attempt to record them as the beginnings of the emergence of Britain's contemporary discourses about the EU, rather to identify them as key reference points for the users of this discourse. Whether they be politicians or officials, journalists or football commentators, the British have used their past military experiences to mould (linguistically and metaphoric-ally) their cognitive understandings of their place in or outside 'Europe', especially as the institutions of integration were born and developed after 1950.

If the 'norm emergence' stage is difficult to pinpoint in terms of dates, it is a little easier to determine the tipping point between stages 1 and 2. I have chosen 1988 and Thatcher's Bruges speech, for all the reasons outlined above. After that moment, those who identi-fied themselves as critics or sceptics of the EEC began to harden and popularize their opinions of the 'Brussels-led' domination of Britain. As Holmes put it in his recapitulation of Thatcher's ideas on the Bruges Group website:

The speech had a major effect on informed opinion and helped fire
those who wanted to forge a different kind of Europe. Academics,
politicians, economists, journalists and other opinion formers were
convinced by its logic and consequently felt free to express their own
disquiet with the bureaucratic juggernaut that the European Community had become. (Holmes undated)

In stage 2 of the Britain and EU norm life cycle, the ideational
momentum Thatcher gave the sceptic cause was given concrete expression. The norm became institutionalized and commercialized in
a variety of ways, including through the creation of bodies like the
Bruges Group and in more publicly available ways by the support she
was able to drum up from leading newspaper proprietors and within
the media more generally. An accident of timing helped, because the
speech just preceded a period of intense debate about widening and
deepening integration after the end of the Cold War in 1989. The
Maastricht Treaty negotiations prompted the Thatcher agenda to be
given a full airing by those elements of the political elite and media
outlets hostile to 'Europe' generally or the EEC specifically. We are
compelled here to think of a counter-factual: what if Maastricht had
never happened? This is important because the 'pro' bits of Thatcher's
speech have been almost totally forgotten at the expense of the
(admittedly longer) critiques of the EU she laid out in Bruges. Seeing
the dynamics behind the transition to stage 2 of the life cycle helps us
understand why. What is fascinating about the Bruges speech in terms
of its ideational legacy is not only that it inspired the sceptics but that,
as we have seen, the early part of it was dedicated to explaining the
long-standing British commitment to Europe. This portion actually
appears in *The Pro-European Reader*, where it is inserted to remind
us that the speech 'was not all of one piece' and that this 'warm evoca-
tion of British links with Europe' (Leonard and Leonard 2002: 92)
has been overlooked because of the opprobrium Thatcher heaped on
the EU after 1988, and especially after she left Downing Street in
1990 (for instance Thatcher 2003: 320–59). We need look no further
than the Bruges speech for an example of the ways in which norms,
and the political discourses that help create them, need in stage 1 of
the life cycle to be falling on ideationally and materially fertile ground
for them to take root and grow into publicly accepted ways of thinking and talking about a particular issue. It is possible, but in no way
provable, that without the Maastricht debates of 1990–93 Thatcher's
speech might not have had the impact it did. Context is as important
in stage 2 of the life cycle as the occurrence of the tipping point itself,
because of the wider conditions necessary for norms to resonate with
established with traditions and to cascade and become transmitted
around national, regional and transnational environments.

Stage 3 of the Britain and Europe norm life cycle takes us from the period after the ratification of the Maastricht Treaty to the present. In the years 1988–93 the themes Thatcher showcased became bed-rocks of Conservative Party opposition to the EU, were consolidated in the language of Britain's EU debates and were reified in the topics it became most acceptable to debate publicly. The Thatcher agenda became the default setting, as it were, for the ways in which the British framed, spoke and thought about Europe. Thatcher and the anti-Maastricht campaigners entrenched ideas about British sover-eignty, independence, threats from the EU to a glorious national history, an overweening superstate in 'Brussels', the prospect of a 'European army' and related threats to Britain's ability to play the role of a 'great power'. This was the period in which media interest in 'scare stories' about Brussels 'directives' became a staple diet of the Eurosceptical tabloid press and these have become an important component of Britain's Europe debates subsequently. Stage 3 was, in effect, the period when all the binaries set up between a benign British polity on the one hand and a malign European polity on the other came to prominence within British elite and public debates about Europe. The years after 1993 were those in which the dis-course about a permanent state of war with continental Europe came to feature as the hegemonic discourse. Coincidentally, one year into this third stage of the life cycle Tony Blair took over the leadership of the Labour Party and he and his team started to think about how to reposition the Labour Party and how they would want to position Britain in the world under a New Labour government. The next section explains how I gathered and processed the empiri-cal data on the New Labour information campaign.

II. Discourse analysis

> Discourse consists of coherent chains of propositions which establish
> a 'discourse world', or 'discourse ontology' – in effect, the 'reality' that
> is entertained by the speaker, or meta-represented by the speaker as
> being someone else's believed reality. (Chilton 2004: 54)

This book on the construction of Self and Other identities in the political speeches of Blair and Brown, as well as the ways in which they represented British history, interests and role in the world, has been inspired by various works in the field of discourse analysis and discourse theory. We will open this section by considering the ration-ale for taking a discourse approach and link it to the analysis of the language of government using the work of Norman Fairclough. The study of discourse is porous to methods and approaches from a variety of disciplines and there is no one definition of 'discourse' or 'discourse analysis' that would meet with universal approval (for a survey of definitions see Titscher *et al.* 2007: 25–7). An observation from Jennifer Milliken in 1999 is as apt today: 'no common understanding has emerged in International Relations about the best ways to study discourse' (Milliken 1999: 226). A study of a range of possible definitions shows certain core themes emerging time and again under the general heading 'the close study of language in use' (Taylor 2009: 5). Miguel Cabrera takes discourse to be an 'already extant system of rules of signification that actively mediates between people and social reality and creates the space in which both objects and subjects are forged in any historical situation'. It later becomes: 'the coherent body of categories, concepts, and principles by means of which individuals apprehend and conceptualize reality ... and through which they implement their practice in a given historical situation' (Cabrera 2005: 22–3). Note Cabrera's debt both to Michel Foucault in his emphasis on historical epochs or eras having distinctive sets of discursive practices, as well as to the social theory of constructivism in his emphasis on discourses mediating reality to individuals. Cabrera nails it by later suggesting that 'if it is discourse that provides reality with its objective face, then it also forges the experience that individuals have of that reality' (Cabrera 2005: 48). This is very much the thrust of David Howarth's argument that 'the discourse analyst examines the ways in which structures of meaning make possible certain forms of conduct' (Howarth 1995: 115) and Milliken's view that discourses are 'structures of signification which construct social realities'. That said, discourse theory has a particular *take* on constructivism (Milliken 1999: 229).

Discourses represent and give meaning to ideas and social action; they have a performative element to them. In the words of Gunther Kress:

> Discourses are systematically organized sets of statements which give expression to the meanings and values of an institution. Beyond that, they define, describe and delimit what is possible to say and not possible to say (and by extension what it is possible to do or not to do) with respect to the area of concern of that institution, whether marginally or centrally. A discourse provides a set of possible statements about a given area, and organizes and gives structure to the manner in which a practice, topic, object, process is to be talked about. In that it provides descriptions, rules, permissions and prohibitions of social and individual actions. (Quoted in Fowler 1992: 42)

Kress's definition stresses the part discourse plays in structuring belief systems by moulding the cognitive frameworks through which we experience, interpret and talk about the world around us. Wæver agrees that discourse is the 'dimension of society where meaning is structured', such that discourses about particular objects 'organize knowledge systematically, and thus delimit what can be said and what not' (Wæver 1996: 5). Charlotte Epstein suggests that the performativity of discourses flows from two things: first of all, discourses constitute 'a space of objects', by rendering real things meaningful in particular ways; and second, discourses constitute the identities of social actors, 'by carving out particular *subject-positions*, that is, sites from which the social actors can speak as the I/we of a discourse' (Epstein 2008: 6), for example as 'pro' or 'anti' Europeans. Epstein's allusion to the *productive* possibilities on offer when adopting particular discourses shows them in a positive light. However, the converse is also true. Discourses (intentionally or unintentionally as far as their user goes) can shut off lines of debate and possibilities for action just as they can open them up. As such, the recognition of what Howarth calls the 'limiting conditions of discourses' (Howarth 1995: 129; see also Milliken 1999: 229) draws attention to an important factor behind much work in the field of critical discourse analysis: its goal of human emancipation. This is illustrated in the work of writers such as Norman Fairclough, who takes discourse as a tool of the powerful to exploit the weak or less powerful (for instance Fairclough 2000). Pulling all this together we can see that for discourse analysts the unspoken assumptions which shape language and behaviour are the key area for study. The aim of studying discourse is to get at the hidden wiring behind the textual productions (what is said and written and how) that first create meaning and second garner support for political programmes and policies. That these perceptions, theories and understandings are everywhere in media, political and public discourses yet remain either unacknowledged or, perhaps more perniciously, actively masked from view is equally disturbing and encouraging for discourse analysts. It is disturbing in that discourses are powerful mobilizing forces which can be used for evil ends, yet encouraging in that rival discourses can take their place and be put to creative and progressive uses. Discourses can manufacture and justify consensus but also be used to transform and generate new consensuses (Ricento 2003: 615).

The function of discourse analysis, argues Epstein (2008: 13), 'is not to query whether its statements are true but to study how its "truths" are mobilized and meted out'. It functions only and exclusively at the level of language itself. Fairclough provides a useful step-by-step guide to the why and how of using discourse analysis to study the language of the New Labour government. Fairlcough's logic is compelling. He begins by arguing that government is a form

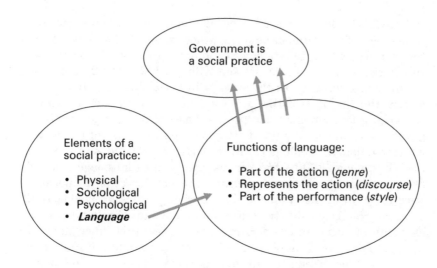

Figure 5. Fairclough on government as social practice (extrapolated from Fairclough 2000: 143–5).

of social practice (figure 5), 'a particular area of social life which is structured in a distinctive way involving particular groups of people (politicians, public employees, welfare claimants, the general public and so on) in particular relations with each other'. Government practices – its various forms of social practice – may alter over time, as can government's relations to other social practices, such as the media or the work of pressure groups. But over time 'it roughly sustains … its identity as one area of social life in contrast with others'. In short, government as social practice exhibits distinctive features that endure despite the comings and goings of even ideologically distinctive administrations (Fairclough 2000: 143–4). Fairclough's next step is to elaborate what he means by social practice. 'Every social practice holds diverse elements of social life together within a sort of network.' The four main parts to the network are: physical (the bodily actions of people and the environment within which these actions occur); sociological (institutional and organizational structures, procedures, rituals and so on, for instance the routines that shape the workings of a political institution such as Parliament); psychological (bodies of knowledge, beliefs, attitudes, feelings and so forth); and finally language (in its most general sense, including not just the spoken and written word but the symbolic gestures and visual images that create meaning) (Fairclough 2000: 144).

Fairclough's last step is to accent the idea that language is just one component of government as social practice, but that it runs through the operations that take place in the other realms (for examples of this in the discourse literature see Milliken 1999: 241–2). Language in this sense features in three ways in social life: it is part of the action, that is, part of the activity that goes on in social practice (governing for example); it represents action through discourses of government; and it is part of the performance, 'part of the way in which particular people perform in particular positions in the practice' (Fairclough 2000: 145). For instance, Blair's language and style as Prime Minister were the defining characteristics of his performance as Prime Minister (on 'performance' in politics see Wodak 2009, especially 9–11). To illustrate how language runs through the other elements of social practice Fairclough argues that when applying physical force (for example in the Kosovo intervention of 1999) militaries do so according to military doctrines, strategies and tactics which are constituted in, by and through language. The brutal physical expression of the force being applied should not detract from the fact that it is force applied with the help of a *language* of force which shapes the why, where, when and how of that force expressed in national and transnational strategic cultures. These develop and take shape in and around the fora in which countries gather to discuss and execute military and military-related operations. These language communities operate around historically contingent and highly context-specific imageries and conventions. They routinely rely on historical analogies and mores that critically shape the other elements of the use of force (see for instance Daddow 2002; Daddow 2003). As Fairclough surmises, we do not need to fall into the trap of suggesting that social life is *nothing but* discourse to recognize nonetheless that it has a pervasive effect on social life as it is played out in all four of the realms of social practice he identifies.

For Fairclough, government does not and cannot happen without language. Yes it involves real people, groups, organizations and institutions doing real things for each other and to each other. There are, yes, real-life actors and those acted upon – there is a real world 'out there' which we all experience. But to divorce those various physical activities and outcomes of government from the sociological, psychological and linguistic elements of government is unnecessarily to tear action from thought. When assessing whether someone qualifies to hold a disabled car parking badge, when fixing the national minimum wage, when setting a target for shorter hospital operation waiting lists and standards of education for primary school children, or when debating about when and where to deploy British troops in support of national foreign policy objectives, language is part of the action, part of the style and part of the performance. Discourse features as the medium by which these various activities of government are constructed and represented and thereby occupies a central position in the study of the very 'reality' these actions are purported to be taking place within and transforming in the process. To wrap up this section, the role discourse plays as mediator of reality is well put by Epstein in her book on the construction of whaling and anti-whaling discourses:

> Discourse confers meaning to social and physical realities. It is through discourse that individuals, societies, and states make sense of themselves, of their ways of living, and of the world around them. A discourse is a cohesive ensemble of ideas, concepts, and categorizations about a specific object that frame that object in a certain way and, therefore, delimit the possibilities for action in relation to it. It is a structured yet open and dynamic entity. (Epstein 2008: 2)

The meaning-giving and meaning-making functions of discourse are more significant for the discourse analyst than are debates about the association that may or may not exist between a discourse about an object (say, whales or the EU) and the reality of that object. (What are whales? What is the EU? For the discourse analyst it does not actually matter – only so far as discourse users answer those questions.) In the constructivist perspective it is false to posit a distinction between the real world and the world of discourse, as Epstein goes on to observe: 'The question is thus not whether material objects exist but how they become meaningful for us' (Epstein 2008: 8). This is not to deny the existence of a physical reality but to highlight that each and every reality exists as a reality *for us* and is necessarily mediated, moulded and made real to us in and through the language we use to describe it, interpret it and speak it.

The study of discourse has therefore been used in this book for three principal reasons. The first and most obvious is that it helps us elucidate the construction of identities at all levels – individual, local, regional, national and supranational – because discourses are 'windows into the lifeways of a culture and society' (Ricento 2003: 630). When we deploy a discourse we are constructing the world for ourselves and for our interlocutors, about ourselves and about our interlocutors. A national foreign policy discourse is, at root, a question of constructing the Other against which, or sometimes with, the state Self intends to act. It is mainly in the hands of policy-makers and elite commentators but, crucially, the written and broadcast media are also engaged in identity creation when they report the 'news' to us and when they comment on it. Discourse analysis can be used to explore the ideological and theoretical assumptions underpinning the writing and speeches of politicians, journalists, expert commentators and leader-writers by helping to answer several important questions. How do these people identify with their audiences and readerships through their narration and reporting of current events? How do they use rhetoric to persuade their listeners? What are their assumptions about who 'we' are and conversely about who 'they' are? What are the artificial closures they have to put in place to make their discourses appear to be the 'truth' about how the world works?

A second reason to use discourse analysis is that it helps us appreciate the importance of what might be called the 'lower case' ideologies running through contemporary political practices – those ideologies that shape discourses but which are not acknowledged in or by them. 'Lower case' ideologies are distinct from 'upper case' ideologies (such as Marxism) in that they work as ideologies without necessarily claiming the epistemic status of ideologies. They are positioned without claiming to be so. Unlike an (upper case) Enlightenment story about the steady progress of reason and freedom, or the Marxist account of class conflict culminating in the proletarian revolution (Jenkins 1997: 70), lower case ideologies are less obviously driven by a metanarrative. Especially since the end of the Cold War and the supposed collapse of the capitalist–communist story, upper case ideology has apparently been in decline, to be replaced by the lower case ideology surrounding the phenomena of 'globalization' and the 'victory' of neoliberalism, which in the reading of many Marxists and neo-Marxists is merely upper case ideology writ small for the purposes of public consumption. As Fairclough pointed out in *New Labour, New Language?* (2000: 23–9), New Labour's uncritical acceptance of the existence and impact of the 'new global economy', a pervasive theme of Third Way speeches, prompted the government to accept equally uncritically the validity and desirability of pursuing post-ideological neoliberal economic policies (for a critique of the New Labour economic narrative see also Tomlinson 2008). A different vision (a different discourse as it were) of the motors of the international political economy might have led to the development of domestic and foreign policies that were more beneficial to Britain, Europe and the wider world, particularly with regard to the actions of multinational corporations. Un(der)stated though it was, New Labour's centre-right ideology was no less prevalent for all the party's much vaunted interest in global development and debt reduction in the Third World, and this comes through clearly in its discourses on the Third Way and globalization.

The third reason why the study of discourse is valuable to the political researcher plays on its emancipatory agenda. Just as discourse analysis highlights the structured and consequently restrictive nature of discourses, it gives hope for change inasmuch as it shows that, with creativity on the part of agents – albeit those agents in positions of relative power or at least with the capacity to mobilize popular opinion by some means – discourses can be altered, and new political possibilities and different futures open up as a result. In an era when the phrase 'it's only of academic interest' has come to imply that dry old theories produced in ivory towers are of no relevance to the practical world of politics, where men and women of action are actually out there *doing* things, changing the 'real' world, discourse analysis helps us make scholarly work relevant to publics, politicians, organizations and businesses. Discourse analysis helps us see the possibilities *beyond* the contemporary dominant or hegemonic political discourses that abound in the world arena. It helps us see through the façade of press and broadcasting objectivity and to think about the conceptual basis of the stories we are told about the world. Discourse analysis helps us think critically about the way the world works, how it could work in the future and how we might go about instigating or bringing about change. It works proudly to a normative agenda, denaturalizing 'dominant forms of knowledge' and exposing to critique 'the practices that they enable' (Milliken 1999: 236), undermining weary positivist claims that all we are given by politicians and news organizations are 'the facts'. By studying discourse we are able to see the elements that go into bringing about states of 'discursive paralysis' (a term from Blain, Boyle and O'Donnell, in Crolley and Hand 2002: 25), and to think critically about how to move the terms of a political debate forward. In writing this book I hope to be able to help us think critically and reflectively about the state of the public debates about the British in Europe and to that end a word on method is in order.

III. Method

To avoid misinterpretation, strip down a policy or opinion to one key clear line before the media does it for you. Think in headlines. (Tony Blair, 1987, quoted in Rentoul 1997: 192)

[P]olitical speeches are now designed to contain phrases that are brief, typical and frequent so that they can be readily taken up as 'sound bites' to be constantly recycled through the broadcast media. (Charteris-Black 2006: 12)

This book studies the discourse element of New Labour's exercise in norm entrepreneurship on the Europe question by answering three research questions. First, how did Blair and Brown use the concept of the national interest to sell the European idea to the British people? Second, how did Blair and Brown use speeches to

construct their own identities as pro-Europeans and how did they
construct the identities of their Eurosceptic opponents? Third, how
did Blair and Brown use history to support their arguments about
Britain being a 'European' country? Data have been collected from
three sets of sources. The main sources the study draws upon are
the political speeches of the two men, which have been analysed
using the discourse method elaborated below. The data extrapolated
from the speeches were put into context using two other sets of
sources. One was the literature I bring together under the heading
of the 'New Labour industry'. This incorporates: primary accounts
(diaries and memoirs) by former government insiders; biographies
and autobiographies of the main protagonists; journalistic commentary and secondary academic literature on the Blair–Brown
years; plus the theoretical literature on Euroscepticism, norms and
discourses. The secondary material was used initially as a point of
departure for describing the key steps in British European policy.
As the study of the data garnered from the speeches got under
way, the secondary material was gutted for work on the speeches
themselves (they receive patchy analysis at best) and the ideas and
thinking behind New Labour's European policy. The other material
came from semi-structured interviews conducted face to face with
current and recent speech-writers and New Labour foreign policy
advisers. I spoke to several people who were involved in devising
and framing British European policy after 1997, so I took the opportunity to ask them questions about Blair and Brown's handling of
this issue. I used the interviews to elicit background information on
the processes and characters involved in making this policy and to
appreciate more about the beliefs and attitudes the Prime Minister
and Chancellor held regarding the British in Europe. I do not claim
that this is an interview-based project in the same way as Anthony
Seldon's or Andrew Rawnsley's work is. That said, the interviews
provided fertile ground on which to test my starting hypotheses and
the results of the discourse analysis as they emerged from the data.
It is to the discourse method that we now turn.

To get at the *sense* of New Labour's European discourses the research progressed through three stages. First, the corpus of texts to
be studied had to be decided upon. There is a plentiful online archive
of speeches on the Downing Street, Treasury and Foreign Office
websites which contains many of what the teams there consider to
be the key speeches delivered by the Prime Minister, Chancellor
and Foreign Secretary. They include set-piece speeches to invited
audiences, statements to Parliament, 'remarks' at launch events and
transcripts of press conferences. In the course of the research the
handover from Blair to Brown in June 2007 led to an overhaul of

both sites, such that Blair became consigned to the 'history' section of the Downing Street website and the Treasury hugely increased the number of texts on its site. The online transcripts, however, remained accessible and the texts did not alter. I wanted to be comprehensive, to tell the story from 1997 as near to the time of study as possible, and to include a comprehensive set of texts (following Milliken 1999: 233). Each speech and statement on the site was categorized as: (a) about the EU; (b) about foreign policy; (c) mentions EU/foreign policy/history; (d) mentions none of the above. Every transcript classified (a) to (c) was included in the study, giving a total of 129 speeches in all: 58 by Blair and 71 by Brown. This main corpus was supported by speeches from other figures such as Peter Hain and David Miliband, taking the total to around 140.

The second stage was to decide how to process the data. Given the large-n sample of speeches studied it might be contended that statistical content analysis would have enabled more efficient analysis of the key data trends in the speeches, especially if it used a generalizable representative sample of key speeches (used to good effect in, for example, Lord 2008 and Dyson 2009a). The value of statistical content analysis is that it offers up numerical snapshots of the key themes that exercise the producers of texts through frequency counts of keywords presented descriptively; the data can easily be broken down for statistical analysis (see Neuendorf 2002). Content analysis was rejected, however, for two reasons. First, at the research design level, content analysis would not help answer the research questions about the *meaning* under the surface level of the speeches. Content analysis could tell us if and how often the Prime Minister and Chancellor talked up their Europeanist credentials, and how much time they spent identifying their opponents. Statistical content analysis could also tell us if and how often the national interest was used to support their rhetorical push for Europe and it could have revealed the frequency with which the 'past' or 'history' appeared in their speeches. Content analysis could help us understand the number of textual signifiers but it is not as well positioned to explain the deployment of those particular signifiers as meaning-making constructions. Our research questions are about *how* Blair and Brown used identity, interest and history to make the case for Europe, not *whether* or *how often* they did. Here I follow Epstein, who argues that discourse analysis is distinct from content analysis inasmuch as meaning 'cannot be derived from the number of occurrences' of keywords, telling though the statistics may be. It works instead by assuming 'the subject position that the discourse presumes and reading critically from there' (Epstein 2008: 173). Content and discourse analysis are certainly not antithetical to each other and could profitably be used in a mixed methods framework if the re-searcher so wished (Titscher *et al.* 2007: 68). Discourse analysis suits this study, however, because it is more interpretative. Second, and for the reasons Epstein identifies, it was felt that content analysis is of greater value to the researcher when approaching a corpus of texts for the first time, in other words when they are largely 'unknown' quantities to the researcher. The idea behind this book was to study how New Labour devised its rhetorical case for Europe by building on a survey of the existing secondary literature. As the researcher, I was already 'inside' the story when I designed the questions and had spent three years researching various New Labour foreign policy speeches for other publications. Wanting to find out about the *meaning* of the New Labour speeches meant that discourse analysis was the most appropriate method to answer the research questions. I already had a stock of knowledge about how New Labour had tried to position itself on the issues of British identity, the country's relation-ship to its past and its world role, so it was a case of developing the empirical data rather than starting from scratch.

The third stage was to execute the method by coding the speeches for the textual signifiers of the Blair–Brown approach to interests, identity and history (on coding principles see Taylor 2009: 39). The choice for all coders is: by hand or computer package? The search for meaning and context was all important in this study so I decided to code by hand to generate familiarity with the texts as I dissected them. That I was not interested in the number of occasions given words or phrases appeared in the speeches meant that counting using computer coding was unnecessary; electronic searches were, however, useful in locating the existence of each keyword. A computer keyword analysis tool was used to help find 'keywords in context' (KWIC) when the coding scheme had been finalized (Hoskinson. net, undated). The speeches were coded around the themes neces-sary to help answer each of the research questions: about national interests; about personal and national identity; and about history (see appendix 1 for the full coding scheme). Coding for these themes was carried out by identifying individual words around which Blair and Brown worked their arguments about the British in Europe. For example, the word 'lead' was coded and then the electronic package could find all occasions through the speeches where the word 'lead', its grammatical extensions ('leading', 'leadership' and so forth) and its collocations featured in the speeches. That it appeared in many forms ('leading', 'leader' and so on) and in many collocations (a 'leading power' or 'leading partner in Europe') made for a beguiling array of findings and it was critical to capture these through KWIC searches. Writing up the findings centred on grouping the keywords together and trying to make sense of what their discursive utterances could tell us about the webs of belief they had created about the story of the British in Europe, and comparing this with evidence from the existing literature and from the elite interviews.

Appendix 2 shows a speech with the codes applied. What it reveals is that analysing discourse entails making a series of epistemological choices about how to grasp the 'meaning' of a text from the words it contains, and this is tricky. One cannot code for every word or concept in a speech, otherwise it would just be a case of reproducing each of the 140 or so speeches selected for analysis and letting the reader interpret them how he or she wishes. There is inevitably an element of selectivity involved in determining which linguistic 'facts' are salient to the study, which are tangential and which are extraneous altogether. The success of a coding scheme rests on how far the textual residues left behind when a speech has been poured through the coding sieve captures the data to help answer the research questions for the study. Naturally, on occasion, the coding scheme threw up irrelevancies such as Blair talking about the British Council ('Brit' being the search term, relating to British national identity) – this can be the case with proper nouns, particularly country names. But in Appendix 2 we can see that the coding easily flags up when Blair spoke about British identity with regard to the Commonwealth and EU, about his brand of 'enlightened patriotism', about national interests and economic interests, about the uses of the past in the present and about the mistakes in Conservative Party policy towards Europe he wanted to reverse. The possibility of empirical gaps opening up in this study has been mitigated by being as comprehensive as possible in terms of the number of speeches chosen and the coding system used. By remaining faithful to the original appearances of the keywords as they were deployed in the speeches, I hope I have managed to convey the thrust of Blair and Brown's key foreign policy ideas and messages as creatively but also as accurately as possible. Through the use of the KWIC tool I have tried to flag up variations in New Labour's use of keywords, while retaining an overall argument that its discourses were remarkably stable over time as well as prolonging traditions of discourse that were prevalent prior to 1997. By the end of the book the reader should have a good picture of New Labour's discursive construction of British national identity, interests and the role of history in putting its case for Europe.

Summary

[O]n the Tibetan prayer-wheel principle, repeat it enough and at some point something unspecified but miraculous will come to pass. (Pynchon 2007: 174)

This chapter began by applying the norm entrepreneurship model of Finnemore and Sikkink to the case study of Britain and Europe. It sought to identify the tipping point at which the hegemonic norm in Britain about Europe being a hostile Other across the English Channel cascaded and became internalized. We found that the most viable date and event was Thatcher's Bruges speech of September 1988. Thatcher ran with established themes in British discourses about Europe going back decades, not to say centuries. She gave profile and credibility to what would become in the 1990s a popular and populist set of Eurosceptic agendas that observers both inside and outside Britain would readily identify as being 'classical' British interpretations of the aims, objectives and policy practices of the EU. Her discourse crucially picked up on the *Zeitgeist* of the time in Britain, was spurred on by practical policy developments in the early 1990s centred around the Maastricht negotiations and became institutionalized in material ways. For example, it led to the establishment of organized pressure groups such as the Bruges Group, which were created to impose the sceptical themes of her speech onto mainstream political and media agendas. In theorizing the nature of the discursive and political environments in which Blair and Brown made their interventions after 1997 it was argued above that they were trying to create a new norm life cycle to replace one that had existed implicitly for hundreds of years, and formally in terms of Thatcherite discourse for nearly a decade. We can therefore appreciate the difficulties they faced in generating and spreading a new norm about the British in Europe.

The second section reviewed the nature of, and rationale for, using discourses as lenses through which to see the cognitive construction of policy at work. Discourse analysis of the Blair–Brown speeches allows us to answer questions about speaker identity, the identities which they attributed to their political opponents, and the wider sets of concepts, ideas and linkages between them that they posited as central to an understanding of the policy challenges they faced. Secondly, we highlighted the critical discourse idea that government is a social practice, foregrounding language as a critical part of that practice. In Fairclough's terms, language does not represent policy in any simple sense *after the fact* of that policy being worked out; language is integral to all government work. Language is part of the action, it represents the action and finally it is part of the performance. Without language there is, in effect, no such thing as government – governing and governance are not possibilities. New Labour used speeches both to describe policy and to shift it in the government's preferred directions. Discourse analysis illustrates how Blair and Brown did this and what meanings they attached to the keywords and phrases they repeated over a number of years. As Nicholas Jones has put it, the speeches might have been quite formulaic 'but they were formulaic for a reason' (interview with Jones). Discourse analysis, I contend, following Ole Wæver, is the most appropriate methodological tool for studying New Labour's foreign policy repertoire as expressed in ministerial speeches on foreign policy. Like all political argumentation, New Labour's messages were founded on a 'basic conceptual logic' available in society at large, but – in acting as norm entrepreneurs – Blair and Brown were simultaneously 'reproducing or modifying this conceptual code, thereby setting the conditions for the next political struggle' (Wæver 1996: 7). It is against this background that the final section considered the method of discourse used to understand the linguistic strategies New Labour developed to 'talk Europe' and put the 'pro' case to the British people. The next chapter is the first empirical chapter of the study, presenting the evidence on the ways in which the Prime Minister and Chancellor discursively constructed the Europe question as a matter of protecting and/or advancing vital British national interests.

Chapter 4

Interests rate:
economics, influence and security

TB wants a crude appeal on the basis of jobs plus an intellectual argument on the question of influence. The problem is that we don't have a clear script for everybody to read from. (Price 2005: 157–8, entry for 7 November 1999)

To cut ourselves off from the major strategic alliance on our doorstep would be an act of supreme folly. (Blair 2000h)

Selling a political argument, policy or vision of the future requires leaders to possess a combination of instant appeal and a persuasive case to help shift public opinion in the direction they want. Blair and Brown believed that the precondition to winning the argument about the EU was altering subterranean British attitudes to matters 'European' more generally. Meanwhile, sweetening the pill of British membership and clearing the way for potential further engagement with the EU across a range of policy sectors meant bringing home to the British people what the EU meant to them in economic, influence and security terms. In Lance Price's words above, the 'crude appeal' of 'jobs plus...' was the propaganda part of the message Blair and Brown put out to alter short-term public opinion. The 'argument' aspect involved reasoning that Britain lost influence by being outside core European decision-making circles and, therefore, could be more influential by being closer to the heartbeat of the European project. There was an additional factor that Price ignored: education. Sometimes, Blair and Brown felt they needed to tell the British what the EU had done for them historically speaking with regard to security, working from the assumption that 'we are pretty poorly educated about it really' (interview with Morgan). Closely intertwined with proselytizing the economic benefits EU membership brought Britain, it is noteworthy that Blair and Brown felt the need to retell post-Second World War European history to their British audiences. This chapter will start by considering how Blair and Brown sold the EU to the British public in economic terms. The second section will explain how they tried to win the argument about the potential loss to Britain's European and global influence that would come about through the 'supreme folly' of cutting Britain off from Europe. The third section covers the methods by which New Labour tried to educate the British public about the successes of the European project in terms of peace and security. By the end of the chapter we should have a sophisticated understanding of the interests-based case New Labour put for the British in Europe – a classically rationalist cost–benefit approach beloved by many a previous government.

I. Economics

The economic benefits of EU membership featured prominently across the corpus of speeches by Blair and Brown. Three factors explain the high profile of the financial case for membership in their discourses. First, the key European issue confronting the New Labour governments, certainly in the early years, was the vexed question of Britain's policy towards the single currency. This was a debate about economics as much as politics (as Blair is at pains to point out – see Blair 2010: 537), certainly as far as Treasury opposition to the single currency went, and Blair–Brown disagreements played out in the first term and a half, at least until the publication of the Treasury verdict on the five economic tests in June 2003 (Bulmer 2008: 603). If economic concerns were a selling point for the public they were additionally a reflection of New Labour's internal debates about the relative merits of staying out or joining the eurozone.

The second factor has historic roots in the strategies Britain's leaders have used to generate support for their European policies. Blair was well aware that in the realm of foreign economic policy, and especially controversial initiatives such as this, any argument for the EU had to be couched in terms of the national interest, in this case the national *economic* interest. On all previous occasions when a British premier was putting the case for closer British relations with the EEC or EU, economic factors weighed heavily both in the government's decision and in its public explanation. For example, when Harold Macmillan announced to Parliament in July 1961 that he would be undertaking accession negotiations to join the EEC, the political character of the organization was not hidden. However, it was conveniently downplayed, with greater proportions of his speech given over to the need to use EEC membership to bolster Britain's global economic position. The alternative arrangements Britain had put in place by helping found the European Free Trade Association (EFTA) in 1960 had, he argued, not benefited the British economy as much as the Conservative government would have hoped (on Britain

and EFTA see Ellison 2000). By contrast, the Rome Treaties had
generated huge economic growth for the six founder members of the
EEC. It was logical, therefore, for the British to consider joining the
rival bloc:

> On the economic side, a community comprising, as members or in
> association, the countries of free Europe, could have a very rapidly
> expanding economy supplying, as eventually it would, a single market
> of approaching 300 million people. This rapidly expanding economy
> could, in turn, lead to an increased demand for products from other
> parts of the world and so help to expand world trade and improve the
> prospects of the less developed areas of the world. (Macmillan 1961)

Derek Scott, Blair's economic adviser, argues that the Macmillan
approach 'set the pattern for the way in which Europe was presented
to the British people on many subsequent occasions by the leaders'
(Scott 2004: 191) and he may well be correct in view of the extent to
which economic considerations came to feature in the 'hard sell' on
Europe.

For instance, Harold Wilson made a more or less parallel statement regarding the Labour government's decision to apply for
British EEC membership on 2 May 1967. He explained that:

> the Government's decision has been motivated by broader consider-
> ations of economic policy ... all of us are aware of the long-term
> potential for Europe, and, therefore, for Britain, of the creation of a
> single market of approaching 300 million people, with all the scope
> and incentive which this will provide for British industry, and of the
> enormous possibilities which an integrated strategy for technology,
> on a truly Continental scale, can create. (Wilson 1967)

Wilson prioritized future economic possibilities arising from British
access to a single market of 300 million people and the attendant
economic benefits which that huge outlet would bring British
industry and the British economy (on the role of economics in both
applications see Daddow 2004b). Of course, each premier has had his
or her pet ideas to push. In Wilson's case, for example – pre-empting
Blair and Brown by some thirty years – his project was the modernization effects to be gleaned from opening up British industry to the
'white heat' of European technological cooperation (see Young 2003).
Distinctive as these concerns were to respective Prime Ministers,
the point is that the economic case for British membership has never
been far from the surface of the argument because the political
dimensions of European integration have proved so off-putting to
the general public. Compare Macmillan's and Wilson's statements
with this from Gordon Brown in 2001:

> Getting the economic future for Europe right matters for Britain
> because over three quarters of a million UK companies now trade

with the rest of the European union [*sic*]. When we joined Europe
in the 1970s, less than £8 billions of our trade was with the rest of
Europe. Today it is £138 billions – more than half our total trade –
with 3 million jobs affected. (Brown 2001c)

It is fair to say that the 'crude' economic appeal is one with an established and recognizable heritage in Britain's European discourses.

The third factor that may explain the economics-led discourse of
British leaders lies in a pragmatic 'what do we get out of it?' British
approach to Europe. The tangible economic benefits have to be seen
to be coming back to Britain to make any further entanglement in
the process seem worthwhile, especially when a negative slant is so
frequently put on the political implications. Why else did Thatcher
generate so much popular and political support for her demand
that Britain get its 'own money' back in the tortured budget rebate
negotiations in the early 1980s? Standing up to Europe politically,
the argument goes, entails standing up to it – and getting the best
deal from it – economically, and that in turn depends on a practical
grasp of the basic financial 'facts' of the matter. It is far from easy to
prove this point empirically but there is evidence that British leaders
such as Blair and Brown both reflected and worked this alleged
national characteristic to domestic and foreign audiences alike. For
example, during his February 1999 statement to Parliament restat-
ing the government's 'wait and see' position on the single currency,
Blair commended his statement to the House by saying that: 'We
have a vision, but it is a vision that is practical. We should have confidence, both in our vision and our pragmatism' (Blair 1999a). Here,
the idealist, visionary Blair came up against the realist, pragmatic
Blair. His statement merged the aspirational and the progressive
with the practicalities of tradition in the country's Europe debates.
It was only to his audience in Ghent the following year that he could
elaborate on why he mixed them. 'The British on the whole are too
pragmatic to believe in visions' (Blair 2000b); the empiricist in them,
he suggested, needs to see or at least be able to calculate, in concrete terms, the effects of membership on their daily lives. If it was
predictable that economics would feature in New Labour's European
discourses it is nonetheless instructive to see exactly how, so let us
take a detailed look at the evidence from the speeches.

The Prime Minister and Chancellor rested their case for the EU
on a variety of facts and figures that helped make it attractive to the
British people financially, while carefully making sure the economics
of the single currency were bounded off from this discourse strand
via the 'five tests'. The two most common sets of statistics they gave
related to jobs and trade. Together they formed the bluntest side of
the 'crude appeal' – proselytizing the EU's capacity to bring practical

benefits to the ordinary person in the street. The employment case flowing from access to the single market was put starkly, right from the beginning. 'Europe is where we are, where we trade, and where we make our living ... 3.5 million jobs depend upon it' (Brown 1997a and repeated almost word for word in Brown 1997b; see also Brown 1997c); this became the New Labour figure of choice on the employment effect: 'Three and a half million British jobs depend on our membership of the EU' (Blair 1999f; Blair 2000h). At times they could be hazier, arguing that 'Over three million British jobs' were dependent upon Europe (Blair 2000b; Blair 2002c; Brown 2001a; Brown 2004f) or that 'up to 3.5 million jobs are directly affected' by it (Brown 1999h).

Along with jobs, the government publicized patterns in national trade, an echo of the earlier pushes for Europe by Macmillan and Wilson, which had been prompted by and sold as grudging acknowledgements of the relative shift in Britain's trading patterns from the Commonwealth towards the EEC economies. 'Europe was seen as a last resort, a final resting place for a country which had run out of options' (Bogdanor 2005: 693). Depending on whether they were talking about British trade with partners inside the single currency zone (usually the lower figures), or with EU partners more generally (the higher figures), the New Labour government was flexible in its calculation of the trading benefits to Britain. The figures ranged upward from '50%' (Blair 1999a; Brown 2005e); 'over 50% of our trade' (Blair 1999f); '53 per cent of our total imports of goods and services are from Europe, 50 per cent of our total exports of goods and services go to Europe' (Brown 2004f; see also Brown 2006c); '55 percent of our trade is with the European Union' (Brown 2005b); 'Nearly 60% of British trade is with the rest of the European Union' (Blair 2000b; Blair 2001d); or, the highest figure, '60% of our trade is with the EU' (Blair 2002d). Only in his New Year's message in 2003 did Blair estimate that under half the British economy's trade was reliant upon Europe ('almost 50 per cent of our trade' – Blair 2003a) and that was out of line with the general tenor of the figures, which increased with his time in office. Brown was initially more bullish than Blair, either saying that 60% of British trade was with Europe (Brown 1997a; Brown 1997b) or that 60% of British exports went to Europe (Brown 1997e; Brown 1998b). He was known, though, to give a lower figure of 58% (Brown 1997c), or 55% (Brown 2005b), and gradually settled in his discourse for 'over' or at 50% (Brown 1999h; Brown 2001a; Brown 2004b). In the US and to the British TUC audience 50% was Brown's chosen figure (Brown 1998c; Brown 1999b; see also Brown 2000c). The statistics may have altered with the speech but the message was consistent: Europe is 'where we do half our trade' (Brown 1998f). For that reason New Labour wanted to make sure that 'we are in Europe and in Europe to stay' (Brown 1999d), helping the Union become more outward looking and internationalist – more British – in the process. It is worth adding that such statistical anomalies were not confined to coverage of the Europe question. For example, in February 2005 Brown said that Britain produced over 11% of the world's 'most cited scientific papers' – left undefined (Brown 2005d); in May the proportion had risen to 12% (Brown 2005e). Are these discrepancies insignificant, or did the real number of citations *actually* rise by 1% over a three-month period, or do they reveal a government obsessed with quantifying the world the rationalist way without ever being able to conceptualize the object or operationalize the measure?

In and around the employment and trade figures, the Prime Minister and Chancellor wove a variety of other economic indicators which played to the particular audience they were addressing. A feature of the Chancellor's speeches to British business organizations such as the Confederation of British Industry (CBI) was that Brown would regale his audience with the history of Britain's growing economic interconnectedness with the continent (Brown 1999h). The government would then use the specifics of this regional narrative to put the case to the general public and Parliament. For example, in his euro statement of 1999 Blair turned to financial statistics to bring home the routine, day-to-day benefits of the euro to big and small businesses alike by discussing the practical point that British businesses were starting to use the currency in their accounting (Blair 1999a). Both in content and in form the following passage indicates significant input from Gordon Brown and the Treasury. In content it is full of dense swathes of statistics and indicators, for which Brown was notorious for packing into speeches. In form, the usual clipped, staccato sentence paragraphs Blair liked to use were replaced with fatter paragraphs more common in Brown's proto-academic tracts (Routledge 1998: 233):

> Not just big business like British Steel, Ford, Philips, ICI and Unilever. Surveys by the Treasury's euro Preparations Unit show that some 45% of SMEs [small and medium-size enterprises] in the UK have trading links with Europe and they are already having to prepare to deal with the euro. The same survey showed that nearly half of all SMEs thought that the single currency would affect their business. Last autumn some 14% of SMEs were already planning to use the euro, and the latest survey by APACS [Association for Payment Clearing Services] showed that 247,000 companies intended to open euro accounts. 86% of large retailers have suppliers in the eurozone and 44% say they are planning to pay eurozone suppliers in euro from 1999. The euro is now an everyday reality for British business, large and small. (Blair 1999a)

At the CBI in November 2003 the Prime Minister talked only in general terms about the economic consequences of EU membership because these were presumably familiar to his audience, but he still hit them with the view that: 'You know that to be anti-Europe is to be anti-business' (Blair 2003h; see also Brown 1997a). The ambiguous 'You know' at the beginning could mean one of two things. On the one hand it could be a way of saying 'One knows', followed by a pause, revealing that Blair is thinking about this from a Labour Party perspective, as in 'we all know that being anti-European is to be anti-business and Labour is the party of business'. On the other hand it could be an injunction, a warning almost: 'You *know* that anti-Europe equates to anti-business' – and it is therefore in your basic interests to be pro-European and supportive of the government. It was also in 2003 that Blair began to make the case for monetary union by reeling off Treasury findings from its 1,700-page June report (the eighteen accompanying studies are available online – see HM Treasury undated) on the preparedness of the British economy for membership of the single currency. This is further evidence, if any were needed, of the Treasury input to Downing Street speeches, an exemplar being the Prime Minister's July 2003 speech in Tokyo, reproduced in part in box 2.

Box 2. The Brown in Blair

Blair's 2003 speech in Tokyo (Blair 2003f) was packed with economic statistics on the nature of and potential future scenarios for the British economy. Gone was the visionary European Blair. In his place was Blair the economist, making the case on the back of hard-headed calculations about Britain's national economic interest. At the heart of his appeal lay the voluminous report on Britain's potential adoption of the euro by Brown and his Treasury team.

'So the direction of policy is now clear. The economics must be right, but if they are we will recommend membership, and in the meantime we will work to ensure the economics are indeed right. And the reasons are plain. Our Treasury estimates that the combination of lower transaction costs, reduction in economic uncertainty, and the attendant increase in trade that monetary union can produce, raises the UK's growth rate by around one-quarter of a percent. That doesn't seem much, except when the magic of compound arithmetic means that after 30 years the nation garners an annual benefit of between 5–9% of GDP. To put that figure in context, the UK spends around 7% of GDP [gross domestic product] on healthcare, so we are talking about a very significant addition to the nation's wealth. Or alternatively the benefit may be seen as similar in magnitude to what we currently spend on state pensions and education combined. So the Treasury studies have established that over the long term monetary union is in the national interest.'

After 2003 Blair and Brown bolstered the economic case for British EU membership by pointing to more than just jobs and trade figures, though they remained a mainstay of the government's case. For example, in his parliamentary statement on the EU Constitutional Treaty in June 2004 the Prime Minister noted the 'extra 1.8% of GDP [gross domestic product] that membership brings us every year' alongside the now established array of economic benefits (Blair 2004b). By 2005 the Treasury had calculated the case for reform in the EU by working out that a 1% growth in the eurozone 'can give an extra fifth of a per cent of growth in Britain' (Brown 2005e). Bringing all this together we can see that around the core benefits EU membership brought Britain, Blair and Brown carefully tailored their messages to their audiences for a given speech. They increasingly shot their arguments through with dense economic material and used these to push the case for EU reform but, tellingly, against a sudden British push to join the eurozone. In effect the Treasury held the whip hand and Blair was acknowledging this in coded fashion by incorporating so many of its facts and figures in his speeches. Other things were going on in these multilayered speeches so we will now turn to the New Labour take on British influence in Europe as a way of illustrating the political dimensions of the Chancellor's and Prime Minister's European discourses.

II. In or out? British influence

New Labour's discourse on the question of British influence in Europe had three main strands to it. First, Britain would be affected by developments in Europe whether the country was inside or out of the EU. Second, Britain would find it easier to reform the EU from inside rather than from the margins. Finally, Britain would be better able to act out its traditional role in global affairs using the EU as a platform. What stands out across New Labour's discourse on influence is how infrequently it referred to the European ideal to back its case. The first strand combated the argument that Britain could or should withdraw from the EU and exercise its sovereignty as an independent state by 'going it alone'. The second strand effectively suggested that being inside Europe was beneficial only inasmuch as it helped Britain exercise leadership over the debates about the EU's future economic direction. The third case leap-frogged from the EU as an end in itself to what the EU could do to help Britain act out its Churchillian role as a bridge between the US and Europe. Both Blair and Brown worked the rationalist 'what the EU can do for Britain' line of thought that pervaded the economic dimensions of British

European discourses explored above. It was only when it came to the wider, security-oriented case for Europe that Blair lived up to his reputation for being a Europhile, but even then national interests still floated to the surface, as we shall see in the next section.

The first of New Labour's arguments in and around British influence was that Britain could not afford to stay out of the EU, economically or politically, as Blair's injunction from 1999 well shows: 'Europe is not marginal to the British economy. It is fundamental to it and each day becomes more so. To quit Europe would be an act of economic mutilation' (Blair 1999f). Earlier that year Blair encouraged his British audience to face up to the facts of the post-single currency EU. 'The euro is a reality. It exists. 11 out of 15 other EU members are in it. It represents 20% of world income, as big as the US. It will be the currency of 290 million people.' After rehearsing the economics of the eurozone, Blair confronted those who predicted or willed that the single currency would never get off the ground: 'It has begun and, on the whole, it has begun well.... And those who predicted it would never happen or would launch itself in disaster, have been proven wrong.' The euro, said Blair, was just the latest in a line of European schemes that the British wrongly thought would never come off, certainly not without British input or participation. Time and again, he said, the doubters have been proved wrong and Britain must, as a country, wise up to the continental will to deliver on new and ambitious plans for deeper integration. Hence, Blair continued, 'it will have a major impact on Britain, in or out. That much is obvious. That alone would rebuke those who would like to pretend it isn't there' (all from Blair 1999a). In this speech Blair the realist was again to the fore: the euro was an empirical fact and policy now had to adapt to the altered circumstances it had brought about.

In May 2003 Blair used lessons from the British experience to educate an audience in Warsaw about the perils of sniping from the sidelines about Europe's integrative projects. 'But let me advise you as a friend to avoid the mistake of British foreign policy towards Europe for around half a century' (Blair 2003c; Seldon 2007: 122–3 rightly notes that Blair was following Hugo Young's 1998 *This Blessed Plot* in framing the narrative in this way). It is unclear if he included the New Labour years in his litany of British mistakes. Blair usually commenced his historical stories about the EU with the Monnet–Schuman years, in the 1950s, but it cannot be out of the question that he was building the early New Labour years into his story of Britain's missed opportunities in Europe arising from the mistaken propensity 'to think that by hanging back in Europe we can avoid the debate; that if we participate we get contaminated by contrary arguments'. The nub of the matter for Blair was that the

EU existed and was materially affecting the British economy and society, like it or not. 'In truth we are in the debate anyway. Europe affects us, in or out. Economically, we are integrated with Europe. Politically, it is absurd to think Europe's decisions do not affect us.' For the Prime Minister, as for Hugo Young, the story pointed in only one direction: 'For Poland as with Britain, our strategy should be: get in, make the most of it, have the confidence to win the debate not be frightened by it' (Blair 2003c). Attacking the naysayers was one element of Blair's discourse, but in terms of the overall time devoted to the question of British influence in his speeches he was at least as interested in discussing the prospects for Britain once wholeheartedly inside as opposed to outside the European club: 'I say to you simply: we will only get reform in Europe by being part of Europe.... we know Europe needs reform and we are fighting for it.... Europe can reform and Britain can and should play a leading part in it' (Blair 1999f). The rationale for British participation in the debates about EU enlargement to the east and institutional reform was framed in realist terms, Blair saying that: 'Shaping their outcome is vital to our national interest' (Blair 2002d). Brown was vigorous in putting the same case. Of the Lisbon summit he said 'Britain is leading Europe with our reform proposals', which 'would mean more business and jobs for Britain' (Brown 1999h). Ironically, of course, New Labour's construction of Europeans as an 'out-group' (on which see Risse *et al.* 1999: 154–5) reified the British–European binary the government sought to transcend. This points up the latent power of day-to-day British ways of speaking Europe into existence, entrapping speakers even as they seek to escape particular discursive shackles. Brown enthusiastically supported the Prime Minister on the reform agenda by arguing: 'our distinctive British qualities have much to offer Europe in our national interest and in Europe's interests [*sic*]' (Brown 1997c).

New Labour's European agenda during Blair's first term centred on trying to generate a Third Way reconciliation between what the government took to be two threatening propensities within the EU: federalism and regulation (Brown 1997c; see also O'Donnell and Whitman 2007: 262). Into its second and third terms New Labour alighted on reform of the EU's decision-making machinery as its point of attack, which became channelled through the Constitutional and Lisbon Treaty negotiations. In both cases British influence was held to be at stake. In October 1999 economic reform was taken to be about switching EU policies 'away from regulation to job creation' (Blair 1999f), such that after the Lisbon summit in March 2000 Blair could argue that Britain's active involvement in the process (explored in Hopkin and Wincott 2006: 54; Bulmer 2008: 608–9)

had helped push the EU in the direction of 'co-ordinated structural reform'. This process, Blair held, 'will create jobs in Britain
and throughout Europe'. Britain naturally came first in the list of
economic beneficiaries from Lisbon, but just as importantly Blair
said: 'The point I am making is far wider than the Euro. It is that
Britain's interests demand we help shape European policy rather
than, passively, be shaped by it' (Blair 2000h). Here, Blair indicated
his preferred leadership model, driving things forward rather than
sitting in the back seat being driven along by the desires and ambitions of others, possibly in unwanted directions. Blair developed
this point a year later when he summarized the principal lesson of
the history of British European policy as he read it:

> What does this history mean? Not that we go along meekly with what-
> ever the rest of Europe decides. On the contrary, it shows we must get
> in on the ground floor of decision-making so that the decisions are
> ones we are happy with. (Blair 2001d)

By 2006 Blair felt he had achieved his goal. 'It's a new Europe. We
are part of it, in at the ground floor. It's where we should have always
been. Now we're there, we should stay there' (Blair 2006a). Departing from the usual 'journey' metaphor of the European project being
a train, bus or boat (see the political cartoons in Daddow 2004a: 63,
65, 67; for a fine example see Checkel and Katzenstein 2009: 1), Blair
depicted the EU as an edifice under construction whose foundations
the British needed to help lay if it were to pass muster with the inspectors from the building regulations department.

Blair's experience of helping shape European defence cooperation
at the St Malo summit in 1998 had clearly helped him to this view of
the need for British influence in Europe. 'I decided Britain should not
hang back but step up front and shape it', he said, not forgetting to
add, after a pause, 'in partnership with France' (Blair 2001d; Blair
2006a; on St Malo see Bulmer 2008: 602, 609–10). With Europe something of a moving target, always under construction ('an unknown
beast' to Diez 1999: 598), it was commonplace that new policy discussions would open up, sometimes unexpectedly and not always
to Blair's liking, compelling him to manage discussion of Britain's
possible participation in a fresh scheme for further integration. His
assumption was that Britain had succeeded in shaping European
defence discussions so why could it not repeat that success on every
other issue? As the Constitutional Treaty debate got under way, for
example, Blair argued that Britain should be seeking to shape the
debate in favourable terms. 'Now is the very moment for Britain to
participate fully in the Europe of the future. Now is the least pro-
pitious time for delusions of self-detachment.' It was not, for Blair,

that the Constitution would or could be imposed on Britain, or that everything coming out of the Giscard d'Estaing discussions looked amenable – far from it in fact. Yet the EU clearly needed to reform, so 'the answer is to get in and change it, not opt out of it' (Blair 2003g). It was to the lessons of British policy on European defence that Blair tended to look to shape his thinking, rather than those from the euro, a pick and choose approach which smacked more of wishful thinking than a realistic assessment of what Britain could hope to achieve in leadership terms while it remained outside the eurozone.

To wrap up on New Labour's approach to the question of British influence we can see in this corpus of speeches some consistent themes emerging and settling into place after 1997. First, Blair and Brown subscribed to the Europeanist assumption that Europe was 'on the move' in political and economic terms. The popular journey metaphor (on why such metaphors are popular among politicians see Charteris-Black 2006: 198–201, 207–9) representing the EU as a boat, bus or train was supplemented in Blairite discourse by a construction metaphor (a favourite Blairism; see Charteris-Black 2006: 156–7). The premise was that the EU was 'on the move' and the British would be failing to help steer it in the right direction or build it on a sound enough footing if the country remained aloof from the process. Blair's nightmare was to repeat what he saw as the gross error of past policy-making on Europe: to be stood on the harbour waving the Europeans off on their next voyage of discovery only to suddenly decide to join them and have to swim frantically to catch up. This fatally risked not being invited aboard, as humiliatingly happened at the hands Charles de Gaulle in the 1960s. The second theme of New Labour's discourse on influence was that Britain would be affected by goings on inside the EU whether or not it was an EU member. It was therefore in the national interest to be a part of the discussions about the EU's everyday decision-making and future direction alike. Third, New Labour struck an uneasy balance between on the one hand the need to be 'in there' participating in EU discussions and showing leadership, and on the other maintaining a certain set of 'red lines' or 'opt-outs' that Britain would not give up during these negotiations (Smith 2005: 717). This, note commentators, was a 'habitual tactic' for New Labour negotiators (Boulton 2008: 214), appearing 'to evoke memories of previous Conservative governments' (Opperman 2008: 186). On the single currency, for example, the government consistently maintained that it may well be beneficial for the British to be involved, but only when the country was ready. In 1999 Brown spoke of 'our robust stand defending London's interests in the European Savings Directive' (Brown 1999d). Red lines on tax harmonization were repeatedly drawn during the negotiations that led to the Lisbon Treaty (see Menon 2003: 977; Seldon 2007: 570). Brown identified that 'tax competition is an essential element of the economic reform agenda' (Brown 2003g) and routinely threatened to 'take the fight on deregulation to Europe' (Brown 2006b). Blair and Brown the Europeanists were everywhere confronted by the limits placed on them by domestic opinion, which impelled them to put the national interest ahead of any personal enthusiasm they had for taking on those more cautious within the Cabinet, party and country at large. To sum up this uneasy compromise in their speeches we can use Blair's November 2003 Lord Mayor's Banquet speech:

> After 6½ years in office, let me express to you the British Prime Minister's European dilemma: do you hope that Europe develops of its own accord in Britain's direction before participating; or do you participate at the outset in the hope of moving Europe in Britain's direction? The risk of the first is that you forfeit influence; of the second, that you are tied to something you don't like. And again on the basis of my experience, my view is clear. You participate. Sometimes, as with the single currency, there may be reasons of economics to hang back. But never do it for the politics of Euro-Scepticism. (Blair 2003g)

New Labour had to strike a delicate balance between what was desirable and what was practical. The government's advice was to get in there and 'participate' – unless perceptions of what was in the national interest dictated otherwise. In setting out a defence of the national interest Brown was more forthright than Blair both domestically and in European settings. Cleverly, Blair and Brown wrote off the politics of Euroscepticism as a motivator of the government's decision-making, in effect suggesting that Eurosceptics could not be trusted to act in the national interest – but that the New Labour government could. Their thinking on this subject was shaped by a wider perspective on what 'Europe' had achieved since the Second World War in terms of peace and security, and it is to the most openly educational aspect of New Labour's discourse that we now turn.

III. Educating the public: peace and security

> We talk of crisis. Let us first talk of achievement. When the war ended, Europe was in ruins. Today the EU stands as a monument to political achievement. Almost 50 years of peace, 50 years of prosperity, 50 years of progress. Think of it and be grateful. (Blair 2005b)

This chapter has so far presented the discourse data on how the government framed the Europe issue as being, at heart, about the pursuit and safeguard of the British national interest. This slippery term referred primarily to economics when speaking of the single currency and to vaguer notions of British influence when talking about the broader, philosophical case for Britain being an active and wholehearted member of the EU. In expounding the case for the economics of membership, however, never far from the government's mind was the Europeanist claim that the birth of the EEC, followed by the transition from the EEC to the EU, had helped bring greater freedom, peace and prosperity to the continent of Europe (and by extension the British people) both during and after the Cold War. Overcoming Franco-German enmity by meshing together first their capacities to make war and then other sectors of their economies has, the official story goes, been both the cause and the bedrock of European integration. As the EU tells its history on its website: 'The historical roots of the European Union lie in the Second World War. Europeans are determined to prevent such killing and destruction ever happening again.' The use of the present tense is telling: history and future vision are brought together in one simple message. With the Schuman Plan, the formal processes of escaping the past could begin; 'none can on its own make the weapons of war to turn against the other, as in the past' and this set in motion the moves to ever closer union in the EEC (all from Europa undated).

New Labour regularly turned to history education of this kind to inform its audiences of the EU's achievements (Seldon 2007: 122–3). The government was responding to what it saw as a hole in the British public's knowledge about the EU in the belief that the more they knew about the EU as an *idea*, the quicker they would feel comfortable inside the EU and with a government that wanted to anchor Britain firmly within it. Blair's fullest account of the EU's achievements came in his 'Committed to Europe, reforming Europe' speech at Ghent in February 2000 (Blair 2000b). His lesson began with the European Coal and Steel Community (ECSC), which, he said, had had one key objective: 'to end the feud between France and Germany that had been at the heart of one European and two world wars in less than a century'. His verdict was that 'The project has succeeded brilliantly' because it helped the two countries become partners, not enemies. But, he went on, the EU has done much more than that, of which three achievements stood out. First, 'It has provided the framework for Europe's prosperity, not just free trade in Europe, but a single market and, increasingly, a single economy'. Second, 'it has provided a clear path forward for countries emerging from political dictatorship and centrally planned economics', helping both Spain and Portugal 'turn their back [*sic*] on dictatorship' in the 1980s 'not by force of arms, but by force of example'. Third, the EU has not only promoted democracy within its member states, but has acted as a force for good on a civilizing mission in the wider world:

It was the European Union and with it the vision of a prosperous, democratic, European Germany that helped bring down the Berlin Wall, so setting off the chain reaction that ended the Cold War. And it is the hope and promise of European Union membership that is now driving political and economic reform across eastern Europe and the Balkans, from Latvia to Bulgaria, from Poland to Croatia.

In sum: 'The European Union is on the threshold of achieving the dreams of its founders. Of reuniting the continent in peace, democracy and prosperity.' (All from Blair 2000b.)

Blair's vision of the EU as a civilized regional power on a global civilizing mission recurred throughout the corpus of speeches explored in the research for this book. Later in 2000, for example, the Prime Minister ranged further back over the past to identify European history with the history of great wars: 'the Hundred Years War, the Thirty Years War, the Seven Years War, the Napoleonic Wars, the First and Second World Wars, and finally the Cold War'. The emergence of the EU, he suggested, helped redirect countries' energies away from nationalism and conflict and its history is the history of peace. 'Within the EU, not only have we not fought each other for more than 50 years but we cannot even imagine fighting each other' (Blair 2000h). Almost a decade into his premiership he was still educating an audience in Oxford that: 'Europe..., 60 years on, is the biggest political union and largest economic market in the world, whose citizens live in democracy, peace freedom and prosperity' (Blair 2006a). From 2001 the EU as promoter and guarantor of security became linked in Blair's mind to the emerging threat to EU and American populations from extremist global terrorists. This found echoes in Blair's repositioning of his arguments concerning the EU's achievements. More than ending state-on-state wars, he wanted to highlight the part the EU's promotion of interdependence between states had played in making it 'much harder than ever before in European history for any one country to become a rogue state' (Blair 2001d). Now, the reconciliation between France and Germany was seen as a necessary precursor to policies being developed at EU level to tackle terrorist groups and states accused of harbouring terrorists and their training facilities. The changing context was encapsulated in a new Blair mantra that 'Europe is in Britain's international security interest', adding to his pre-existing one that 'Europe is in Britain's economic interest' (Blair 2001d). Blair was in effect historicizing the EU's past to make the case for a new Anglo-American-European approach to upholding global security and the norms of international society in the post-9/11 world, with the threats *from* globalization entering a discourse which up to that point had tended to privilege the benefits to be embraced

(Sherrington 2006: 71). Conveniently for Blair, the interdependence that had helped states transcend their nationalism could help those same states police their populations more effectively in the face of these emergent threats:

> on crime, especially organised crime, there is simply no way that we can handle the international nature of these challenges in the twenty first century on our own. We can tackle issues such as organised crime and illegal immigration only through policies shared on a Union-wide basis. (Blair 2001d)

Blair and Brown rarely shied away from putting the case for Europe in blunt national interest terms, and setting immigration and organized crime alongside the established themes about Europe as harbinger of security helped them underscore this element of their discourse after 9/11. In some speeches, they spoke as if the entire European project was barely about the principle of unity for collective purposes at all, but was really about what Alan Milward dubbed 'the European rescue of the nation-state' (Milward 1992). For instance, Blair explained to Europe's parliamentarians in June 2005 that 'The idea of Europe, united and working together is essential for our nations to be strong enough to keep our place in this world' (Blair 2005b). A few months later the Prime Minister worked the same theme. 'I don't support ever closer union for the sake of it; but precisely because, in the world in which we live, it will be the only way of advancing our national interest effectively' (Blair 2006a). Brown had previously 'placed' the EU on New Labour's political agenda by arguing from 1997 that 'the nation state is and will remain the focus of our British identity and our loyalty.... The nation state will continue to represent our national interest. That is why we reject federalism' (Brown 1997c). Behind all the talk of the country's European heritage, the basic facts for the Chancellor were that 'extending the Single Market is in the British national economic interest' (Brown 1999h) and that 'A Europe of self-governing states working together for common purposes is in Britain's interests' (Brown 2004f). The domestic legislation and externally oriented defence policies put in place in Britain after 9/11 caused rebellion both within the PLP and in the country at large. New Labour increasingly had to make the case that with interdependence and globalization came downsides as well as upsides. For example, in his New Year broadcast in 2003, shortly before the coalition invasion of Iraq, Blair identified the multitude of 'dangerous problems' Britain faced and the 'risks' that came with increasing economic and cultural interconnectedness around the globe. 'All of this means that for many people the defining characteristic of the modern world is insecurity': fears of terrorism; economic insecurity and its negative effects on jobs and pensions; and anxiety over asylum and domestic social cohesion. Make no mistake, he suggested, 'whether we survive and prosper or decline in the face of this insecurity depends crucially on the political decisions Britain now takes'. What he meant, of course, was that the outcome relied on the decisions *he and his government* would take on behalf of 'Britain', and this would require 'strong leadership and direction' (Blair 2003a).

From telling the official story about the EU as a solution to the systemic upheaval caused by war and conflict, New Labour after 2001 swung if anything more towards an appreciation of the negative effects of globalization. The EU as guarantor of peace through interdependence had become part of the problem of insecurity, for example in relation to cross-border immigration and organized crime. This posed a very real issue for someone, like Blair, steeped in the metanarrative of the EU as a haven of peace, prosperity and democracy. In a changed post-9/11 context, the free movement of people and goods and services seemed to be enhancing the ability of those individuals and networks working outside of Blair's moral compass to engage in the kinds of destabilizing activities that curtailed the government's ability to safeguard the national interest. This fear was heightened by the terrorist attacks in Madrid in March 2004 and London in July 2005. These, 'and the discovery of local terrorist cells in countries across the EU, have opened the eyes of EU governments to the immediacy and seriousness of the internal threat that they now face. Terrorists, especially those who are EU citizens, can move easily around a porous EU' (Niblett 2007: 633). There was no longer a single menacing Other lurking behind the Iron Curtain, but rather a series of shadowy, vaporous Others, which had come to haunt the EU from within its supposedly secure zone of freedom and security. This worried Blair and perhaps reflected the conventional construction of a national narrative in Britain that had not historically included a prominent immigration strand, as in many other European states (Citrin and Sides 2008). This was something New Labour had looked to challenge through its discursive emphasis on the merits of multicultural Britain after 1997 (Jones and Smith 2006: 1082). However, the element of double-speak involved was never satisfactorily resolved by the government. Just as Blair and Brown managed to maintain vague yet broadly positive discourses on Britain's cooperation with Europe, the choice the government made to ramp up British involvement in Iraq compelled the Prime Minister to favour 'the transatlantic alliance as the bedrock of our security' even as he favoured a reformed EU economy as 'the path to our prosperity' (Blair 2005a). In effect Blair fell back on the lesson learnt by many a previous British premier, that in times of crisis and conflict it is safer to privilege the Atlanticist over the European dimension of Britain's relations in defence and foreign policy discourses.

Summary

This chapter opened by studying the no-nonsense use the Prime Minister and Chancellor made of economics to persuade the people of New Labour's case for Europe. It went on to consider two more philosophically inclined arguments that featured in their discourses: one, that Britain could more easily exert influence over the EU from the inside than from the fringes; the other, that it was in Britain's basic security interest to be an active member of the EU. Different times and different audiences all, of course, shaped the messages Blair and Brown emitted during any given speech, but two themes emerge with some degree of clarity from this account of what might be called New Labour's 'crude-plus' or 'crude+' appeal to the British people to accept a European future. First, the events of 9/11 altered the nature of the history lessons Blair and Brown felt they wanted to teach their audiences. In the earlier years they were happy selling the EU's official line that peace and security had been forged by the founding fathers out of the rubble of the Second World War. However, 9/11 demanded new thought on the security effects globalization and interdependence were having on, and within, the EU. We saw this in Blair's drive to push through reform of the EU's policies on cross-border crime and in his hardening stance on immigration controls and asylum legislation towards the end of his tenure in Downing Street. The story of the transcendence of Franco-German enmity became replaced by a story of the search for new enemies within the EU itself. Second, the use of economics, influence and security arguments points up how much Blair and Brown's respective brands of Europeanism were heavily driven by realist calculations about the national interest. Quantifying the interests–values balance struck in their speeches would clarify the picture from a statistical perspective, but is a task that lies beyond the scope of this study. What we have been able to establish from a qualitative perspective is just how much time Blair and Brown spent spelling out the case that, at heart, the question of Britain in Europe was not about what they wrote off as 'starry-eyed' idealist or utopian visions (Blair 2010: 502) but the preservation of the British economy and political capacity to act on the world stage. These arguments were constructed as antithetical to those the Prime Minister and Chancellor perceived as Eurosceptics,

who had 'got their history wrong' and who would therefore undermine the national interest by remaining aloof from the EU. In the
next two chapters we will learn more about how New Labour 'fitted'
into existing British discourses on Europe by considering how Blair
and Brown constructed their authority to speak as 'pro-Europeans'
by fixing the identities of their 'Eurosceptical' opponents.

Chapter 5

Context III. A permanent state
of discursive war

> Finding new identities is painful and slow. The old narrative contin-
> ues to cast a long shadow over political debates.... (Gamble 2003: 39)

When Tony Blair and Gordon Brown assumed the role of norm entrepreneurs on the question of Britain in Europe they recognized that
they were stepping into, and trying to alter the terms of, a distinctive and 'deeply unhelpful' (Blair 2010: 534) national narrative about
what it means to be 'British' and 'European'. The aim of this chapter
is to establish the key facets of this debate *as Blair and Brown saw it*.
The discourse analyst is not, it is important to observe, trying to be
a psychologist, interested in establishing intentionality, 'the thoughts
or motives of the actors, hidden intentions or secret plans'; instead,
a discourse approach 'searches for structure and meaning exactly at
the level where meaning is in reality generated in the first place: in
the discursive universe' (Wæver 1996: 2, 6, respectively). Nor is discourse analysis concerned to establish whether agents were correct
to ascribe to the views they did, but it is important to note that there
were many types of Euroscepticism left out of Blair and Brown's discourses altogether. This is the point of political discourses. They are
selective re-presentations of a complex reality which do not necessarily give a direct insight into what policy-makers really believe, or what
a population believes, 'but what are the codes used when actors *relate*
to one another' (Wæver 1996: 7; emphasis in original). For Blair and
Brown their opponents cleaved to an outmoded, nationalist rendering of British history, one of recurrent conflicts and disputes with
individual nations or groups of nations on the continent. New Labour
ministers were commonly critiqued for erecting straw men to knock
down in their speeches (for instance Scott 2004: 17–18) and I leave it
to the reader to decide how far the data I discovered in New Labour's
discourses tell the whole story of Britain's debates about Europe. The
task of the discourse analyst is the more modest one of mapping the
cognitive life-world inhabited by the agents whose texts are under the
microscope. To establish this case the chapter is divided into three

sections. The first introduces the idea that, in Blair and Brown's view, the British have, damagingly, been kept by core elements of the press and Eurosceptics in a permanent state of discursive war with the continent, even though the chances of 'hot war' between nation states has become remote to the point of non-existent. The second section spells out how the fault-lines have been drawn in this story between a British 'us' and a continental 'them'. The third section looks to wider cultural markers showing how Britain has Othered Europe, in terms of opposing both national rivals such as France and Germany and the EU as an organization. By the end of the chapter we should have an appreciation of the discursive environment into which Blair and Brown believed they were stepping. We will carry this forward into the subsequent chapter, which explores the empirical data on how the Prime Minister and Chancellor constructed their identities for the purposes of positioning themselves in Britain's European debates.

I. A never-ending battle

If you are trapped in an imaginary state of war with an Other, you are likely to interpret every action or decision taken by that Other as part of an ongoing and perpetual conflict with your Self. A person could live in a state of war with the world and be constantly on the defensive about the meanings of the actions of everyone and everything within it. In not dissimilar fashion, treating the state as a unitary actor, Blair and Brown believed the British people were ensnared in a permanent state of war with Europe, with every directive emanating from the European Commission, every European Council summit and every parliamentary debate in Brussels or Strasbourg refracted and reported against the backdrop of Britain's martial past. This tendency makes British public discussion of EU politics less than the sum of its parts. Viewed through the lens of military conflict, clear-sighted analysis of any EU policy proposal or piece of legislation takes a back seat to arguments about what this means for the future survival of the British as a sovereign nation on the world stage.

Image 4 shows the front page from the *Daily Mirror* newspaper the morning before the England football team's semi-final encounter with Germany during the Euro '96 football tournament. It illustrates what Blair and Brown had in mind when they identified their opponents as perpetuating a permanent state of war with the continent. Thirty years on from England's 1966 World Cup final victory against the same opponents, two England players, Stuart Pearce (always characterized as a passionate English 'lion') and play-maker Paul Gascoigne, were mocked up in Second World War army helmets

Image 4. Front page of the *Daily Mirror*, 24 June 1996.

warning the German team ('Fritz') that its time in the tournament was about to come to an end (on the fallout from this article see Crolley and Hand 2002: 21–2). The cause of much ire and distaste, this article illustrates the extent to which – still – key elements of the popular British press are 'incapable of referring to today's German football teams without mentioning past wars' (Beck 2003: 401–2). The message we get from this and related sporting iconography is that where the British are concerned, the very mention of Europe and/or its key nation states (especially 'foes' such as Germany) means the potential for war in one form or another. This brings to mind Carl von Clausewitz's dictum that 'War is merely the continuation of policy by other means' (Howard and Paret 1976: 87). Turn this on its head and we have a leitmotif for the hegemonic discourse on British European policy: politics is the continuation of war by other means, linguistic ones, where each and every EU policy initiative becomes another piece of barbed wire to be cut, another reason to baton down the hatches and step up to the plate to fight off the intruders with pride and self-sacrifice for the good of the mother country.

The test of New Labour's strategy for affecting a real and lasting shift in Britain's relationship with the EU would therefore be a discursive one. Could the government unpick and restitch the webs of belief within which the British encountered Europe so that instead of existing in a permanent state of fear the British would feel at home living alongside their European neighbours? Could the British confidently adopt a national identity that coexisted with a higher-order European identity? To answer this question we need to acquaint ourselves with the kinds of attitudes to the past and to British national identity that Blair and Brown felt they had to confront to make the case for Europe hold water. There is no need to retell 'one thousand years' of British history, nor to investigate in detail the component parts of Britain's national identity since 1945. What we can usefully do, however, is sketch the plurality of ways in which the British and in particular the English have treated Europe and Europeans as inimical 'out-groups', as a means of building and coming to terms with their collective self-identity as 'Brits'. We will do this by working the concept of 'heterotypification', which entails 'the formulaic characterisation of the Other in discourse' and con-trasts with 'autotypification', the discursive characterization of Self (Crolley and Hand 2002: 44). The two clearly go hand in hand, with processes of creating out-groups through heterotypification con-stantly interacting with, and thereby co-constructing, autotypified self-groups. Examples of political, social and cultural heterotypifica-tion will be followed by analysis of four pillars of the British national story that have created this sense of Otherness about Europe: the 'island story'; religion; militarized discourse; and binary thinking. Together, they sustain the crucial link between history and national identity that Blair and Brown felt necessary to break, or at the very least modify, to alter the conceptual prisms through which the British people encountered the EU. The nature of this association will be considered in the final section of the chapter.

II. Europe as Other

> If you think about it, it's precisely because people are different from others that they're able to create their own independent selves. (Murakami 2008: 19)

To begin with, we need to establish what it means to talk of Europe being Othered in British political and public discourse. It is worth noting in advance that the British (if we can assume a collective agent for the time being) are not unique in Othering Europe as a means of defining their complex, multilayered English, Welsh, Scottish and Northern Irish identities. The building of identity is, fundamentally, a permanent process of Othering:

> Self-definition (like 'truth'...) necessarily involves *exclusions*: it's by excluding some 'other' that we differentiate our selves; it's by seeing the rest of the world as background that we foreground ourselves, and it's by cutting ourselves off from that background – seeing ourselves as separate entities – that we are enabled to constitute our own identities. (Southgate 2005: 100–1; emphasis in original)

If this is true of personal identity constructions then it is no less so of the processes that constitute local, regional and national identities. If we start from Benedict Anderson's well known description of nations as 'imagined communities' (Anderson 2006) we immediately see that all countries are constructed entities. They rely for their sense of cohesion and togetherness on a people's shared will to believe that because they happen to be born and live within a (usually but not always) well defined and fixed territorial border they are bound by ties handed down from time immemorial. In the process of identity-building at the aggregate level, perceptions of what went on in the past are key because societal discourses on nationality and nationhood flow directly from 'the ideological uses of history' (Riishøj 2007: 513). Anna Horolets, for example, has noted that 'at the discursive level history still divides rather than unites the European nation states due to the high symbolic potential it possesses and openness to interpretations' (Horolets 2002: 15). This is the nub of the matter. 'For all the talk about eternal nations, they are created not by fate or God but by the activities of human beings, and not least by historians' (MacMillan 2009: 83). The *essence* of a nation for writers such as Margaret MacMillan and Walker Connor is psychological, a 'bond that joins a people and differentiates it, in the subconscious conviction of its members, from all other people in a most vital way' (Connor, quoted in Lawrence 2005: 185). John Armstrong, too, argues that 'groups tend to define themselves not by reference to their own characteristics but by exclusion, that is, by comparison to "strangers"' and the focus of his work is on the 'myth- and symbol-defined boundaries and the communicators who codify these differentiating perceptions' (quoted in Lawrence 2005: 187). National identities are thus constructed in the selective edit of historiography and 'are usually rather sticky and only gradually subject to change' (Risse *et al.* 1999: 156). As such, 'all people, and all nations, live in the past as well as in the present. And modern Britain is no exception to this general rule' (Cannadine 1988: 9).

From this work on individual and national identity construction we see the part constructed national pasts play in furnishing identities which are, in effect, stories (the myths Armstrong refers to) we tell ourselves and others about who we are, what we stand for and where we fit in the stream of global history. In terms of the British Othering of Europe, geography and history have been important components of these stories:

> nation-building is often a matter of positioning the nation in a larger cultural–geographical context and whereby 'Europe' is used as a stereotype in the construction of both 'Us' and 'They', of self-identification and of distinction of 'the Other'. Such auto-stereotypes and xeno-stereotypes reinforce each other. (Malmborg and Stråth 2002: 23)

Mikael af Malmborg goes on to argue that all countries use Europe in this way, exhibiting 'a clear awareness of "We" and "They", of an "Other" that possesses certain European features that the "We" is exposed to or wants to acquire' (Malmborg 2002: 58). In Britain it is the downbeat 'Us being exposed to' element that predominates in Eurosceptic discourse, as opposed to the enthusiastic 'We want to acquire' connotation of the term 'Europe'. As we shall see in chapters 6 and 8, Blair and Brown's discourses were set solidly against the former conceptualization of Britain's relationship with Europe. However, they rarely diverged far enough from it, or often enough, to suggest that they wanted the British to acquire European characteristics. New Labour consistently pushed for EU reforms to make the project more palatable to British sensibilities. The government argued for the British to be part of Europe, as long as that Europe in its EU form came closer to aping the British way of doing things, as far as economic and social policies were concerned. This, writes Philippa Sherrington, was a form of 'defensive engagement' (Sherrington 2006: 72) that appealed to what Taggart and Szczerbiak would identify as 'soft' Eurosceptics in Britain (see chapter 6).

There is a plethora of commentary on the symbolic techniques by which the British have Othered Europe. They coalesce around the idea that, in Andrew Gamble's words, the British have constructed their identity against 'a suitably frightening manifestation of Europe' (Gamble 2003: 108). How has this come to pass? In 2004 Robert Harmsen and Menno Spiering took identity as a social construction, mired in the sense we have of ourselves and others through our education, upbringing, national political traditions and so forth. They pointed out that national context (the way Europe is framed in and by its various member sates) was all important when considering the creation of public attitudes to Europe and the EU. Taking

a comparative perspective, their evidence suggested that the experience of 'cultural alterity' was more sharply defined in Britain than it
was in other European countries. According to their research, 'only
in the British case does a sense of belonging to Europe, rather than
"Europe", appear to raise politically significant questions' (Harmsen
and Spiering 2004: 17–18). In other words, where other countries they
included in their study – France, Germany, the Netherlands, Ireland,
Austria, the Czech Republic, Poland and Switzerland – all took the
'being European' part for granted and debated the merits of different
EU trajectories and policies, in Britain the debate over belonging to
this wider entity, the landmass of 'Europe', was found to be far from
settled. Spiering developed this point in his country study, where he
identified the causes of this sense of British 'differentness' as lying
in the British electoral and party political system, 'the condition of
the press and a tradition of regarding the country and people as distinct from Europe and the Europeans' (Spiering 2004: 127; see also
Risse *et al.* 1999: 161). In his analysis we see the very real problems
of claiming exceptionalism for Britain on the grounds of having a
unique parliamentary and electoral system, unique national traditions, a unique 'way of life' or any other supposedly unique quality.
By definition all countries could claim exceptional experiences. The
question is, therefore, what is it the British tell themselves about the
national character that makes the British way of doing things seem
incompatible with a European way of life? We have to look elsewhere,
to deeper structural undercurrents in the British story, for the particular causes and expressions of the national Othering of Europe
that marks Britain apart, and there are four main elements in the
mix: geography, religion, war and binary thinking.

The first is geographic, picking up on the theme of Britain's island
status. In the nationalist narrative this has fed a sense of psychological remoteness from the continent, a perception Blair and Brown
looked to challenge by arguing that 'our unity as a country cannot
be based merely on memory or geography' (Brown 1999a). The
story goes that the British would always have trouble identifying
with, and feeling a part of, a grand experiment in a trans- or multinational coming together inscribed in any move towards European
union, because of the uniqueness of living on an island set apart
from mainland Europe – described by William Shakespeare as a
'sceptr'd isle ... set in a silver sea' (quoted in Haseler 1996: 14–15)
(on the 'island story' in English literature see Paxman 1999: 33–4).
As the Eurosceptical former Labour peer Peter Shore expressed
it, in the disputes between Britain and France over how to handle
Germany, 'we have simply reflected our island geography and the
separate history that that geography, particularly the Channel

and the Atlantic – the sheltering seas – have enabled us to shape'
(Shore 2002: 228). Spiering termed this the tendency for Brits to see
Europe as 'abroad' and, paradoxically, the US as being much closer
to Britain, pointing up the part values play in constructing and vali-
dating identity-based discourses (Spiering 2004: 144). The General
Secretary of the British Council of Churches expressed the paradox,
without realizing it, in 1964: 'We British feel we only belong in a
very partial way to Europe. It is not only our island state.... It is
that our lines have gone out to Canada and Nyasaland [Republic of
Malawi], to New Zealand and India every bit as much as across the
narrow straits of Dover' (quoted in Coupland 2006: 138). From this,
we can assume that what is important in Britain's debates about
Europe are not the realities of the geographical distances between
Britain and Europe, Britain and the US and so on, but the relative
emotional distances created by these physical separations. The gap
in values and the deeper emotional attachment to things American
or Australian than to things European is what really appears to
create the discursive separation of Britain from the continent. It has
manifested itself in what Nicholas Crowson describes as a 'crude
"superiority" complex' that shapes Conservative Party and arguably
other party debates about Europe (Crowson 2007: 11–12), the line of
reasoning being that British interests are global rather than confined to petty arguments of narrow regional importance.

    The geography–memory–identity nexus casts valuable light on
the links between discourses on national identity and the creation
of out-groups such as the actor called 'Europe' we see appearing in
Britain's national foreign policy debates. 'The importance of national
identity in politics and international relations can be overstated ...
but should not be ignored in the case of British Euroscepticism. In
Britain the tendency to see Europe as an undifferentiated "abroad"
is deeply ingrained' (Spiering 2004: 144). From the sixteenth
century, Spiering has argued, the terms 'Europe' and 'European'
began to be used to denote an outside, alien entity. What is remarkable about the British case is not the use of foreigners to help define
the British national identity but 'that one of those out-groups is,
and has been for a long time, the Europeans *en masse*. In other
European countries such a differentiation makes no sense' (Spiering
2004: 145). If we look to Linda Colley's analysis of the origins and
development of British national identity the picture is similar but
not identical. Where Spiering sees a British process of Othering that
has centred on lumping Europeans together, Colley points out that
in many ways the French were (and may be still today) the original
Other against which the British liked to define themselves culturally,
politically, economically, socially and, the second of our underlying

causes of Britain's psychological distance from the continent, in religious terms. 'One of the recurrent arguments of *Britons* is that the overwhelming Catholicism of large parts of continental Europe, and especially France and Spain, provided a newly invented Britain with a formidable "other" against which it could usefully define itself' (Colley 2005: 16; see also Haseler 1996: 23–5). In increasingly secular and diverse multi-faith societies in Western Europe today, the religious aspects of the construction of a putative pan-European identity have been rather lost. Yet it is significant that religious differences helped ingrain the idea of a separation between Britain's identity on the one hand and a supposedly cohesive 'continental' identity on the other. For example, suspicion of the Christian Democratic religious persuasion of the states that founded the EEC in the 1950s helped turn a generation of British decision-makers off throwing their lot in with Europe in its formative years. Philip Coupland has argued that religion might not have been the cause of Britain's divergence from European unity in any simple sense, but as a key component of identity construction going back hundreds of years it was invested with sufficient emotional capital in and around the time of the Second World War and immediate post-war years to help reinforce British scepticism about European projects. Far from British Christians seeking to reach out across the Channel they in fact acceded to the government's view in the middle of the 1940s that 'the continent would be too weak and divided to be a viable political unit and, therefore, they looked to a world order built around an Anglo-American axis' (Coupland 2006: 46–7). Where prominent theologians and the branches of organized religion could have contributed to a more constructive and engaged European policy in those vital years, Coupland suggests they were instead co-opted by the organs of state and ended up coming to 'share much of what passed for "common sense" in the Foreign Office's worldview too' (Coupland 2006: 76).

'In a very real sense, war ... had been the making of Great Britain' (Colley 2005: 322). On top of religion, Colley points out that British national identity has been forged by the experience of war, so representations of the nation's martial past – particularly the idea of defiantly 'standing alone' against all the odds – constitute the third of our focal points here. Britain's 'traditional enemy across the Channel' (Colley 2005: 312) through the eighteenth and nineteenth centuries was France (of the many references to British–French antagonism see Colley 2005: 1, 5, 17, 24–5, 33–6, 78–9, 86–90, 99, 172, 198, 215–17, 240, 250–3, 285–9, 305–8, 310–31, 322, 358, 368–71). France has been called Britain's 'ancestral' or 'historic enemy' (Paxman 1999: 25, 237). French–British rivalry still features in British discourses on national identity and helps us refine Spiering's image of an undifferentiated European Other. 'Time and time again', writes Colley (2005: 5), 'war with France brought Britons, whether they hailed from Wales or Scotland or England, into confrontation with an obviously hostile Other and encouraged them to define themselves against it.' Jeremy Paxman sums up British chauvinism against the French by writing that 'We all need enemies, and the French are so wonderfully convenient – near to hand and yet apparently oblivious to the interests of anyone else' (Paxman 1999: 28). If France was the early source of those military confrontations, then in the twentieth century Germany became the principal protagonist (Beck 2003), with the French assuming the mantle of untrustworthy, potentially devious and, most significantly, politically and militarily unstable partner across the Channel. During the Second World War these perceptions came to be imprinted onto the popular imagination as the rhetorically gifted Churchill encouraged Britain to reinvent itself as a beacon of freedom and goodness, promoting liberty by 'standing firm against tyranny' (Brown 2005h; Brown 2006a). As a critic of the nationalist tradition, Stephen Haseler has wryly commented that during 1939–45 'Englishness … had a very good war'. It was a period when 'The fires of patriotism, and nationalism, were re-stoked as war reinforced the sensibility of not only a separate but also a virtuous English and British identity' (Haseler 1996: 53). Gamble agrees that the Second World War quickly 'came to rank with the defeat of the Armada and the defeat of Napoleon in the national myth' (Gamble 2003: 73). Perhaps when the British talk of 'Europe' they are really referring only to two big countries – France and Germany – countries with which military conflict is kept alive through the way they are positioned in the web of everyday discourses about Europe in Britain.

It is useful at this juncture to follow Paxman, who sees in the received wisdom about the evacuation of British troops from Dunkirk shortly before the fall of France in 1940 a kind of physical enactment – as well as the cause and explanation – of Britain's suspicions of 'Europe'. This is a story that in its telling and re-presentation through written and visual history has come to symbolize something much more than a tactical military rescue designed to save the lives of 338,000 British soldiers (figure from BBC 2000). 'It is because the island mentality is so deeply ingrained in the English mind that the Dunkirk evacuation of May 1940 has such a powerful hold on memories of World War Two' (Paxman 1999: 32). Why? First, because it speaks to Britain's sense of separateness from the continent. That the British could escape across the Channel meant they could mentally pull up a drawbridge, as across a moat into a castle. Second, it became a potent and much-needed metonymical mythologization of the few representing the heroics of the many in the face of extreme adversity: 'a towering monument to British bravery' (BBC 2000). Third, 'it demonstrates to the English what they have known for centuries, that the European Continent is a place of nothing but trouble, and that their greatest security is behind the thousands of miles of irregular coastline around their island home' (Paxman 1999: 33). Evoking the 'Dunkirk spirit' has come to be used to stir up tales of national patriotism, heroism, passion and a 'British bulldog' resolve to stand up to aggressors when the odds are stacked in your opponent's favour. Paxman identifies Dunkirk both as a turning point in developing the British sense of self and as a crucial explanatory factor in the creation of Europe as an out-group. As such, representations of Dunkirk show the geography–memory–identity nexus in its sharpest relief, as well as accenting the role Britain's martial past has played in forging an extra- or contra-European identity for Britain. Vernon Bogdanor puts it well: 'For Britain, the war seemed to have shown not the weakness of nationalism and the need for supranational organization; rather, it had shown what could be done with the force of British patriotism' (Bogdanor 2005: 691).

The fourth and final factor that helps explain Britain's heterotypification of Europe concerns the fabric of domestic political life. Here the issue is twofold (drawing on Spiering 2004: 137–8). To begin with there is the country's 'winner takes all' electoral system, meaning that slender margins at the polls translate into disproportionately larger majorities in the House of Commons for the victorious party. The first-past-the-post system has historically tended to invite polarization between the two main parties of government and, it could be argued, opposition for the sake of it over many areas of policy. As Bogdanor (2005: 697) describes it:

> The procedures of Westminster are geared to informing the electorate of issues in dispute between government and opposition, and they imply the existence of two disciplined armies in the House of Commons articulating two quite different philosophies.... EU legislation does not conform to the binary pattern of politics which is dominant at Westminster.

British European policy has historically been remarkably consistent through successive governments (if not the tone or the language that accompanies that policy), even though the party of government has switched back and forth between the Labour and Conservative parties. Opposition parties have, meanwhile, done just that: oppose. The most radical expressions of doubt or fundamental opposition to EU institutions and policies have been confined to the backbenches and fringe parties, such as UKIP, which garner much support, for a variety of reasons, at mid-term secondary elections. For example, at the European Parliament elections in June 2009, the sitting Labour government secured just over 15% of the national vote, putting it in third place behind the Conservatives and UKIP (BBC 2009). The party most consistently supportive of the EU inside Parliament has been the Liberal Democrats, but in electoral terms it is well behind the two main parties of government and has only got into power in the post-1945 period as part of a coalition after the 2010 election that returned a hung parliament, a point to which we will return in a moment. The Us/Them dichotomy that characterizes British discourses about Europe is mimicked in the domestic Us/ Them debates that have for so long taken place over the House of Commons despatch box. As Southgate has noted of national foreign policy discourses, the use of divisive Manichean terminology by politicians is encouraged by the 'need clearly to distinguish their own people from any others, their friends from their enemies, the right from the wrong' (Southgate 2005: 69) and this has applied as much to the two tribes facing each other in the House of Commons as it has to the British facing the Europeans across the Channel. There is more than a sense in which, Andrew Jordan argues, 'For a variety of reasons..., the British do find it difficult to speak the language of European integration. To a large extent, they still see the EU as a zero-sum game played out between sovereign states' (Jordan 2006: 238). According to this line of reasoning, sovereignty and power are like finite commodities to be haggled over rather than increased and shared through pooling and cooperation: more 'power' to the Commission equals less 'power' (or sovereignty) for Britain, or, as Aspinwall puts it, 'a little more Europe means a little less Anglo' (Aspinwall 2004: 7).

From the impetus towards binary thinking that comes from the British electoral system we can add a second factor: the leading British political parties – until 2010 – have not been accustomed to forming coalition governments, which are more common in European democracies. As Aspinwall has pointed out (covered in Spiering 2004: 138) the proportional representation voting system tends to offer up results that offer radical or smaller parties the chance to form governments, sometimes as key 'swing' parties, with mainstream parties of the centre. In England (less so in Scotland and Wales since the creation of devolved assemblies after 1997) the Conservative and Labour parties have not been used to negotiating power-sharing arrangements with members of even like-minded parties such as the Liberal Democrats, let alone radical parties, were the latter to be elected in significant numbers to the House of Commons in first-order elections. The discussions in the lead-up to the 1997 election and early on during the Blair years about whether to include Paddy Ashdown and/or other Liberal Democrats in the New Labour Cabinet, and even to start 'merger talks' (Campbell 2007: 179–80, 256–7), were gently scotched when the two parties could not agree on how to reform the electoral system. The Liberal Democrats wanted a thoroughgoing move to proportional representation while Labour wanted to maintain the status quo more or less intact. Behind this breakdown was the fact that the top echelons of the Labour Party realized they had managed to create a broad-brush progressive party of the political centre without needing the support of the Liberal Democrats. Such talks as did take place smacked more of a plan B than a plan A. 'With a majority of 179 it was simply not possible, even for Blair, to tell his party that they needed to share power' (Boulton 2008: 7; see also Jenkins 2007: 230). In short, there appears to be something of a politico-cultural factor at work here. The long uninterrupted history of the British two-party system, the country's 'unwritten' constitution and unbroken democratic tradition backed by a winner-takes-all electoral system have made for a situation in which British policy-makers and politicians do not *get*, cannot quite *grasp* the need for, or the practices of, coalition government and shared decision-making responsibilities, even in the post-devolution era in the UK. This plays out in a general stupefaction with the loose coalitions that make up parties that sit together in the European Parliament and a hesitancy about engaging in the sort of horse-trading that characterizes European-level policy-making: 'fighting with foreigners' (Wall 2008: 58) is merely a replication of adversarial domestic tactics projected onto the European stage. Domestic events in 2010 may work to change attitudes, but it remains to be seen how long the coalition will last and how long attitudes to coalition government will take to alter perceptibly as a result. And in any case, altered beliefs about two-party government may not work to affect overall attitudes to European affairs if other beliefs within the tradition remain unaltered.

Box 3 reproduces exactly, including spelling, grammar and syntax, a selection of comments posted on a 2008 *Daily Telegraph* online forum commenting on the desirability of holding a national 'Britain in or out' referendum on the EU, to replicate that held on EEC membership in 1975. As we would expect of people logging onto a forum maintained by a newspaper that is no great supporter of the EU, the vast majority of the posts were sceptical about the EU, about Gordon Brown's handling of the 'referendum' question and about that on the Lisbon Treaty in particular. More pertinent, however, than the numbers of 'pros' versus 'antis', was the jargon used to express opposition to the EU, the three examples appearing in box 3 being particularly interesting. Peter Watson took the war theme on

Box 3. Verbatim extracts from a 2008 *Daily Telegraph* online forum about a putative EU referendum

Does Britain need an 'in or out' referendum on the EU?

Nick Clegg has urged Conservative MPs to back an 'in or out' referendum on Britain's relationship with the EU, ahead of today's parliamentary vote on the Lisbon Treaty.

In a letter appealing to Tory MPs for support, the leader of the Liberal Democrats argued: 'Surely it is right that this is the debate that engages the British people through a referendum, not the technicalities of a minor revising Treaty.'
...

Do you agree with Mr Clegg that Britain needs an 'in or out' referendum on Europe, and not just a vote on the Lisbon Treaty? Will he do more harm than good by attempting to thwart the Lisbon referendum? Do you trust parliament to negotiate our relationship with the EU in the best interests of the British people?

vivian jones
06/22/2008 12:50 PM
Great Britain has always been a thorn in the sides of Europeans the french and germans are not pro british, the wars we have fought to retain our heritage have left a nasty taste, and we now have to do what the people we beat say we must do, I see a dictatorship being born in the EU and we must be the loosers.

Peter W Watson
03/06/2008 01:08 PM
gordon Sturman on March 6, 2008 10:19 AM asks how many understand it and says there is too much emotion. Those of us who have studied the matters EU in detail since it was the EC, then the EEC then the EU are incandescent with rage precisely because we do understand it. We understand it in the same way the people in London understood the meaning behind the air raid sirens in the Blitz.

Patricia Kenny on March 06 2008 at 09:17am
03/06/2008 09:17 AM
Surely the Queen should be taking to task this inept subprime PM. To opt out of the EU if this treaty stands will necessitate four countries approval of Britain leaving the EU, we will not be able to decide our own future. Okay bring it on, riots and civil unrest and the EU army and police here with their tear gas, batons and guns. I am sure the People will find the Dunkirk spirit and resist. Remember May the 1st, use your vote to register yoiur disgust at labour and liberals.

Source: *Daily Telegraph*, 5 March 2008 (print and online) and subsequent posts (www.telegraph.co.uk/news/yourview/1580797/Does-Britain-need-an-in-or-out-referendum-on-the-EU.html???, last accessed 9 September 2008).

by referring to the Blitz of 1940, another big British 'moment' during the Second World War when the brave few resisted the onslaught of the many. His view is that if one experienced the horrors of the Blitz, today's EU only exists to be resisted, just as the Germans were all those decades ago. Patricia Kenny doubted if the current EU lets the British 'decide our own future', but she had faith that the British people retained enough of the 'Dunkirk spirit' to help them resist such incursions. In another post, Vivian Jones summed up the dichotomy well. Note how let down she felt by the French and Germans not being 'pro-British' and note also the place the wars (fought to 'retain our heritage') occupy in her discourse. Her sense of disappointment extended to having (as she saw it) to submit to 'the people we beat' who form a 'dictatorship'. It would be rather like the Conservative Party winning a landslide election victory and then having to dole out Cabinet posts to Liberal Democrats!

Two principal points emerge from this investigation of the causes behind Britain's tendency to Other Europe. The first is a general one concerning the complex processes through which national identities develop and are sustained. I have concentrated on the Othering part of this process less than the self-generated, internal or organic components of British national identity because that was the aspect of British identity that Blair and Brown both wanted to reformulate in their foreign policy speeches after 1997. Britishness in their eyes was not to be defined as an identity antithetical to a European identity but could be melded *with* that higher-level European identity. By attacking popular attitudes towards the legacy of Britain's wartime experiences, towards zero-sum power games and the like, they were acutely aware of the Othering of Europe prevalent in nationalist discourses. The second point is that many different causes are said to be at the heart of this British Othering of Europe. Here, we have only covered four of the most popular. That commentators cannot agree on which one best explains Britain's semi-detachment from Europe is less important than the fact that they agree that this process has been occurring for a number of years and that we can see its remnants today in the way the British represent 'Europe' discursively. Wolfram Kaiser nicely sums up the post-1945 era:

> Elite assumptions about the Second World War as a triumph of 'the British way of life' and its political institutions and about an almost moral right to a continued world power role combined with widespread popular feelings of contempt for Continental European political and cultural traditions to strengthen the imagined 'otherness' of 'the Europeans' and the idea of British singularity, over and above the real differences in the economic situation and political commitments. (Kaiser 2004: 11)

Box 4. Stephen Wall on the national psyche

Sir Stephen Wall was British ambassador to Portugal 1993 to 1995, the UK
Permanent Representative to the European Union from 1995 to 2000, and
from 2000 to 2004 he was head of the European Secretariat in the Cabinet
Office in London. Near the end of his book *A Stranger in Europe* (2008) he
points out that the common response of Whitehall departments to a piece
of legislation is 'no, unless…', compared with a 'yes, if…' default setting
observable in the legislatures of Britain's fellow EU members. Why?

> 'It is rooted in our national psyche, the psyche of an island nation which
> has lived by resisting Continental encroachment; whose sixteenth-century
> Reformation was about politics as well as worship; which fought against
> the very countries who are now our partners to establish its imperial
> supremacy in the eighteenth and nineteenth centuries; which did do
> something remarkable for European liberty in 1940, and which, unlike
> much of the rest of Europe, emerged from war in 1945 with its pride in
> its national institutions enhanced. However flawed it may often have been
> in practice, England was the model of liberal political philosophy until
> the newly born United States of America took on the mantle in the late
> eighteenth century.'

Source: Wall (2008: 210).

To bring home Kaiser's point about the intensely felt British sense of
separateness from continental Europe, and to illustrate the overlap
between collective national values and day-to-day practice in Whitehall, note the appearance of all the issues explored so far in this
section in box 4, which showcase's one recent and very senior EU
adviser's take on the instinctive Whitehall response to legislative
proposals emanating from the EU. For Wall, history is *the* single
most important explanation for Britain's aloofness from Europe.
Echoes of the past weigh as heavily on the civil service and elite
decision-makers as on the members of the public who process European affairs through the conceptual lens of Britain's martial past.
The next section will develop two of the themes covered above: everyday culture and militarized discourse in Britain. This will help us
understand just how common it is for the British to speak of Europe
as a quirky, suspicious Other, whatever their views on the costs or
benefits of being an EU member state. It will further highlight the
extent to which New Labour was trying to shift not only short-term
opinions but also more deeply held attitudes and values, expressed in
the way the British *think* and *talk* about Europe – public and policy-
makers alike.

III. Otherness as cultural product

We should dismiss the notion that our history suggests being British
is synonymous with being anti-European. (Brown 1999b)

Jeremy Paxman has remarked that 'England remains the only
European country in which apparently intellectual people can use
expressions like "joining Europe was a mistake" or "we should leave
Europe" as if the place can be hitched to the back of a car like a
holiday caravan' (Paxman 1999: 29). Overlooking the conflation of
English with British – is it *only* the English who talk about Europe
in this way, or do the Scots, Northern Irish and Welsh participate
in the linguistic wrenching of Britain from Europe too? – Paxman
has alighted on the power of language to reveal perceptions of the
world we may not even realize we hold, together with the specifics
of the ways in which Europe can be Othered through discourse.
People talking about Europe in this way are referring to the EU bit
of Europe, but that does nothing to diminish the significance of a
pervasive cultural tendency to see both the organization and the
continent of Europe more generally as, variously: foreign, hostile,
threatening or potentially subversive to the British people and British
way of life. An issue that looms large in any analysis of Britain's
discursive construction of a European Other is the extent to which
it is driven by xenophobia against specific countries or against EU
'foreigners' in general. This would have to be investigated on a case-
by-case basis with textual signifiers indicating xenophobic prejudices
clearly conceptualized in advance; I do not intend to conduct such a
study here. What I will say is that the kinds of attitudes Paxman
pokes fun at, and the linguistic constructions I detail below, indicate
that many people who talk this way do so not consciously wanting
to denigrate European publics or nation states, but because it is the
British way to 'speak about Europe' to each other in this fashion.
They reside in a national structured language community in Britain
that permissively Others Europe. In some cases these attitudes do go
hand in hand with racist and/or xenophobic attitudes, but to label a
whole nation or group of nations xenophobic because of the way they
have been brought up to speak about Europe would be going too far.
What this powerful set of constructions does do is pose a very real
challenge to any government wanting to create a new norm about
Europe and the EU in Britain.

Paxman's idea that Europe is construed as something the British
can take or leave demonstrates that it has been constructed by the
British as an entity 'over there', separate and separable *from* Britain.
It thus establishes the validity of Harmsen and Spiering's arguments

that, 'While Euroscepticisms are principally played out in the arena of party politics, one must not lose sight of the fact that these arenas are themselves embedded in wider cultural contexts'; and such scepticism 'finds expression not only through party politics but in a rich vein of literary and cultural commentary as well' (Harmsen and Spiering 2004: 33, 16). Two examples suffice to make the point that the political discourses featured in this book are reflective of, and shaped by, wider cultural currents expressed through a linguistic universe that entrenches an 'abiding sense of alterity' (Harmsen and Spiering 2004: 16). The first picks up on the values of liberty and freedom and is explored by Paxman through the medium of the pages of *This England* magazine; the second is expressed in the way football commentators and pundits use a notional European identity to cast light on the way the British, especially the English, conceive of and play their football – and therefore how they construct their Self identities as antithetical to a European identity.

This England magazine has been published quarterly since spring 1968 and boasts a worldwide readership of nearly 2 million people. Its name comes from a passage in Shakespeare's *Richard II* in which the dying John of Gaunt eulogizes 'This blessed plot, this earth, this realm, this England, this nurse, this teeming womb of royal kings' (quoted in Paxman 1999: 77). Gaunt's words head the website details about the magazine, which sets itself up to be 'an ambassador for everything English', accompanied by picture postcard images such as cricket being played on a village green in front of thatched cottages, and a river gently meandering under a Roman aqueduct in the hazy spring sunshine (*This England* undated). By the later 1990s, Paxman notes, the magazine's sales figures were outstripping the combined sales of each edition of the *Spectator*, *New Statesman*, *Country Life* and *Tatler*; the publisher was also making money from sideline sales in 'St George ties, tieclips and lapel badges' (Paxman 1999: 77–8). What is interesting is that *This England*'s homily to the quiet, decent, honest folk strolling around parks and gardens and sipping real ale in country pubs everywhere 'cloaks a torrent of outrage' (Paxman 1999: 78) stemming from the belief that this is an England that will not exist forever if our quisling, traitorous politicians have their way. Accompanying the nostalgia for the national past – a characteristic feature of Thatcher's post-resignation discourse (see Beck 2003: 406) – comes vitriolic abuse against a possible European future which in its imagery and reference points calls to mind precisely the Eurosceptical attitudes Blair and Brown took it upon themselves to subvert after 1997 (on the perils of nostalgia see Brown 2004g). This warning from an edition of *This England* published after Blair came to power is worth quoting at length:

We are in the middle of a carefully-crafted plot going back many years which is designed to create an easily manageable, European super-state to be run like a socialist republic. That means one overall (but unelected) government, one puppet parliament, one federal army, navy and air force, one central bank, a single currency and one supreme court of law. Our precious Monarchy will be replaced by a President on the Continent, the Union Jack will be banned in favour of that horrid blue rag with those 12 nasty yellow stars and we shall all have to sing the new Euro anthem to the tune of Beethoven's *Ode to Joy* ... except that its title will really mean 'Goodbye Britain'. (Quoted Paxman 1999: 78–9)

Note firstly the sense of persecution: the plot by an aggregated mass of 'Europeans' to destroy the English way of life. Note secondly the qualities ascribed to the European system of governance the author of this piece so despises: unelected, federal, puppet, anti-monarchy, horrid flag/nasty stars. For each evil European style of governance there is an implied, morally superior British opposite: democratically elected, Westminster-centred, legitimate, monarchy, Union Jack. Note thirdly the suspicion of military cooperation with the Europeans in the form of a possible European 'federal army' that would replace the sovereign British armed forces. Note finally the conflation of English with British in the final line. We can conclude that this article is calling to mind the exact same dangers the *Sun* and *Daily Mail* warned (see chapter 1) would result should Britain sign up to the idea of a United States of Europe through the Lisbon Treaty. The idea that Europe and Europeans threaten to impose political, economic and military conformity on the British is a constant refrain in the pages of all these publications.

The second example of what Harmsen and Spiering might designate Eurosceptical cultural commentary in Britain is of a different and arguably more influential kind, given its location: press reporting of football matches. This example reinforces the idea being pursued in this book that Euroscepticism, while clearly having its own dynamic as a transnational political phenomenon, helped not least by the existence of a directly elected European Parliament which facilitates the coming together of parties of all shades of opinion about the EU, has distinct national-level characteristics that can be observed in arenas notionally outside the conventional domains of party and parliamentary political debate. Football is one such crucible. Why? Here, the cue comes from work on football and popular culture by Liz Crolley and David Hand, who have published a comparative study of press reporting of football in England, France and Spain (Crolley and Hand 2002). They covered the reporting of both national league matches and international matches; here we will study the international arena. They begin with the work of

J. A. Mangan, who argues that sport 'is far more than a national and international entertainment: it is a source of political identity, morale, pride and superiority. It also sustains political antagonisms, hatreds and prejudices' (quoted in Crolley and Hand 2002: ix). In this take on sport we are invited to see it as more than a source of entertainment, isolated in some way from the politics of the day, but as an integral part *of* that politics. Of central import is the link between football and national identity:

> Match reports ... do not contain only dry facts.... European print media discourse on football may also be said to play a significant part in the construction of national, regional and group identities. For linguistic and commercial reasons ... match reports and related articles frequently take on the characteristics of literary narratives ... and they may be read, therefore, partly at least, as weaving a story about how Europeans interact with each other and how they reflect upon their own national and regional identity. (Crolley and Hand 2002: 1–2)

From the general portrayal of football reporting as cultural constructs they move to the specific, by noting that the contents of a press report on the performance of the English national team 'is inextricably bound up with wider psychological, cultural and ideological processes, and it therefore also provides information about concepts of Englishness itself' (Crolley and Hand 2002: 8). The principal way in which the football reportage they studied reflected and reinforced national identities was through the cultural stereotype: racial, sexual and by British region, the last organized as a 'north versus south' dualism. Stereotypes 'may be regarded as social constructs or shared cultural artefacts' which rebound around individual nations diachronically and synchronically, 'passing unchanged, unhindered and frequently unchallenged from, say, sport to the cinema and from literature to politics and back again' (Crolley and Hand 2002: 9). Put another way, a stereotype is 'a cognitive construct concerning the properties of a social agent' (Chilton 2004: 38), a form of 'cultural shorthand' which reduces the characteristics of diverse individuals from other countries to a single, stable set of supposed characteristics that define each and every person. Many different citizens from the same country are, in a stereotypical view, taken to share supposedly typical, static, uniform looks and character traits, with countries as a whole anthropomorphized, or treated as people, so that they in turn become owners and bearers of these traits. The convenience of stereotypes is that they 'classify human diversity into a set of instantly recognisable and largely reassuring categories' (Crolley and Hand 2002: 10) which can remain remarkably durable over time.

Crolley and Hand's treatment of football as cultural commentary gives us genuine pause for thought, not least because the reports they studied were penned in the later 1990s – exactly the period when New Labour came to power attempting to denationalize such hegemonic interpretations of the English/British national identity. The essential points from their work as far as the football–identity–Europe nexus goes are as follows. First, there is Crolley and Hand's description of the characteristics ascribed to an archetypical English national identity. 'The picture of "Englishness" painted in the football writing under consideration tends towards a stereotype and is probably best summarized by the phrase "bulldog spirit"' (Crolley and Hand 2002: 19). The idea of the English possessing 'bulldog spirit' calls to mind the patriotic, determined English fighting for their nation's future in a world of injustice, tyranny and sometimes plain evil. It does not take much for this patriotism to blend seamlessly into narrow national chauvinism and the 'jingoistic denigration' of foreigners from the point of view of the 'superior' English. Crolley and Hand's account of how German, Italian, French and Spanish players in the English Premier League are represented and reported through the medium of national stereotypes in the English press – tabloids and broadsheets alike – amply demonstrates this point (Crolley and Hand 2002: 46–59). Their research revealed 'a certain English attitude of insecurity when faced with the significant European "Other" … written in a more general climate of British Euro-scepticism towards the increasing integration favoured by most in the European Union'. This was in no small measure down to 'a wider belief in Great Britain's historical superiority over its European neighbours' (Crolley and Hand 2002: 22–3; the same sport–Eurosceptic link is drawn in Beck 2003: 395). If it was evident in press coverage from the 1990s then it was apparently no less obvious over halfway through Blair's second term in office, when Denis MacShane put anti-German chanting by English fans during the Euro 2004 tournament down to 'a sense of superiority which has always been the Achilles heel of Britain through the ages'. He blamed Eurosceptics for giving 'overt encouragement' to xenophobically inspired constructions of the British national self (quoted in Sylvester 2004).

The second point from Crolley and Hand's investigation concerns the frequent recourse in football reportage to the language of war to describe events on the pitch that are, of course, very far removed from the metaphors through which they are communicated to their readers. As a competition between two opposing teams it is not unnatural that 'war' has become an organizing frame for sports re-porting, but what strikes Crolley and Hand is just *how* frequently this type of language gets used in the English case. Drawing on Mangan's work they give four reasons why. First, it reflects an Empire-era conception of war as national duty, which lingers in the collective psyche and translates, today, into the idea of sport as national duty. Second, and related, there is a martial aspect: the necessity for warriors and therefore sportsmen and women to possess positive attributes such as physical strength and leadership qualities as well as a sense of self-sacrifice, hence the term 'putting your body on the line for the team' or 'taking a hit for the team'. Third, they recognize the role sport came to play as a medium through which these supposed English characteristics came during Victorian and Edwardian times to assume stereotypical qualities. It was particularly the case at English public schools, which were then the leading recruiting grounds for the institutions of government that oversaw the management and expansion of the British Empire. Finally, there was a tendency not only for sport to be reported as a form of war but also for the reverse, for war to be construed as a form of sport, whereby, in Mangan's words, 'colonial battlefields [became] exotic versions of the playing fields of Eton'. Crolley and Hand conclude that football has been intimately bound up with a 'broader, socio-cultural and historically-determined perception of a typically aggressive and virile form of "Englishness"' (Crolley and Hand 2002: 29) which rose to prominence during the nineteenth century but which lives on in accepted and easy stereotypes of what it is that constitutes Englishness today.

The sport-as-war metaphor lends itself to constructing a good Self opposing a bad Other and features prominently in Crolley and Hand's analysis of the football writers' lexicon. The memory of the British evacuation of Dunkirk, discussed in the previous section, the Battle of Rorke's Drift in 1879 (immortalized in the 1964 film *Zulu*), the Battle of Britain and other 'moments' in Britain's martial past seem to live on in the country's psyche as defining features of a national identity which has the ability to transform a disappointing and costly defeat into a cause for celebration of patriotic defiance and a heroic refusal to surrender to a potentially overwhelming opponent (Crolley and Hand 2002: 31). The England national team's many dramatic exits from international football tournaments over the past twenty years, notably against two old foes, Germany and Argentina, have offered up ample opportunity for the Dunkirk myth to be trotted out as evidence that while the battle may be lost the war is not yet over, and as an example of the country's ability to turn apparent defeat into unlikely victory. We can support Crolley and Hand by turning to a related genre of sporting literature: football autobiography. The example chosen is that of the Liverpool and England midfielder Steven Gerrard, ghost-written by Henry Winter of the *Daily Telegraph*. In an otherwise unremarkable book we are treated to several asides on the qualities that distinguish 'British' (meaning English) from 'foreign' (sometimes, but not always, European) football culture. Of Wayne Rooney's sending off during England's quarter-final against Portugal at the World Cup in Germany 2006, for example, Gerrard suggests that before the flash-point that led to Rooney's red card we saw classic underhand tactics being deployed against the English:

> If Wayne had acted like most foreigners and fallen over at the slight-est contact, England would have got the free-kick. But we're England. We don't cheat. We take the knocks ... we don't complain or pull stunts like foreigners. (Gerrard 2006: 415)

Here, the general outcry following England's departure from the tournament is channelled into a casual xenophobia which typi-fies the English playing by the rules but being undone by wicked 'foreigners' – a moment of defeat recast as a moral victory of sorts, and with the implication that there will always be a rematch on another battlefield another day. Reading other football biographies and autobiographies has confirmed that Gerrard is not alone in expressing such cultural stereotypes that pertain to 'foreigners', including key international football nations and players alike. The use of clichés and stereotypes, a haughty ignorance or disdain for the world outside Britain, and the language used to create Self and Other identities are a stock-in-trade of this type of football writing and commentary. Take another example from football autobiography, this time former Liverpool striker Robbie Fowler. Russian League 1 side Vladikavkaz, against which Liverpool played a European club match in the 1995–96 season, is written off as 'some godforsaken Eastern European shithole', while Fowler mourned the fact that under manager Gérard Houllier it was all 'new faces, every one a foreigner who seemed soooo serious' (Fowler 2006: 177, 261). Books like this are clearly a genre in themselves and they are discursively structured to hit the very notes and create the very meanings with which the authors believe their intended football-fan readerships would connect. The culture of football and the football commen-tary culture work symbiotically off each other to promote a sullen resistance to the world outside England's so-called 'beautiful game'. In Crolley and Hand's work, as in football literature, we see the football–politics overlap in sharp relief, with a dangerous and unfair world 'out there', in Europe and beyond, perpetually undermining saintly English ambitions.

Military metaphors pervade journalistic (and political) accounts of sporting contests involving British and European teams and this is significant, notes Charteris-Black, because they:

have the power to arouse emotions that are associated with physical combat such as pride, anger and resentment. These emotions then evoke strong feelings of antipathy towards an identity whom they identify as 'the enemy' – or the villain – and strong feelings of loyalty and affection towards a 'hero' figure, typically themselves. (Charteris-Black 2006: 22)

It is noticeable that British leaders wanting to back their claims to be able to safeguard the national interest at European summits and negotiations can fall back on the language of 'no surrender' to describe their policies, knowing that its underlying message will be understood and well received by critics of the EU. See, for example, Blair's speech at the CBI in May 2006, when he assured his audience that 'We will not agree to anything that surrenders our opt-out on working time' (Blair 2006d). This was the logical extension of Brown's pledge three years earlier to 'resist inflexible barriers being introduced into directives like the Working Time Directive, we will … remove unnecessary regulations and restrictions' (Brown 2003e). Ever a favourite of Brown, the checks came in the form of three more tests: the 'costs' test, the 'jobs' test and the 'is it really necessary' test (Brown 2003f; see also Brown 2004d). Five tests on the euro, three tests on regulation; it seems nothing that came from Europe could avoid being fed through the Treasury's accounting machinery, which was some task because Brown's calculation was that 40% of new regulation in Britain 'comes from Europe' (Brown 2004c). New Labour slotted its discourses into a militarized discourse on British–European relations which suggested that responsible British governments 'fight for British interests in Europe' (Brown 2004b). After all, 'it is in the national interest that we continue to resist inflexible regulation from the European Union' (Brown 2005b). The government, Blair and Brown suggested, could always be trusted by British businesses to report back from duty on the front line that they have 'won the battle' (Brown 2004f) against the latest continental ploy to undermine British interests or sovereignty, whether this be the European Savings Directive, moves to harmonize European tax systems (Brown 2004h) or creeping federalism more generally.

The significance of this line of discursive reasoning returns us to sport and politics. Crolley and Hand observe that the framing of football reports (not only in England, it should be added, but in France and Spain also) undermines the federalist ambitions of the founding fathers of the EEC and EU by promoting the idea of a 'Europe of nations' differentiated in perpetuity by both geographical and psychological frontiers. MacShane's 2004 observation (quoted above) that Eurosceptic vocabulary and the mode of thinking it betrays were a reflection of latent or not so latent xenophobia was no isolated outburst during the New Labour years. For example, a BBC documentary broadcast in 2005 picked up the idea that the 'English disease' of football hooliganism from the 1970s might have been caused by the slippage from aggressive national patriotism into national chauvinism. In fact, it judged, 'these aggressive displays of identity would become the football equivalent of Euroscepticism'. One interviewee, the singer-songwriter Billy Bragg, commented that 'I think that these people must get their worldview from the opening credits of [the British situation comedy] *Dad's Army....* It does say something about English culture, I think, that we cling to the past in that sense.' (We return to an appreciation of the significance of *Dad's Army* for an understanding of Euroscepticism in chapter 8.) The documentary was significant because it was replete with references to the power of the past to limit the ability of progressive forces to shape the kind of 'modern' identity for Britain of which Blair and Brown frequently spoke (BBC 2005). When any and every encounter with the continent in political, economic or sporting terms is depicted as a military expedition it does rather tend to heighten the sense of Europe being an Other. When that logic of Otherness becomes a part of a nation's linguistic universe it becomes all the more difficult to chip away at its appeal. Blair and Brown faced a huge task to create consensus around a new discursive norm of pro-Europeanism.

Summary

It is often said that there is a thread running through British history, from Magna Carta to the Bill of Rights and the great Reform Acts – one of individual liberty, the individual standing firm against tyranny and the state's arbitrary exercise of power. And Britain has always rejected the ideologies of state absolutism and excessive individualism. (Brown 2000f)

This chapter has considered the mechanisms by which Europe has, historically, been heterotypified as a hostile Other in popular discourses on an 'exceptional' British identity. It did so by sketching some of the attitudes and opinions Blair and Brown felt they had to overturn to put their case for Europe. We first explored the basis of the well known 'island story', a geographical fact that critically shapes the psychocultural milieu within which the British think of themselves and their role in the world. We then worked through some of the less well aired cultural commentaries on England and Englishness that rebound through the pages of specialist publications such as *This England* and in journalistic coverage of international football matches. The aim of the chapter was to set the scene for a consideration of New Labour's European discourses by painting a picture of the linguistic environment into which Blair and Brown were venturing. We can see from the evidence in the chapter just how widespread the British heterotypification of Europe is – and the Prime Minister and Chancellor were well aware of the national story they needed to rewrite. The island story, Dunkirk, the 'bulldog spirit' and so on provide the 'moments' of Englishness around which fables of the national character have been built, tested, revised and rebranded. In and around these moments we have the routine ways of talking about Europe and Europeans as always 'over there', usually 'different', often 'quirky' and sometimes plain 'threatening'. Eurosceptic discourses have a natural affinity with the way the British *talk* about the world. We saw this most acutely in the literatures explored above when commentators talk of football hooliganism being a physical manifestation of a Euroscepticism that finds its benign counterpart in political and press discourses of Otherness and a 'Europe of nations'. The next chapter will explore the theoretical literature on Euroscepticism and then spell out how Blair and Brown defined this key term as a way of identifying their political opponents in their European discourses from 1997.

Chapter 6

Identities: New Labour and the Eurosceptics

Of particular relevance perhaps is Britain's persistent identity crisis in the wake of both empire and Cold War, most notably the difficulty of equating Britishness with toleration and openness rather than xenophobia and chauvinism. (Beck 2003: 409–10)

In the previous chapter we considered the British propensity to heterotypify European countries and the EU's system of governance through discursive constructions which set British national identity permanently against that of the EU's leading member states and the EU as political practice. The argument pursued was that not all discursive Otherings of Europe are necessarily expressions of opposition to the EU, or born out of xenophobic prejudice. The diversity of everyday Otherings of Europe in the way the British speak about going on holiday *to* Europe or discuss football matches played 'in Europe', for example, does not automatically betray Eurosceptical attitudes on questions relating to Britain's involvement with the EU – but it can do. A respect for the British liberal tradition, its political institutions, the beauty of its countryside and its heritage may or may not prompt one to oppose Britain's membership of the EU – but it might. The point is that in trying to overturn accepted ways of thinking about Britain and Europe, Tony Blair and Gordon Brown were having to engage with binary modes of expression (things 'British' on the one hand versus things 'European' on the other) that have a huge influence over the shape and nature of Britain's EU debates. The simple fact appears to be that in Britain this is a 'natural' way of talking about Europe and calling it to mind for the purposes of everyday conversation and public debate. From the worlds of sport to top-selling public quarterly magazines and through discussions between politicians and diplomats in the Palace of Westminster and the corridors of Whitehall, we saw in the preceding chapter just how wide and deep the cultural Othering of Europe is in Britain and thereby gained an insight into the size of the task facing New Labour's leaders in winning the propaganda war.

The vital issue as Blair and Brown saw it was to try at least to undermine and, ideally, break the organic link that had apparently developed between passion for nation on the one hand and Euroscepticism on the other. The former, they believed, could be a precursor to the development of *greater* passion for things European if Britain's Self identity was recast to be composed of several layers, one on top of the other, rather than as an exclusive national-based identity, perpetually constituted against a continental Other. That a love of country or support for the England football team does not necessarily render one a Eurosceptic makes it pertinent at this stage to pause and unpack the meaning of that crucial word by reflecting on the language used to describe the particular expression of opposition to Europe and/or the EU that Blair and Brown felt they had to engage. This will be achieved in three sections. The first two study a variety of scholarly efforts to define 'Euroscepticism', from those informed by historical assessments of British European policy in the first section, to formal modelling of attitudes to the EU and 'Europe' in the second. The conceptual problems associated with trying to arrive at an agreed definition demonstrates the ideologically loaded nature of the term, which flows straight from descriptors such as 'Euroscepticism' being so malleable as to defy almost all our efforts to fix signified through signifier. Politicians, of course, cannot deal in such detailed wordplay. However, it is vital to appreciate the ideas Blair and Brown held about Euroscepticism (the identities they ascribed to their opponents) as a way of understanding the currents of thought they challenged and the techniques they used to dislodge the narrative force and mass discursive resonance of Eurosceptical ideas. The third section of the chapter therefore uses extracts of speeches by Blair and Brown to determine how they fixed their Eurosceptical opponents in their European discourse, and how in the process they constructed their positions within this debate as 'Europeanists'.

I. Euroscepticism in the academy

The words 'Euroscepticism' and 'Eurosceptic' come weighed down with meaning and using them in any objective or universally applicable sense is impossible. So far have these words travelled, and so flexible are they, that Clive Church has even wondered whether 'Euroscepticism may not be ... a serviceable term' (Church 2004: 288). That the word gets used in party political debates in a non-EU member state such as Switzerland, the national case study he uses in his research, immediately alerts us to the force of his argument, which rests on three propositions (from Church 2004: 285–8). The first is that the term 'Eurosceptic' is as commonly ascribed *to* an agent or group of agents as it is used *by* those agents to describe their position within a country's debates about the EU. In fact, notes Church of the Swiss Eurosceptics, in making an intervention on this subject 'it is rarely seen as Euroscepticism by those involved' because of the EU-positive agenda they advance. The second proposition relates to the national connotations that necessarily come with the term. Church finds that in the Swiss case Eurosceptics do not have an 'ideological phobia based on Europe. It is broader and more Swiss-centred than this', posing real problems for any academic wanting to develop a comparative model of Euroscepticism that permits generalizations about its character and functions within domestic polities, while at the same time remaining sensitive to the discursive nuances across distinct national contexts. Church's third proposition is that politicians, publics and the media can use the language of Euroscepticism as a tool of popular mobilization without necessarily believing in the cause they are rhetorically advancing. In this light, Church sees opposition to Europe in Switzerland as 'a form of anti-establishment politics' – a device deployed in domestic power struggles over the nature and pace of the government's external policy after the later 1980s. Church's study of Euroscepticism in Switzerland shows: how national contexts are all important in determining how the label is used; that it may change its meaning in response to key events or policy changes at the domestic or European level; and that apparent expressions of Euroscepticism may in some, perhaps many, cases be more indicative of the dynamics of domestic party politicking than those same parties' 'true' opinions about Europe and/or the EU. Concluding with a warning note to students of the British case, Church remarks that 'European integration clearly helps to mobilize politics beyond the narrow confines of the EU and the candidate states.... In other words, the term is wider and harder to pin down than many British usages assume' (Church 2004: 288). The word 'Eurosceptic' can, it seems, be as meaningful or as meaningless as we want it to be.

So how might we go about defining Euroscepticism? This opening section will outline some of the contentious issues in the existing literature and the chapter moves on in the second section to consider two academic models that have been developed to explain the phenomenon, each with its own strengths and weaknesses, uses and potential drawbacks. Part of the problem in developing a serviceable model of Eurosepticism, and the reason Church trains his fire on the British-centricity of the term, is that the word itself was apparently first used in British politics and has since spread and been taken on by a variety of users in other member states. In other words, a nationally defined concept has since taken on transnational connotations that may be anachronistic to those changed contexts. Harmsen and Spiering argue that the term entered the British political and journalistic lexicon and hence public consciousness in the mid-1980s, tracing its first usage to an article in *The Times*. From here, they suggest, 'Euroscepticism' has mostly been used to imply 'opposition to UK membership of the European Union and its antecedents, rather than a milder lack of enthusiasm for the project' (Harmsen and Spiering 2004: 16). Their argument is that British sceptics may support the idea of integration but not the specific processes enshrined in the 1957 Rome Treaty and its successors. Later in the volume Spiering digs deeper into the British case by breaking down 'Euroscepticism' into its component parts. The 'Euro' part refers to the institutions of the EEC and EU and the 'sceptic' part means 'doubtful'. This would also limit the meaning to scepticism about the current form of integration as practised in the EU (Spiering 2004: 128).

Identifying an 'origin' of Euroscepticism is, however, fraught with difficulty and points up the fact that for all writers on this topic periodization is a contentious issue; we can clearly see this in the work of Martin Holmes and Anthony Forster. In his 2002 collection, which brought together an array of Eurosceptical voices from the British establishment, Holmes, like Harmsen and Spiering, saw a 'rebirth' of Euroscepticism after Thatcher's Bruges speech in 1988 – the tipping point we discussed in chapter 3. Before that time, he suggests, the 1975 referendum had effectively made it 'dormant, subdued or outside the political mainstream'. Thatcher's intervention 'transformed the issue from sideshow to centre stage' and it has since become a 'permanent feature of the political landscape' in Britain (Holmes 2002: 1). For Holmes, contemporary events at the time of writing were everything and he went straight on to investigate the prospects and prognosis for scepticism under the second Blair government of 2001–5. Euroscepticism in this connotation is the stuff of elite, party political manoeuvrings since the later 1980s. Anthony Forster took a more inclusive approach to the history of Euroscepticism in Britain. In 2002 he pointed out that in its popular guise it generally 'has been employed as a generic label that defines a negative point of view towards the European Union' (Forster 2002: 1–2). For Forster, Euroscepticism meant something more than the 'rather narrow and contemporary understanding' centring on the Conservative attack on the transition from the EEC to EU in and around the time of Thatcher's Bruges speech and the Maastricht Treaty. Forster amplified the term both in terms of time period, tracing the roots of contemporary scepticism back to the Second World War, and in terms of party, pointing out that such opposition has not been confined to the Conservative Party. Hence, he wrote, 'the term needs to be seen as a particular manifestation of a school of sceptical thought about the value of Britain's involvement with moves towards supranational European integration' (Forster 2002: 2). The Bruges speech, he suggested, saw a crystallization of existing trends in scepticism rather than providing the *source* of scepticism in any simple sense. It was, in fact, the second of three historical periods in post-war British scepticism. The first was book-ended by Harold Macmillan and Harold Wilson's failed attempts to take Britain into the EEC in the 1960s and the referendum on continued membership in 1975. The second was the Thatcher period itself, from 1979 to 1990, culminating in the Eurosceptical activity surrounding her Bruges speech. The third period spanned the evolution and ratification of the Maastricht Treaty in the 1990s (Forster 2002: 3). What we see in Forster's work is an attempt to avert our gaze from the Holmes-esque homage to Thatcher that comes from stressing the Conservative–Thatcher–Maastricht dimensions of scepticism. A groundswell of opinion in Britain against post-war European integration had, Forster argues, existed for many years prior to the Iron Lady popularizing it so vocally. Even if they were not calling themselves 'Eurosceptics' they expressed ideas and attitudes that might legitimately be called 'Eurosceptical'. Tacit support might be found for Forster's position in the work of the historian Melissa Pine, who uses the term 'Euro-sceptics' to refer to Labour politicians such as Barbara Castle and Tony Benn, who were hesitant about, if not outright opposed to, Britain's second application to join the EEC under Harold Wilson in the 1960s. On first usage Pine puts the word in quotation marks, a sign that she sees it possibly being used out of context, but as her historical narrative progresses the quotation marks disappear and later in the book it is written 'anti-European'. Pine takes the terms to mean general opposition to certain aspects of British European policy, in much the same way that Forster does, and she is happy to use the descriptors interchangeably (Pine 2007: 32–3, 177, 179; 'anti-European' appears on 141–2).

Spiering took issue with Forster by arguing that to classify every expression of opposition or doubt about Europe as a sign of Euro-scepticism, before the term had readily entered popular jargon, was to render the concept 'almost meaningless' (Spiering 2004: 128). Spiering's view was that we have to be sensitive to both chronological and ideological contexts, and that the word refers to something more than any vague doubt about 'Europe' expressed in post-war British politics. He gave two arguments in support. The first was that the term has been used as a 'badge of honour' by groups such as the Campaign for an Independent Britain (CIB), which campaigns for

Box 5. Euroscepticism and the Campaign for an Independent Britain: extract from the organization's website

The Campaign for an Independent Britain is a non-party political campaigning organization of people from all walks of life who recognize that continuing British membership of the European Union poses grave threats to our liberties, independence, and economic prosperity.

We believe that Britain should leave the European Union and that the corrupt, undemocratic, obsolete and fraud-ridden EU should be superseded by modern, democratic structures that enable the peoples of Europe to co-operate without loss of any nation's freedoms and way of life.

The Campaign for an Independent Britain seeks the repeal of the European Communities Act 1972 under which EU directives take precedence over UK law. Once self-government has been recovered, the United Kingdom would be free, as an independent state, to co-operate and trade with its neighbours in Europe and with countries elsewhere in the world without the restrictions imposed by EU membership.

Britain's relationship with the European Union is one that sits above party politics and one doesn't have to be a member of any particular political party to be concerned about the ever-growing power of the EU. In Campaign for an Independent [Britain] we have members from all the major political parties, trades unionists, environmentalists, businessmen, students, journalists as well as members of both Houses of Parliament who are united in their belief that Britain's membership of the European Union has been a great error for this country.

Source: CIB (2008b).

British withdrawal from the EU 'and for a positive future for our country as an independent, self-governing nation' (CIB 2008a). It was founded in 1976 as the Safeguard Britain Campaign. The organization's website claims 'it is not too much of an exaggeration to say that without CIB not only would no-one have heard of the word "eurosceptic"' and that without it 'the mass opposition to the European Union that now exists in this country simply would not exist' (CIB 2008b; see further box 5).

Spiering's second argument was that while groups such as CIB proudly proclaim their Euroscepticism, the term is just as often eschewed by individuals and groups in Britain that are critical of the EU but that do not advocate withdrawal from it. They prefer softer-sounding labels, such as 'Eurorealist' or 'Europragmatist' (Spiering 2004: 129–30). As opposition to Europe and the EU has grown so, it seems, has the number of descriptors on offer. For instance, in his 2001 analysis of British critics of the euro, Lord Haskins used 'Eurosceptic' interchangeably with 'europhobes', 'ultranationalist europhobics' and 'euro critics' (Haskins 2001: 51–4), while Stephen Haseler has equated 'eurosceptic' with 'europhobic' (Haseler 2001: 71). Blair and Brown had equal trouble arriving at soundbite definitions for their positive approach to the EU, as we shall in section III.

Spiering concluded his assessment by writing that 'although Euroscepticism can and is used in a general sense, as a label for all views more-or-less critical of the EU, in Britain the term has always had radical connotations' (Spiering 2004: 130). He thus leant towards the Stephen George line, that 'it has to be said that in Britain the term has come to refer to a rather stronger position which is hostile to British participation in the European Union' (quoted in Spiering 2004: 128–9). The wider national context within which Eurosceptical positions have been shaped and articulated has often been lost in works that focus on debates that have occurred among politicians and diplomats. In this collision between elite and public discourses we see persistent Otherings of Europe that hint at a multifaceted phenomenon assuming different guises according to language user and language hearer. In such a situation perhaps the need to periodize is less compelling because what parties and people say about Europe might not, in fact, be what they *mean* or *intend* to mean. For example, expressing opposition to the Social Chapter and/or the single currency and/or the Lisbon Treaty might be a genuine expression of concern about a particular EU policy by an individual otherwise in favour of European integration. It could be interpreted, however, as an expression of dissatisfaction with one's country remaining in the EU as it currently stands, or even with the whole idea of integration. Context is vital and any person expressing such opinions is not in control of how his or her utterances will be received among the wider political, media and public listenerships. This is the problem with nouns and adjectives as signifiers: they may cue attitudes or images that are unintended by the user but are all too obvious to an interlocutor. Garton Ash (2001) has therefore argued that we should rewrite 'Europe' as 'EU-rope' to convey the ambiguity and the conceptual confusion that lie at the heart of British debates about 'Europe' and I would tend to agree.

Spiering's analysis is useful because it provides a way into the tangle of words and definitions that academics who have tried to model the concept have had to contend with, whether they are dealing with a single-country case study or a larger-n comparative study. 'Euroscepticism', 'Eurorealism' and 'Europragmatism' are just some of the signifiers used by politicians, journalists and campaigners to capture in soundbite form their policies and/or attitude towards Europe and its processes of integration. The loose terminology is both reflective of (and feeds back into) confusion in

---

Box 6. Some student definitions of Euroscepticism

Hayley Conboy. 'A term to describe a person's distrust of national activity at the European level and a belief that the disadvantages of European integration outweigh the advantages.'

Georg Huber. 'A political tendency, not particularly connected to any specific political party or current, that questions the legitimacy and necessity of European Integration either as such, or its depth, scope or specific aspects of it.'

Annie Poole. 'Eurosceptism takes many forms and means different things to various nations. Britain is labelled eurosceptic for its refusal to belong to the euro and its reluctance to act on any European initiatives.'

James Fuller. 'A fear of European integration in a political and economic sense. Politically about devolution of sovereignty towards Brussels, and economically the anxiety over a move to a single European currency.'

Verena von Eicken. 'A critical or rejecting attitude about the project of the European Union, whose advocates use arguments like the loss of national sovereignty and identity, the insufficient political participation of citizens and the lack of transparency of European Union politics.'

Stephen Wilson. 'A fear and general opposition to European integration often coupled with a strong national identity. A fear of the loss of sovereignty and law making ability.'

Holly Grey. 'Someone who is wary or against the EU, fear for national sovereignty, may prefer the British-American relationship.'

Sam Gould. 'Not a believer in the "European project".'

---

and outside Britain about just what it is British 'sceptics' are opposing. What muddies the water still more is that 'Europe' is a moving target and Euroscepticism has to be in perpetual motion to keep up with it. A snapshot of undergraduate student opinion on how we might define Euroscepticism makes this all too clear. For the past few years I have been running a final-year undergraduate optional module on Euroscepticism in Britain to a mixture of thirty UK and Erasmus exchange students per semester. To get discussion under way at the opening session of the 2008/9 academic year students were asked to define Euroscepticism, to identify a Eurosceptical individual, party or campaign group, and to think of an image, symbol or word associated with Euroscepticism. It is the definitions that interest us here and box 6 reproduces a representative selection of the students' ideas. The plethora of reference points, keywords and terminologies the students came up with shows the problems of putting together a definition that applies in a national context, let alone a pan-EU one. Sam Gould's 'not a believer' in the European project could imply scepticism either about the EU approach to integration or the idea of pooling sovereignty among European states in an organized, top-down way. Hayley Conboy's focus was on the cost–benefit analysis of the disadvantages of membership outweighing the advantages; the pressing question then becomes how to judge the benefits and costs of being part of the various segments of the EU's activities. Georg Huber stressed the non-partisan roots of scepticism, Annie Poole pointed to the essential slipperiness of the word and Holly Grey alluded to the pull for British policy-makers of the 'special relationship'. Throughout their interventions key themes presented themselves: sovereignty, identity, nationalism, particular EU initiatives and policies such as the single currency and the CAP and, finally, words such as 'fear' and 'wary' call to mind representations of Europe as an Other we explored in the previous chapter. In the student definitions we see the general eliding with the specific, as well as the economic with the political, and there was many a reference to the perception that EU-level activity is somehow more questionable or lacking in legitimacy and accountability than national-level activity in the same policy domain. Several academics have tried to clarify matters using formal modelling techniques and we now study two of the most popular.

II. Modelling attitudes to 'Europe'

Having unpicked the word 'Euroscepticism' in a general sense, we can now explore two of the leading efforts to make sense of its meaning from a theoretical perspective: the models proposed by Paul Taggart and Aleks Szczerbiak on the one hand and Petr Kopecký and Cas Mudde on the other. Having reviewed each approach we will see how they map onto the usages of the term in Blair and Brown's speeches. It will be argued that, for New Labour, a Eurosceptic (or anti-European – the terms were used interchangeably) was someone, frequently but not always of the Conservative right, whose opinions are built on the twin pillars of national superiority and British-best assumptions that denigrate anything and sometimes everything European. That is, it denoted someone at the 'harder' end of the 'sceptic' spectrum the academics have devised to capture the meaning of this conceptually problematic phenomenon.

Arguably the best-known effort to pin down different strains of Euroscepticism has been that of Paul Taggart and Aleks Szczerbiak, whose opening gambit was a 2001 working paper on Euroscepticism in what were then the candidate states of Central and Eastern Europe (Taggart and Szczerbiak 2001). Founders of the Opposing Europe Research Network (OERN), since renamed the European Parties, Elections and Referendums Research Network (EPERN), their judgements were quickly tested by the other network members and this has resulted in a productive process of dialogue and theoretical refinement (Taggart and Szczerbiak 2002; Szczerbiak and Taggart 2003; Taggart and Szczerbiak 2004). Such alterations as have been made, however, are less important than the labels they gave to the different strains of scepticism they found in those countries – for two reasons. First, as we shall see below, their 'hard/ soft' distinction has become an integral part of the academic lexicon of scepticism as the 2000s have progressed. Second, dissatisfaction with that early terminology prompted Kopecký and Mudde to develop their alternative model of attitudes to Europe. The starting point for Taggart and Szczerbiak in 2001 was the observation that expressions of opposition to Europe within EU member states cut across national boundaries and party borders. Across Europe there are many parties, or factions within parties, that express opinions that we could classify as sceptical or, at the extreme, hostile to European integration. Taken together, these collected Eurosceptics constitute a range of very different political parties and factions from extreme left to far right via the new left and the new populist right. In what were then EU candidate states, Taggart and Szczerbiak observed a gradual weakening of the consensus behind accession, to the point that 'it is no longer safe to assume a compliant and supportive mood of public opinion' (Taggart and Szczerbiak 2001: 6). The dearth of comparative work on Euroscepticism up to that point came as a surprise and, they felt, required a distinction to be drawn between different strengths of scepticism. This would aid an appreciation of the differences between national scepticisms and help show similarities across states which might form the basis for generalizations about the dynamics of opposition to Europe in EU candidate states (Taggart and Szczerbiak 2003: 9). It is important to reiterate that at this juncture Taggart and Szczerbiak were focusing only on countries in Central and Eastern Europe, although in talking in general terms about Euroscepticism they surely saw the potential for their labels to 'travel' to any state home to opposition to Europe and/or the EU.

The question is, where did the hard/soft distinction come from and what do those labels imply for our understanding of the term 'Euroscepticism'? Already in 1998 Taggart had written that Euroscepticism 'expresses the idea of contingent or qualified opposition, as well as incorporating outright and unqualified opposition to the process of European integration' (quoted in Taggart and Szczerbiak 2001: 9). In their 2001 paper the authors added flesh to those bones by distinguishing between two varieties of scepticism. 'Hard Euroscepticism implies outright rejection of the entire project of European political and economic integration and opposition to their country joining or remaining members of the EU.' They readily admitted a problem with this definition. 'Theoretically hard Euroscepticism encompasses those with principled objection to the idea of any European economic or political integration. In reality such a position is too abstract to be applicable.' The result was a somewhat looser definition of the term: 'the principled objection to the current form of European integration in the EU' (all quotes here from Taggart and Szczerbiak 2001: 10). By contrast, soft Euroscepticism 'involves contingent or qualified opposition to European integration' and can be broken down into two forms, both of which imply opposition not to the existence of the EU or European integration itself but opposition to a particular sector of EU policy or proposals to extend the EU's competence into a new policy arena. 'Policy Euroscepticism is opposition to measures designed to deepen significantly European political and economic integration (e.g. EMU [Economic and Monetary Union]) or is opposition to an existing policy and is expressed in terms of opposition to specific extensions of EU competencies' (all from Taggart and Szczerbiak 2001: 10). A policy sceptic might appreciate the economic and security benefits of pooled sovereignty in a European body but have qualms about the provisions of the Lisbon Treaty. Not opposed to integration in general, policy sceptics are wary of wider or deeper integration for reasons that will be contingent upon the specific nature of the proposed policy and the prevailing environment of national debates about integration. The second type of soft Euroscepticism is national-interest scepticism, which involves 'employing the rhetoric of defending or standing up for "the national interest" in the context of debates about the EU'. Key here is that this kind of scepticism 'is compatible with support in principle for the European project' but that it is used by those who deploy the rhetoric of scepticism 'to shore up their domestic political base' (Taggart and Szczerbiak 2001: 10–11). This is arguably the 'thinnest' type of scepticism, in that we see it being wheeled out not for ideological reasons or on grounds of principle, but mostly for short-term political gain or rhetorical effect. The authors provided a pithy summary of the distinction between hard and soft variants later in the article. Soft scepticism, they say, 'offers a qualified criticism of European integration either on grounds of particular national concerns or for particular policy reasons, than the "harder" outright rejection of European integration' (Taggart and Szczerbiak 2001: 29).

The authors revisited the hard/soft distinction a year later to shore up their meaning across the twenty-five states used in a fresh study. Hard Euroscepticism in this formulation became '*principled opposition to the EU and European integration and therefore can be seen in parties who think that their countries should withdraw from membership, or whose policies towards the EU are tantamount to being opposed to the whole project of European integration as it is currently conceived*'. A party was identified as a hard sceptic party if it was a single-issue anti-EU party or if its 'opposition to the EU is framed in language that stresses that it is too capitalist/socialist/neo-liberal/bureaucratic, depending on ideological position (communist, conservative, socialist/populist)' (all from Taggart and Szczerbiak 2002: 7; emphasis in original). Fundamental to the reworked defini-tion of hard scepticism was that they were starting to look *through* the official policy discourse of the parties concerned to make infer-ences about their real, underlying or intended motive for resting their opposition on the grounds of conditional or qualified support for the EU. Taggart and Szczerbiak showed themselves alert to the ironies of double-speak and reception theory as they apply to the study of politi-cal discourse by suggesting that rhetorical support for the EU could be so conditional 'that it is tantamount to being *de facto* opposed to EU membership' (Taggart and Szczerbiak 2002: 7). The politician might say one thing, but the cues this gives the notional audience for a speech or policy document might be – and might cleverly be intended to be – altogether different. Soft Euroscepticism in the new definition '*is where there is NOT a principled objection to European integra-tion or EU membership but where concerns on one (or a number) of policy areas lead to the expression of qualified opposition to the EU, or where there is a sense that "national interest" is currently at odds with the EU's trajectory*'. This variety, they contend, constitutes 'real scepticism about the way European integration is currently develop-ing'. The crux, as it was in 2001, is that the definitions of hard and soft scepticism each related to 'an ideal type that will, in some cases, become blurred but it may be useful to identify the two forms as poles on a spectrum with some parties moving between them' (Taggart and Szczerbiak 2002: 7–8; emphases in original).

It is unnecessary to critique the Taggart and Szczerbiak model, or to showcase the various iterations they went through in developing these concepts (on which see Taggart and Szczerbiak 2003). Rather, it is useful to observe that the hard/soft distinction has become a hugely popular theoretical accompaniment to empirical work on Euroscepticism both within and outside the British context. Two examples help make this point. First, Menno Spiering remarks that the most common strains of Euroscepticism in Britain 'must be classified as "hard". A British Eurosceptic aims to withdraw the UK from the EU, or perhaps one should say "promotes the idea that Britain withdraw".' The category could include post-Prime Minister Margaret Thatcher, who has apparently come to see withdrawal from the EU as the only sensible way forward for Britain but who has not explicitly advocated this course of action (Spiering 2004: 130). Inferring intent from the content of policy utterances picks up the 2002 Taggart and Szczerbiak sentiment that the attribution of Eurosceptical attitudes can truly be in the eye of the beholder. The second example is from Andrew Geddes, whose assessment is that over the past two decades the Conservative Party has evolved into a 'hard' Eurosceptical party, which at the 2005 general election placed so many conditions on its proposed engagement with the EU that withdrawal seemed the only likely outcome had the party won the election. The party's vulnerability to losing votes to a genuinely hard Eurosceptical party, in the form of UKIP, backs the argument that even if the Conservative Party as a whole might not be Eurosceptical, certainly a significant and potentially vocal minority would have it that way (Geddes 2006: 129–33). As critics of Taggart and Szczerbiak would point out, such examples of the tentacular spread of the hard/soft distinction through the literature on Euroscepticism are not necessarily testament to the validity or general applicability of their model. However, it does demonstrate how this early academic effort to pin down usable working definitions of different strains of scepticism has taken off among political scientists. Of considerable note for this study is the tendency to see British Euroscepticism as, more often than not, of the 'hard' variety.

Two co-authors taking a different approach are Petr Kopecký and Cas Mudde, whose 2002 'The two sides of Euroscepticism' article provides a contrasting methodology and typology of party positions on Europe (Kopecký and Mudde 2002). It also used comparative data, from the Czech Republic, Hungary, Poland and Slovakia. These authors began by advancing a critique of Taggart and Szczerbiak's work, centring on four points of attack (all from Kopecký and Mudde 2002: 300, unless otherwise stated). First, they critiqued Taggart and Szczerbiak's definition of 'soft' Euroscepticism, saying it is so broad that 'virtually any disagreement with any policy decision of the EU can be included'. Second, they saw insufficient delineation between the two strengths of Euroscepticism when Taggart and Szczerbiak can include in their 'hard' category 'objections to *the current form* of European integration in the EU' (Taggart and Szczerbiak's emphasis). Third, on the method used, Kopecký and Mudde were unclear about what criteria were in play 'to connect and to separate the two forms of scepticism', making it tricky to explain where, when and why the two forms might appear. Fourth and finally, Kopecký and Mudde saw a lack of depth or nuance in the hard/soft typology, which, they believed, downplays a subtle distinction between ideas about European integration on the one hand and about the EU as practice on the other. Søren Riishøj summarizes the gist of Kopecký and Mudde's critiques by touching on the 'danger of conceptual stretching', whereby simple articulations of the national interest come, erroneously, to be labelled expressions of scepticism (Riishøj 2007: 507–8). Conceptual concerns fed directly into a terminological dispute, with the label 'Euroscepticism' being wrongly applied by Taggart and Szczerbiak 'to parties and ideologies that are in essence pro-European as well as to those that are outright anti-European'. From these critiques of the hard/soft model we can accent some key themes that then emerged in Kopecký and Mudde's article. They professed a general interest in mapping party positions on Europe, whether they be supportive or oppositional; they used a greater number of labels to account for a greater range of opinions about Europe, from the two of Taggart and Szczerbiak to their four; and they wanted less definitional overlap between their categorization of party positions. What stands out from the article is the lengths to which Kopecký and Mudde went to finely grain their typology of party positions – they especially wanted to remove the definitional confusion to which they believed a two-point spectrum gave rise. This led to the addition of a whole new academic jargon for characterizing party positions on the EU and 'Europe', themed around a new set of discursive signifiers for this essentially contested concept. It is to an exploration of their typology that we now turn.

Kopecký and Mudde's inspiration came from David Easton's work on different types of support for a given political regime. In the first place there is 'diffuse support', meaning 'support for the general *ideas* of European integration that underlie the EU'. Then there is 'specific support', meaning 'support for the general *practice* of European integration: that is, the EU and how it is developing' (Kopecký and Mudde 2002: 300; emphasis in original). Moving on, they argued that there are two dimensions through which we can study support for, and opposition to, European integration. Plotting these dimensions against each other brought into existence their 2×2 matrix. The first dimension, which features on the x-axis of their matrix, roughly equates to Easton's diffuse support. This they called 'support for ideas of European integration' and here there is a separation between the 'Europhiles' and the 'Europhobes'. Europhiles believe in the concept of institutionalized cooperation at the economic and/ or political level, 'regardless of how European integration is defined and realized in detail'. This group can include Jean Monnet-type supranational federalists as well as those who may limit their support to the creation of a single market. In Kopecký and Mudde's terminology, therefore, the earlier Margaret Thatcher could be classed a Europhile, on the basis of her European policies as they developed during the 1980s, especially towards the Single European Act (SEA) (Kopecký and Mudde 2002: 301). Europhobes, by contrast, oppose (or at least do not support) the general integrationist ideas underlying the EU, whether for nationalist or ideological reasons, 'or simply because they believe the idea of European integration is a folly in the face of the diversity (and "thus" incompatibility) existing among European states'. Europhobes may be in favour of interest-based cooperation between nation states at some level and in some form, but not in the EU, either as it exists at present or as it is predicted to develop in the future. In Britain, UKIP might be an example of a Europhobic party (Kopecký and Mudde 2002: 301) because although it does not technically oppose the current process of European integration, nor even the EU, it does not want Britain to remain within the organization. As its general election manifesto from 2005 put it, 'We are not *anti-European*; we just believe the best people to run Britain are the British' (UKIP 2005: foreword; emphasis in original).

The x-axis, then, plots diffuse support for integration. The y-axis maps positions flowing from Easton's 'specific support' for the EU, which for Kopecký and Mudde divides the EU-optimists from the EU-pessimists. EU-optimists 'believe in the EU as it is and as it is developing'. They are satisfied with the way the EU has been set up, how it functions and are sanguine about the future direction of its development. Kopecký and Mudde pointed out that a critical attitude towards a certain area of EU policy does not mean a party cannot still be labelled EU-optimist, on the grounds that it is rare to find a party agreeing with the scope and direction of the EU *in toto*. A party might see the CAP as a wasteful and inefficient use of the EU's own resources (and/or as contributing to poverty in the developing world) but still see the EU itself as a valuable multilateral forum in which nations come together to pursue political, social, environmental and security-related cooperation (Kopecký and Mudde 2002: 302). EU-pessimists, by contrast, do not support the EU in its present form, or worry about its potential future direction. They do not necessarily object to EU membership per se but can 'simply consider the current EU to be a serious deviation from their interpretation of the founding ideas of European integration'. EU-pessimists want to alter the EU in a way that takes it closer in institutional terms to their perception of the earlier mainsprings of the integration idea (Kopecký and Mudde 2002: 302), for instance by promoting an intergovernmental conception of the EU.

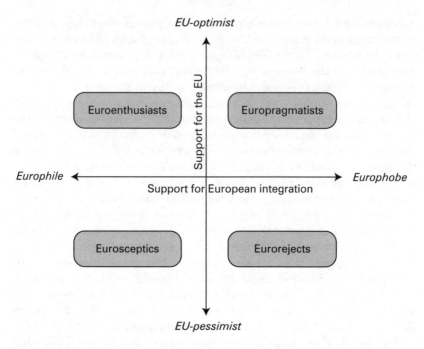

Figure 6. Kopecký and Mudde's typology of party positions on Europe.

Mapping the x-axis of diffuse support for the general idea of integration against the y-axis of specific support, Kopecký and Mudde arrived at four ideal-type categories of party positions on Europe, as illustrated in figure 6.

First (all the following from Kopecký and Mudde 2002: 302–3) there is the 'Euroenthusiast' category, which combines Europhilia with EU-optimism. Euroenthusiasts support both the principle of European integration and see in the EU the best vehicle for its institutional realization. Below it, in the bottom left quadrant, are the 'Eurosceptics', who combine Europhilia with EU-pessimism. They are in favour of the general thrust of European integration as a principle but are sceptical about the EU's ability to deliver these ideas in reality. Across in the bottom right corner we find the polar opposite of the Euroenthusiasts – the 'Eurorejects', who combine Europhobia with EU-pessimism. They are neither in favour of the principle of European integration nor of the EU as a set of institutional practices or source of legislative outputs. Finally, there are the 'Europragmatists', parties which oddly blend Europhobia with EU-optimism. Kopecký and Mudde describe their strangest category as follows: 'They do not support the general ideas of integration underpinning the EU and they do not oppose them either; however, they do support the EU' (Kopecký and Mudde 2002: 303). Europragmatic parties 'do not hold a firm ideological opinion on European integration' and take pragmatic decisions on whether or not to express support for the EU, depending on their reading of what is in their party or local constituency interests.

We have now been introduced to the two most popular academic theories of Euroscepticism. On the one hand we have Taggart and Szczerbiak's hard/soft Euroscepticism and on the other hand Kopecký and Mudde's four-fold typology of party positions on European integration. We will now begin to shift the focus from the realm of academia to political practice by way of four comments on the epistemologies of these attempts to capture and model the complex phenomenon of Euroscepticism. This will set the scene for a consideration of the light the models can shed on how Tony Blair and Gordon Brown identified and described the opposition to Europe they sought to challenge in their European discourses after 1997. The first point is that, *as models*, they provide us with quite different vocabularies for grappling with attitudes to European integration. Taggart and Szczerbiak initially wrote in fairly general terms about Euroscepticism and their hard/soft distinction was intended to partition the hardened opponents of European integration from the softer critics of particular EU policies or trajectories. For Kopecký and Mudde a Eurosceptic is someone who appreciates the general idea of integration but who is specifically concerned about the EU manifestation of this vision. The problem with the latter's typology is that it does not map comfortably onto popular usages of the term, and this becomes apparent when they agree with Ronald Tiersky's point that 'all Eurosceptics are Europhile', that is, not opposed to 'realistic advantageous cooperation among various groups of European states for greater peace and prosperity' (the latter quote is from Tiersky, in Kopecký and Mudde 2002: 304). At first glance it seems counterintuitive to equate Europhilia with Euroscepticism when in political and public discourse about Britain's relations with Europe they are so commonly opposed in a binary. Kopecký and Mudde might retort that Eurosceptics are akin to Taggart and Szczerbiak's soft sceptics and their Eurorejects equate to Taggart and Szczerbiak's hard sceptics.

The second point is that the two articles I have covered here led the sets of authors into a dynamic process of discussion, development and methodological refinement. Their exchanges brought out considerable areas of agreement and overlap, but also resulted in a hardening of divisions in certain other regards. For example, Taggart and Szczerbiak have admitted that their 'soft' category was initially too broad, but they have picked up on the disjunction between the

Kopecký and Mudde use of 'Euroscepticism' and its popular usages (Taggart and Szczerbiak 2003: 8). More seriously from a theoretical perspective, they cannot think of any party that would fit into Kopecký and Mudde's 'Europragmatist' category of opposing European integration in principle but supporting a proposed or possible extension of the EU's competencies. Moreover, they further find the 'Euroenthusiast' category too expansive, grouping together strange bedfellows such as the German Christian Democrats and the French Gaullists. The problem as they see it (Taggart and Szczerbiak 20003: 9–10) is that the more fine-grained and in-depth a typology is, the less useful it is as a shorthand or efficient way of categorizing parties, especially when the terms have to travel across a wide range of national borders. There will always be a tension between the political scientist's desire to create a general theory and the simplifying and distorting effect this necessarily has when set against an in-depth reading of the complex texts of the social world.

The third point is methodological and speaks to the diachronic–synchronic versions of the comparative method. As snapshots of party positions at given times these models are good at giving us spatial coverage of snapshot moments in party position. One question might be (if we take changing party positions over time), can the models accommodate dynamic, diachronic comparisons as party positions on Europe alter over periods of years? Take Kopecký and Mudde, for example. Is it possible to map the same party in different boxes depending on what it says in European elections, during local elections and general elections, and would this add anything to our understanding of the believability, or otherwise, of political parties' European discourses? What we are getting at here is the issue of when we can legitimately believe we have found the 'true' or 'accurate' textual or symbolic representation of a party's position. This is more a problem the narrower the terminology we use and the fewer documents we scrutinize to garner information about a party's position on Europe.

The fourth and final point is that these models have been developed to capture party positions. Can they be used to label up the positions of individuals? In this study I am assuming they can – especially when the individuals in question are leaders of their parties and in powerful positions to set agendas and to shape policies and language through their strategic communications. However, the same epistemological problems of knowing when we have found an accurate representation of an individual's 'true' sentiment about the European question will remain. The same individual such as Margaret Thatcher could be positioned in several boxes in the Kopecký and Mudde typology, depending on whether we take her stance out of government prior to 1979 (Euroenthusiast), in government on the SEA (Europragmatic) or after the Bruges speech (Euroreject). The shifting sands of time bring about changes to political cultures and the terms of national debate; these in turn may change leadership perceptions of what is in a party's best interests, prompting those leaders to deliver different messages, sometimes simultaneously, to assorted audiences in the same speech.

III. From theory to practice: language in use

Our approach is, and will continue to be, considered and cautious – one of pro-euro realism. (Brown 2001a)

The two models considered above offer novel ways of identifying and classifying party positions on European integration. It is now useful to pick up the baton Taggart and Szczerbiak have handed us regarding the extent to which academic classifications have resonance in the 'real world' of political manoeuvrings, and we will run with it over two stages. We will first consider the academic validity of these models as a way of appreciating the nuances of Britain's debates about Europe. We will then apply them normatively to the question of their application outside the confines of academia, in the 'real world' of politics and public policy.

The two main criteria for judging the quality of measurements of a concept, in this case Euroscepticism, are validity and reliability. It is validity that concerns us here: 'the degree to which one actually measures whatever concept (or "construct") the measurement procedure purports to measure' (the discussion and quotes in this paragraph are from Pennings *et al.* 2006: 67). Measurements of Euroscepticism therefore need, ideally, to possess all three types of validity: face validity, correlational validity and predictive validity. Face validity holds when measurements are perceived as 'indisputable facts' by the scientific community at large; this is sometimes seen as occurring when the measurement results accord with 'common-sense expectations, regardless of the precise definitions of the concept'. For example, if you set out to measure speed in kilometres but end up measuring revolutions per minute it should be pretty obvious that your study will fall short of even a simple test: on the face of it, does it look right? Correlational validity is obtained as the tools used for measurement get more and more precise. The example from Pennings *et al.* is that an electron microscope should be able to reproduce the measurements shown up by a lens microscope more accurately, but more importantly the new results should correlate with the old ones. Predictive validity obtains when the measurements help us make 'correct predictions about real-world phenomena'. It is 'probably the most important hallmark of validity, since it relates the usefulness of the obtained measurements to the context of prevailing theories'. In the case of Euroscepticism, predictive validity would be achieved when measurements of the attention given to 'pro' and 'anti' statements about Europe in party manifestoes correspond with the level of attention given to each strain of opinion by the party leadership in speeches, party political broadcasts and in campaign leafleting.

The two models we have explored in this chapter possess all three types of validity, rendering them internally valid *as theories* because their measurements hold for the cases under the microscope (for more on validity see Langdridge 2004: 34–7; Graziano and Raulin 2007: 181–5). In comparative research the question is, does the model 'travel' well to include other cases? I would argue that, given the robust methods and underlying data-gathering techniques that are the hallmark of both models, they can easily be transposed onto other member states not included in the original studies and still remain internally valid. However, if we turn it around and ask if the models have validity from the point of view of public policy-makers such as Tony Blair and Gordon Brown, who routinely deployed labels such as 'Eurosceptic' and 'anti-European' in their discourses on Europe, the picture is rather more mixed. Let us take a look at some of the techniques New Labour employed to bound its approach by constructing the identity and attitudes of the Eurosceptics, and then see how we might map these back onto the academic models discussed above. Blair used the terms 'Eurosceptic' and 'Euroscepticism' loosely to contrast with his own position, clearly spelled out in his June 2005 speech to the European Parliament: 'I am a passionate pro-European. I always have been' (Blair 2005b). The Prime Minister could be vague about whom he saw as sceptics and about the conceptualization of his key terms, but he knew 'Euroscepticism' was not a stance he wanted to take when, for instance, in 2006 he talked dismissively of it as 'foolish' and 'the surest route to the destruction of our true national interest' (Blair 2006h). This was Blair about to hand over to Gordon Brown and he did not need to spell out what he meant by Euroscepticism because he had established it in earlier speeches. Blair was more studied in his early years in power, when he was seeking to construct and then challenge his opponents on the Europe question – he left it to Brown to denounce the sceptics as 'extremists' (Brown 1997a) who put about 'myths often sustained only by prejudice and dogma', as opposed to the New Labour government, which operated only on 'fact and evidence' (Brown 1999h). Blair's earliest effort to clarify the terminology came in his foreign affairs speech in December 1998, when he identified two forms of

Euroscepticism – he would cleave to this distinction throughout his time in office. He had least sympathy for the first form ('unintelligent scepticism'), which 'looks at anything that happens in Europe as an excuse to be anti-European. It was a minority sport in the last Government. It is where, sadly, the majority in today's Conservative Party seems to be' (Blair 1998f). Eight years later he described this form of scepticism as 'plain old anti-Europe, probably anti-foreigner. They just detest the whole business', and he pinpointed the view of a UKIP Member of the European Parliament to illustrate those he identified with this position (Blair 2006a). Brown took to denouncing 'those anti-Europeans who continually pose Britain against Europe' (Brown 2000b) and in 2003 trod a Third Way for the government between 'unacceptable federal assumptions rooted in the past and anti-European prejudices of the present' (Brown 2003g).

Blair's second variant was 'intelligent scepticism', which 'realises Europe is of vital importance to Britain, but is anxious about the direction Europe is taking' (Blair 1998f). These people, he said, are 'ideological sceptics', opposed to the principle of supranational integration. 'Their objections are intellectually pure, albeit practically outdated. They reject sharing sovereignty, accepting common rules, majority voting and so forth. The more honest among them admit that this means rejecting EU membership itself' (Blair 2006a). There is a partisan dimension to that form of scepticism because: 'It fears, if I am again being frank, that because centre and centre left governments are now in the ascendancy in Europe, there will be a return of old Labour' (Blair 1998f). At the French National Assembly earlier in 1998 the Prime Minister reflected on a wider 'concern amongst our peoples as to how they make sense [of] and relate to the new Europe' (Blair 1998d). The British, he said, worry about the loss of national identity, find 'Brussels and the European institutions often remote and unsympathetic' and cannot see on a daily basis 'what Europe does for them'. It is interesting here that Blair used the language of the Eurosceptic ('Brussels' to denote the European Commission for example) to show sympathy for the sceptic cause at the same time as he sought to assuage sceptic concerns and assert his credentials as an 'intelligent' student of European politics in the rest of the speech. The same technique resurfaced in his 'Clear course for Europe' speech in Cardiff in November 2002, when he said:

> We fear that the driving ideology behind European integration is a move to a European superstate, in which power is sucked into an unaccountable centre. And what is more a centre of fudge and muddle, bureaucratic meddling, which in economic terms could impede efficiency and in security terms may move us away from the transatlantic alliance. (Blair 2002d)

This was reworked in his Lord Mayor's Banquet speech a year later as 'Europe has too much bureaucracy, is too little focussed on the economic and social concerns of its citizens, too distant' (Blair 2003g). Occasionally Blair used the descriptor 'anti-Europeanism' to mark an approach to British pride and patriotism he saw as 'an out of date delusion' (Blair 2003c). More often than not, however, he used 'sceptic' as shorthand for a person or party who wants to 'bring European integration to a halt' (Blair 2003g).

Pinpointing Blair's position in the debate proved somewhat difficult in the research undertaken for this book, because he was better at identifying what he stood *against* than what he stood *for*, especially during his first term in office. Using the above data we can see that he mapped the terrain of British scepticism in December 1998 by taking what we might deem a detached, 'academic' approach. He removed himself from the hurly-burly of the debates on the ground and objectified the two variants as a dispassionate observer. From the point of view of the theoretical work considered earlier, Blair effectively preceded Taggart and Szczerbiak. His first variant (the general 'anti-European' approach) would translate into their 'hard' scepticism, while his second variant (critique founded on specific EU-related concerns) would translate into their 'soft' scepticism. However, more is going on in the 1998 piece than initially surfaces. Blair not only identified the two variants, he identified *with* the second one – the 'intelligent' critique of the EU, as did Brown, who had argued the previous year that Britain's decisions over Europe needed to be taken 'on the basis of intelligent, well-informed debate' (Brown 1997a). New Labour clearly positioned itself both on the intellectual high ground and on the rational side of the debate, as we can see in the Prime Minister's aside on hard scepticism – 'for which I have no time' (Blair 1998f). His normative approach was to crystallize attitudes on Europe into two camps: a 'rational/me/right' one and an 'irrational/not-me/wrong' one. As we can see, in his later speeches Blair spent no little time elaborating his justification for taking what could be seen as a 'soft' sceptic position, both by identifying with the sceptical agenda and by deploying Eurosceptical language to generate empathy for his dilemma from his British audiences. For example, in February 2006 he talked of a strain of scepticism that could not easily be dismissed (presumably because it came from him):

> ... practical scepticism. This is a genuine, intellectual and political concern about Europe as practised not about Europe an ideal or a vision or even a set of values. This is not xenophobia, nor devotion to undiluted national sovereignty, but a worry about Europe's economy being uncompetitive; its institutions too remote; its decision-making too influenced by the lowest common denominator. (Blair 2006a)

None of this is to suggest that Blair was, or would label himself, a soft sceptic, even when he showed himself vexed 'with what can be a maddening process in Europe' (Blair 2006g). It was a tactical ploy to create a relationship with his audience so they could then be led to see the rectitude of his stance on Europe by understanding more about where he was coming from. He would normally follow his criticisms of the EU with a 'but' or an argument for a more posi- tive British policy, the implication being: I understand your concerns but I do not necessarily believe in the same solutions to our shared problems as you do. For example, he told the CBI in November 2006: 'Now, I know there will be many sceptics here about the European Commission and its propensity to regulate. The only thing I would say is this ... we've got a better chance than we've had for some time of making a difference in this area' (Blair 2006g). The main reasons Blair would never go the whole way to identifying with the sceptics were first the obvious one that he did not see himself as a sceptic and second that it was a party political issue. He led a government committed in its manifesto to improving Britain's relations with the EU and wanted to delegitimize Eurosceptical arguments by associating them with the 'hard' sceptics of the Conservative right. As he saw it, the Conservatives were to blame for marginalizing the British in Europe through their trenchant opposition to treaty reform in the 1990s and their principled opposition to any and every directive emanating from their bogey men in 'Brussels'. That Blair felt able politically and personally able to identify with some of the elements of the 'soft' sceptical position meant that, according to the logic running through his speeches from 1997 to 2007, he probably did not see principled opposition to the EU as widespread enough either in Parliament or in the country at large to warrant it being set up as his enemy for the purposes of his speeches on Britain and Europe. We can therefore attempt to position Blair in the Kopecký and Mudde typology (2002) according to how he constructed his position on Europe, using the following logic.

Figure 7 reproduces Kopecký and Muddes' typology, this time with the addition of some specific subject positions. Blair is located in the top left quadrant, a self-declared Euroenthusiast who believed in the ideal of European integration and in the form that process was taking in the EU. The arrow down into the bottom left Euro- sceptic quadrant indicates that Blair could empathize with those he called the 'intelligent' or 'soft' sceptics, who support the principle of integration but who worry about some of the specific policies and practices of the EU in its current and possible future form. Blair also used language, imagery and political rhetoric which chimes with Kopecký and Mudde's Eurorejects, who oppose the general idea of

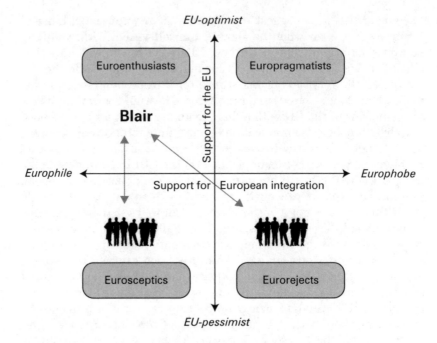

Figure 7. Blair in the Kopecký and Mudde typology.

integration and who, it follows, do not support the EU either as it is in the present or as how it might develop in the future. However, note that the arrows are two way. While Blair could temporarily talk himself into being a sceptic or a reject, he was using that to help fix his identity as an integration enthusiast.

It is unnecessary to try to divine from its discourses the 'truth' about New Labour's 'real' attitude towards the EU and British European policy. What I have tried to do here is more modest, in that I have used Blair's efforts to define Euroscepticism to help us see how he went about constructing New Labour's 'We' position on Europe and how that framed, and worked off of, the discursive construction of its Other political opponents. One thing we can be certain about is that, when critiquing the 'sceptics', Blair and Brown were projecting onto them negative qualities and character traits that contrasted – sometime tacitly, sometimes openly – with their vision of a Britain leading from the front in Europe. We can see this in Brown's tortuous attempts to set up the government's second-term 'pro-euro realist' policy after the 2001 general election:

Pro-euro because ... we believe that, in principle – membership of
the euro can bring benefits to Britain. Realist because to short-cut or
fudge the assessment, and to join in the wrong way or on the wrong
basis without rigorously ensuring the tests are met, would not be in
the national economic interest. (Brown 2001a; see also Brown 2001b;
Brown 2001c; Brown 2002b)

What Brown seems to have been trying to convey was that New
Labour's approach to the euro was built in his own image: economically rational, interest-based, cool, calculating and above all
grounded in an expert appreciation of the reality of the situation
Britain found itself in. Having said that, Brown sporadically felt
compelled, most likely under pressure from Number 10, to call
himself a 'pro-European' (Brown 2002c; Brown 2003g). However, on
the first occasion it was ambiguously phrased as 'for a pro-European
like me' (emphasis added) and on the latter occasion it was couched
in terms of being pro-European as long as radical reforms of the
organization were put in place or, as he put it to the CBI in November
2004, the EU moved 'from being a Trade Bloc Europe to being a
Global Europe' (Brown 2004h). A year on, the focus on what he saw
as narrow regional concerns within the EU had become a secondary
reason for Brown declaring his pro-Europeanism – it was now about
'pro-economic reform' and 'pro-Global Europe policies' (Brown
2005e). By 2006 Brown was defining his position in even more convoluted terms as 'pro-Britain, pro-business and pro-European single
market' (Brown 2006b).

It seems New Labour's leaders were always more comfortable
elucidating what they did *not* stand for on Europe than what they
did, an observation made of New Labour discourses more generally
(see Marquand 1999: 233). For example, in 2005 Blair held that
sceptical 'nations' wanted to 'huddle together' to 'avoid globalisation' and 'shrink away from confronting the changes' around them
and wanting to 'take refuge' in easy solutions to present problems.
In the process they 'risk failure ... on a grand, strategic scale' (Blair
2005b). We are left to infer what that meant in terms of positive
policy prescriptions. The upshot was something of a yes/no policy
on the single currency which Brown outlined at the Transport
and General Workers' Union conference in March 2002: 'in principle in favour of the euro; in practice the five tests have to be met'
(Brown 2002a). Other members of the New Labour governments
encountered similar problems in defining their attitudes to 'Europe'.
For example, former Cabinet minister David Blunkett called his
approach to Europe 'positive scepticism' (Blunkett 2006: 25–6).
What this meant was far from clear and it does raise the question,
assuming Blunkett's approach was cooler than Brown's and Blair's,

how *much* cooler and what did this mean in practical policy terms in Cabinet discussions (if there were any)? Did the government ever discuss the semantics? For New Labour, the semantics did not appear to matter. Blair and Brown were more concerned to establish their intellectual credibility to make the right decisions for the good of the long-term British national interest. They were quick to objectify their sceptical opponents as pie-in-the-sky dreamers who put anti-European prejudice ahead of cool, calm, rational calculation of the benefits to Britain that accrued from being 'in' Europe. Prime Minister and Chancellor would side with the sceptics for tactical reasons but always couch such limits as they placed on their ambitions for the British in Europe in the context of the broader 'renewal' mission they had embarked on. Thus, at Mansion House in 2001 Brown spoke simultaneously of the government's commitment to building an EU in which 'independent nation states work together to shape the decisions', not a 'one size fits all' Europe, but also of the 'great cause' that Europe represents in terms of peace, prosperity and security. The renewal aspect would come through Britain leading a major process of 'economic and institutional reform', which would be better for Europe but more crucially for Britain (Brown 2001a).

Summary

Given New Labour's penchant for setting up linguistic dualisms, the Taggart–Szczerbiak hard/soft dichotomy was always likely to appeal to the government more than a nuanced approach, such as Kopecký and Mudde's typology. The latter maps attitudes to Europe across two dimensions, taking in both positive and negative attitudes to integration. This results in a finer-grained model with more shades of grey than the black and white binary approach. However, what it gains in detail it loses in the capacity to travel to the 'real' world of policy because there are now four different labels to account for. Kopecký and Mudde's 'sceptics' are Europhiles in a general sense but disdainful of the EU, equating to Taggart and Szczerbiak's 'soft' sceptics. From the evidence derived from the discourse data in Blair and Brown's speeches, they saw a sceptic as someone in the 'Euroreject' category, critical both of the general principle of integration and of the specific practice of integration in the EU. For rhetorical purposes, Blair occasionally showed sympathy with 'soft' and 'hard' sceptics but did so only to help them understand his own position.

I am assuming, for the purposes of this book, that the 'scepticism' Blair and Brown addressed in their speeches, rightly or wrongly, was of Taggart and Szczerbiak's 'hard' type and Kopecký and

Mudde's 'Euroreject' type. The government specifically targeted its European campaign *not* at supporters of the integration ideal who were critical of some aspects of the work of the EU, but at those who did not accept either premise and who consistently showed themselves in Eurobarometer and domestic opinion polling to be doubtful of the idea that Britain was a 'European' country in the first place – 'Europe as Other' thinking. Brown spelt out the official New Labour definition of Euroscepticism in 1999 by arguing that anti-Europeans had drawn incorrect conclusions from Britain's wartime experiences. What the past showed him and Blair was rather the converse, that 'Britain did not and would not relinquish our role in Europe or abdicate responsibility for the progress of the continent. Europe, by virtue of history as well as geography, is where we are' (Brown 1999b). In 2003 this was shortened to: 'At no point in our long history has Britain ever been prepared to relinquish our responsibility and interest in Europe's future' (Brown 2003e). It was the construction of Europe as a pernicious Other (and thereby 'evil'), outlined in chapter 5, that New Labour was attacking, not the nuanced sceptics who were generally supportive of the principle of integration yet sometimes critical of the EU. This would make sense for Prime Ministers Blair and Brown, who saw that to alter attitudes to the EU they needed to change attitudes to 'Europe', such is the discursive slippage between the two, both in a technical and in an everyday sense. In the next chapter we look more closely at how memories of the past featured in these ostensibly progressivist New Labour discourses.

Chapter 7

Context IV. New Labour, old history

Yes the past happened, but it's over. Isn't it? (Anderson *et al.* 2007)

These words from the film *The Darjeeling Limited* could easily have been in the back of Tony Blair or Gordon Brown's mind at any time during one of their speeches or press conferences designed to win over the British public to the idea of their nation being not a 'stranger in Europe' (Wall 2008) but a constructive and engaged participant in the integration process. At the European Parliament in 2005, for example, Blair passionately defended the principle of British membership of the EU against Nigel Farage, then leader of UKIP, who had depicted the budget settlement of that year in zero-sum terms: a loss for Britain and a gain for rival EU member states such as France. Blair accused UKIP of living in the past, wrapping itself in the Union Jack more as a shield against the outside world than as a display of patriotism. 'You sit there with our country's flag – but you do not represent our country's interests', Blair said. 'This is the year 2005, not 1945. We are not fighting each other any more' (quoted in Watt 2005). Coming at the end of the second time Britain held the Presidency of the EU under Blair's premiership (July to December 2005; the first was January to June 1998), Blair was applauded in Europhile quarters for finally standing up to the Eurosceptics. Unfortunately, as the *Independent* pointed out the next day, Blair found it easier to show this level of commitment to the European ideal when he was talking to a broadly sympathetic EU audience in Brussels than when he was faced with a hostile British media pack. Back in Downing Street at his end of year press conference the Prime Minister was reluctant even to mention the EU, let alone the details of the budget agreement that had sparked his combative outburst just hours earlier. The paper's leader opined that 'Britain's EU presidency over, it seems, the dangerous subject of Europe can be consigned to the back burner, where this avowedly pro-European government prefers to keep it. What a difference the audience makes' (*Independent* 2005).

Here we see why the words from *The Darjeeling Limited* script say more about New Labour's European discourse than either Blair or Brown might have wanted to admit – it ends full of doubt. New Labour's audiences were routinely emolliated with statements of intent like 'the past happened, but it's over – let's move on' and yet the same speeches would be packed with diplomatic references to the nation's great history, the Second World War, Churchillian flourishes on the pivotal role Britain could play in global affairs and the like. There is no better example of how New Labour saw itself as heir to Churchill's globalist pretensions for Britain than in the second line of Gordon Brown's speech to the Commonwealth Finance Ministers' meeting in Ottawa in September 1998. There, he played on Churchill's famous wartime line 'Never has so much been owed by so many to so few' (see Churchill Centre undated) by stating: 'Never in all of economic history have so many depended so much on genuine economic cooperation among all the nations of the world' (Brown 1998d). Summoning the memory of Churchill would have created *pathos* for Brown among members of that particular audience and located New Labour at the pinnacle of international efforts to restructure the international political economy for the twenty-first century, or what he called in the title of the speech 'the new global age'. The Chancellor reworded it slightly for an equally appreciative American audience a week later (Brown 1998e). Another of Churchill's famous sayings – that 'those who build the present only in the image of the past will miss out entirely on the challenges of the future' – Brown repeated so frequently it could have been a New Labour motto (see Brown 1999e; Brown 2000b; Brown 2001b; Brown 2002d; Brown 2003e; Brown 2005b; Brown 2008a; Brown 2008b). 'The Churchill syndrome', Richard Toye has found, features heavily in post-war Anglo-American exchanges across all sorts of texts, not always for cynically manipulative purposes (Toye 2008). The manner in which Brown summoned the memory of 'the archetype of idealised leadership' (Toye 2008: 369) inevitably suggests he felt Churchill had something to offer his attempts to shape his personal reputation – and potentially his push for the premiership – as well as enhancing New Labour's credibility to be at the heart of the process of global economic reform.

Of greater significance for this study, however, is that Blair and Brown's veneration of Churchill symbolizes New Labour's infatuation with memories of the past even as the government endeavoured to instigate a 'new' approach to foreign and economic policy. Outwardly wanting to modernize attitudes by getting over Britain's obsession with the past, inwardly Blair and Brown seem constantly to have been asking themselves: 'The past *is* over isn't it?' This chapter elaborates this point by considering two key facets of the New Labour project:

its take on the Labour Party's past and the lengths to which it went to win the support of key segments of the British press. It advances the argument that the architects of New Labour represented, literally *re-presented*, the image of the Labour Party by repackaging core elements of the party's and the country's recent past. A huge part of this re-representation involved currying favour with a media establishment that had been broadly hostile to Labour in the 1980s and early 1990s. Blair and his team worked assiduously to persuade media magnates such as Rupert Murdoch that 'New' Labour was not (like) 'Old' Labour. The problem the government encountered was that many of the same elements of the media it needed to woo to achieve success at national elections were the most sceptical about British membership of the single currency and cool on the 'Europe' idea in general.

I. New Labour on history

[T]he past is central to the modernising project. The past needs to be turned into history, the thinking being that only by boxing it up neatly can its deadening, its unifying, effect be neutralised....

History, then, may be no less illusory, no less useful, than the past. New Labour needs Old Labour. A new, improved version must have an old, unimproved one from which to distinguish itself. (Bale 1999: 199)

That New Labour was a product of both the Labour's internal party past and the national past almost goes without saying. Every individual, family, institution, organization, political party, community, region, nation comes from *somewhere*, so the more interesting question is how we define these traditions, how we relate to them, and how we identify ourselves and act towards others accordingly. It is here that the past-as-history dichotomy comes into play. In this view there is the past on the one hand and there are histories of that past on the other. In defining our identity, in understanding who we are and in bringing into being some kind of theory of social action and interaction (a theory about what the world is and how all of its component parts mesh together) it is our perceptions of the past that matter, not the events of the past themselves. These perceptions are shaped by a combination of written, oral and visual histories, which provide the theoretical contexts for action because they shape who we think we are and who we think other peoples are. Writers such as Tim Bale are interested in the uses to which the past was put in the Labour Party's effort to write itself into the history books as a coherent entity and a political project. The principal tactic New Labour architects brought to bear, as Bale notes, was to contrast New Labour with Old Labour. In this process of setting up binaries around 'new' and 'old' we see history being used in the service of the present, as new renderings of a tormented past came to frame the New Labour project as radical and full of promise. New Labour was thus constructed against an idealized and much maligned Old Labour, a party that had become unelectable by virtue of 'Image, ideology and constitution' (Jenkins 2007: 206). 'Erroneous' and 'casual' this repackaging may have been, but it 'did not prevent the revised name gaining wide currency' (Wring 2005: 137). The juxtaposition of 'New' against 'Old' came to be interwoven with other techniques of turning the past into history, many of which conveniently carved up historical time for New Labour's interlocutors. Bale wryly talks of the New Labour supposition that there was a period 'BG': 'Before Globalisation' (Bale 1999: 200). New Labour spoke of globalization unquestioningly as 'an objective social process that requires states to adopt certain reforms' (Bevir 2005: 128), in the process constructing itself as modern, fashionable, innovative and forward leaning, in contrast to both Old Labour and the Conservative Party, which spoke only to the dusty relics of the past. 'In the first instance it was about being modern', recalled David Hill, one of those 'present at the creation' of New Labour in 1991. 'This required a change to the way in which everything the Labour Party did was presented. It required thought about language. It required thought about vehicles' through which process and content could work symbiotically to present the party as fitting 'modern' British ideals at the turn of the twenty-first century (interview with Hill). This section explores some of the influences upon the thinking of New Labour's architect-historians. It centres first on Blair himself and his attitude to 'tradition' and second on the construction of New Labour as a transcendence of the ills that had bedevilled the Old party. By the end of the section we will have identified the paradoxical part history played in constructing the New Labour 'myth' (Marquand 1999: 226) and how it was designed to 'ditch traditional images of Labour' (Routledge 1998: 154).

It may be stretching things to explain New Labour's approach to history as a by-product of Blair's idiosyncrasies or personality. However, there is certainly a point worth making that, as leader from 1994, Blair led a party that appears, certainly as far as his close political and advisory appointees went, to have been highly suspicious of certain British traditions and establishment ways of thinking and making decisions. Before coming to power he made a play of his 'anti-establishment' credentials with comments such as 'If you think I'm not a radical, you're wrong' (quoted in Mandelson 2002: 58). Such reformist zeal helped New Labour to the view that a modernizing agenda would have to go hand in hand with a wholesale rethink of the meaning of the British past: socially and culturally as well as ideologically and politically. Geoffrey Wheatcroft suggests that in taking on and critiquing establishment Britain Blair was playing up to Rupert Murdoch, the media baron Blair believed held the key to helping New Labour into government with a sufficiently large majority to implement its reformist vision for Britain. 'Murdoch shows that it is possible to combine an intense love of the capitalist system with antipodean contempt for custom, both of which Blair shares: he is a true spiritual Australian. In Ensor's phrase, Blair is ignorant of history and indifferent to English political tradition' (Wheatcroft 2005: 271). Overlooking the national stereotyping in this quote (are *all* Australians contemptuous of custom?) Wheatcroft draws our attention to two aspects of Blair's personality and political outlook that require analysis: his indifference to custom or tradition and the sources of his historical knowledge.

The anti-establishment point is crucial because, in psychological terms, it surely made it easier for Blair and his team to think about overthrowing established ways of 'doing' politics in Britain if they saw themselves neither as products of that system nor as wedded to aspects of it. Insider accounts and biographies of Blair make many a reference to his critique of 'establishment' Britain, his fondness for can-do entrepreneurs and 'guys' in the military over 'amateur' politicians, 'bureaucratic and soft' civil servants and the 'hidebound' public sector (Rawnsley 2001: 90, 298–9; Kampfner 2004: 22, 92, 235). We can combine these insights into Blair the person with those we have already seen in this book about the centralization of foreign policy (and other) decision-making under Blair, to paint a credible picture of someone who, if not an outsider, certainly felt at home in Downing Street only insofar as he was surrounded by his own people and could do things his own way. If this meant ignoring, by-passing or working around the civil service, Cabinet colleagues and ambassadors abroad, then Blair was comfortable if the ends justified the means. It is pushing things to argue that Blair mimicked Murdoch just to get him onside because this does not seem to have been all an act. Blair, it seems, wanted to transpose onto his working methods in government those he had honed in opposition to get things achieved efficiently and quickly. Part of the explanation for Blair's approach to establishment Britain might reside in his relationship with history more generally. This is a somewhat convoluted argument because it assumes that the more we know about history the more we respect it. The logic of the argument is that 'Blair the historian' would have been more appreciative of tradition and the conventional ways of 'doing' politics in Britain than 'Blair the non-historian'. Simon Jenkins touches on this point when he writes that Blair's ignorance of history could be a spur to radicalism; yet it was also dangerous 'when the going becomes tough and a sense of the past might shine light on the future' (Jenkins 2007: 9). Many commentators, not only Blair critics, note that the Prime Minister 'was not interested in venerating Labour or Britain's history' (Boulton 2008: 15). Nor did he profess much of a passion for history in the mould of a Churchill, Macmillan or even a Gordon Brown, and this gets linked to his wider approach to the British establishment.

Roy Jenkins described Blair's approach to history as follows: 'He is interested in history rather than particularly knowledgeable about it. Suddenly he will seize on something in history, but his knowledge is vague' (quoted in Seldon 2005: 34). Jenkins is in a good position to judge because he was used by Blair as an unofficial 'history tutor' (Naughtie 2002: 74) to get him up to speed on key issues in Britain's recent past, notably the history of the Labour Party, progressive politics in Britain, and post-war foreign policy centring on relations with the EEC and EU. Jenkins was a vocal exponent of the 'missed opportunities' school of thinking about British European policy of Hugo Young *et al.* According to this interpretation the British had suffered economically, politically and strategically by not playing a greater role in Europe's various schemes for integration after 1945. Remaining aloof from the ECSC, the European Defence Community and then the EEC itself were, in this story, just the first stages in the unfolding of a frosty relationship that had taken the British to the unhappy position they found themselves in with regard to the EU by the time Blair came to power (an interpretation studied further in Daddow 2004a). Jenkins, himself a former President of the European Commission, chastised policy-makers from both leading parties in Britain for failing to take the country 'wholeheartedly into Europe' (Jenkins 1990: 8) and he was held in high regard by Europeanists on the continent (see for example Prodi 2002). Putting together an interest in, but no great knowledge of, contemporary global history and being taught by a history tutor steeped in the 'missed oppor-tunities' interpretation of British European policy, we can see how Blair would have been getting authoritative support for his view that New Labour's modernization strategy needed to create a progressive consensus around a positive approach to Europe.

Having dealt with Blair's views on establishment Britain as a function of his approach to history more generally, we have seen great impetus from within his own belief system behind the idea that things in Britain needed changing if the country were to adapt to life 'AG', or 'After Globalization', to play on Bale's terminology. In this view Blair was ably supported by the team he put together around him. No great fan of Blair or New Labour, Peter Oborne surmised that 'New Labour is hostile to tradition, class, existing institutions, history. This hostility is based on three things: ignorance, hope and, ironically enough, New Labour's own tormented past' (Oborne 1999: 158). 'Hostility' may be too strong a word but Oborne's point is well made because he draws our attention to the uneasy connection the 'New' Labour project had with the 'Old' party. Some of this unease came from the multifarious ways in which 'Old' Labour had picked up negative associations in the minds of the electorate in Britain. Old Labour, in this rendering of the party's history, was the party led by Michael Foot, which, in electoral terms, consistently let down its voters in the 1980s and again in 1992 under Neil Kinnock, when it appealed to narrow sectional interests, notably the trade unions, at the expense of the wider populace. As Mandelson put it, 'New Labour was shaped by the experiences of the 1980s and 1992 election' (Mandelson 2002: xxvii; see also xlviii–xlix). From the later 1980s Kinnock had begun to address the image and policies of the party via a thoroughgoing review, in which Europe featured as a central motor of change (well covered in Daniels 1998: 76–8). Blair and New Labour took it as axiomatic that the Labour Party was perceived as 'soft' on defence and law and order and as chauvinistically anti-European. The architects of New Labour believed all these characteristics would have to be overthrown to give it mass appeal and make the party electable, and there 'were times when it seemed there was nothing in Labour's past from which New Labour did not want to dissociate itself' (Gamble 2003: 192).

In a book first published prior to the 1997 election, and which served as a beefed up election manifesto, Mandelson set out the seven-fold distinction between New and Old Labour (see table 3). Even though it was largely economically focused one can see the political implications that flowed from them (all the quotes below are from Mandelson 2002: 21–8 – the 'revisited' edition of the book – unless otherwise stated). First, 'New Labour firmly rejects the notion that centralised planning and state control are the route

Table 3. New versus Old Labour

Old Labour	New Labour
1. Preferred mixed economy	1. Prefers capitalist market economy
2. Was hostile to big business	2. Encourages the pursuit of profit
3. Favoured nationalization	3. Favours privatization
4. Was dominated by trade unions	4. Will reduce trade union influence
5. Defined equality too narrowly	5. Will judge equality more subtly
6. Put too much emphasis on the state	6. Will redefine notions of community
7. Was dangerously anti-European	7. Will be pro-European

to economic success'. This highlighted New Labour's commitment to creating a dynamic market economy as opposed to Old Labour's commitment to a mixed state–private economy. Second, succeeding in a dynamic economy involved recognizing that 'substantial personal incentives and rewards are necessary in order to encourage risk-taking and entrepreneurialism. Profit is not a dirty word'. This sent out a signal that New Labour would be as friendly to big business and private enterprise as the Conservative Party was perceived to be. Third, some market regulation is important and effective but 'New Labour does not regard public ownership of industry as necessary in order to manage the economy'. This was a restatement of the stance that had led to the removal of Clause 4 (on nationalization) from the party's constitution (White 1994). Fourth, 'New Labour has shed 1970s ideas of "corporatist government" taking decisions with pressure groups and in alliance with certain vested interests, over the heads of the public as a whole – a process more akin to bargaining than to governing'. Mandelson argued against trade unions exerting such a strong influence over the policy, direction and ideology of the Labour Party. Fifth, public expenditure would be 'economically and socially productive' under a New Labour government, rather than being set at a proportion of GDP whatever the economic and social conditions of the day. Equality in this view is more about equality of opportunity rather than equality of financial inputs alone; in other words, more public expenditure does not always lead to improvements in the quality or quantity of public services. Sixth, 'New Labour emphatically does not seek to provide centralized, "statist" solutions to every social and economic problem. Rather it aims to enable people to work together to achieve things for themselves and their fellow citizens.' This implied a new definition of 'community', around the ideas of rights and responsibilities, and had implications for economic management and public expenditure, in terms of both the size of the outlay from central government and the expectations on or duties of citizens receiving state payments.

Finally, Old Labour back as far as Hugh Gaitskell in the 1960s had an 'instinctive dislike of what was felt to be a continental cartel of capitalist-oriented Christian Democrats'. In adopting at home the fundamental economic reforms set out in the previous six points New Labour would be able to adopt a more positive approach to Europe because the British would be both structurally and ideationally more in line with EU policies and practices. Even though Europe featured last in the Mandelson rendition of the changes New Labour had made to party policy, it is clear that the party's Europeanization preceded rather than followed many of the changes it made to its economic orientation. According to this line of thinking Europe was both a tool for modernizing the Labour Party's image and was integral to the Labour Party's strategy on how best 'to pursue many of its policy objectives, particularly in the economic sphere', from the Kinnock years on (Daniels 1998: 92).

The construction of a divide between 'new' and 'old' was of substantive and symbolic importance for the Labour Party under Tony Blair and we can date its 'conversion to a pro-European policy' back to the perception that anti-Europeanism was one of Old Labour's most damaging failings (Bulmer 2008: 598–9). 'I tell you honestly that [the] Labour Party of the 1980s was wrong and irresponsible to become, contrary to its history, an anti European party and to ignore the central importance of our European connection to our prosperity and employment' (Brown 1999h). In substantive terms, real and lasting alterations to the party's constitution, its approach to economic management, its intended relations with big business and entrepreneurs and a renewal of the party's commitment to 'community' spoke volumes about what New Labour people had in mind when they talked about creating a 'modern' Britain for the modern world. 'Europe', we can infer from the Mandelson manifesto examined above, played a decisive part in this story of party re-invention and national renewal because of the Labour Party's and the country's historically difficult relationship with the EEC and EU. The balancing act Blair and his team had to pull off was to tell this story of modernization and renewal without simultaneously trashing the very history and traditions that the British people held dear. This comes through quite clearly in the memoirs of Peter Hyman, Blair's adviser and speech-writer who ran the SCU in Downing Street. He has described the tension between the need for a future-looking vision and respect for the past when he notes that 'most of us want to blend the old with the new. We want to celebrate our great history and traditions whilst carving out a new role for the country. In other words *old Britain was not nearly as unpopular as Old Labour*' (Hyman 2005: 59, emphasis added). Here we see where many of the problems for New Labour lay. The party had to encourage voters to forget Old Labour and 'old' Britain while, paradoxically, being able to lay claim, discursively, to the guardianship of the nation's heritage and the promotion of the 'great' aspects of Great Britain in the wider world. In New Labour's hands Europe featured as something of a paradox because 'Europe was the great national question that could not be allowed to become the great national question' (Naughtie 2002: 130). Having opened up this problem area, the next section will first detail how New Labour attempted to address it, principally through a rapprochement with key organs of the press, and will then analyse the textual strategies the government developed to lay claim to the past while promising future national greatness. It will be argued that even before coming to power New Labour was finding it hard to marry the idea of a more wholehearted engagement in Europe with the idea that the party respected Britain's national history and traditions. As we have seen, it was widely perceived that the former logically entailed the denial of the latter and New Labour was no more able than any of its predecessors to change that perception.

II. Making friends in the media

We did not then have that solid block of the Black, Murdoch and Rothermere presses going full steam all the time, with which many of my successors have had to contend. (David Hannay, Ambassador and Permanent Representative to the European Communities, 1985–90; Hannay 2004: 21)

[E]verything has to be fed through their anti-Europe frame of mind. (Hugo Young, describing Alastair Campbell's take on the British press during a telephone conversation, March 1999; Young 2008: 594)

New Labour's campaign to win over the elements of the British press that were avowedly anti-Labour and/or pro-Conservative before and after the 1997 election is well documented by government insiders (Price 2005: 100–1) and outside commentators alike (for example Wheatcroft 2005: 214–15; Seldon 2005: 250–4). Robin Cook went so far as to call it an 'obsession' (Cook 2003: 23) and Clare Short talks of a 'media-dominated system of decision-making' (Short 2005: 50). Oborne describes New Labour as the 'first ever Media Class opposition. In due course it became established as the first ever Media Class government with Tony Blair installed in No. 10 Downing Street as the first ever Media Class Prime Minister' (Oborne 1999: 112). Seldon argues that back as far as the 1987 general election Blair, Brown and Mandelson were all 'agreed that the party had to distance itself from the trade unions, warm up relations with business and the right-of-centre press, and appeal beyond Labour's traditional heartlands'. The following election, 1992, reinforced in Brown's mind in particular the idea that Labour needed to shed the image of being a 'tax-and-spend' party (Seldon 2005: 659, 661). In the previous section we concentrated on the construction of New Labour as antithetical to an outdated Old Labour. In this section we will survey the well documented efforts by New Labour's architects to court the right-of-centre press and showcase an example of the way in which closer relations with the press would impinge directly on New Labour's discursive management of the Europe question when in power.

Labour's strategy centred on convincing hostile press barons and political editors that the party had changed and now had mass electoral appeal. It resulted in such a turnaround in favour of New Labour that during the 1997 general election, Oborne has estimated, 70% of the newspaper market supported Blair and his party, a complete reversal of the 1992 situation. Significantly, the widely read *Sun* had come on board (Oborne 1999: 145). It was one of two newspapers that New Labour targeted in its offensive, the other being *The Times*. Both are part of Rupert Murdoch's sprawling News Corporation (or News Corps), which also owns the *Sunday Times*, the *News of the World* and Sky television. The *Daily Mail* and the *Daily Telegraph* both featured prominently but were not, it seems, quite as highly prized (Price 2005: 13; Short 2005: 25, 30, 36, 49, 102–3, 272, 279), the *Sun* being described by Kampfner as 'Downing Street's favourite organ' (Kampfner 2004: 288). According to Short, Blair agreed with the *Sun*'s self-congratulatory assessment that its support for John Major helped him win an unlikely victory in 1992 (Short 2005: 36). It is difficult to prove or disprove this hypothesis, but what is clear is that the Murdoch press was, and still is, a vaunted source of support for any political party in British politics that can secure the magnate's personal backing. A recent estimate is that the Murdoch-dominated News Corporation has over 30% of the UK market by circulation (Tunstall, cited in Hutchison 2009: 54).

Despite wanting their support or at least their acquiescence in a New Labour victory which would oust the Conservatives from office in 1997, Blair found neither the *Telegraph*, *Daily Mail*, *The Times* or *Sun* to be in favour of his idea of encouraging Britain to be a more wholehearted participant in the EU. This has been consistently reflected in their coverage of European and international affairs more generally over the years (see for instance Crowson 2007: 102–3, 183–6). Ian Bache and Andrew Jordan have described the context in which the public lacked a firm steer from the government after 1997, which meant that 'a largely hostile press has been given free rein to highlight the weaknesses of EU membership and in doing so deepen the sense of scepticism' about the EU (Bache and Jordan 2006: 5). Peter Anderson found that, under the stewardship of Conrad Black in the 1990s, the *Daily Telegraph* and its stable mate the *Sunday Telegraph* became vigorously Eurosceptical, in line with Black's personal predilection for the 'special relationship' and the North American Free Trade Agreement (NAFTA). Their reporting showed particular opposition to closer defence cooperation at the European level because this was seen as a threat to Britain's relationship with the US and the position of NATO as the lead guarantor of European security, as well as constraining British sovereignty over its defence policy (Anderson 2004: 163–4). While the Telegraph Media Group never advocated withdrawal from the EU, Anderson suggests its superficially moderate position hid a 'covert agenda', namely that, over the long term, membership of the EU would do Britain more harm than good (Anderson 2004: 168). Wheatcroft adds that in appointing editors such as Max Hastings to the *Daily Telegraph* (editor 1986–95) and Charles Moore to the *Sunday Telegraph* (editor 1992–95; he replaced Hastings as editor of the *Daily Telegraph* 1995–2003), Black was doing so in the knowledge that they shared his Atlanticist convictions. 'Most of these tweedy chaps were ardent admirers of free-market capitalism and the American model' and both editors had supported the Eurosceptic John Redwood against John Major during the 1995 Conservative Party leadership contest (Wheatcroft 2005: 225, 229). Insights into the kind of attitudes to Europe that pervaded the pages of the daily and weekend editions of the *Telegraph* can be gained from the titles of books by former journalists for those newspapers, such as John Laughland's *The Tainted Source: The Undemocratic Origins of the European Idea* (1997) and Christopher Booker's *The Castle of Lies: Why Britain Must Get Out of Europe* (1996). Laughland, for instance, sees EMU as 'unpolitical and anti-national' and sees the wider EU project as rooted in Nazi ideas about how Germany could dominate Europe using France as a pliant accomplice. Construing the EU as a threat to British freedom, sovereignty and statehood has been a staple of the Conservative-supporting *Telegraph*'s coverage of EU and international affairs.

The *Daily Mail* can be grouped with the London *Evening Standard* for the purposes of analysis because until January 2009 they were both part of Lord Rothermere's Daily Mail and General Trust (Sweeney 2009). They took parallel approaches to the question of the British in Europe. While the *Daily Mail* obviously sold more copies nationally, 'London's *Standard* is taken very seriously in Downing Street because it helps set the agenda for the national papers the next day' (Oborne 1999: 3). Robin Cook testified to the influence these staunch Tory outlets had within the newspaper market in the 1990s; New Labour had to take action to counter some of the viscerally anti-Old Labour ways of these papers (Cook 2003: 260–2). It does not seem as if Blair felt he could ever win 'tribal Tories' over to the New Labour side (Blair 2010: 274), or dissuade them from criticizing the EU, but in trying to expand Labour's voting base he had to play to their 'middle England' sympathies (Oborne 1999: 177–8). Ultimately, it seems, New Labour failed to make anything other than a short-term impact on the owner or editors, but that did not deter the government from trying, especially through Blair's assistant, Anji Hunter (Naughtie 2002: 239–40). Writing in 2001, Toynbee and Walker argued that 'Long after the *Daily Mail* had turned to devoting itself daily to trashing Labour, its editor and his wife were to be found at an intimate Downing Street dinner. Even he asked on that occasion why Tony Blair bothered. "I will always be a Tory" he told the Prime Minister in no uncertain terms' (Toynbee and Walker 2001: 237).

Where the support of the Telegraph and Mail groups were deemed helpful bonuses to the New Labour cause, winning over the Murdoch-owned newspapers, *The Times*, *Sunday Times*, *Sun* and *News of the World*, formed the central plank of the strategy. This meant tackling a press empire which, by purveying 'a pure stream of Euroscepticism' (Naughtie 2002: 369), had helped establish a news agenda with 'a greater component of scepticism and outright hostility than that in any other member state' (Morgan 2003: 44). As Naughtie observed:

> A great deal of energy was devoted to the reassurance of Murdoch and his editors – Alastair Campbell has a nervous system that is tuned carefully to the *Sun*, and a pen that is always ready to dash off a signal article by the Prime Minister saying that the national interest will never be sold off. (Naughtie 2002: 145)

This, says Sally Morgan, was only to be expected: it was Campbell's job to keep the press supporting the New Labour project (interview with Morgan). The causes of Rupert Murdoch's antipathy towards the EU are not entirely clear. His unhappy experiences trying to set up a Europe-wide satellite channel in the 1980s surely did not help. In the end his ambitions had to be scaled back and Sky television was rolled out only in the British market (Chalaby 2003: 15). We have to remember that Murdoch is in the media industry to make money, not for ideological reasons (Wheatcroft 2005: 218–19), and it is the demands of global capitalism that drive the Euroscepticism of the Murdoch press outlets (Anderson 2004: 156). Hence, the commercial and economic factors in Murdoch's antipathy to the EU loom large for many a commentator – its rules and regulations on monopoly ownership have regularly conflicted with his desire to dominate the European media markets. Lance Price, for example, noted that, three and a half years into the Blair years, Murdoch was 'still a sceptic on Europe, of course, but has good business interests of his own for being less hostile to Europe generally' (Price 2005: 276). Ultimately, argues Anderson, 'Murdoch fostered a style of reporting and commentary that ... constructed a coherent nationalist framework to use as a vehicle for his ideologically and commercially-driven non-nationalist opposition to the European

Union' (Anderson 2004: 166). Through this pseudo-nationalist discourse Murdoch hoped to prompt his British readers to come to the same conclusion as him about the damage closer integration within the EU could do them. As Murdoch's perception of his pecuniary advantages regarding operating in the EU altered so, apparently, did his views on Europe.

Two themes become apparent when studying New Labour's relationship with the Murdoch press. One concerns Murdoch's Euro-scepticism having to be balanced against his support for Blair as Prime Minister on a personal level; the other concerns New Labour's pro-Europeanism having to be watered down to keep Murdoch on its side. They were two sides of a rapidly spinning coin. As political–press relationships go, this was a marriage of convenience rather than love, prompting writers such as William Wallace to speculate about the existence of a 'Faustian pact' between New Labour and Murdoch, whereby News International newspapers would support the government and in return the government would stay unenthusiastic about the EU (Wallace 2005: 63). Insider accounts from the period more than hint at the potential European *policy* implications of Blair and Murdoch being so close. For instance, in November 1998 Price recorded in his diary that 'News International are under the impression we won't make any changes [to the wording of European policy] without asking them' (Price 2005: 45). That said, News International gaining the impression of having influence and it actually having influence are two quite different things. From Price's words it seems as if New Labour at that stage was keen to dispel any such notion in public, if not quite so forcefully to Murdoch and his acolytes behind closed doors. It might, therefore, be stretching the argument to say that Murdoch set the European agenda, just as it would be to argue that in 1997 *The Times* became New Labour's mouthpiece (Oborne 1999: 174). Blair's advisers were of the opinion that the Prime Minister never set out to 'appease' Murdoch or influential political editors for the *Sun* such as Trevor Kavanagh; Blair would actively put the Europe case and argue things through with them. It was different with the Mail Group, such that by 2001 Downing Street had judged it was unlikely to change its opinion on New Labour or the EU and 'pretty much stopped speaking to them', although Brown and the Treasury continued to court the *Daily Mail* after that time (interviews with Morgan and Hill; Blair 2010: 494–5, 518, 655).

The official line therefore had it that no Faustian pact was ever agreed between New Labour and the Murdoch press. However, in both his tabloids and broadsheets, Murdoch's instinctive Euro-scepticism was toned down because of his personal support for Blair. Of the *Sun* Oborne writes:

Its readers were starkly presented with two contradictory propositions. On the one hand they were informed that federal Europe presented an apocalyptic menace which had to be fought with ceaseless vigilance. On the other they were reminded daily that Tony Blair, the man set on leading Britain towards that feared destination, was not merely a genius of outstanding gifts, but also a secular saint. (Oborne 1999: 175)

At *The Times* a similarly schizophrenic attitude prevailed. At the same time as Eurosceptical Tory thinkers 'thrived' and the possibility of a closer relationship with the EU taken was taken to be an 'abomination', its readership was informed that Blair was 'as fine a Prime Minister as Thatcher' (Oborne 1999: 175). Anderson fleshes this point out by noting that Peter Riddell covered EU affairs for *The Times* in 1997–98 and he is hardly a renowned sceptic. However, in the main, the discourse of the newspaper was found to be ideologically Eurosceptical, containing 'a strong focus on British sovereignty' and 'a clear suggestion that the EU was a major threat to this' (Anderson 2004: 160). The greater vehemence about Europe in the *Sun* can be explained at the level of language, inasmuch as the discursive constructions of an Other in tabloids tends to be more vivid, reactionary and lacking the perspective we might expect in a paper written for an 'establishment' readership and a higher reading age. Seldon highlights a practical reason too: Murdoch was more 'hands off' with *The Times*, such that its editors could indulge their own views more readily. By contrast, the *Sun* was 'the only British paper that he himself sought seriously to influence' (Seldon 2005: 252). In a way this worked against Blair as far as both he as premier and his European policy went, with *The Times* given free rein to be more critical of both. During the 1997 election, when the *Sun* backed Blair, *The Times* 'opted to advise its readers to back the most Eurosceptical candidate in their constituency, regardless of party' (Seldon 2005: 253). We can conclude from this that the *Sun* and *The Times* were schizophrenic about Blair, New Labour and the EU. The *Sun* paraded Blair as a great leader while at the same time damning any prospect of joining the euro as an abhorrence to be fought by the British people with every sinew in their bodies. *The Times* was more open to Europhile comment in its pages, but again the 'positive' side of its schizophrenia was less in evidence than its routinely 'negative' attitude towards the EU. As Blair's sparkle faded through the later part of his first term and into 2002 and beyond, neither newspaper had any cause or desire to alter these deeply held perspectives on British European policy. By 2006 Blair was quite up front about his travails: 'the fevered frenzy of parts of the British media don't exactly help. I have long since given up trying to conduct a serious debate about Europe in certain quarters' (Blair 2006a).

This section has argued that the Murdoch press adopted a pro-Blair and anti-EU line simultaneously. It was empirically impossible, however, to prove the existence of a Faustian pact between New Labour and Murdoch, although elements of an apparent unwritten understanding between them can be found, especially in the pages of the *Sun*. That Murdoch remained heavily engaged in shaping the position of his key tabloid newspapers in Britain throughout the Blair years is documented by Seldon, who notes that in 2004, when the sceptical press was campaigning hard for a British referendum on the proposed Constitutional Treaty, the *News of the World* ran the headline 'Traitor Tony Blair is to let Britain be run by ten unelected bodies in his EU splendour'. It later emerged, notes Seldon, that 'Murdoch had personally argued for the use of the word "traitor"' (Seldon 2007: 266). Thus, while it may be going too far to argue that Murdoch had a direct, observable influence on *policy* per se, it must have been constantly in the minds of New Labour decision-makers what the Murdoch (and other media) reaction to steps in a proactive European policy might have been. Many a commentator would agree with Toynbee and Walker that, in the main: 'The media were un-doubtedly biased, even the BBC was dragged by newspaper impetus into running stories critical of European situations' (Toynbee and Walker 2001: 150–1). It is with this in mind that we can usefully look at the paradox from New Labour's vantage point. Blair and Brown wanted to enact an enthusiastic policy towards the EU while keeping the backing of the Murdoch and 'middle England' press outlets by convincing them they had nothing to fear from New Labour. 'With a general Eurosceptic predisposition in the British press and public' (O'Donnell and Whitman 2007: 263) it was unlikely Blair or Brown would have wanted to tackle the controversial issue of Europe in the lead-up to any of the general elections New Labour fought. During the 1997 election, for example, 'Labour maintained its essentially pro-European stance' yet on key issues such as the single currency and treaty reform 'it ensured that there was little ground between it and the Conservative Party' (Daniels 1998: 81). A telling medium in which we saw this paradox at work was an article Tony Blair wrote for the *Sun* shortly before the general election in May 1997, one day before the day of St George, patron saint of England (image 5).

In this piece Blair speculated that 'Europe' might be a present-day manifestation of the dragon that St George had to slay to protect the country from attack hundreds of years ago. He engaged in some party politicking by highlighting Conservative in-fighting over Europe, before turning to his own position: 'I will have no truck with a European superstate. If there are moves to create that dragon I will slay it.' The potential dragon as Blair depicted it was

Image 5. Blair, Europe and the *Sun*.

a federalist EU and he reassured his *Sun* readers that he would not allow this monster to destroy Britain, such that 'National identities will be protected and not submerged'. As far as the single currency went, Blair pointed out that there were 'formidable obstacles' in Britain's path to joining the euro, but that ruling out membership would damage British influence over the process; 'Therefore we keep our options open'. He pledged to hold a referendum if Cabinet and Parliament agreed it was in the country's best economic interests to join. After that, Blair set down a list of what would later become the government's 'red lines' on Europe: over tax, fiscal policy

(Brown 2004f), asylum, immigration policy and so forth. He argued, however, that Labour, through its domestic party unity, would be a 'tougher negotiating force' abroad than the Conservatives had been and therefore was the real patriotic party of the British people, standing 'ready to lead'.

The article rapidly became something of a stick with which to beat Blair for undermining the pro-Europe lobby in Britain by setting out too many 'defensive' disclaimers, which prevented the articulation of a sustained 'positive public interest case in support of integrationist measures' (Sowemimo 1999: 348, 354). According to Johann Hari (2004) the article was 'preposterous'; Robert Peston said Blair was exploiting a nationalistic symbolism that 'verged on the absurd', an impression reinforced by the well known Europhile Peter Mandelson leading out a bulldog at a pre-election press conference (Peston 2005: 196). Sowemimo judged the piece 'damaging' because it re-inforced and legitimized British hostilities to the single currency while at the same time limiting the government's future room for manoeuvre (Sowemimo 1999: 358). It is evident that the thinking behind this and similar articles was the need to 'avoid alienating the Murdoch press' (Wall 2008: 162) by staying cool on the question of British membership of the single currency. As Powell has observed, 'there was a certain amount – before the 1997 election – of trying to buy off the Murdoch press and Associated [Press] on Europe' (interview with Powell). On an issue of low electoral salience, like Europe, Blair surely believed he could afford to send out mixed messages to different audiences and not risk losing the support of any of them. Our interest in the article, then, is threefold. First, does it show the existence of a Faustian pact? Arguably not, because while Blair hardly came across as supportive of the single currency project, he refused to rule it out altogether and, given his views on the EU, Murdoch would surely have liked him to go much further in that direction. In interview, Powell denied anything as formal as a pact, saying 'I don't think [articles like this] actually constrained what we did subsequently' (interview with Powell). Second, this was part of an ongoing process of policy development within New Labour circles. The government had come to power with firm ideas about what it what it wanted to achieve but with few concrete plans in place to deliver on its promises and pledges. If this was true of critical aspects of policy such as health and education it was even more so in the foreign policy realm, where the New Labour team was not just inexperienced but almost oblivious to the demands of enacting a modern, progressive agenda. By the end of 1997 'keeping our options open' on the single currency had mutated into the 'wait and see' approach cobbled together with the Treasury in response to the confusion surrounding British policy towards the euro that October (see chapter 2). Third and finally, we see examples of how Blair played to his audience through his discourse. The imagery around St George and the dragon, man-in-the-street colloquialisms such as 'no truck with' a superstate, and words associated with Eurosceptic discourse such as the idea of states being 'submerged' in Europe would all have chimed with the intended readership for this article. The overall sense we get is that New Labour could be trusted to 'protect' the British from European interference in its sovereign law-making powers. But perhaps as importantly, Blair set himself up as a latter-day St George, who is tough, can 'prevent' bad things happening and who will 'protect' the English, specifically, as well as the British. Through the article Europe was Othered using national-ist discourse. There was no effort to educate, inform or engage with Europe: it was simply fended off, pending another battle another day.

Summary

In the past politicians – indeed I and my predecessors – have been accused of saying one thing to one audience and another thing to another. (Brown 1999h)

This chapter has investigated the ways in which Blair, Brown and the architects of New Labour set about rebranding the party to give it credibility in the eyes of the media and the electorate. The former was seen as a key target that needed hitting to enable the refashioned party to attract widespread popular support from centre-ground voters. In prising 'New' Labour away from the legacy of 'Old' Labour, Blair and his team carefully crafted an image based on a repudiation of key policies as well as the history of the Old party. New Labour's use of history in this process was ironic because while it needed to recount history (in this case a particular version of Labour's past) to rebrand the party, it was also claiming to be a party that would move on from the past and into the future, taking the British with it, reluctantly or otherwise. So history in the New Labour story was the ghost at the banquet: ever present but also a thorn in its side; there but not really there; influencing New Labour but not needing to be seen to influence it *too* much. This troublesome balancing act played out equally as much with regard to European policy as it did over the party's identity. Having crafted a fresh iden-tity for itself, Labour then had to convince key media outlets that they could safely back Blair and his party without risking losing readers and/or viewers by uprooting their instinctive political out-looks or challenging their orthodox editorial lines.

We discovered above that the approach to New Labour and the EU in the pages of the broadly Eurosceptical newspapers Blair courted most heavily, particularly the Murdoch press, came to be characterized by something approaching schizophrenia. On the one hand they backed Blair as leader of the Labour Party and as British Prime Minister, but on the other they consistently warned against the dangers the EU posed to a Britain led by a Europhile premier. Blair for his part played upon press schizophrenia by adopting an electorally sensible but policy-restricting stance on issues such as the single currency, such that he gave the readers of different newspapers what they wanted to hear: both in policy terms and discursively. As far as the argument of this book goes, I suggest we can empathize with Blair from a personal, party and political perspective. However, from the point of view of implementing a modern, progressive European policy, actively cultivating this level of ambiguity right at the heart of New Labour's foreign policy discourse was always liable to hold it back from achieving its objectives. The ensuing chapters will demonstrate that Blair and Brown struggled to 'place' or 'contain' history in their foreign policy speeches as successfully as they managed to repackage the story of Labour's past. The principal reason was that where the media and public showed themselves to be generally supportive of the transition from Old to New Labour, they were not as enthusiastic about making the same journey from Old Britain to New Britain.

Chapter 8

Escaping the past?

History. The more of it you have the more you have to live it. (Updike 1991b: 555)

The previous chapter detailed New Labour's paradoxical attitude towards the Labour Party's and Britain's past. It was argued that while on the one hand the New Labour architects sought to present the refashioned party as having instigated a decisive break with all that was ideologically unsound and electorally unappealing in Labour's past, on the other hand they needed to historicize that very past in order to make such claims hold water. This resulted in something of a dilemma for Blair, Brown, Mandelson and Campbell, in that it raised the question, how *much* history needed to be included in the new party narrative to keep traditional Labour voters on side, while at the same time attracting a fresh batch of voters to the new party? A wider set of questions about the role of history in British public life also reared its head. Was a public brought up on stories of national greatness and a global leadership role ready to jettison that past in favour of a modernized national identity focusing on a narrower European role, albeit one in which Britain would retain its element of uniqueness in the world by acting as the 'bridge' between Europe and the US? New Labour might not have been in love with its past, but the British certainly seem to have been comfortable with theirs, and this led to an ongoing tension in New Labour discourse between the will to escape the past and the need to be seen to embrace it. As John Updike suggested, getting over the legacy of the past is never easy, especially if that history comes in the form of a national narrative dating back (however mistakenly) a 'thousand years' and more.

This chapter will study how the legacy of the past haunted Tony Blair and Gordon Brown's discourses on British European policy. It will be argued that New Labour was living history and living with history just as much as the governments that preceded it, because it never made a decisive enough discursive break with the past, and this went for Brown the historian as well as Blair the non-historian, or even anti-historian (Beckett 2007: 5–6). History featured heavily in New Labour ministers' speeches, regardless of their personal knowledge of or respect for the past, and it did so because diplomacy has come to be seen as an exercise in divining current and future foreign policy strategy from the so-called 'lessons' we can learn from recent international history. Even in some of Blair and Brown's most progressive speeches on British identity and attitude to the EU, history was always there, holding them back, like quicksand swallowing up an unwary traveller in a foreign land. In trying to pull themselves free of history, Blair and Brown found to their discomfort that it was only through an appreciation of the lessons of the past that British diplomacy functioned in policy and discursive terms. The conditions of the existence of New Labour's foreign policy discourses placed strict limits on what Blair and Brown were able to say and do in the foreign policy arena.

We will chart New Labour's uneasy approach to history in three sections. The first will show the government at its most revisionist, most challenging as it were, calling on the British not to be dragged back by their past, to get over their history and move on. This was a particular facet of the early years, 1997–2000, when the government's confidence in its ability as an agent to shape a modern British foreign policy was at its zenith. Even then, however, Blair and Brown were of the mind that history needed to be valued for what it was and what it taught us, so the second section of the chapter will study the government's traditionalist approach to the 'lessons of history' and what the leaders had learnt about Britain and Europe from their study of the past. Blair and Brown's confidence in the ability of the past to offer up lessons was severely shaken by the events of 9/11 and we can see from later in 2001 a more nuanced, critical approach to history taking shape. The final section will link what Blair and Brown said about Britain needing a fresh approach to history to what they had to say about the psychological courage needed to make this break. They identified the 'confidence' needed to develop a modern British identity and contrasted it with a Eurosceptical position that shied away from pursuing active British involvement because of a lack of belief or faith in the modernizing project. In this element of their discourse Blair and Brown were projecting the image of confident, patriotic leaders, able to re-vision the past against weak small 'c' conservatives too timid to stand up and change the course of history. Whether the Prime Minister and Chancellor were as radical or reforming as they liked to set themselves up to be is open to doubt, however, when we compare the elements of change with the elements of continuity in their overall logic of history.

1. Coming to terms with the past

> From the standpoint of the political centre, embracing Europe has
> also implied an embrace of 'modernity' defined in centrist terms.
> (Ludlow 2002: 121)

New Labour encouraged the British people to call time on their retrograde obsession with the national past, 'to fight on our merits not on
our past' (Blair 2006d). Although the government made this point
more frequently than its predecessors, Piers Ludlow's remark above
is apt: British leaders making the case for Europe have routinely
couched their policy in the argument that 'joining Europe' would be
beneficial for Britain in terms of modernizing or updating attitudes,
practices and the nature of the country's set of global relationships.
Put in these terms, the country is portrayed as lagging economically
behind the other members of the EEC/EU, or it is suggested that it
is losing the ear of the Americans by remaining outside the club, or
it is implied that its security is being damaged by not helping shape
European defence and security policies. Economics always features
heavily in the modernizing discourse of British premiers. Perhaps
most memorably, in his speech to the Labour Party conference in
1963, Harold Wilson 'talked of reinvigorating British industry
through the "white heat" of a "scientific revolution", whereby the
improved application of technology, alongside better government
planning, expanded higher education and an end to restrictive
practices, would improve Britain's economic prospects' (Young 2003:
96). Wilson was responding to particular concerns then being expressed in Britain about the country's increasingly shaky scientific
research and development base, about Britain's 'brain drain' to the
US, and about European companies' relative lack of competitiveness
compared with multinational corporations in the US. Although the
context might shift, holding out the prospect that 'Europe' can help
modernize Britain has been a constant refrain in British foreign
policy discourses, particularly during periods of introspection and
perceived national decline.

After eighteen years in the electoral wilderness it was under-
standable that New Labour proclaimed its ascent to office meant
'the new chapter opening in British history – a time of change that
will become a time of renewal' (Blair 1998a). Blair and Brown were
not planning to write a new history book altogether; instead they
were tacking a new chapter onto the end of the old edition, and
this casts doubt on the precise nature and size of the break they
intended to make, or could make, from the past. This is the main
argument of Simon Jenkins's *Thatcher and Sons* (2007), that New
Labour – mostly at home but abroad too – represented not so much

the negation of Thatcherism but its logical extension. It is hard to disagree when we observe Brown in 2000 describing his task using words reminiscent of the Conservatives: 'there has not been enough competition, dynamism and entrepreneurship in many areas of our economy' (Brown 2000b). Rather than deconstruct New Labour's Thatcherite domestic policy agenda, however, we will concentrate on the international dimension by considering what Blair said in a speech in Japan in January 1998, eight months into his premiership, called 'New Britain in the modern world' (Blair 1998a). He began by setting out the argument for taking decisions that would be beneficial for the country in the long term instead of what he called 'the political expediency of the quick fix and the destabilising economics of boom and bust'. His mission was 'simple: to build a modern Britain in which prosperity, and a decent, fair society go hand in hand'. He wanted to work 'with globalisation', identified as an actor with agency in its own right (Blair 1998a; see also Brown 2003b). It was a consistent Blair–Brown refrain that globalization 'is a fact and here to stay' (Brown 2006b; Brown 2006d); the only choices were over 'the values that govern it' (Blair 2006c) and how to manage it in the face of the threatening 'forces of protectionism' (Brown 2006d). New Labour suggested that countries should be in 'a state of permanent modernisation' to garner the full benefits of globalization (Blair 2006d) and to keep pace with 'this bewilderingly fast period of change' (Brown 2005e). Blair went on in his 1998 speech in Japan to identify the ways in which the government would promote British business, encourage inward investment and improve the quality and skills base of the workforce. On European policy, Blair quoted from Brown's October 1997 statement on the single currency and said the government had 'made it clear there is no insuperable constitutional barrier to our joining' but that it had to occur when the economic time was right; that time had not yet arrived, he said, but preparations for joining were well under way both inside and outside government. The Prime Minister was confident there had already been 'a transformation of attitudes to Europe by the New Labour Government ... a positive, constructive approach to Europe, widely welcomed by our European partners' and that Britain could play a 'leading role in Europe' (Blair 1998a).

For the Chancellor, Britain's leadership role was also less reality than aspiration, but the message was simple, 'we must play a leading role in shaping Europe's future', and he presented just that case in a series of speeches through 1997 (Brown 1997b; Brown 1997c). Like Brown, in 1998 Blair was confidently publicizing the government's commitment to taking the tough economic decisions that would make the dream of a modern Britain leading in Europe a reality. 'The uncertainty, introspection and half-heartedness of the last few years have gone. We are building a modern, dynamic and outward-looking Britain for the 21st Century.' We indeed see a new chapter rather than a new book being written by Blair when he recapped British history from the 1980s, a decade that he said had also been 'a time of change' with regard to labour market flexibility and the increase in privatization within the economy as a whole. 'Those reforms will remain in place', he said, but Britain is 'now embarked on a new transformation, a second wave of reform' to address the weaknesses ignored in the (alluded to, but unnamed) Thatcherite agenda. This parting description of the journey on which he was taking Britain relentlessly included the New Labour keywords one after the other in a cascade effect: 'new', 'transformation', 'second wave', 'reform'. The momentum built up through the 'wave' metaphor was inserted to make this journey appear inevitable, unstoppable, like a tsunami sweeping everything before it. This was one example of how Blair managed to create the image of an apparently decisive discursive break from the past and why more than the odd writer credited Blair and New Labour with bringing about the very transformation in British attitudes to the past the government's publicity claimed it could achieve. For instance, referring to the outdatedness of the 'three circles' model of British foreign policy in 2005, Beverley Southgate put it as follows:

> Winston Churchill's confidence, as late as 1952, that 'We [British] stand erect as both as an island people and as the centre of a world-wide Commonwealth and Empire', now, some half-century on, stands as little more than some historical curiosity on a par with the patriotic proclamations of Shakespeare's Henry V.

However, at the beginning of the twenty-first century, he argued, things had radically altered:

> The island people, who were once both naturally (and providentially) defended from external threats and also able to define themselves against those continental 'others', with their erratic philosophies and gastronomic oddities, have become (or at least are becoming) more or less assimilated into a cosmopolitanism against which the 'English' Channel provides little defence. (Southgate 2005: 101–2)

Southgate was as optimistic in 2005 as Blair had been seven years earlier about the Prime Minister's ability to bring into being a sig-nificant rupture with the past. It would have entailed a new mode of thinking in Britain about everything from the public–private mix in the economy on the one hand to the national character and global outlook on the other. Southgate also echoed some of Blair's pessi-mism, however, that the history of the British economy and society could be overcome so easily. Where Blair proclaimed that a 'young' country had been born in 1997 he also recognized that he was building on and extending Thatcher's legacy from the 1980s. Southgate was confident that the reformist vision could be implemented but still recognized the potential of the English Channel and associated ideas about British separateness from continental Europe to act as some sort of defence against the forces of cosmopolitanism and globalization sweeping Blair's proposed changes through the country.

Blair's 'New Britain in the modern world' speech offers many an insight into the discursive concepts and techniques the Prime Minister deployed to sustain the momentum of the New Labour project in office. His claims about modernity, globalization and the future rested on the philosophical argument that respect for past traditions and values could easily mutate into a small 'c' (and, on a party political note, a large 'C') c/Conservative veneration of that past which constrained progressive thought about how to improve society for the better. Blair's speeches on many topics – domestic and international – particularly in the early years, were replete with warnings about the dangers of repeating the past. For example, just weeks into his time in office, in May 1997, Blair spoke at the signing ceremony of the NATO–Russia Founding Act, which stated that 'NATO and Russia do not consider each other as adversaries' and pledged to 'build together a lasting and inclusive peace in the Euro-Atlantic area on the principles of democracy and cooperative security' (NATO 1997). 'Newness' was not just confined to the New Labour project and Blair projected it onto the 'new European landscape' which he saw being 'reclaimed from the battlegrounds of the 20th century' by the Founding Act. The crux for the Prime Minister was that the signatories were transcending the stultifying outlooks and policies of previous generations. Their coming together, 'born out of the vision and courage of nations determined not to repeat the past, is historys [sic] gift to our future' (Blair 1997c). Five months later, at the Commonwealth Business Forum, Blair allied his push for a modern Britain to the push for a Commonwealth 'for the 21st century. A Commonwealth that is modern and forward-looking, that learns from its history rather than re-living it' (Blair 1997f). Days later he was back on his favourite topic of wanting Britain to be forward-looking, pointing out that 'I also do believe that we allow an old-fashioned image of Britain occasionally to obscure the new fashions of Britain to our detriment'. However, 'Properly followed', Blair's principles of a modern foreign policy 'do allow Britain to escape from the legacy of the past and shape an exciting future for ourselves' (Blair 1997g).

New Labour's interpretation that countries and regions needed to escape the past to make it into the future held for Britain, the EU, the wider Euroatlantic area and the Commonwealth alike. In 1999 Brown specifically turned on New Labour's opponents a national-ist language forged in war by arguing that it is wrong to 'believe Britain does best when we stand alone, free of long-term continental attachments' or that 'joining Europe was one of the wrong turning points of our 20th century history'. For Brown, as for Blair, a mis-reading of Britain's past military glories represented all that was wrong with the argument that 'Britain's future lies outside Europe' (Brown 1999b; on the 'standing alone' component of the British national narrative see Gamble 2003: 110). Identifying other occa-sions on which New Labour took the line that history can prevent progress towards the promised land of 'modernity' will be sufficient to consolidate our understanding of this aspect of Blair and Brown's logic of history. It will, moreover, set the scene for a consideration in the following section of some apparently contradictory messages they sent out about the past, sometimes in the very same speeches. A good example of their logic at work came in November 1998, when Blair became the first British Prime Minister to address the Irish Parliament. His familiar counsel that day was that historical baggage could prevent the peace process from moving forward. The 'troubles' between the Catholic and Protestant communities had to be overcome by moving on from the past towards a future built on power-sharing in government between the main parties. 'No one should ignore the injustices of the past, or the lessons of history. But too often between us, one person's history has been another person's myth.' He implied that understanding the empirical 'real world' was possible and could lead to a virtuous, liberal truth emerging, where each side could see what it shared with the other side. By contrast, the mythical sectarian Other version of history somehow obscured from view this realm of truth and therefore set back the chances of peace and reconciliation in Northern Ireland. As he went on: 'We need not be prisoners of our history'; Britain and Ireland 'can try to put our histories behind us, try to forgive and forget these age-old enmities'. As the ties between the countries increase, 'so the past can be put behind us' and through closer bilateral cooperation 'we can finally put the burden of history behind us' (all from Blair 1998e). In this speech we see Blair both placing himself in the stream of history between the two countries ('I feel profoundly … the history in this event') and trying to step outside that stream of history, to tell it impartially and thereby fix its meaning for his audience.

Blair's words at the Irish Parliament told of the wider New Labour logic of history and as such his discourse on the dangers of being stuck in the past warrants three remarks. The first is that the New Labour government was hooked on the idea that an obsession with history could be damaging to a series of collective endeavours: first, to forge a common home in the UK through the peace process in Northern Ireland; second, to build a common European home with Britain comfortably at its heart; and finally, to secure a stable international society. That each level overlapped with the next came from New Labour's take on the essential interconnectedness between external and domestic politics in a globalized world. 'Foreign policy should not be seen as some self-contained part of government in a box marked "abroad" or "foreigners". It should complement and reflect our domestic goals. It should be part of our mission of national renewal' (Blair 1997g). The second point is that in order to create a discursive break between New Labour/Britain/world on the one hand and this mythical past of Old Labour/Britain/world on the other, Blair and Brown represented history as a 'thing' or object we can choose to enter or carry around with us or not, as we see fit. In this sense their discourses were reminiscent of a certain British approach to Europe which sees it as an optional add-on, a holiday caravan to use Paxman's metaphor (see chapter 5) which can be fastened on to traditional conceptualizations of the British identity. It was the implied separation of Britain from Europe that Blair and Brown questioned when they pointed out that Britain had always and forever been a part of Europe, in or out of periods of war and conflict. The third point to make is that there was an overt morality to the government's use of history which can be deduced from the way it framed this 'history' and its effects, to the point where in 2003 the Prime Minister constructed history as an other-worldly deity. In an emotional speech at the US Congress Blair staunchly defended the Iraq invasion: 'That is something I am confident history will forgive'. Inaction against Saddam, he said, would be 'something history will not forgive' (Blair 2003e).

New Labour's objectification and attribution of a certain agency to history reveals something about the logic underpinning its European discourses. Talking about escaping from history (a prison metaphor), or carrying history around (a weight metaphor), enabled New Labour to position history as a dangerous place to get stuck in, or a pernicious thing to be burdened by. Both call to mind a further (light–dark) metaphor about the dangers of being stuck in the shadow of history and there is clearly an ethical dimension to such a discourse. For Blair, in particular, obsessing about history was tantamount to a form of criminality and in taking that line the Prime Minister seems to have been making a powerful claim about the perils of being backward-looking as opposed to forward-looking. For example, in Brazil in August 2001, Blair discussed how Britain could progress economically using the slogan: 'Reform, not retreat into the past, is the answer' (Blair 2001b; 'We have ceased to be a nation in retreat' was a favourite Thatcher refrain after the Falklands War – see Jenkins 2007: 76). A constant Blair refrain was 'to embrace globalisation not retreat from it' (Blair 2006d). The word 'reform' is key because of the prison metaphor it conveys. One of the reasons society sends convicted criminals to prison is to rehabilitate them to live by the rules of society when they return after their spell in prison, cut off from 'normal' society. By implying that reform is the binary opposite of retreating into the past, that past – history in other words – is construed as a prison: a place for the tainted and morally bankrupt. Constructing history figuratively as either a prison or a burden, New Labour positioned itself as a metaphorical prison guard who held the keys to the door of the jail. It was New Labour, the suggestion seemed to be, that could show the British, Irish and the world, no less, how to release themselves from their unhealthy obsession with the past, or at least a distorted version of that past, and how they could walk tall into the future. History in this sense formed a vital part of Blair and Brown's construction of their virtuous leadership qualities, which were in turn projected onto the role the two men wanted to carve out for Britain in the world.

II. Learning the lessons of the past

> While Britain's relationship with Europe has neither been exclusive nor constant, any study of our history does show not just that we have always been a European power but that Britain has been European for good pragmatic reasons. (Brown 1999b)

History, policy-makers tell us, has the capacity to teach lessons about the way we should think and act in the present to help carve out a better future for ourselves as individuals, communities and nations. For people subscribing to this view, 'history' is constituted as something approaching an empirically accurate and verifiable chronicle of events, handed down to us from the past by historians acting out the role of quasi-omniscient reporters of 'the facts'. Treating historians as impartial narrators, and the history they produce to be 'straight' sequences of the 'this then that happened' variety, enables policy-makers who live by the dictum 'history teaches...' both to learn from the sense of the past they glean from the history books and to educate their publics about the nature of these lessons. In an era of uncertainty, flux and unpredictability brought about by globalization and complex interdependence, we are told, turning to the past can provide us with some measure of certainty: 'the lessons of the past seem even more relevant in an age in which communications play an unprecedented role' (Cull 2008). In this section we will begin by establishing how Blair and Brown accepted the 'lessons of history' idea in their speeches and then study the kinds of lessons about British European policy they felt they had learnt. In assuming that lessons could be gleaned from the past, they took on a standard Europhile approach to the history of Britain's 'missed opportunities' in Europe since 1945. The questions New Labour shied away from asking or answering fell into two categories. First, why were the history lessons they had learnt more accurate than the history lessons sceptics liked to propagate about Britain as a great, sovereign power independent from Europe's integrative processes? And second, did the events of 9/11, after which Blair apparently lost faith in history to teach lessons, invalidate the government's wider approach to the uses of history? The government could usefully have asked these questions, because a different and subversive take on the lessons of history represents the past as being as malleable as we wish it to be when we historicize it. This explains why interpretations of history hold a fundamental place in discourses on the nation: they can be used to support almost any point we wish to make about contemporary political challenges. Nor were the follow-up questions ever asked by Blair or Brown; these included: How do aggregated organizations of individuals and bureaucracies that make up states actually go about *learning* lessons? Or, was the 'we' who learn lessons in fact a rather small portion of people at the top of the New Labour machine (for instance Brown 1999g)? Is a historical record from which *any* lesson can be learned of any practical use at all other than as a prop to achieve a halo effect for a particular political ideology or policy? And why do some lessons of history become better learnt and garner more popularity than others? In terms of presenting a logic of history, Blair and Brown might have gone further towards answering these important questions.

Let us begin with an illustrative exception from the broader pattern of continuity found in New Labour's logic of history. On only one high-profile occasion did Blair lose confidence in his ability to learn lessons from the past. His moment of weakness came during the same speech to the US Congress introduced above, where he reflected on international security in the opening months of the invasion of Iraq, saying: 'There has never been a time ... when, except in the most general sense, a study of history provides so little instruction for our present day' (Blair 2003e). We can but speculate on why his faith had been so shaken: the sheer trauma of the events of 9/11; the problems of identifying 'new', seemingly invisible security threats from Al Qaeda; the need to achieve empathy with his US audience; and a personal view that 'everything changed' after 9/11 (for example Blair 2006f). All these factors may have prompted Blair to depart from the opinion he commonly espoused, that a knowledge of history could help guide national decision-makers in the present, in moral, spiritual and policy terms. Blair had briefly rehearsed the idea of a post-9/11 historical rupture in his 2002 Lord Mayor's Banquet speech, which, unlike all the others that covered British foreign policy generally, was entirely given over to how to combat these 'new threats' and 'new dangers' in 'new times' (Blair 2002c). The year before, in a speech to the Press Club in Washington, DC, in December 2001, Brown had moved to the view that 'no historical analogies can ever be exact' but he did not elaborate on the reasoning behind this statement (Brown 2001e). He in fact always took a conventional line on the lessons of history, for example by arguing that a 'new' (Brown 2001e; Brown 2003e; Brown 2003g) or 'modern' (Brown 2003a; Brown 2005i) Marshall Plan could help solve the world's security and economic crises. This would be a 'global new deal' built in 'new times' but 'rooted in the Marshall Plan's enduring values' (Brown 2004a), the goal being to bring together 'developed and developing countries' to solve issues such as poverty and debt and to work together on climate change (Brown 2005a). Such analogies came straight from the 'history as teacher' tradition. In sum, these post-9/11 wobbles on New Labour's part were just that: short-term deviations from an otherwise steady, predictable state. The radical sentiments about history that Blair expressed in Washington, and Brown's thesis on the flaws of analogous thinking, were out of line with New Labour's wider thinking on the role of history in the present. Neither Blair nor Brown seriously developed this line of reasoning, for the obvious reason that – developed to its full – it ran counter to the government's entire project of historicizing Labour Party, British and global history.

Blair and Brown thus showed themselves to be firm advocates of the Hugo Young line, that 'a historical view helped greatly in seeing where you were' (Brown 2005h). They propagated the view that New Labour had learnt the correct lessons from the past where their political opponents had faltered, summed up in Brown's critique of Thatcher: 'She recognised the importance of an appeal to enduring British values. Sadly her view of Britishness was too narrow, and she learned the wrong lessons from the past' (Brown 1999a). In his 1999 'Doctrine of the international community' speech in Chicago Blair took it as axiomatic that the history of European wars yielded one simple lesson: 'We have learned twice before this century that appeasement does not work. If we let an evil dictator range unchallenged, we will have to spill infinitely more blood and treasure to stop him later' (Blair 1999d). Blair rooted himself firmly in what

Mikkel Rasmussen (2003) has described as a hegemonic Western metanarrative about security and peace-building, especially as far as the Balkans region was concerned. Whether or not such historical analogies are applicable is less pertinent than the fact that Blair was clearly signed up to the idea that history lessons can be learned and the 'anti-appeasement' lesson would shape many of the Prime Minister's pronouncements, both on Kosovo and, later, on Iraq. By 2006 Blair had come to equate the scale and difficulty of executing the war on terror with the lead-up to the Second World War, 'In 1939 when Britain declared war on the Nazi tyranny'. Using language reminiscent of Churchill, he identified 'a struggle of a very different nature, but it will determine our collective future'. Here, the situation after 9/11 fed into a war narrative favoured by many Western foreign and defence policy-makers (Blair 2006c). This and other data from the speeches show a Prime Minister who packed his speeches with memories of history and historical lessons.

We have already seen how Blair warned the Irish Parliament not to ignore 'the lessons of the past' (Blair 1998e). At the World Economic Forum in Davos two years later he urged his audience to avoid the dangers of running boom–bust economies by being 'mindful of the lessons from history' regarding the need for fiscal discipline, stability and transparency. He argued that 'History teaches us' that counter-arguments about the perils of free trade do not 'just go away', and that 'The 20th century was a brutal lesson in the need for tolerance, understanding and commonsense [sic] about human nature' (Blair 2000a). At the turn of the millennium, New Labour embarked on a spree of historicization which put the events of the twentieth century in their place, as both history and history teacher. They were gone but not forgotten, always on hand like a subpoena witness in the twenty-first century to give 'evidence' when necessary (Blair 2001a). Even in speeches which went against the grain of what could be considered populist national history by encouraging the British people to think about the merits of a European future, Blair felt the need to pay due reverence to history: 'I value and honour our history enormously' (Blair 1997g). In upholding the conventions of international statecraft and diplomacy by metaphorically bowing down to history, Blair was infusing the progressivist elements of his European discourses with more traditionalist elements. What Prime Minister could reasonably stand up and *not* pay tribute to British history in this manner? After all, as Blair put it at Davos in January 2000, 'nations are a product of their own individual history' (Blair 2000a) and at the Scottish Parliament two months later, Britain's values and interests 'have grown up from our history and our shared experience' (Blair 2000c). There are some things it seems that leaders have to say in foreign policy discourses, and homage to the national past is one such element. A foreign policy discourse without history is, simply, *unimaginable*.

So nations are products of their past, but which past? The progressive elements of New Labour's European discourse usually featured as the explication of different lessons New Labour people had learnt from the past compared with those learnt by their Euro-sceptical opponents. To follow Blair and Brown's logic of history their British audiences needed to take two steps: first, they had to make sense of their history; and second, they had to use that made-sense-of-history wisely to build a European future. The first step the Prime Minister and Chancellor took was to urge their British listeners to 'make sense of our history' primarily with regard to Empire, Commonwealth and the nature of Britain as a 'dynamic multi-cultural, multi-ethnic society' and also with respect to Britain's status as a 'global player' because of the material and ideational legacies of the national past (Blair 1997g; see also Brown 1997c). Blair was forthright in his first Lord Mayor's Banquet speech on foreign affairs, putting the view that the 'facts' of the Empire were safe in his hands. 'There is a lot of rubbish about the Empire. In my view, we should not either be apologising for it or wringing our hands about it. It is a fact of our history' (Blair 1997g). Having one day set himself up as an Empire man, the next day (at the CBI annual conference) Blair suggested that memories of Empire could eclipse the prospects for a European future. In this regard he identified New Labour as having promoted, as early as November 1997, 'fresh confidence and optimism: fresh understand-ing of the joys of our history but also the prospects for our future' (Blair 1997h). It was this idea of a 'fresh understanding' of history that the Prime Minister believed he could sell to the British people, a classic Third Way *via media* between Empire as fact-of-the-past and a revivified Commonwealth as precursor-to-the-future. He ex-pressed the same idea to the US State Department in February 1998, when he undercut the 'quaint' or 'old fashioned' stereotype of Britain, 'A country of pageantry and ceremony, bowler hats and stiff upper lips', and set out his vision for a 'new Britain' under New Labour. 'Britain today is defined by a lot more than its history' (Blair 1998c). Changed times and circumstances, the Prime Min-ister told his audience at the Polish Stock Exchange in October 2000, necessitated a change in mentality, meaning 'it is time to overcome the legacy of Britains [*sic*] past' (Blair 2000f). History should not be jettisoned altogether (too radical) or clung to in the vain hope that the world as it really is will cease bothering the British island people (too c/Conservative), but should be used to tread a Third Way that combined reverence for the past with creative renewal of the best British traditions.

The way in which Blair and Brown suggested the legacy of the past could be overcome was to use it more effectively to build a 'post-imperial' future for Britain in which the country could secure its 'national interests as part of the European Union' (Brown 2006a). Repackaging the actuality and legacy of Empire would allow the people to respect the past for what it was but more importantly to use that reinterpreted past to point them towards a new – European – future. This seems to have been what Blair had in mind when he talked in his 1997 Lord Mayor's Banquet speech about 'using the strengths of our history to build the future' (Blair 1997g) and it was a theme that would bounce around through his foreign policy speeches. In December 1998 he described it as 'building on the strengths of our history; it means building new alliances; developing new influence; *charting a new course for British foreign policy*' (Blair 1998f; emphasis added). In 2001 he was back urging: 'Let us in Britain use the strengths of our history – our place in Europe, our alliance with the Commonwealth, our traditional ties with the Arab world, India, China or the Commonwealth – to build a solid future of influence for our nation' (Blair 2001c). Blair explained how to use history subtly and sensitively in a 2003 speech at the Foreign Office in London, where he spoke favourably about the 'reach given by our past', 'the strengths of our history, unique in breadth for a country of our size' and an Empire which 'left much affection' as well, unfortunately, as 'deep problems to be overcome' (Blair 2003b). As he saw it, the useful residue of Empire consisted of formal and informal connections around the globe which put Britain in a privileged position, able fully to play the role Churchill had described in 1948. 'Our very strengths, our history equip us to play a role as a unifier around a consensus for achieving both our goals and those of the wider world', said Blair. However, it was only by *placing* history correctly that Britain could play this role. As he saw it history is a source of strength only 'provided we lose any lingering traces of imperial arrogance and recognise countries will only work as equals' (Blair 2003b). Remember the Empire, but lose imperial arrogance; take pride in history, but do not venerate it at the expense of the future. These classic Blair doctrines played out in the final lesson of history he felt his various audiences (but mainly those in Britain) needed to learn: Europe is the future. The philosophical underpinnings of this position can be seen in the parting shot to one of the most stridently Europhile speeches of his premiership, from November 1999, when the Prime Minister said that 'The real denial of our history would be to retreat into isolation from the continent of Europe of which we are a part and whose history we have so intimately shaped' (Blair 1999f). The everywhere-ness of history in this sentence stands out, with Blair suggesting that it would be a distortion of reality or truth to deny that Britain has always been a European player. To reject the EU would not just be a denial of the New Labour project but would be a denial of the logic of history itself.

New Labour's will to historicize everything in its European discourse is therefore evident in the premium Blair and Brown placed on learning from the past. There are two other ways in which we see its will to historicize at work in the data: first, in its periodization of the past for the purposes of popular consumption; and second, in the ways New Labour categorized the errors of the past it wanted to avoid repeating. Beginning with periodization, Blair would often construct himself and his party as taking forward the work begun by another great reforming Labour government, that of Clement Attlee, of 1945–51. This tendency was most noticeable in, but not confined to, speeches in his first year in office. On the steps of Downing Street in May 1997 he spoke warmly of the domestic achievements of the Attlee governments: 'It was a previous Labour Government that formed and fashioned the welfare state and the National Health Service. It was our proudest creation. It shall be our job and our duty now to modernize it for a modern world' (Blair 1997b). Brown used the NHS experience to draw a general lesson for Britain fifty years on: 'when we pool and share our resources and when the stronger help the weak it makes us all stronger' (Brown 1999a). He extended this argument a year later in a lecture on civic society delivered to the Arnold Goodman Charity, when he said that under the Attlee governments 'a new relationship emerged between the state, the individual and the community' (Brown 2000f; on Brown's admiration of Attlee see Bower 2007: 40–1). On the external front, Blair was taken with the actions of Attlee's Foreign Secretary, Ernest Bevin, who, by helping to create NATO, helped bring security and stability to the Western world in the early years of the Cold War: 'a very, very considerable achievement from an earlier Labour government' (Blair 1997d; see also Blair 1999b). Those days might be 'now distant' but Blair credited Bevin with a great act of leadership and foresight (Blair 2000h). Added to these well documented domestic and international achievements Blair also played up the Attlee government's record on promoting human rights through the European Convention on Human Rights, using this memory to underline the size of the step he proposed to make to incorporate the Convention into British domestic law (Blair 1997e). The Prime Minister was also proud to note that 'it was under a Labour Government that India secured her independence' (Blair 1997i). It is clear from the consistent references to Attlee that Blair wanted to position himself in the stream of Labour success stories, and that he wanted to silence memories or talk of the – as New Labour had it – disastrous Old Labour party of Harold Wilson, James Callaghan and Michael Foot.

New Labour's veneration of the Attlee years took in both domestic and foreign policy. However, as far as European policy was concerned, Blair and Brown saw no reason to exclude Attlee from their most popular lesson from British history: that the country's leaders had failed the nation by remaining aloof from the European integration process which gathered pace in the early years after the Second World War. However, the government could never quite settle on how best to describe the history and its periodization of this litany of mistakes went back either fifty years or twenty years, depending on the speech. On the one hand Blair implicitly included the Attlee governments by saying that the tragedy extended back five decades. 'The blunt truth is that British policy towards the rest of Europe over half a century has been marked by gross misjudgements, mistaking what we wanted to be the case with what was the case' (Blair 2000f). At the Foreign Office in 2003 he argued that fifty years of hesitation 'never profited us' (Blair 2003b). Occasionally, however, Blair would tend to be vague when writing off past trends in British European policy, by speaking, for instance, about 'the mistakes of the past' (Blair 1999f) or 'the sterile confrontations and isolationism of the recent past' (Blair 1999c). In 1997, Brown had criticized British isolationists for denying Britain's outward-looking character on the basis of a 'negative' and 'anti-European' reading of the immediate past (Brown 1997a) which would mean 'cutting ourselves off from Europe' (Brown 1998b). Perhaps the best example of New Labour writing off everything that had preceded it came during Blair's rallying call behind Britain's EU Presidency of January to June 1998, when he wanted to demonstrate 'That the indecision, vacillation and anti-Europeanism of the past have gone' (Blair 1997j).

On the other hand, when New Labour wanted to make partisan points about European policy it narrowed the period of policy errors and short-sightedness to the two decades prior to 1997 – coterminous with the Conservative years of Margaret Thatcher and John Major. For example, at the Lord Mayor's Banquet in 1997 the Prime Minister said 'we must end the isolation of the last twenty years and be a leading partner in Europe' (Blair 1997g). This was sometimes narrowed further, to focus on Blair's recent rival over the House of Commons dispatch box, Major. For instance in Poland in 2000 Blair described the 'reality' of his government's inheritance on Europe as 'foolish' marginalization and isolation, 'despite the efforts of John Major' (Blair 2000f). In his March 2002 Commons statement on the

Barcelona European Council he said that the previous government had made Britain dangerously 'marginalised, without influence appropriate to our weight and size, *in the isolation room*' (Blair 2002a; emphasis added). In the back-handed compliment to Major from 2000 we note that Blair was more interested in discrediting the Conservative Party as a whole rather than its leader, for whom he had no little personal respect (Blair 2010: 2). Perhaps Blair saw in the miserable later Major years something of his own predicament, an 'outsider' struggling to impose his vision on a recalcitrant set of backbenchers. Similarly, he damned Thatcher's Bruges speech with faint praise, castigating the effects it unleashed on British European policy (making it 'withdraw into its shell') rather than the speaker herself (Blair 2000b). He admired Thatcher's tactics, her 'genuine' reasons for giving the speech and especially her penchant for 'adding lustre' to Britain's self-perception of its role in the world (Stephens 2004: 104).

It was rare to find New Labour departing from one or other of these two periodizations of British history. One occasion came in Chicago in April 1999, when Blair proclaimed that 'For the first time in the last three decades we have a government that is both pro-European and pro-American' (Blair 1999d). It is unlikely that Blair would have wanted to remind his American hosts of the Wilson–Johnson arguments over British troop commitments to Vietnam in the 1960s so we can only assume he meant the Edward Heath governments from 1970. This would imply a period of errors in British European policy spanning back two and a half as opposed to three decades but, as we have seen in this book, New Labour's use of quantitative data to support its arguments was notoriously lax and could be stretched to the point of numbing vagueness. Working the theme of British economic history, Brown would periodize slightly differently from Blair but the morality tale about the British in Europe was the same. The Chancellor stressed that the government had learnt lessons from 'the political mistakes of the last forty years', making New Labour determined to maintain tough strictures on government spending and inflation to end the nation's economic cycle of 'boom and bust' (Brown 2000c; Brown 2000d; four specific lessons were elucidated in Brown 2000e; on Brown's economic lesson learning see also Brown 2003d; Brown 2003f). To make a party political point at the expense of the Conservatives in the run-up to the 2001 general election, Brown firmly fixed his sights on the '18 years of boom and bust' and the short-termism, 'the quick-fixes' that led to 'the stop go, boom bust economy, the ups and downs, of the past' (Brown 2000g) in an effort to convince the unions of Labour's economic competence in government. His periodization might have been different from Blair's but his will to *periodize* was exactly the same, speaking of a government that actively sought to distance itself from its predecessors, Old Labour and Conservative alike.

Thus, New Labour's veneration of the Attlee government stopped abruptly at its European policy, where its failures were historicized into the metanarrative of 'missed opportunities'. However, Blair and Brown saved most of their ire for the Conservative governments after 1979. Throughout, the government characterized the mistakes of the British in Europe using a number of metaphors, some of which are worth visiting now in some detail for the light they shed on the ways in which Blair and Brown projected their self-images and ideal-type leadership traits onto their ambitions for the British in Europe. We saw above how Blair worked the idea that the Conservative governments had put Britain in the 'isolation room'. This spatializing concept underpinned his argument that, in contrast, his government was, and would be, 'Internationalist not isolationist' (Blair 1998c). At times the government's suggestion that the British could somehow help create and define globalization could reach the point of farce. For example Brown claimed in May 2005 that 'we were internationalist even before the word was first heard' (Brown 2005e)! This dovetailed with what New Labour saw as the inexorable rise of internationalist centre-left governments in Western Europe and the US in the later 1990s (Blair 1999d), the discourse supporting his strategy of building consensus around a Third Way approach to social democratic governance. Later, when Blair was seeking to generate consensus around a strategy for European reform, the spatializing metaphor was again to the fore when he rued, over the Constitutional Treaty, that 'instead of bold policy reform and decisive change, we locked ourselves in a room at the top of the tower and debated things no ordinary citizen could understand' (Blair 2006a). The soundbites used to convey the desire for Britain and the EU to be 'out there' changing the world may have altered, depending on context, but New Labour saw 'engagement not isolationism as the only serious foreign policy on offer' (Blair 2001c; Blair 2003g). Alternatively, as he put in the first of a series of three valedictory speeches on foreign policy in March 2006, 'a policy of engagement not isolation; and one that is active not reactive' (Blair 2006b; see also Blair 2006e).

The Prime Minister's thinking on foreign policy over the course of his final year or so in office came to settle on the idea that in the world, as he saw it, there was a 'true division in foreign policy' between 'those who want the shop "open", or those who want it "closed"'. The former want to be 'out there, engaged, interactive', while the latter 'think the short-term pain of such a policy and its decisions, too great' (Blair 2006b; Blair 2006c; see also Blair 2006d). The open/closed idea was the logical extension of Blair's thinking as it had developed both as personal philosophy and as national outlook since 1997.* In both realms, the 'doctrine of benign inactivity' as he called it (Blair 2006b) was trumped by the 'doctrine of international community' that 'both embodies, and acts in pursuit of global values' (Blair 2006e). The former spoke of not-so-splendid isolation and retrenchment, the latter of interest- and value-driven alliance-building and held out the possibility of humanity's progress, through the hawkish idea of 'progressive pre-emption' and 'the necessity of a common value system to make it work' (Blair 2006e). To News Corps in July 2006 Blair set out the economic counterpart to 'open/closed' thinking: 'The response to globalisation can be free trade, open markets, investment in the means of competition: education, science, technology. Or it can be protectionism, tariffs, tight labour market regulation, resistance to foreign takeovers' (Blair 2006f).

Significantly, we can see that the open/closed idea guided Blair's European discourses throughout his premiership, when he would contrast the Conservative policy of being closed with the idea of Labour's open, proactive approach. We saw above that in his statement on the Barcelona European Council Blair accused the Conservative government of 'indecision, vacillation and anti-Europeanism'. He regularly deployed these and related descriptors in his indictment of British policy before 1997. In Ghent in February 2000 he talked unfavourably about the British tradition of 'miscalculations', which meant 'We opted out of the European Coal and Steel Community. We opted out of the European Economic Community. We opted out of the Social Chapter' (Blair 2000b). The cascade of opt-outs Blair identified was responsible for what he described in November that year as 'weakness and isolation' – which could be overcome by the reverse policy of 'Leadership and influence' (Blair 2000g). Being an 'observer in Europes [sic] development, not a player' (Blair 2000b), 'British ambivalence to Europe' (Blair 1999e), hesitancy, 'retreat to a common market' (Blair 2005b), 'hanging back in Europe' (Blair 2003c) and joining schemes late (Blair 2000b): these were the negative aspects Blair identified in the history of British European policy. He summed them up in his November 2002 Cardiff speech on the subject. 'For 50 years, we have chosen to follow, first in joining; then in each new departure Europe has made' (Blair 2002d). Worries about possible failure had outweighed, as Blair saw it, the assertiveness needed to get involved and shape the process to suit Britain's interests. This lack of confidence was mixed dangerously with the arrogant belief that European unity was not possible without British involvement. 'At each stage, Britain thought it won't possibly happen

* I am grateful to Philip Collins for pointing this out to me in interview.

and held back. And at each stage it did happen and we were faced
with the choice: catching up or staying out' (Blair 2000f). Or as he
put in 2001 of the ECSC: 'So we said that it wouldn't happen. Then
we said it wouldn't work. Then we said we didn't need it. But it did
happen. And Britain was left behind.' And of the EEC: 'We said that
it wouldn't happen. Then we said it wouldn't work. Then we said
we didn't need it. But it did happen. And Britain was left behind.'
And latterly of membership in 1973: 'Already, politicians across both
major parties wanted to pull out. They still said that it wouldn't
work, and that we didn't need it.' (All from Blair 2001d.) Another
cascade effect, this time produced by split repetition, called to mind
the British vainly trying to plug a leaky dam: resistance, resistance,
resistance – but ultimately the pressure that built up was too much
and the inevitable 'did happen'. The Chancellor identified the same
plot to the story of the British in Europe (Brown 1997c), his moral
being that divisions over Europe succeeded only in marginalizing
British influence and 'denied us a national economic consensus'
(Brown 1997e). For New Labour, the only foreign policy option on
offer was to be open to new alliance-building projects with like-
minded partners, not shut off from them.

A signal departure from the idea that Britain had 'sinned' by
staying in the isolation room came towards the end of Blair's time
in office, when he was apparently irritated and exhausted trying
to generate a pan-European consensus around reform of Europe's
social model and institutions, as well as seeking to correct the EU's
democratic deficit. In a speech on the future of Europe in February
2006, Blair turned the tables by arguing that Britain's exclusion
had come to be expensive not so much for the British but in fact for
the Europeans: 'we [British] think of what might have been for us.
But there is a distinctive way of looking at it; what might have been
for Europe' (Blair 2006a). His thinking was that Europe without
Britain had become too inward-looking and obsessed with the drive
for institution-building. 'At the outset this was not just natural but
necessary. But over time, it became almost self-perpetuating and
certainly self-absorbing' (Blair 2006a), blinding European decision-
makers to the need to keep Europe responsive to the wants and needs
of the peoples it was set up to help. The key reason for the switch in
emphasis at this juncture appears to have been that during his final
year and a half in office Blair developed his foreign policy thinking
around the idea, explored above, of states and international organizations being either 'open' or closed', and he was infuriated with the
EU's prolonged bout of institutional navel gazing which he believed
was keeping it 'closed' and blinding it to the bigger politico-economic
challenges in the international system. What we can see therefore

is a different Tony Blair in 2006 than in earlier years, when he was playing supplicant to the EU rather than spokesman for it.

In the main, therefore, we can see how Blair and Brown bought into the 'missed opportunities' thesis about British European policy, and how this featured as a series of spatializing metaphors in their political rhetoric. Their characterization of the past failings in British European policy allowed them to create the discursive space in which to construct their policy and ambitions for New Labour's policy towards the EU. In the next section we will see how they themed their approach around the idea of 'enlightened patriotism', or what Brown described as 'mature patriotism' (Brown 1998b; Brown 1998c; Brown 1998f).

III. The moral of the enlightened patriots

[I]t seems to me that no matter how far we go – or rather the farther we go – the things we discover are more likely to be nothing more than ourselves. (Murakami quoted in Rubin 2005: 227)

In their discourses on the British in Europe, Tony Blair and Gordon Brown trod a careful path between respect for the past and a re-evaluation of the meaning of that past for the present and future of British foreign policy. Prime Minister and Chancellor frequently put the view that the British needed to come to terms with the legacy of their past in order to create a modern and exciting future for themselves; this was sometimes expressed as a call for the British to 'get over' their past. This process of 'coming to terms' with history (which for New Labour straightforwardly overlooked theoretical questions associated with how the past *becomes* history) involved a psychological acceptance on the part of the public, media and political elites that the disparate events woven seamlessly into the British national story could be unpicked and stitched back together to create a quite different image of the meaning of the past in the present. From New Labour's perspective, the British national story had to be recast as a tale not of separateness from Europe but as coterminous with that entity, a version of global history that re-evaluated the meaning and interactions of whole sets of events, personalities and processes. At the same time, New Labour took a traditionalist view, widely held by British politicians and diplomats, that history could provide moral, political and practical lessons for the present. Brown put this line most clearly in January 2006, when he described his vision of the place national history should occupy in the British education system: 'And we should not recoil from our national history – rather we should make it more central to our education. I propose that British history should be given much more prominence in the curriculum – not just dates, places and names, nor just a set of unconnected facts, but a narrative that encompasses our history' (Brown 2006a). In taking this line Blair and Brown had to confront a persistent problem: that New Labour was by no means in the majority in placing a progressivist, European-oriented reading onto British history. Prime Minister and Chancellor had apparently learnt different things from their readings of history than had the Eurosceptics and others in the anti-European camp, who read into the idea of Great Britain many more reasons to stay remote from European integration than to get involved with it. This prompted some in the latter camp to question Blair's sense of patriotism and national duty. A partisan critique from the right of the Conservative Party it may have been, but nonetheless it was potentially damaging to any Prime Minister, who first and foremost must have the moral authority to speak about, and have the credibility to safeguard, the national interest.

The anti-patriot charges became louder as the pressure mounted for a referendum on first the single currency and then the Constitutional and Lisbon Treaties. The premise of the calls was, as Christopher Booker put it in 2001, that British Prime Ministers have knowingly concealed the sovereignty-degrading aspects of the EEC and the EU from the British people, and done so over a prolonged period – since joining in 1973. Blair, in this view, was:

> [the latest to] lead them step by step into exchanging their own country and political system for another, totally different; and to pretend at every stage that none of it is really happening. And it is that fundamental dishonesty which in the end accounts for that ubiquitous culture of deceit which now permeates every corner of our dealings with the European project. (Booker 2001)

High-profile commentators in national newspapers came to the same opinion, with one example standing out (image 6): a 2003 comment article by Richard Littlejohn in the *Sun*, headlined 'How dare Tony Blair call *us* unpatriotic' (Littlejohn 2003). Littlejohn put pen to paper on the back of Blair's argument in his May 2003 Warsaw speech, put together with the help of an array of Europeanist thinkers outside Whitehall (Naughtie 2002: 152–3), that 'anti-Europeanism … is itself a symptom not of national pride but a lack of confidence about just how strong Britain can and should be' (Blair 2003c). Blair suggested that 'standing up' to Europe was not always the patriotic thing to do; a true patriot knows when to engage with the EU as well as when to say 'enough is enough'. In other words, the Prime Minister was trying to pass on the lesson he had learnt from history by countering the hegemonic, Eurosceptical reading of the national past discussed in chapter 5. For Littlejohn, this was 'the most despicable

Image 6. Littlejohn article and Gaskill cartoon.

speech ever made by a serving British Prime Minister'. Blair's take on patriotism was a 'monstrous slander' on the people he had been elected to lead. 'How does sticking up for the right to defend our borders, pass our own laws and run our own economy make us unpatriotic?', Littlejohn asked, when 'That is the very essence of patriotism'. An outraged Littlejohn went on to imagine what Blair might have done as British premier at the outbreak of the Second World War: 'Presumably [he] would have thought the patriotic thing to do would be to hand over the keys to Hitler.' As well as being angry, Littlejohn was perplexed: 'I simply don't understand why anyone goes into politics to destroy their own country and hand it over to foreigners.' In the famous words of Labour leader Hugh Gaitskell, delivered over forty years earlier to describe his opposition to the idea of a federal Europe, Littlejohn chastized the premier for hating 'this country' and for being 'hell-bent on destroying 1,000 years of history'. Quite simply, Littlejohn continued, the French and Germans 'are not people you can do business with'. His fairy-tale description of the non-choice for the British people in a possible referendum on the European Constitution was telling. 'Certainly, given the option, most British people would rather live in a free, benign kingdom nominally ruled by a kindly old granny than in a federal superstate run by foreigners, with their tidy minds, armed with their railway timetables and oppressive "human rights" laws.'

Throughout the article Littlejohn blurred the boundary between history, nostalgia and popular culture. The cultural context was clearly brought through in Dave Gaskill's accompanying cartoon. In it, a horrified Blair castigates the cast of *Dad's Army* for trying to defend Britain at the famous landmark of the white cliffs of Dover looking out over the English Channel. This popular British situation comedy ran for nine years from 1968 and over eighty episodes; it followed the travails of a group of men from the fictional town of Walmington-on-Sea on the south coast of England, who set up their own Local Defence Volunteers, later to become the Home Guard. It was turned into a feature film in 1971, a stage show in 1975 and adapted for radio too. In the period before digital and satellite television its audience figures numbered tens of millions and episode repeats remain hugely popular today, such that it 'is never placed opposite a major television production' (Dad's Army Appreciation Society 2009b). It even has a dedicated museum that houses a collection of artefacts similar to those you can find for Britain's 'real' military experiences around the globe (Dad's Army Appreciation Society 2009a). Set around tales of this bumbling, amateurish, ill-organized but fiercely patriotic group, the show played upon memories of the heroic English standing up to the latest continental enemy, well captured in the show's song lyrics: 'who do you think you are kidding Mister Hitler / If you think old England's done?' (Dad's Army Appreciation Society 2009c). Sporting a badge reading 'I love Brussels', Blair is telling them: 'Don't be so unpatriotic!' An affront to the well known and much loved fictional *Dad's Army* is, it appears, an affront to the British 'in reality' and this would have been the overarching sentiment *Sun* readers that day would surely have taken from Gaskill's cartoon and Littlejohn's article.

The lesson Littlejohn had learnt from his study of the past was that the British should 'stand up' to, fend off and remain aloof from everything 'Europe', its nation states and their suspect integrative practices. He may not have expressed the association in full but Littlejohn equated patriotism with an anti-Europeanism that flowed directly from a martial, conflict-ridden interpretation of the British experience of 'Europe'. The ideological divide between Littlejohn and New Labour opened up over the latter's acceptance of the always-European dimension of the British national identity in the past and the present. It can be seen very simply in Blair's take on the populist interpretation that closer integration into the EU represented the possible end of a 'thousand years' of British history. To my knowledge Blair never responded by pointing out the historical inaccuracy of the claim that Britain as an entity has actually existed for that period of time; in fact he used the phrase in his retort that as early as the 1960s policy-makers had recognized 'that "a thousand years of history" were not enough. Because yesterday's heritage did not guarantee today's influence or tomorrow's prosperity' (Blair 2001d). Where the nostalgia for the 'thousand years' was the cause of Littlejohn's scepticism about the EU, for Blair it was the very reason for his proactive integrationism. Blair preferred to look to the next 'thousand years' rather than the last, and it was on the shifting sands of history that each located his definition of the national interest, political leadership on the Europe question and national duty. It is to New Labour's concept of patriotism that we now turn.

Understandably during his formative years in power, Blair liked to be clear about the extent to which he could be trusted with representing Britain on the world stage. He had already staked out his claim in his pre-1997 election St George's Day article in the *Sun* (see chapter 7) and was quick to remind the British people when in office that: 'In the end I am, simply, a patriot. I believe in Britain' (Blair 1997g). It was in his speeches on European policy that he felt he had to clarify his position most frequently. Hence in his 'New challenge for Europe' speech in Aachen, May 1999, Blair said he wanted to be 'very frank about my feelings about Britain and Europe. I am a patriot. I love my country' (Blair 1999e). Five months later, at the relaunch of Britain in Europe, he put the case that he was fronting 'a patriotic cause. The people here represent a patriotic alliance that puts country before Party' (Blair 1999f). What kind of patriotism was Blair espousing? He described it as 'enlightened patriotism' and contrasted it with the kind of inward-looking, jingoistic, blinkered or nationalist-fuelled isolationism he identified in the Eurosceptical positions he was set on demolishing through his government's foreign policy: 'Patriotism based not on narrow chauvinism but on the right values and principles', patriotism in a country that 'does stand for the right values and can give something to the world' (Blair 1997g). Three years later Blair was back to confronting the isolationists:

> To show that the patriot is not the person who pulls up the draw-bridge and sits in his tower musing on the errors of the world; but the person who recognises that today no drawbridge makes a nation safe and that we are better out in the world, fighting for what we believe in; that tough choices over how to act are a better way of life than the soothing illusions of inactivity. (Blair 2000g)

The Prime Minister's argument rested on his favourite concept of engagement, 'whatever the criticisms' (Blair 2000h). He cast the isolationists as ducking for cover in the face of hard political decisions and suffering from the 'delusion that the tide of change can be turned back' (Blair 2006f). He wanted to evoke the image of people with closed minds sitting idly by in an English castle, twiddling their thumbs while the world turned around them. Blair depicted his critics as backward-looking, stuck in the past, and he sought to pre-empt just the sort of nostalgic notions of the British past of the fairy-story type Littlejohn would later eulogize in his pieces on Blair's dearth of patriotic credentials.

Blair spent a good deal of time trying to undermine the zero-sum appreciation of foreign policy, that 'anything that pleased Brussels was bad for Britain' (Blair 2010: 533). For example, in his 1998 *tour d'horizon* on foreign affairs he noted that:

> today I read, in the front page headlines of one of our broadsheets, that being positive and constructive in Europe, amounts to me issuing orders to the Government to 'bat for Brussels'. So that when I say to the Government – get close to our allies in Europe, I am somehow batting for Brussels. I see it as batting for Britain. (Blair 1998f)

He put his case rather more forthrightly in February 2000, when he spoke about ongoing discussions about EU reform.

> To withdraw ... is not patriotic; it is an abdication of our true national interest. Other countries playing a leading role in Europe do not see the European Union as an alternative to the nation state; indeed, they see it as a way of enhancing their national interests. (Blair 2000b)

By 2003 he had even less patience with his detractors.

> My passionate belief in Europe is not born of any diminishing of my belief in Britain. On the contrary, I believe in Europe because I believe membership of the European strategic alliance is a crucial part of the British national interest. Anti-Europeanism is not British patriotism. It is an out of date delusion. (Blair 2003c; see also Blair 2003b)

This was the first of several occasions when Blair, from the middle of his second term in office, began to turn the tables on his

Eurosceptical opponents by labelling *them* unpatriotic, or at least cleaving to a misguided interpretation of patriotism, hence his exchange with Littlejohn. It was in 2004 that he really went on the offensive, this time over ten 'myths' that had come to surround the Constitutional Treaty (Blair 2004b). He argued that the Eurosceptical opponents of the Treaty would 'put in jeopardy' everything the EU had achieved to date in terms of greater freedom, security and prosperity, just 'for the sake, not of any real British interest, but of a narrow nationalism which no British government has ever espoused or should ever espouse if it has the true interests of the British people at heart' (Blair 2004a). The implication was that Blair was on the side of truth, reality and the British people, while the sceptics were on the side of error, delusion and self-interest. As the negotiations over the treaty progressed through 2004 Blair said: 'I am told to leave our allies in the lurch, walk away from the argument, retreat into a eurosceptic sulk and call it "standing up for Britain". And why? Because we have confused identity with isolation; the more "alone" we are, the more purely British' (Blair 2004c).

Blair's increasing irascibility on the issue of patriotism (i.e., who possessed the authority to 'speak' for Britain) surely testified to his confidence after two landslide election victories, to a Prime Minister increasingly frustrated with press coverage of his foreign policy but increasingly assured of his judgement to take bold foreign policy initiatives, such as over Iraq, which did not always sit well with either the public or the media, not to mention his own advisers, Cabinet and backbenchers. What is interesting throughout these passages from the Prime Minister's speeches is how they chimed with New Labour thinking on leadership, European policy and, critically, how to ingrain leadership *into* European policy. He put British hesitancy about the EU as being down to:

> a chronic lack of self-confidence we suffer from sometimes as a nation, failing to believe in ourselves properly, so we think we will lose arguments in Europe, when actually when we put our minds to it, we usually win. We should have more self-confidence because we are a leading European power, always have been and always will be. (Blair 2002d)

This was an echo of Brown speaking at the Smith Institute in April 1999 on the British needing to become 'more confident in our culture' as a diverse, multiethnic society (Brown 1999a) and suggesting in his July 2004 British Council Annual Lecture that in the post-war era 'a loss of self confidence' was 'becoming part of our history' (Brown 2004g). In 2003 Blair diagnosed anti-Europeanism as 'a symptom not of national pride but a lack of confidence about just how strong Britain can and should be' (Blair 2003c). He urged that Britain must 'have the confidence to stride

forward' because: 'There are real battles.... But they are battles we
can win' (Blair 2003d). Blair's inadvertent use of military jargon
to describe Britain's summitry in Europe should not obscure the
point he wanted to make about the sceptic line on Europe, that it
was born out of a loss of confidence in the British as a people to get
what they want from the world by prudent diplomacy and persuasion
rather than military conquest. In 2005 he diagnosed the same ill at
the supranational level, calling for a 'confident Europe' instead of
one that might 'become more narrow, more introspective' by sacri-
ficing 'European idealism' at the altar of 'outdated nationalism and
xenophobia' (Blair 2005b). Blair described anti-Europeanism using a
health metaphor, that it was a medical condition suffered by people
who had become addicted to outmoded policies and practices, a
'sickness that has afflicted Britain's relationship with the project of
European integration ever since it joined the European Community
more than thirty years ago' (Blair 2006a). British Eurosceptics were
ill because they clung to memories of Empire. In Europe, meanwhile,
the infirmity took a different form – an idea of 'protectionist bloc
Europe', whose proponents refused to contemplate radical reform of
the EU, particularly of the social model (Blair 2005b). Blair's pre-
scription to both sets of patients was that they needed to adapt to the
demands of the modern, global era and, by implication, to share his
'complete inner-confidence in the analysis of the struggle we face'
(Blair 2006f). Reclaiming a centre-ground interpretation of patriotism both from the extreme right BNP and from the nationalist wing
of the Conservative Party became a preoccupation of Brown as it
looked more and more likely that he would take over from Blair. In
his Fabian Society speech in 2006 he added to the Blair line a view
that patriotism was about more than identity but about the 'values
of liberty, responsibility and fairness'. By reclaiming these values,
Britain could finally grasp the leadership of Europe by helping force
upon it 'the next stage of Europe's development' (Brown 2006a).

Summary

There is, therefore, a combination here of a modern approach, recognizing the importance for a medium-sized country like Britain of
working with and through the EU, with a more traditional emphasis
on Britain's independent global role. It will be important to observe
how the balance or tension between these two emphases develops.
(Hughes and Smith 1998: 95)

This chapter has studied three key elements of New Labour's European discourse as far as history goes: first, the way the government
encouraged the British people to move on from the past; second, New

Labour's views on the lessons of history; and third, the government's concept of 'enlightened patriotism'. These themes appeared time and again in Blair and Brown's speeches over a long period, a sure sign that they were never fully fledged doctrines but nonetheless convictions that were firmly held and required constant iteration as critics tried to subvert them for political gain as Blair and Brown charted Britain's path into the twenty-first century. New Labour's turn to history clumsily blended the traditionalist and the radical. Blair and Brown were firmly in line with established diplomatic convention in constantly referring to history as a source of lessons. In objectifying it as having an existence and an agency all of its own, the government would also put its spin on the ontological nature of history, construing it as some form of deity which can 'forgive' us mere mortals, or not, as it sees fit. History was both a subject of Blair and Brown's speeches but also an object of them, giver and given, with a force and direction of its own. In 2006, by way of example, Blair noted that EU enlargement was manifestly right because it worked with the prevailing force of globalization and because 'the new members are themselves the product of a history that impels them towards a Europe that is open, free, Atlanticist and ready, willing and able to compete' (Blair 2006a). Spotting the tides of history and moving with them, rather than swimming against them, was one of Blair's favoured leadership qualities. He was at his most prosaic on history when addressing audiences in North America and it was there that we witnessed the only occasion on which the Prime Minister lost faith in history as a moral guide.

For Blair and Brown, the national story pointed to one end-state for Britain, whereas for their sceptical critics it pointed in a different direction. As the chapter progressed we saw how the two men projected elements of their own personalities and leadership styles onto New Labour's vision for Britain in Europe. Their take on the psychology of patriotism was that their opponents lacked self-belief and direction, whereas they could take spiritual courage from the knowledge that they were treading the correct path, both for themselves and for the country. In the next chapter we will develop the idea that New Labour's leaders used their foreign policy speeches to project their personality and beliefs about leadership onto British foreign policy and see how this played out in New Labour's discourses on Britain's role in the world.

Chapter 9

Projecting an image:
New Labour, the EU and the wider world

> It is certainly true that one of the more significant qualities of a
> national leader is the ability to tell a country 'stories' about itself
> which make sense of what a leader and a party are trying to achieve.
> (Rentoul 1997: 398)

Chapters 7 and 8 traced the progressivist elements of New Labour's
discourse on British European policy with reference to the place perceptions of history occupied in Blair and Brown's speeches on foreign
policy. The Prime Minister and Chancellor called on the British
people to 'make sense of their past', which, for them, is and always
has been a European one. Through a study of their historical lessons
we gained insight into what this book calls New Labour's 'logic of
history'. For those people and parties New Labour fixed in its discourse as the government's opponents over Europe, British history
was a long unfolding story of aloofness from, and reciprocated hostility towards, a continent, group of states and, latterly, supranational
processes of integration. As Blair and Brown interpreted it, British
Eurosceptics believed that the EU threatened to replace British identity and sovereignty with a hotch-potch, unimaginable, unrealizable
but, most importantly, unwanted *faux* European identity. Blair and
Brown's reading, shaped by New Labour's take on globalization and
interdependence, was that world history speaks not of the continued
primacy of nation states but of their coexistence with other loci of
power in the international system, both above the level of the nation
state and below it. Nation states may not be dead or even in their
death throes, but they do have to share the global stage with a whole
host of other actors to bring about common solutions to shared
problems. These opposing readings of the meaning of the past for
the present and future raise real and lasting questions about the
quality of the 'lessons of history' argument as it was deployed so
often by New Labour in political and public debates about the value
of history. Only on one prominent occasion, at the US Congress
in 2003 (see chapter 8), did Blair question the appropriateness of

taking this line on history. However, his wobble was all too swiftly
forgotten because diplomacy of the kind Blair was engaged in during
his speeches placed such emphasis on a reverence for the past.

Blair and Brown's logic of history entailed three propositions,
which become increasingly more contentious as we read down them:
first, that the past matters in the present; second, that the study of
history offers up lessons for the present; and third, that their reading
of the past was the 'correct' version. We can only assume that in
asking the public to make sense of their past Blair and Brown were
encouraging them to make the same sense of the past that they had.
New Labour did not want the British people to arrive at their own
sense of the past because this was in fact the source of the problem
as Blair and Brown saw it – that in being left to make their own
connections to the past the British people had been misled by the
illusions of Eurosceptic and/or nationalist histories. They went to
great lengths in their speeches to rehearse the meaning of the past
for their audiences, simultaneously making sense of it for the public
and imposing their own personal agendas onto that past. What we
increasingly saw through the preceding chapters was that Blair
and Brown were projecting something of *themselves* – in the form of
personality, leadership qualities and moral codes – onto their interpretations of the interconnections between the past, present and
future for British foreign policy. As figurehead of New Labour and
leader of the country between 1997 and 2007 this was particularly
the case for Blair as Prime Minister, and it fitted his character to
personalize his discourses in this fashion. This, Stephen Dyson, has
argued, is because the Prime Minister possessed 'a very high belief
in his ability to control events', compounded by 'a highly personalistic
style, in which Blair regarded the prospects for progress on an issue
as a function of his personal involvement in it'. A 'great persuader'
such as that, in the words of a Blair aide, was always likely to project
his own personality onto his speeches in a noticeable way, especially
when the essence of leadership for Blair was to be 'forward leaning'
(all from Dyson 2009b: 237). This chapter studies Blair and Brown's
projection of their self-images onto their discourses about the British
in Europe in two areas: in their ideas about European 'leadership';
and New Labour's positioning of Britain as a 'bridge' between the
US and the EU. The analysis of each set of data sandwiches a study
of how we can see New Labour's leadership psychology at work
through its words on Britain and Europe.

1. European leadership in Blair's global strategy

The people of Europe are speaking to us. They are posing the questions. They are wanting our leadership. It is time we gave it to them.
(Blair 2005b)

If one of Barack Obama and David Cameron's favourite keywords is 'change' then Tony Blair and New Labour's buzzword was surely 'leadership'. It was not the only one, of course, with 'new', 'modern' and 'change' itself all featuring prominently in New Labour speeches and policy documents. Yet 'leadership' as a theme stands out as *the* powerful idea behind the changes the government hoped to bring to both politics at home and Britain's relationships abroad. Blair and Brown never spelt out precisely what they meant when they talked about Britain assuming a European leadership role. However, a senior government source told Matthew Sowemimo that it was Blair's early ambition that by 2007 'Britain would wield the same influence in the EU as France and Germany' did in 1997 (Sowemimo 1999: 344). In his 1997 Downing Street victory address the Prime Minister spoke of wanting to give Britain 'strength and confidence in leadership both at home and abroad' (Blair 1997b), while just two and a half weeks later the Chancellor was, rather ominously, threatening to 'unleash the potential of the British people, to lead in Europe and in the world in the 21st century' (Brown 1997a; see also Brown 1997e). Blair managed to lever the prospect of British leadership into each and every statement or speech he made on the subject of Britain in Europe. For example, in his December 1997 speech on the British Presidency, 'leadership' appeared with a question mark hovering over it, Blair asserting that the Presidency represented: 'A test for Britain to show that we can and do offer strong leadership in Europe'. It was a direct challenge to goad the country into action. Not just Britain, but the Europeans too needed 'every bit of leadership and purpose we can muster' at a time of 'immense challenge' (Blair 1997j). In Japan in January 1998 Blair showed the wide applicability of the term when he told his audience that the aim of the government's education policy was 'high standards, the pursuit of excellence, discipline and leadership' (leadership on whose part was not totally clear). When he turned to foreign policy that day he harked back to his Downing Street address by stating that he wanted Britain to be 'confident of a leading role in Europe', having already talked of wanting to build 'a country at home in Europe, leading in the world' (Blair 1998a). This would be done, said Brown, by using the qualities of the British genius 'to show leadership abroad' (Brown 1997a) because 'Britain will do best if it takes leadership in Europe' (Brown 1997c). Playing a leadership part was, it seems, the best way to help the British feel comfortable with their country's role in the world.

Blair and Brown variously spoke of Britain being 'a leading player in Europe' (Blair 2001a), a 'leader in Europe' as the EU faced up to the challenge of globalization (Brown 2003e) and about Britain's 'destiny' or 'future' as a full and 'leading partner in Europe' (Blair 2000b; Blair 2000e; Blair 2000f; Blair 2000h). This they contrasted with being 'a bit player' (Blair 2000h) because 'Half-hearted partners are rarely leading partners' (Blair 1999e). Occasionally the leadership and partnership ambitions were conjoined as, for example, when the Prime Minister played to domestic and inter-national audiences alike by suggesting that 'Britain's proper role is as a leader and partner in Europe' (Blair 2002a), a 'key player in Europe' (Blair 2000d) or a 'key partner' in both Europe (Blair 2000f) and the world's major alliances (Blair 2000h). As with other attempts to tone down Britain's leadership aspirations, the context of Blair's switch to 'key partner' in his speech to the Polish Stock Exchange was telling because it articulated not his ambition, in fact, but what was then the current state of play in British–European relations. 'From Europe's perspective, Britain as a key partner in Europe is now a definite plus not a minus' (Blair 2000f). For Blair, being a key partner was a staging on the post on the way to becoming a leading partner, which was, as he put it later in the speech, after all 'Britain's future' in Europe. As Blair saw it, Britain had to build up gradually to its leadership role after the Conservatives had let it slide into neglect during the earlier 1990s. Being a 'key' partner in the present was the way to resuming the country's leadership role in the future. The data suggest that Blair's speeches contained an interesting admix of lofty European rhetoric and naked statements about Britain's will to lead Europe. The Prime Minister clearly valued the perception of Britain being a 'key partner' not as an end in itself but as the means to the longer-term goal of fashioning a post-imperial global leadership role for his country.

In stressing the leadership angle of its European policy New Labour was helping appease a sceptical domestic audience. As Sowemimo has put it, 'by asserting a leadership role, Britain's European engagement could be presented in a more patriotic, even nationalistic light' (Sowemimo 1999: 350), a point backed up by Pauline Schnapper, who has suggested that whichever party we study, 'British politicians' discourses on Europe ... remain burdened by a vision of national identity which remains largely defined along national, if not nationalist, lines' (Schnapper 2011: 2). We can see this in two important ways in Blair's speeches. First, Blair rou-tinely equated Britain playing a 'full part in Europe' (Blair 2001c;

Blair 2003a) or a 'full and complete part' (Blair 2002d) with the country being a 'leading' partner. This theme emerged as early as 1997, when he said at the Lord Mayor's Banquet that 'Britain is a part of Europe. It must play its full part in leading it' (Blair 1997g). This was a rather paradoxical take on the idea of partnership, which implies joint or compromise decision-making rather than one partner dominating the other. Is a partnership in which one power leads the other really a partnership at all? Perhaps Blair was transposing his experience of London's supposed 'partnership' with Washington onto his reading of British–European relations. It is noticeable that for his French audience in March 1998 Blair toned it down by suggesting that the future for Britain was as 'full partners [sic] in Europe' (Blair 1998d). This watering down shows not that Blair had changed his mind but that he perhaps would have encountered political difficulties standing up in Paris and talking up the prospect of the British leadership of Europe. By 2004, however, Blair had dropped the idea of being a 'partner' altogether when he described Britain as 'a leading member' (Blair 2004c). It seems that by passing the staging posts of being 'true' and 'key', Britain had been able to fulfil its leadership role in Europe and thus he could drop the pretence that the relationship between Britain and the EU was one of equals, or that a genuine partnership had been achieved.

The second way in which New Labour used the EU as a vehicle to carry Britain's national ambitions was through its emphasis on 'reform' of the organization. Brown tended to lead on the economic side and meant four things by it: structural reform, regulatory reform, a less protectionist trade policy and alterations to EU budgetary policy (O'Donnell and Whitman 2007: 256–61). Reform of the EU's economic and political 'vision' via the Lisbon process, New Labour suggested, entailed a shift in priorities from the 'continental' economic model to an outward-looking 'Anglo-Saxon' posture. This favourite Blair–Brown dualism has been critiqued as overplaying the distinction between the two models (Hopkin and Wincott 2006). The later Blair even publicly recognized that such caricatures actually harmed the debate by positing a false choice between the two models of Europe's political economy (Blair 2005b). The EU needed to reform in other areas too, said New Labour. For example, at the Council of Europe in October 1997, Blair said that although there was an amount of 'catching up' to do he hoped that, in time, Britain could 'lead the way' in terms of the protection and extension of human rights and freedoms, by bringing decision-making closer to the people (Blair 1997e). Likewise at the Hague at the beginning of 1998, the Prime Minister spoke of developing 'a reformed social model of which [sic] Britain can not only take part, but take a lead in helping to create' (Blair 1998b). Finally, at the relaunch of the Britain in Europe campaign the same sentiment persisted, that Britain could and should be playing a 'leading part' in European reform: of employment policy, structural reforms, European defence, on crime and pollution, and in widening and deepening the EU: 'Europe can reform and Britain can and should play a leading part in achieving it' (Blair 1999f).

What does this analysis of the data on 'leadership' reveal about New Labour's European discourses? The first finding is that Blair and Brown did not necessarily see Britain being 'at the centre of Europe' (Blair 2003b; Blair 2003e) or 'at the heart of' Europe (Blair 2004a) as the final point of their country's journey. They instead had it in mind that Britain needed to be at the centre of the EU in order to fulfil its foreign policy ambitions of being the privileged interlocutor of the US and thereby exercise its moral capacity for global leadership. 'Europe gives us weight and strength', Blair told the Lord Mayor's Banquet in November 2006 (Blair 2006h). A second finding is that New Labour saw the British being at home in Europe *only* if they could feel they were leading it and only if it was a different EU/Europe from the one currently in existence. Again, the implication was that the EU needed to think and act more 'British' and this would make it a more appropriate forum in which Britain could advance its national interests and exercise global leadership. The third finding revolves around the choice of 'reform' as a New Labour keyword. This was telling because when it talked about the changes it wanted to make to Britain's economy and society the government usually spoke of a 'modernizing' rather than a 'reform' agenda, implying a judgement on the relative ethical positions of the two entities as actors on the global stage. The ambition to 'reform' has stronger connotations than 'modernize' because where the latter implies something basically works and just needs tweaking, the former implies something is significantly wrong and needs urgent attention. Britain in this view basically *worked* but was in need of a little updating to make it fit for purpose for the twenty-first century. Europe, by contrast, had *gone off the rails* like a wayward or out of control teenager, liable to be dangerous to international society if not 'reformed'.

Having examined New Labour's thinly disguised leadership ambitions for Britain we can start to home in on a theoretical conception of discourse as a study in leadership psychology in action. The next section will illustrate how, using the data from the speeches.

II. Political discourse as personality projection

The purpose of bringing in Blair's implied moral codes when he spoke of the British in Europe has been to bolster what was said in earlier chapters about New Labour's binary 'good–bad' construction of British identity, interests and place on the world stage. But more than that, we have started to see how New Labour discourses on the EU actually projected something of Blair and Brown themselves onto the objects of their discourse.

We see in figure 8 what it means to say the two men were projecting their idealized self-images onto their construction of global politics through their speeches. When discussing the need for the British to be more 'confident' in their dealings with Europe, when talking of 'leadership' and 'reform', when articulating the government's desire to be ready to play a full part and get engaged with the EU, Blair and Brown were projecting onto the actor that is 'Britain' a huge measure of their own political outlooks. In their self-perceptions and their personal characteristics *were* both their leadership qualities and the embodiment of their political outlook as New Labour; in urging a dynamic, outward-looking and engaged

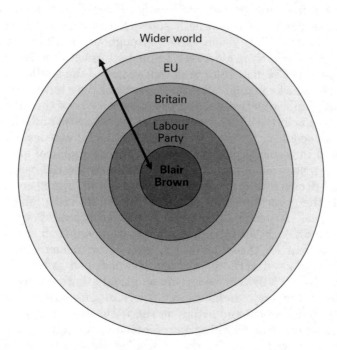

Figure 8. New Labour's target: global leadership.

British foreign policy Blair and Brown were urging the country to follow their lead – to perform more like they did. Ultimately this was a worldwide vision, in that rendering the EU more like Britain would enable New Labour to safeguard the British national interest but also impose the government's moral and political codes on the rest of the world through an expressly globalist foreign policy. Helping Britain lead the EU would make the world a safer, more congenial place for Britain and for Blair and Brown. In figure 8 the darker the shading of a given circle in the target, the closer Blair and Brown believed the actors in that circle were to agreeing with their shared belief system. Obviously the darkest circle is the innermost one: Blair and Brown themselves, leaders with moral purpose, humility and inner belief. 'For a leader, don't let your ego be carried away by the praise or your spirit diminished by the criticism and look on each with a very searching eye. But for heaven's sake, above all else, lead' (Blair 2006f). The next circle out was the Labour Party, the reform of which had been vital for both men, though perhaps Blair in particular, who had spent several years trying to reform the party from within, both as a member of the shadow Cabinet through the early 1990s and then as leader from 1994. It is fair to argue that by the time he became Prime Minister Blair saw the Labour Party as mostly but not totally reformed to the extent he would have liked. Hence, while it supported him as leader he had not imposed the 'Blair vision' either throughout the PLP or on the grassroots membership. Moreover, in his battles with the Brownites in and outside Cabinet, Blair was well aware of the shallowness of the foundations he laid for 'Blairism' over the longer term. Next out, and lighter still, was Britain, representing the size of the task New Labour had before it to modernize opinions, attitudes and values to prepare the country for the twenty-first century, at elite level, in the media and in terms of public opinion on the key political questions of the day. Next out and more elusive still was the EU, where the Blair and Brown's 'reform' agenda came up against significant opposition. If the government struggled to impose its vision on British society it was naturally a harder and lengthier process to achieve a parallel ambition in an extra-national environment such as the EU. The same went for the wider world, where New Labour's vision of the reform of key international organizations such as the UN and its efforts to exert British leadership on global affairs naturally had to confront the unpredictable and powerful consequences of the actions of other states and actors on the world stage, as well as the limits that came from working out of a medium-sized economic and geostrategic power base. The double-headed arrow denotes the idea that the Blair–Brown vision worked both ways: it came from within

Blair and Brown the people, the politicians, the Prime Ministers, the British patriots, the European leaders and world statesmen, but these identities were constantly being negotiated and constructed through their discursive and day-to-day practical dealings with all the actors involved in the game.

Taking all that together, we can see how hard it is to talk of Blair or Brown in the singular, as 'finished' politicians with settled views regularly and consistently set out in speeches. Having said that, we can – and have in this book – identified keywords and concepts that made up the Blair–Brown (and hence New Labour) life-world as it was expressed by them in their speeches. They featured on one side of a binary, as set out in table 4, themed around: personal qualities, leadership skills and political vision. The words on each side of this table come from three facets of New Labour's European and foreign policy discourses. The first are the words Blair and Brown actually used to describe their policies in their speeches, whereby they spelt out both sides of the equation for us, such as 'internationalist' or 'engaged' on the one hand versus 'isolationist' on the other. For example, in the second of his valedictory foreign policy speeches in March 2006 Blair said: 'We need to construct a global alliance for these global values; and act through it. Inactivity is just as much a policy with its own results. It's just the wrong one' (Blair 2006c). Here the 'action as good' versus 'inaction as bad' judgement is plainly stated in the speech.

More often than not, however, they gave us one side of the binary (in the column on the left) but it was left to the audience to infer the matching word on the opposite side. The point of binary discursive constructions is that hearing just one side of them can do the work for us, so politicians do not always need to spell out the other side. The second and more common tactic, therefore, was to use terms such as 'modern', 'practical' and 'pragmatic'. These were ways of generating authority and legitimacy for New Labour policies because they were positive descriptors of its thinking and policies. By implication, those who disagreed with Blair and Brown found themselves portrayed as holding negative or ill-thought-through positions associated with the words on the right of the table. For example, when the two leaders criticized others for living by illusions or being half-hearted they were implying that they were the reverse: grounded and wholehearted. When Brown spoke of 'mature patriotism' he was delegitimizing his nationalist or Eurosceptical opponents by implying they were being immature or childlike in their approach to the EU, insufficiently developed mentally to appreciate the complexities of the situation (Brown 1998b; Brown 1998c). The third facet comes from the inferences we can draw about Blair and Brown's

Table 4. New Labour's binaries

Tony Blair and Gordon Brown	Blair and Brown's 'Others'
Personal qualities	
Modern	Dated
Progressive	Stuck in the past
Value-driven	Interest-driven
Intelligent	Unintelligent
Pragmatic	Doctrinaire
Practical	Theoretical
Rational	Irrational
Grounded	Delusional
Target-oriented	Lacking focus
Spots opportunities	Misses opportunities
Principled	Opportunistic
Modest	Arrogant
Reads tides of history	Misunderstands history
Leadership skills	
Confident	Lacking confidence
Courageous	Faint-hearted
Self-belief	Anxiety
Strong	Weak
Proactive	Reactive
Engages	Hangs back
Decisive	Indecisive
Purposeful	Directionless
Player	Observer
Wholehearted	Half-hearted
Flexible	Dogmatic
Forward-looking	Backward-looking
Patriotic	Unpatriotic
Political vision	
Internationalist	Isolationist
Outward-looking	Introspective
Post-imperial	Imperial
'Cool Britannia'	'Rule Britannia'
Europeanist	Nationalist
Britain first	Party first
Long-term	Short-term
Unifying	Alienating
Radical	Conservative

life-world from the concepts they deployed to rationalize their ideas
and outlook. For example, when they spoke of 'stepping up', 'delivering', 'history teaches...' and 'reform not retreat' we can assume that
these are qualities they valued and liked to convey to their audiences
as guiding principles behind their political actions. 'Stepping up'
speaks of confidence and engagement, especially through its military

connotations, as in stepping up to the plate; 'delivering' speaks of reliability, proactivity and practicality; 'history teaches...' speaks of being knowledgeable, informed and insightful; 'reform not retreat' speaks to the 'get up and go' image New Labour liked to convey to the public. We could expand the table by using more examples from each of these elements of New Labour's political discourse, but the point should be clear. These binaries served first of all to organize New Labour's thinking by helping Blair and Brown organize their own, Britain's and Europe's identities. They secondly helped New Labour create the discursive space in which Blair and Brown could generate moral authority and legitimacy for the government's European policy. Like all linguistic dualisms Blair and Brown did not need to state openly that there was a negative Other when they talked, for example, about being 'future-looking' ('backward-looking') or 'purposeful' ('directionless'); the cues in the language did that for them.

However, in trying to communicate and impose their shared vision, Blair and Brown had to confront the significant obstacle that many people both in Britain and in the wider world were not ready to share that vision, nor inhabit the same cognitive life-world as they did. New Labour's discourses on leadership were performatively constituted to shift the terms of the political landscape in Britain. However, they could never depart decisively from that landscape as Blair and Brown saw it, and the mixed messages they emitted reflected this problem of combining progressive and traditionalist takes on the British role in the world. We will turn finally in this chapter to a consideration of one of the most frequently commented upon paradoxes of New Labour's European discourses: the concept of Britain as an EU–US 'bridge'. The bridge idea represents perhaps the ultimate example of the difficulties of using discourse to construct a progressivist, Europeanist foreign policy in Britain.

III. The old in the new

New Labour never saw Britain's relations with the EU as locked in a competitive game with Britain's relations with the US. The closer Britain was to the heart of the EU, the government argued, the more influence London could exert over Washington. Rather than zero-sum, then, the two were mutually reinforcing, and achieving New Labour's EU ambitions would help Britain play the part of a bridge across the Atlantic; they were thus an important component of Blair and Brown's global ambitions for British foreign policy. As the Prime Minister put it to US President Bill Clinton in May 1997: 'a Britain that is leading in Europe is a Britain capable of ever closer relations also with the United States of America' (Blair 1997d; see also Blair 1999d). Note how the prospect of 'ever closer union' of EU member states was there linked to the Anglo-American 'special relationship', which perhaps says something about Blair's subconscious preference for the latter. The Prime Minister held that the EU end of the bridge needed to be constructed only to a minimum level necessary to carry Britain's weight across the Atlantic. For example, at the University of Northumbria in November 2000 one of the challenges Blair said the country faced was: 'To give leadership in the world, and develop Britain as a leading player in Europe and the world' (Blair 2000g). Here, the Europeanist principle was fixed between the desire for leadership in the world and leadership over that same European project – hardly Heath-style Europeanism and unlikely to appeal to Britain's key EU partners.

New Labour's thinking on Britain's role in the world updated a powerful establishment view that Britain occupied a unique position in world affairs, the product of its extensive diplomatic contacts – a legacy of the days of Empire – and its moral capacity to shape international practices in a positive, progressive direction. The Labour Party's internationalist heritage (see Vickers 2003; Hughes 2009: 34–5) provided one possible mode of expressing this approach to foreign policy but it tended to be overlooked in the New Labour rush to disassociate itself from Old Labour. In fact, New Labour looked more to Conservative rather than Labour figures for its foreign policy ideas. The idea of Britain acting as the 'fulcrum' of the international system was popularized (but by no means instigated) by then opposition leader Winston Churchill in his speech to the Conservative Party conference in 1948. His theme was how to provide for national security when 'the state of the world and the position of our country in it, have sunk to levels which no one could have predicted' (Churchill 1948: 149). Churchill argued that the British had a unique role to play in the world by virtue of being 'the only country which has a great part to play in every one' of 'three great circles among the free nations and democracies' (all quotes in this paragraph are from Churchill 1948: 153). Churchill's first circle (figure 9), 'naturally', was the British Commonwealth and Empire, which he had earlier in the speech described as 'the foundation of our Party's political belief'. The second circle was 'the English-speaking world in which we, Canada, and the other British Dominions play so important a part'. The third and apparently final circle was 'United Europe'. The ordering of the circles, with Europe very much last on the list, could be taken as symbolic, especially given the time Churchill devoted elsewhere in his speech to the need for close ties between London and Washington and his comments on the significance of Empire. What gets forgotten

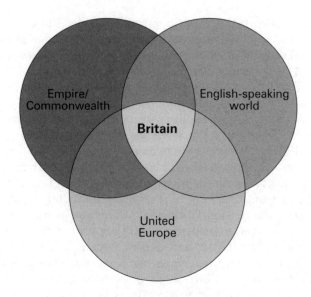

Figure 9. Churchill's three circles of British foreign policy.

is that earlier in the speech Churchill eulogized the principle of European integration by stressing that 'there is absolutely no need to choose between a United Empire and a United Europe. Both are vitally and urgently necessary.' More evident in the speech than any denigration of the European ideal was Churchill's view that, of all the countries in the world, Britain was uniquely placed to hold the circles in place because 'we are the only country which has a great part in every one of them', an 'Island at the centre of the seaways and perhaps of the airways also'.

Revisiting the original Churchill model is instructive for two main reasons. First, it is worth noting how little time Churchill devoted in his speech to elaborating his idea of three circles: about 14 lines from a nearly 500-line speech, or under 3%. It does not appear as a fully fledged concept but a series of empirical takes on the state of Britain's main strategic partners as Churchill recognized them in 1948. Second, although Churchill's opinion was already in wide circulation, his model refreshed and added yet more legitimacy to this dominant paradigm in British foreign policy thinking. Perhaps Churchill's speech was a 'tipping point' to use the norms literature, drawing on a bank of material and ideational support to establish the 'Britain as unique' perspective in domestic and international discussions on the conduct of post-war international relations. However, little attention has been paid either to the original context

of the speech or to its wider applicability after the early Cold War
years. As an empirical concept developed in the later 1940s too few
policy-makers and academics have asked some important questions
about it. Is it generalizable? How relevant is it to contemporary practice? Can we draw a straight line between Churchill and Blair? This
is pertinent when we note that it is with the former Conservative
Prime Minister, Anne Deighton argues, that 'Blair's foreign policy
also starts' (Deighton 2005: 5; see also Menéndez-Alarcón 2004: 103).
Blair and Brown were clearly in awe of Churchill and deploying the
'bridge' concept allowed them to tread Churchill's path fifty years on.
Fondly remembered for his wartime heroics, skilful rhetoric, English
eccentricities and, crucially, his stubborn, nationally unifying resistance during the Second World War, Blair and Brown's espousal of
Churchill was most in evidence when they visited the US or Canada
(for example Blair 2001a; and Brown 2002b: 'His words ring with
relevance in our own times') or when they spoke to US audiences in
Britain (for example Brown 2000b). For New Labour, Britain could
maintain its centrality in world affairs by being a Churchill-esque
point of contact, the privileged interlocutor, between Brussels and
the national capitals in Berlin, Paris, Rome and so forth on the one
hand, and Washington on the other. New Labour was a government,
it seems, that saw itself, like Churchill, transcending the hurly-burly
of domestic party politics and sitting above partisan sniping to
guard, quite simply, the national interest.

New Labour's commemoration of the three-circles model took one
of two forms in its European discourses: it was either an empirical
fact of international life (Britain is a bridge) or a target for British
foreign policy (Britain can be the bridge). In its first guise Blair
and Brown were at their most confident, proclaiming that Britain
was already acting as a bridge, a conduit or honest broker between
the US and the EU, usually when addressing a British audience. In
November 1997, for example, Blair said: 'We are the bridge between
the US and Europe. Let us use it. When Britain and America work
together on the international scene, there is little we can't achieve'
(Blair 1997g). Note that Britain was *the* bridge, not *a* bridge, or one
of several routes the US might wish to use into the EU, emphasiz-
ing Britain's unique positioning as an interlocutor between the EU
and the US (see also Blair 1999d: 'We have finally done away with
the proposition that we must choose between two diverging paths').
Brown cemented the economic foundation of the British bridge by
arguing that 'Britain is well placed as the bridge between America
and Europe.... We are indeed the bridgehead from which [American]
companies trade in mainland Europe' (Brown 1999h). He repeated
this injunction almost word for word in later speeches, albeit

replacing 'bridge' with 'vital link' (Brown 2001a; Brown 2001b; Brown 2001c). Matching Blair's take on the politics of the bridge, America as Brown constructed it had one main trading route into Europe: Britain.

In its second guise New Labour's ambition had not yet been achieved but the vision was in place, the government tailoring its message carefully to audiences abroad, especially in Europe. Even in speeches where Blair pushed the British to accept a European future he could not resist the bridge analogy: 'we are stronger in Europe if strong with the US. Stronger together. Influential with both. And a bridge between the two' (Blair 1999f). In June 2000 Blair concentrated on the economic dimension by arguing that: 'We believe Britain can become the European hub of the emerging global economy. In Europe, a bridge to America.... In effect, Europe's corporate headquarters' (Blair 2000d). He resolutely pushed the 'influence' argument throughout that year: 'our strength with the US is not just a British asset, it is potentially a European one. Britain can be the bridge between the EU and the US' (Blair 2000f; Blair 2000h). Brown articulated the rationalist, interest-based argument for bridge-building by arguing that: 'The more influence we have in Paris and Bonn, the more influence we have in Washington. Our Atlantic Alliance is not in contradiction with our European commitments. British interests are best served by being strong in Europe' (Brown 1999b; see also Brown 1999h). Blair's unwavering public support for George W. Bush's decision to undertake military operations to overthrow Saddam Hussein in March 2003 caused huge controversy within European–US relations and aroused hostility towards the British and Blair personally across the EU. In the months preceding the war Blair toned down his language slightly, such that to the Foreign Office in the January before the invasion he said: 'We can indeed *help* to be a bridge between the US and Europe and such understanding is always needed'. Recognizing the problems his policy on Iraq had caused his bridge-building ambitions, Blair urged that 'Europe should partner the US not be its rival' (Blair 2003b; emphasis added). The Prime Minister was still expounding the 'bridge' idea in November 2004, albeit with slightly less confidence than he had done in previous years. 'We have a unique role to play. Call it a bridge, a two lane motorway, a pivot or call it a damn high wire, which is often how it feels; our job is to keep our sights firmly on both sides of the Atlantic' (Blair 2004c).

We saw in the previous chapter that Blair and Brown were not Empire men to the extent that Churchill or previous generations of British politicians were. Yet New Labour refused to write off Empire (as Commonwealth) as a source of British prestige and 'reach' around

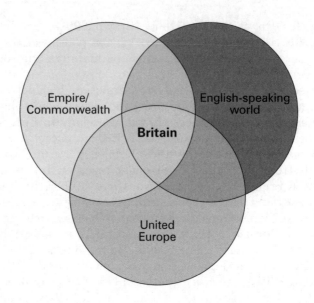

Figure 10. Blair's three circles of British foreign policy.

the globe (Brown 2005f; Brown 2006b). In figure 10, therefore, the Empire/Commonwealth circle has faded into the background but not gone altogether. Britain in the New Labour view could still make use of its imperial contacts and networks to promote British interests in the other two circles. 'Note that they [the circles] are very Anglo-centric, but that the argument is that New Labour thought that the Third Way/Triangulation could be achieved between the three circles as much as Churchill did' (Deighton 2005: 6). In Deighton's view Blair's pursuit of the Churchillian agenda meant painting a new gloss on a traditional aspiration of those who made British foreign policy. Robin Cook would have agreed with Deighton because he argued that 'The concept of a bridge is perfectly tailored for New Labour, as a bridge cannot make choices, but by definition is in the middle' (Cook 2003: 133). Bache and Jordan have also agreed that the bridge concept 'did not eliminate the Atlanticism of the past. Rather, the third way involved transcending such dilemmas' (Bache and Jordan 2006: 8; see also Gamble 2003: 231–2). Riddell was more scathing, writing that back as far as Suez British leaders had always sought to duck the issue rather than lead on it: 'It was the avoidance of a choice elevated into a new national strategy' (Riddell 2005: 129). Wanting to construct a Euro-Atlantic area around a shared set of Anglo-American values was hardly a new goal for British foreign policy, as William Wallace made amply clear in a 2005 article in *International Affairs* (Wallace 2005). If that was not bad enough, commentators have noted that whatever Blair said, his policies *in practice* showed up the emptiness of his rhetoric, and that when push came to shove he was always prepared to remain closer to the US than to his European allies, leaving the EU end of the bridge to crumble in a state of disrepair. David Marquand perspicaciously pointed out back in 1999 – before 9/11 and Iraq – that Atlanticism – in particular the influence of the New Democrats under Clinton (see Bevir 2005: 42–3) – had inspired much New Labour thinking in its formative years. 'Its rhetoric is American; and the influences which have shaped its project are American, as is its political style. When American and European interests diverge, New Labour can be relied on to show more tenderness to the former' (Marquand 1999: 239). And so it proved.

> In so far as Britain was a bridge, it was carrying traffic from West to East across the Atlantic and not the other direction. The idea that the British government might seek to take the lead in achieving a common EU view before taking that view to the United States was never seriously entertained. (Wall 2008: 215)

Perhaps the problem for New Labour was that it made the mistake of treating the 'US' as a single, unitary actor. Blair and his team might have been able, on occasion, to persuade President Bush of the merits of taking a multilateral approach, for example over UN Security Council Resolution 1441 of 8 November 2002 (Seldon 2005: 586), which gave Iraq one last chance to meet the disarmament obligations imposed upon it by previous resolutions (UN 2002). However, the influence of the 'hawks' in Bush's team, who seem to have had the President's ear, such as Donald Rumsfeld and Dick Cheney, seems to have outweighed the influence of the 'doves', such as Colin Powell and, to a lesser extent, the wavering Condoleezza Rice. We can conclude this survey of critiques of the bridge strategy with the words of two people who worked closely with Blair. First, Clare Short judged that, in the final verdict, Blair's Iraq policy not only showed a Prime Minister unwilling to act out this role for Britain, but demonstrated his 'total incapacity to act as a bridge' (Short 2005: 273). Second, Christopher Meyer, from his vantage position in the Washington embassy, felt that, by the time of Blair's meeting with Bush in January 2003: 'Transatlantic relations were in a trough. Blair's famous bridge between Europe and America was sinking beneath the waves' (Meyer 2006: 261).

In sum, critics of the bridge strategy argue that it was undesirable in theory, or that it was impossible to execute in practice, either because Blair did not mean what he said or because he was unable to exercise enough of a calming influence over US policy in the war on terror. What we could add from our study of the language New Labour used in its speeches is that the 'Britain as bridge' idea was never likely to be one that appealed to Europe's leaders because it spoke of outmoded and haughty pretensions for British foreign policy – a classic failing of British European policy that Blair and Brown both recognized. Nevertheless, through Blair and Brown's foreign policy discourse we saw them using the bridge concept both as a prop to Britain's 'global player' aspirations and as a way of developing a basically Atlanticist foreign policy. They might not have seen that a choice needed making, or they might have believed they could transcend it through the New Labour method of triangulation. Unfortunately other leaders, most notably in Europe, did see that a choice needed to be made when US and European policies towards Iraq and the war on terror began to diverge so rapidly after the end of 2001. We can further remark that the bridge idea gave British voters nostalgic for 'Old Britain' what the government felt they wanted to hear: that the country could still be a global player (as long as it took its European policy more seriously). Blair and Brown maybe managed to sustain the illusion but only at the expense of mixing their messages on the EU. From apparently being an end in its own right, Blair and Brown would commonly shift to a *realpolitik* position which took engagement with Europe first and foremost to be about the pursuit of an alliance in the British national interest (Stephens 2004: 105, 111). This use of Europe for national ends helped quell criticism of the more proactive elements of the government's European policy – on defence and the 'European army' for example – but does call into doubt what exactly they believed they could achieve by mixing the progressive and traditionalist messages about British foreign policy.

Summary

In these times, caution is error; to hesitate is to lose. (Blair 2006f)

If successful political leadership is all about the development and projection of a credible image that resonates with, and garners support from, the public, then it seems we can discover in New Labour's European discourse the clues as to the type of leaders Blair and Brown wanted to be, and the type of government they envisaged New Labour being. Having taken a reluctant Labour Party from Old to New after 1994, Blair and Brown set about imposing their style of politics on what they saw as a small 'c' conservative Britain after 1997. As he became more settled domestically, Prime Minister Blair revelled in playing the role of world statesman and this encouraged him to project his values and outlook onto the global stage, ably supported in the first instance by Chancellor Brown. New Labour wanted the EU to play two not necessarily reconcilable roles in British politics. On the one hand the government saw Britain's embrace of the EU as a vital test of Britain's ability to reconstitute Britishness and to remodel itself as a 'young country'. On the other hand Blair and Brown saw the EU not as an end for Britain in the sense that more ardent pro-Europeans in Britain might have done, or to the degree that partners such as France and Germany might have wished. Instead, the Prime Minister and Chancellor took the EU to be a vehicle through which Britain could achieve quite traditional foreign policy goals. Thus we had the odd scenario whereby Blair and Brown's European discourse sought to overcome outdated notions about Britain's relations with Europe in order to bring about the fulfilment of the very Churchillian ambitions that had led large segments of the public and political elites to disavow the idea of 'Britain as European' in the first place. New Labour never saw (or admitted to) any contradiction between its proposal that Britain could act as a bridge between the EU and the US. Nevertheless, both supporters and opponents of this strategy pointed out that enacting Churchill's idea from 1948 did not necessarily require an enthusiastic embrace of the EU in the New Labour years. Studying the Blair and Brown leadership project in this chapter helped us see what New Labour was trying to achieve with regard to Britain, Europe and the wider world. It also pointed up the immense difficulties the government encountered when it tried to generate domestic, let alone international, consensus around a new set of norms and practices that were context-specific, nationally focused and in many ways highly personal to Blair and Brown themselves. In the conclusion we will reflect on the key themes to emerge from this study of New Labour's logic of history.

Chapter 10

Conclusion

You could hear words like those a million times and understand the
sense of them, but until you were emotionally ready to embrace them,
it was trying to sow seeds on a motorway. (Welsh 2008: 327)

We have found in this book that Tony Blair and Gordon Brown's
European discourses mixed the expected with the novel in peculiar
ways. As the two men saw it, Britain's post-war foreign policy under
both the Labour and Conservative Parties had been driven by an
erroneous reading of the meaning of the country's national past. In
what they took to be the orthodox rendering of the story, Britain was
represented as eternally separate from the continent; this severance
was preferable to entanglement, given that the most common British
experiences of the continent were of military conflict and the associated disaster, death and destruction. The elegance of the orthodox
story was its simplicity, which had two dimensions, the cognitive and
the narrative. At the cognitive level it worked around a series of easy-
to-comprehend binary distinctions. In the orthodox story a British
Us, possessing characteristics such as bravery, honesty, democracy
and liberty, was positioned against a continental Them, exhibiting
the reverse properties of cowardice, treachery, tyranny, totalitarian-
ism and oppression. The binary oppositions erected between Britain
on the one hand and the continent on the other meant that, at the
narrative level, the story could easily account for divisions between
Britain and individual nation states, such as France and Germany,
or (out of 'official' periods of war) between Britain and the EU as a
superpower in the making, another rival, as it were, on the global
stage. The power of the orthodox narrative came from the fact that
it was a retelling of well understood and culturally powerful proto-
religious stories of good versus bad, lightness against darkness, with
any and every European country or integrative scheme slotting easily
into the latter half of the binary, as 'that which must be opposed'.

Blair and Brown took a different view because in their eyes the
British had got their history wrong. Like their opponents, they

believed that history was important and that we could and should learn from it to inform contemporary decision-making. Yet they diverged from the Eurosceptics – as they saw them – when it came to the nature of the lessons the British should learn from the past. Blair and Brown used ideas about globalization and interdependence and imposed them back on to the British past as a way of telling a globalist version of history, with the British marked down as always-and-ever European. For them, world history was a story of the greatness of the seafaring British bringing order to the world and peace to the homeland by being actively 'out there', managing world affairs politically, strategically and economically. The 'isolationism' of the British from Europe after 1945 was, in this view, a nonsensical policy as far as the country's relations with Europe went because it denied the British the opportunity to act out the global role that both the orthodox and revisionist schools wanted Britain to play. By being an active player in Europe, New Labour had it, Britain could finally deliver on its 'great power' promise. Europe could, in sum, be the launch pad from which New Labour could help Britain perform the pivotal role in the international system Churchill had identified for it half a century previously.

This book has traced the contours of each of these stories and the havoc they wreaked upon the government's European discourses after 1997. The orthodox story appears in the 'context' chapters, always framing the New Labour story which was told through the propaganda campaign on behalf of the EU that Blair, Brown and their government colleagues put about in their foreign policy speeches. The central argument pursued in the study was that New Labour was up against it from the beginning in terms of putting out a rival narrative about Britain's role in the world. It came down to the simple reason that Blair and Brown were attempting, over a relatively short period, to change the way the British thought of themselves as a national community. When the kinds of anti-European attitudes New Labour wanted to oppose are found in the very ways in which the British speak of Europe (i.e. in the ways the British call the EU to mind for the purposes of making sense of it as a politico-economic actor), it was always going to be a challenge to transcend in discursive terms the psychological divide between 'Britain' on the one hand and 'Europe' on the other. After studying what New Labour tried to do in this discourse domain we can come to the conclusion that the government's policy failure can be explained in two ways: structurally, by the conditions within which its discourses were devised and reported; and agency-wise, by the recidivist elements *within* New Labour's supposedly progressive, enlightened European discourses. A difficult task was made much harder by New Labour never consistently or radically enough helping wean the British people off the idea of their historical destiny as a great global player. In fact, the government actively promoted that idea and in the process undermined the case for a policy systematically aimed at getting the best out of Britain's regional partners in Europe. This chapter will reflect on three aspects of this clash of rival narratives about the British and Europe, taking in both the theory and the discursive practices explored in the book. It will begin by considering the causes of New Labour's policy failure, move on to consider the utility of taking a discourse approach to British Euroscepticism and, finally, indicate where future research might profitably take us to develop the major themes and issues raised in the book.

I. The Europe campaign that never was

Political parties in Britain have remained prisoners of a discourse on Europe which fails to give it political legitimacy in Britain and continues to dissociate British and European identities.... Attempts to 'sell' the EU to the British public and, more important, to redefine British identity in the European context, were at most half-hearted if even attempted. (Schnapper 2011: 29)

The New Labour government did not set out just to alter British policy towards the EU: it wanted to modify public attitudes, public opinion and deeper public values as they pertained to the Europe question in British political life. Only by taking a restrictive interpretation of success as *policy success* within the EU environment can we argue that the government's European policy bore fruit. British public opinion on the EU remained disconcertingly constant after 1997 and the country still showed itself, at the end of thirteen years of New Labour government, to be among the least enthusiastic supporters of the EU. One of the explanations for New Labour's failure studied in this book involved the media, not least because in waging any propaganda campaign for Europe, the government had to use a broadly hostile media to convey its messages to the public. It is but a small minority of people who visit the Downing Street, Foreign Office and Treasury websites to read the 'untainted' original speeches by Prime Ministers, Foreign Secretaries and Chancellors. If members of the public are interested in European affairs at all they garner their impressions of speeches and policy from newspapers and the broadcast media. In this process of mediating the message, Blair and Brown would find that the speech was either not reported at all, or so heavily 'spun' and commented on by the media that the (admittedly limited) progressive pro-European elements were lost in a storm of opposition, critique and anti-European bluster. Thus New Labour watchers have suggested that the government was always likely to struggle to persuade the British public of the merits of a European future because of the fabric and ideology of the most influential segments of the national media. Many newspapers and broadcasters neither educate British citizens about the EU nor report EU affairs emanating from 'Brussels' in any great detail. Commentators broadly agree that coverage of the EU in Britain is slanted against the twin ideas of the British being a 'European' country and that London should take itself more wholeheartedly into the European project. As Anand Menon put it, summarizing the findings of those who have seen the relationship unfold from within the corridors of power in London and Brussels, 'the tone adopted by the media has done little to fuel either understanding of what the EU is for or how it operates, or sympathy for the integration process' (Menon 2004: 44).

In his memoirs Blair reflected on the media's part in damaging New Labour's European ambitions, writing of the political debate about the Lisbon Treaty: 'it reminded me how far I had to go to persuade British opinion of the merits of being in the mainstream of Europe. As ever, the difficulty was that the Eurosceptics were organised and had savage media backing' (Blair 2010: 501). The media negativity Blair identified (as have British diplomats and many academics) came directly from the narrative tropes through which press outlets frame their EU coverage as a series of British–European conflicts, which keep the British in their permanent state of discursive war with the continent. The lack of public appreciation of the rationale behind and workings of the EU was what Blair and Brown tried to address through the openly educational portions of their speeches which dealt with the EU's achievements in political, economic and security terms. However, persistent press and wider media scepticism surely hindered New Labour's willingness and ability, to get its European messages across. Those who worked with Tony Blair on this issue have remarked on his caution in confronting the Eurosceptics in the media. For example, at the time of the announcement, in February 1999, of the National Changeover Plan which would prepare the British economy and businesses for the possible introduction of the single currency, Lance Price noted in his diary:

> It doesn't look as if he will now say that he plans to recommend that we join the single currency. He's nervous about taking on the press in a big way. He knows what a huge battle it would be and doesn't seem ready to have it now, although most of the rest of us think he should. (Price 2005: 79)

When William Wallace wrote of the 'sullen resistance' to Europe in the British media (Wallace 2005: 56) he could equally have been remarking on the attitude of some of Blair's closest and most influential advisers. 'Campbell, instinctively a Eurosceptic, did not relish an early war with the right-wing papers he had worked so energetically to neutralise' (Rawnsley 2001: 75). In the early months of his premiership Blair had apparently been told by Roy Jenkins: 'I will be very blunt on this. You have to choose between leading in Europe or having Murdoch on your side. You can have one but not both' (Seldon 2005: 315, quoting Paddy Ashdown's diary). New Labour apparently opted for Murdoch over Europe.

The theoretical work on norm entrepreneurship helped us appreciate how difficult a task Blair and Brown faced, given this unhelpful media context. As Finnemore and Sikkink have it, the acceptance of a new norm – in this case the pro-European vision of 'British as European' – requires a combination of factors, only partly under the control or influence of the norm entrepreneur (Finnemore and Sikkink 1998). When we identified Margaret Thatcher's 1988 Bruges speech as a tipping point in the norm life cycle of Euroscepticism in Britain (see chapter 3) we were alerted to the fact that the conditions in which she operated were broadly favourable to the cascade, acceptance and internalization of this norm about the British and Europe. Not only could she use well worn images about the antagonism between Britain and Europe, but her speech coincided with a contentious period in the evolution of the EU's history in and around the time of the Maastricht Treaty. The early 1990s were a troubled period for the Conservative Party on the subject of Europe, but ironically they were also the years that saw the Thatcher agenda find its final embodiment in government policy, in part through the acceptance of that agenda by a significant and vocal minority of parliamentarians in Cabinet and on the backbenches. These fed, and fed off, press scepticism towards European integration, as well as at best muted public support for the idea, and helped reactivate organized pressure group resistance to the European project in Britain, notably in the form of the Bruges Group. Well financed fringe parties such as James Goldsmith's Referendum Party were signal contributors to the anti-European cause and helped popularize the 'Britain versus Europe' attitudes that had become the mainsprings of the nationalist, oppositional norm about the British and Europe by the time New Labour came to power.

If we can argue, therefore, that the material conditions within which Thatcher's Bruges speech appeared were favourable to the cascade of the norm she set down on that occasion, we can argue with equal conviction that Blair and Brown had no such luck. The pro-European consensus they sought to build had little public legitimacy because it was built on, at best, a marginal reading of the British past, found in the odd broadsheet newspaper and academic tracts on the history of the British in Europe. While no doubt worthy works of historical scholarship in and of themselves, in terms of generating support for the European idea they were hardly the ideal tools the government could use to generate support for its new norm. Looking back on the New Labour years, it is very difficult to come up with a single speech or 'event' that could be put alongside the Bruges speech as a tipping point, taking the British debates in the opposite direction from the path down which Thatcher's intervention had led. Blair and Brown delivered more 'pro' messages than many critics perhaps have recognized, but none of their speeches, alone, stands out as a 'moment' in the building of a pro-European consensus. Blair's 1999 Chicago speech on liberal interventionism, by contrast, does stand out as something of a tipping point in a different field, even though it was not followed through as far as Blair might have hoped (Daddow 2009). No equivalent speech exists for his or his government's thinking on the EU, although, had things gone differently, his speeches in Birmingham, Cardiff or Warsaw might have been the big Blair 'moment' on the EU, a doctrine of European community perhaps. However, it is too simplistic to blame external factors such as the press for the death – or stillbirth – of New Labour's European policy. The next section will reflect on the nature of the Eurosceptical attitudes Blair and Brown were confronting and how their sometimes confused policy discourses allowed their opponents to exploit internal government divisions. This was especially relevant to the question of British membership of the single European currency, the early resolution of which via a referendum might have led to a new norm emerging during the New Labour years.

II. Confronting the Eurosceptics

> There's something in the British psyche – up to now – which doesn't want to do it, which believes that because we've not been linked to Europe, it's been to our historic advantage. The Channel is both practical and symbolic of the fact that we have been able to stand alone. (Interview with Hill)

The purpose of taking a discourse approach to the study of New Labour's European policy was to try to empathize with the policy dilemmas *as the government saw them*. Academic studies of Euroscepticism have shown how malleable the word is and how many variations there are in the party arenas of countries both in and, paradoxically, outside the EU. The two principal models of Euroscepticism we studied were those by Kopecký and Mudde on the one hand and Taggart and Szczerbiak on the other (chapter 6). The latter co-authors opted for parsimony in developing a relatively accessible distinction between hard and soft strains; the former opted for a four-fold typology around attitudes to Europe, both favourable and more sceptical. What was interesting about Blair and Brown's approach to the Eurosceptics was that they basically ignored the nuances and constructed their opponents as hard-nosed nationalist Eurosceptics fuelled by 'little Englandism' and no small measure of xenophobia against all things Europe and European. The scepticism New Labour wanted to undermine fell into Taggart and Szczerbiak's 'hard' category and into Kopecký and Mudde's 'Europhobe' category. Many writers have identified dominant strains of Euroscepticism in Britain as being at the 'harder' end of a notional spectrum and therefore in taking this stance Blair and Brown were treading familiar ground. In party political terms this was convenient because they saw in the rump Conservative Party left after 1997 the manifestation of all that had been wrong with British European policy after 1945, and calculated that political points could easily be scored by contrasting the 'modern' Labour Party against the outdated, unfashionable, ageing Conservatives.

The problem with this approach was that the government was never as settled on its brand of pro-Europeanism as its public presentation suggested. Blair and Brown's discourses of stability, vision and internal government agreement actually belied some intense behind-the-scenes policy arguments on questions of Europe. The government machine contained at its heart more than the occasional decision-maker or adviser who was not convinced either about the case for 'Europe' generally or about specific steps in further integration, such as the single currency. This was more than a fault-line between Prime Minister and Chancellor. It divided Treasury from Foreign Office and Downing Street, Blair's team from Brown's and even divided members of the supposedly 'pro-Europe' Blair team. Much comment has come to centre on the figure of Brown as 'sceptic', but this book has served to add nuance to a common misconception that he was the main stumbling block in the way of a positive European policy. Yes, he was taking a well established Treasury in line in showing suspicion towards the single currency and members of his team, notably Ed Balls, were no great fans of the European project. After he wrested control from Blair over the timing of a single currency referendum in October 1997, Brown could effectively determine the pace and therefore the nature of the push for Europe on New Labour's part, while simultaneously joining Blair in his campaign 'for' Europe. Maybe Brown considered this a small price to pay for such an early victory for his department over

Number 10 and Foreign Office. Exacerbating this, Blair did not come to office with a well worked out plan to force home his vision on the European front. Not a foreign policy expert by inclination, the Prime Minister had created a bind for himself by wooing so many sections of the Eurosceptical newspapers – notably Murdoch's *Sun* and *The Times* – to New Labour's side in the run-up to the 1997 election. The short-term expedient of talking about 'slaying Euro dragons' might have helped New Labour win at the polls up and down the country, but it was tricky then to pull back from that position once in office. Combined with the complexity of devising a policy towards the EU on which the whole government could agree, we can start to see that New Labour was determined to fight its European corner but was quite literally not prepared enough to do so.

Through a study of New Labour's European discourse we saw these policy disagreements, uncertainties and frailties of logic tearing through the veneer of certainty the government wished to convey to the public. Discourses in this study (expressed in and through foreign policy speeches) have been taken to be sites of negotiation and policy debate. They are aimed at multiple audiences simultaneously and what is fascinating about them is that they reveal as much about the user as the events, personalities and processes the discourse utterer is intending to construct. Superficially finished, settled and coherent stand-alone entities, the political speeches studied in this book were never quite the last word on a topic, never succeeded in conclusively fixing their targets and were shot through with internal tensions that undermined the messages New Labour tried to convey. We studied three dimensions of the speeches in which we could identify these logical contradictions at work. The first (chapter 4) was the most obviously persuasive, Blair's 'crude appeal' to national interests, backed by Brown's statistical barrage on the economic benefits of EU membership. This aspect of New Labour's European discourse also talked up issues of influence as a way of conveying that Britain was more prosperous and secure inside as opposed to outside the EU. The second dimension concerned identity (chapter 6): who/what did the British think they were? Here Blair and Brown took on those who equated Europeanism with a weak sense of patriotism and created moral distinctions between their proactive policy and the 'retreat' implied by a sceptical policy of retrenchment or 'going it alone'. The two speakers could sympathize with their opponents to create pathos for their position, but theirs was a tactical Euroscepticism, always qualified by a 'but...'. The third dimension we studied was the logic of history running through the speeches (chapter 8). History featured as both cause of the New Labour project and antithesis of it. New Labour needed history to exist as a coherent entity, but showed itself opposed to many facets of the national past which, the government believed, held the British back from charting a new and exciting future for themselves.

The central problem, it appears, was that a majority of British people might not have been fans of Old Labour but they were definitely appreciative of Old Britain. New Labour never succeeded in helping the people make new connections with history. The government lacked the courage to create a decisive enough rupture with the national past to jolt the British into forming a new historical consciousness because – like the people – the government remained imprisoned within popular nationalist discourses of Britishness. Brown the historian took a conventional approach to the lessons of history but we might have expected the less historically minded and anti-traditionalist Blair to provide the groundwork for a veritable shake-up of attitudes. That he never managed to is testament to the part history plays in foreign policy and diplomacy more generally: it is literally *everywhere*, even when the government wished it to be nowhere. The problem New Labour encountered in trying to weave the national and the European pasts together was that it was trying to replace one officially sanctioned discourse about British national history with another. This was never easy, and became less so as trust in Blair personally and the popular appeal of the New Labour project waned through its second and third terms in office, culminating in its removal from office under Brown in 2010.

The narrative power of the government's 'new' story about Britain's interconnectedness and interdependence with the continent did not resonate with a public literally schooled in 'old', official stories of British national greatness, put about by professional historians first to the field of disciplined history and then re-enacted in the pages of the most popular newspapers, even at the turn of the twenty-first century. New Labour's retelling of the national past using disciplined but relatively marginal academic histories to construct a progressive story about the national future may have worked well when Blair and Brown spoke to hand-picked audiences of party supporters and academics at the opening of centres for European research. But what was the point of continually repeating the new official story if no one whose opinion you are trying to alter listens – or cares? Linda Colley's *Britons* might have been staple reading for Gordon Brown but for millions of members of the public it was the *Sun* and the *Daily Mail* that informed their world-views. We are left with a frightening irony. The more New Labour attempted to control the story of Britain's past, the more popular the counter-narrative became, such that the history of Britain's national past became something of a time bomb for New Labour: handling it was difficult and dangerous.

The harder the government tried to contain it within safe, prudent limits, the more powerfully the counter-narrative of British national greatness fought back at them in the press, over the airwaves, on the internet and in Parliament. History was one of the few things New Labour was never to control, try as it might (this argument is expanded in Daddow 2008).

III. Future research

> The dilemma of a British Prime Minister over Europe is acute to the point of ridiculous. Basically you have a choice: co-operate in Europe and you betray Britain; be unreasonable in Europe, be praised back home, and be utterly without influence in Europe. It's sort of: 'isolation or treason'. (Blair 2006a)

As New Labour saw it, Britain was a European country by virtue of its geography and history, but more importantly because of its vital national interests, which it felt were best safeguarded by being part of the EU. The EU featured heavily in the government's strategy for global leadership because Blair and Brown believed that having influence in the EU gave Britain influence with the US and, through that, a voice in the key global institutions and debates shaping the post-9/11 world order. This book set out to study the discourse element of New Labour's European policy and in the process found that there were different New Labours, depending on time and circumstance. We found that the same speech could combine progressive with traditionalist approaches to history, Eurosceptical imagery with pro-European messages and praise for the British national character with calls for the British to re-vision their national past. These speeches were, in this context, treated as sites of cultural production, where we saw Blair and Brown reinforcing the status quo at the same time as they tried to dismantle it. It is the paradoxes inherent in political rhetoric that open the way for a future research agenda, which could usefully have three strands.

The first strand would enhance our knowledge of the *practices* and *sites* of Euroscepticism as they existed in New Labour's Britain. The birth of organized Eurosceptic groups in earlier decades has been well documented by writers such as Forster (2002) and in this book we studied press organs as guardians of the Eurosceptic tradition, keeping the British in a permanent state of discursive war with the continent. What I was not able to research in depth were other sources of scepticism, not just elsewhere in the media, but on the internet, in literature and magazines and at elite level, in pressure groups and fringe political parties. Identifying these other sites of scepticism would be one thing – we would then need to try to measure their scale and impact on the public debates. This would be difficult, but not impossible. The point of developing this strand would be to study on an empirical level the structural barriers facing Blair and Brown when they assumed the role of pro-European norm entrepreneurs. It could be turned around, too, and studied from a comparative perspective, such that Europhile groups and organizations could be brought into the picture. These were the platforms Blair and Brown could have used to spread their messages about the EU and it would be telling to investigate the relative organization and funding in Britain of the 'pro' and 'anti' wings of the debate both in and outside Parliament. To create a norm cascade in favour of the EU, campaign groups such as Britain in Europe would have had to have been co-opted by New Labour and to have worked more effectively as a transmitting mechanism of the Europeanist message than apparently it was able to. Studying the empirical position of the 'pro' groups would have the practical advantage of identifying the potential levers available to policy-makers in their quest to upgrade the 'European' element of British national identity.

The second strand would be part empirical and part theoretical and would involve finding more out about the *life-world* inhabited by New Labour decision-makers. It may seem paradoxical to suggest this as a topic when the post-1997 Labour governments are surely the most contemporaneously commented upon of any British government by both insiders and outsiders alike. The urgency comes from an appreciation of policy-making under New Labour, described by Tom Bower as 'Blair's wilful informality in government' (Bower 2007: 464). 'Sofa government', where policies were devised bilaterally between Blair and Brown, or working in small teams away from Cabinet in the Prime Ministerial den in Downing Street – often without official minutes being kept or note-takers even present – means that when scholars finally get to see the records of formal government discussions released to the National Archives from 2027 onwards they may well be disappointed to find that they cannot paint anything approaching an incisive or detailed picture of New Labour's foreign policy decision-making. Contemporary historians and political scientists might therefore be advised to talk to recently serving ministers and officials using oral history techniques, so that we build up an interim picture of New Labour's ideas, influences and machinations. This is particularly true because of the subject matter involved. New Labour's governance of Britain will be best remembered for a series of contested pieces of domestic legislation (on tuition fees, fox hunting, health and welfare reform) and the foreign policy adventure of Iraq. These are likely to continue to

take the limelight in memoirs and secondary accounts of the New
Labour years, which take a teleological approach to explaining how
Britain arrived at its present state. Students of the less popular EU
dimension will, it seems, have to actively seek out this dimension
of the government's work before it gets lost to the official memory
altogether. Talking to all those involved in devising and selling the
policy will help fill in gaps that are otherwise likely to open up in
our knowledge base of this vital aspect of British foreign policy. Particular questions would have to be asked about New Labour's (non-)
handling of the referendums on the euro and then the Constitutional
Treaty and about the Downing Street–Treasury divisions that
stultified European policy. A top Blair adviser said: 'I personally
don't think Euroscepticism is very deep in Britain. I think it's wide
but relatively shallow and I do actually think it could be changed
quite quickly' (interview with Powell). If Blair was as proactive a
leader as he liked to present himself, then why did he never seize
the day and go for an early referendum on the euro or, better still,
the question of EU membership more generally? Was this a personal
or a party political decision, or was it just that, in the end, Europe
did not *matter* enough to Blair to force him to take a firm line with
Brown on it. On Iraq he showed himself prone to taking unpopular
moves when questions of morality were at stake, so perhaps the fact
that the EU was never seen as a values-based issue (instead, it was
constructed first and foremost in interest terms) militated against
Blair pursuing it with the same degree of conviction and vigour.

The third strand is the *discourse analysis* strand. In this book we
studied New Labour's European discourse from the vantage points
of interests, identities and New Labour's logic of history. These
were just some of the many interesting facets of the government's
foreign policy discourses, before we came to issues of values, ethics,
globalization, international political economy, the use of force and so
on. Through the coding scheme developed in this study we were able
to infer, from the language used, how Blair and Brown characterized the qualities of strong leaders and how, through their speeches,
they imposed that vision, or tried to impose it, on Britain and British
political debates. We discovered at a cognitive level that the New
Labour mind, like individual human minds, worked around a series
of binaries. These were usually set up to be transcended, as in the
Third Way for instance, and they were not always logical equivalents
or natural opposites. The point is that in setting up such dualisms
the government could cleverly construct or frame the dimensions of a
political debate for its audiences without those audiences necessarily
having the inclination or time to question the utility of the binaries
around which the government built its arguments. The value of

taking a discourse approach was normative, in that it allowed us to interrogate the underlying assumptions, the hidden wiring behind New Labour's European discourses. We emerged with the unsettling proposition that Blair and Brown's speeches said less about the EU than they did about Blair, Brown and the New Labour project themselves. As the personal embodiments of the New Labour project, these New Labour figureheads loaded their foreign policy discourses with meaning, but not necessarily in the ways they or we might have expected. Ultimately, their logic might have been compelling but the stories they told about Britain were devoid of meaning.

New Labour after Blair:
British European discourses 2007–10

> I believe that we should have the confidence to engage with Europe
> and make it better and – dare I say it – more British. (Brown 1997a)

Throughout this book we saw how Gordon Brown acted as both
enabler and obstacle to Tony Blair in New Labour's search for a
pro-European consensus in Britain. On the one hand the Chancellor
faithfully sent out identical messages to the Prime Minister about
the need for Britain to be outward-looking, proactive in the world
and a full and wholehearted member of the EU. At its crudest, the
interest-based case Blair made for Europe relied prominently on a
steady stream of Treasury calculations about the material benefits to the British economy of its membership of the EU's single
market. New Labour's ideational case rested on the argument that
the British had always been a European country, always would be,
and that – back to interests again – the British nation would best be
served by paddling with the tides of history rather than swimming
against them. Brown brought all his knowledge of the past to bear in
constructing an identity-based argument around the 'genius' of the
British people. This, he said, would be realized only if the country
pursued an engaged, Europe-come-global foreign policy which would
enable the people 'to meet and master' (depending on the speech)
'tomorrow's challenges' (Brown 2005f) or 'global change' (Brown
2006a). Together, Blair and Brown variously decried Eurosceptics
for their outmoded, xenophobic and isolationist attitudes, which
would hold back Britain from becoming a modern 'young country'.
On the other hand we saw how Brown played the role of inhibitor
by wresting control over Britain's policy towards the single currency
from Number 10 Downing Street as early as October 1997. The self-
styled Iron Chancellor thereafter 'kept almost total control over the
process of whether to join' (Peston 2005: 178).

However, it was never as simple as Blair being 'pro' and Brown
being 'anti' EU or euro. In fact Brown was widely acknowledged
to be a 'pro-European' member of the New Labour team (Smith

2005: 706, 719; Bulmer 2008: 606). Brown certainly took this view in 1998 in a meeting with *Guardian* journalist Hugo Young, who recorded the Chancellor discussing how 'People liked to take these dichotomies – fairness/efficiency, pro-EMU/anti-EMU etc. – and pin each side of them on Blair and Brown respectively. He thought they were artificial differences' (Young 2008: 568). In his biography of the Chancellor, Robert Peston has even characterized Brown as 'pro-European throughout his political life' (Peston 2005: 180). This image is upheld by Clara O'Donnell and Richard Whitman, who, like Julie Smith and Simon Bulmer, argue that 'Brown was considered to be one of the more committed pro-Europeans of the New Labour government elected in 1997' (O'Donnell and Whitman 2007: 254). Others, such as former Foreign Office Minister Chris Mullin, were less sure. Following a meeting on the single currency in July 2002 he confided to his diary: 'as regard the euro, I wasn't clear which side he was on' (Mullin 2009: 301). Maybe things became hazier as time progressed, or Brown was anti-single currency but positive about European integration in principle. What we can establish is that Brown faithfully echoed the Treasury line that British membership of the single currency may not be in Britain's long-term economic interest. Blair was more interested in the political aspects of British–European relations and thus there was a degree of tension between the 'idealist' Blair and the hard-headed, 'realist' Brown.

Most commentary on British European policy under New Labour has tended to foreground these divisions over the single currency at the expense of bringing to the fore the many areas of agreement between the two figureheads over the future for the British in Europe and the world. What this book has shown is that, in many important ways, Brown played a crucial part in helping Blair build his case for Europe, such that where criticism can be levelled at New Labour it needs to be shared between the two men rather than aimed at either of them individually: 'the present incumbent of No. 10 [Brown] is as much the architect of this problematic legacy as his predecessor' (James and Opperman 2009: 290). According to this argument, there are three reasons why a major rupture either to foreign policy discourse or to the thinking behind it when Brown acceded to the premiership in June 2007 was unlikely: the continuity provided by Brown's move into Downing Street; the Cabinet appointments he made; and the depth of the bipartisan consensus on British Euro-pean policy. First, and most obviously, Brown was a key progenitor of New Labour's foreign policy thinking between 1997 and 2007 and his ideas on the subject were both well known and well publicized, and discursively it seemed to *work* for him in terms of how he viewed Britishness and Britain's world role. The (almost) well orchestrated

hand-over from Blair to Brown saw a flurry of Blairite activity designed to establish the New Labour legacy after 2007. Even had he
wanted to, Brown would have struggled to change course swiftly in a
relatively short space of time, a situation made even more difficult by
the relative stickiness of New Labour's discourses on domestic and
foreign policies.

Second, on the patronage side of things, Brown appointed as
Foreign Secretary David Miliband, formerly the head of Blair's
Downing Street Policy Unit. This acknowledged Blairite would
provide symbolic physical and intellectual continuity within British
foreign policy thinking during the Brown years. Brown was also
keen to restore 'trust' in British political institutions by undermining accusations that he might, like Blair, run a presidential-style
government and, as Simon Bulmer argued in an article published
early on in the Brown years, the new Prime Minister had already
'shown a willingness to leave more of European policy to his Foreign
Secretary' (Bulmer 2008: 606). Moreover, the framework of Britain's
debates about Europe during Brown's premiership were radically different from the early Blair years, with Chancellor Alastair Darling
having to focus on navigating Britain's way through the global
credit crisis through later 2007 and beyond. Analysis of Darling's
speeches on the Treasury website showed a Chancellor oblivious to
any need to make the case for Europe and not wanting, as Brown
did before him, to intellectualize the case for Britishness as the
second decade of the twenty-first century approached. New Labour
buzzwords like 'change', 'confidence', 'new', 'reform' and so on litter
Darling's speeches, but they say more about Darling the New Labour
politician and disciple of Brown than about Darling the Europeanist.
About the most revealing Darling statement is a somewhat anodyne
and well established New Labour one: 'Britain will continue to play
a full role in the European Union and in the international response
to financial markets turbulence' (Darling 2008a). Another popular
New Labour theme we saw emerging in the later Blair years, this
time the EU reform agenda on regulation and red tape, came through
clearly in Darling's speech to British business leaders at the CBI in
May 2008 (Darling 2008b). Although foreign policy-making under
Brown awaits further investigation (for coverage of the 1997–2010
period in its entirety see Daddow and Gaskarth 2011), it seems that
the balance of power within the Europe debate had swung back from
the Treasury to the Foreign Office.

The third reason for supposing that continuity rather than
change would be the order of the day under Brown is that it would
be a remarkable break from previous trends in British foreign policy
for an incoming Prime Minister to want, or to be able, to bring

about radical change to the style or substance of Britain's external relations over a three-year period – even if he or she led a different political party, which Brown obviously did not. The two major political parties have come and gone from office over the past six or seven decades, but in terms of policy thinking, if not always the language or tone each has adopted, major ruptures between them have been the exception rather than the rule. Nowhere is this more evident than in the realm of British European policy, where a degree of caution and hesitancy have been the defining features of London's approach to the EEC and EU whatever the colour of the party in power. Even exceptions, such as the Europeanism of the Conservative government of Edward Heath 1970–74, help to prove the rule. Heath never launched a formal application to the Communities, but picked up that left on the table by Labour's Harold Wilson in 1967. Wilson's application was dressed up in the language of a hard-headed calculation of the British national, essentially economic, interest, as was the application launched by Harold Macmillan's Conservative government six years earlier. All governments have had, moreover, to operate in a national environment which has not been hugely receptive to the idea that Britain should integrate itself deeply in a union of European states, and which in some cases doubts Britain's identity as a European state at all.

The broader picture is equally revealing. Churchill's popularization of the 'three circles' model of Britain's supposedly unique role in the world has proved immensely durable. Its appeal to the governing elites and informed commentators has played a part in the persistence – some would say stagnation – of a line of thinking that says Britain is destined to act out the part of privileged interlocutor between the key world states and international organizations the globe over. Seen in this light, the Blair–Brown hand-over in 2007 was unlikely to provide a nodal or radical turning-point in British political history (Tonge 2009: 308). In foreign policy terms the portents were spelt out by Foreign Secretary Miliband in a speech in July 2007: 'After 10 years in government, the Labour Party is seeking under new leadership to set out and deliver a renewed vision for the future of the country that builds on the social, economic and political changes introduced since 1997' (Miliband 2007a). 'Yes' to new leadership and the expected promise of 'renewal', said Miliband, but 'No' to a radical overhaul of the Blair agenda. Not only were they from the same party – whatever the supposed divisions between them and their respective 'teams' personally, politically or stylistically – but they also shared responsibility for launching the New Labour project itself. Given what we have seen in this book of the structured and relatively limited nature of British foreign policy thinking and discourse, such wriggle room as Brown did have would have been highly circumscribed by the conditions of the existence of his inter-ventions with respect to Britain's diplomatic and external priorities.

Prime Minister Brown set out his thoughts on the challenges Britain and the world faced in his preliminary remarks at a press conference with George W. Bush at the end of July 2007, just a few weeks after taking office (Brown 2007b). His nine-point programme was: first, to combat terrorism, 'those who practise terrorist violence or preach terrorist extremism'; second, to bring security and pol-itical reconciliation to Iraq; third, to take forward the Middle East peace process; fourth, to succeed militarily in Afghanistan, not least by encouraging the US to commit more troops; fifth, to stay resolute on Iran's nuclear weapons ambitions and work with the UN to keep effective sanctions in place; sixth, to bring an end to the violence in Darfur; seventh, to achieve the Millennium Development Goals; eighth, to develop and encourage the mechanisms of global free trade; and finally, to tackle climate change and promote sustainable development. Brown's first set-piece foreign policy speech, at the Lord Mayor's Banquet in November 2007, gave the Prime Minister the chance to flesh out his thinking and it is there that we begin to see some distinctive elements beginning to show through. However, in order to appreciate the novelty in Brown's approach we need to identify the similarities with the Blair agenda, so we will begin with those (all the below from Brown 2007c unless otherwise stated).

The first continuity was that Brown followed Blair in perceiving 'globalization' as a powerful 'force for change' with which nation states have to contend in the modern international system. At the end of the Cold War, Brown said near the start of the speech, 'no one foresaw the scale of the dramatic and seismic shifts in economy, culture and communications that are now truly global'. Brown's views on globalization provided the second point of continuity between himself and his predecessor – that states have to live in an 'inter-dependent' world and make the best of it rather than fight against it:

> we cannot any longer escape the consequences of our interdependence. The old distinction between 'over there' and 'over here' does not make sense of [sic] this interdependent world. For there is no longer 'over there' of terrorism, failed states, poverty, forced migration and environ-mental degradation and an 'over here' that is insulated or immune.

In Brown's view, the only successful foreign policy was the one Blair identified as 'engagement' not 'isolation', or in his post-Iraq years 'progressive pre-emption' (Blair 2006e). As Brown expressed it, 'Today a nation's self interest today [sic] will be found not in iso-lation but in cooperation to overcome shared challenges'. Brown expressly wanted to build on Blair's famed 'doctrine of the international community' by pressing for that community 'to discover common purpose'.

Brown's rationale for developing this community provides the third and most obvious point of continuity. It was in the British national interest to head off problems at the pass rather than waiting for them to come to damage Britain or its citizens, wherever they might live in the world. In taking this stance Brown casually mixed interests and values such that they became coterminous: 'the timeless values that underpin our policies at home – our belief in the liberty of all, in security and justice for all, in economic opportunity and environmental protection shared by all – are also ideas that I believe that it is in our national interest to promote abroad'. For both Blair and Brown, 'isolation' from global affairs was not an option for any state, but particularly not for a middle-ranking power such as Britain. 'Retreat' was not a leadership quality Brown wanted to have associated with him any more than Blair did, and the 'engage' not 'retreat' message was also a feature of Miliband's foreign policy discourse (Miliband 2007a). Brown's doctrine of international community went by a different name – 'hard-headed internationalism' Brown called it (Brown 2007c), 'hard-headed' being one of the terms he regularly used to describe his approach to politico-economic decision-making (on 'hard-headed' multilateralism see Brown 2008c). Being hard-headed means one privileges the 'pragmatic', 'practical common sense' and 'business-like' over the 'dogmatic' (for instance over the single currency – see Brown 1997c; Brown 1997e; Brown 1999h). That said, the Blair doctrine was in need of some modification in light of Britain's experiences in Afghanistan and Iraq (Miliband 2007b). But Brown and Miliband both worked the same concepts of globalization and interdependence, and used the same mixture of values and interests as we saw in the Blair foreign policy agenda (for a good example see Miliband 2009b). Brown and his team fully endorsed the later Blair's idea that 'open countries' (and by extension 'open leaders') are more likely to succeed than 'closed' countries or 'closed' leaders (Miliband 2007a).

Just as Brown and Miliband's ontological suppositions about the nature of the international realm were broadly similar, so there were a few telling similarities in terms of underlying philosophy and approach to the past, of which three stand out. The first is that both Prime Ministers Blair and Brown liberally sprinkled their diagnosis of the positive and negative effects of modern global interdependence with the epithet 'new'. New Labour needed Old Labour to give it sense, legitimacy and purpose, and it appears that incoming Prime Ministers need to identify 'new' challenges and aim to build 'new' world orders to mark boundaries between them and their pre-decessors. Nonetheless, just as Old Labour was a crucial part of New Labour, so the challenges Brown talked of as being 'new' (at Mansion House in 2007, for instance, he spoke of a 'new global competition for natural resources' – Brown 2006c) were, in all but name, the exact same international challenges that Blair believed he was facing down on Britain's behalf. This links to a second underlying continuity, which is that, like Blair, Brown spoke of wanting to help write 'a new chapter' in international relations for the twenty-first century: not a new book, a new chapter. The problematic term 'new' is again with us because while the discourse sounds progressive and forward-looking it was actually speaking to a conservative, incrementalist tradition whereby Brown sought to build on past achievements, not overthrow them entirely – evolution, not revolution, would in fact be the order of the day. Not that we should necessarily have expected anything else in terms of foreign policy, but it betrayed a rather less ambitious agenda than the accent on 'renewal' might suggest on first hearing. Finally, Brown and Miliband showed themselves well aware of the power of history to teach lessons and they wanted to be seen as 'learning lessons from the past', with an eye to 'examining the challenges ahead' (Brown 2003d). The last portion of the Prime Minister's first Lord Mayor's Banquet speech in 2007 was packed with lessons: for example, that multiculturalism is the way forward; 'that progress depends upon openness, freedom, democracy and fairness'; and 'that the best route to long-term economic growth lies in action to tackle climate change'. In setting out these lessons Brown showed that his would be a highly conventional approach to diplomatic practice, ably supported by Miliband, who earlier that year set out the case for multilateralism by arguing that 'History suggests the attraction of becoming members of "clubs" such as WTO [World Trade Organization], NATO, or most profoundly the EU, is a powerful one' (Miliband 2007a). Indeed, in a Blair-esque concoction of the old and the new, Brown's final assessment was that it was only by looking to these already learned lessons that we could face the challenge 'in a sustained endeavour to reform and renew our global rules, institutions and networks' (Brown 2007c).

In terms of its ontology and underpinning philosophy, Brown's foreign policy approach can be argued to have been strongly and not altogether unsurprisingly rooted in thinking that developed and came to fruition during Blair's decade in office. However, there were a few innovations in Brownite discourse which indicated a novel contribution to British European policy, albeit that such novelty was relative given the strict confines of British establishment discourses about the nation's foreign policy orientation. Part substance and part linguistic, they might not have been radical but in foreign policy terms even small shifts away from conventional modes of thinking could be considered significant, such was the weight of the dominant traditions of thinking charted in this book. The most prominent discontinuity was Brown's natural affinity for the US as opposed to Blair's instinctive Europeanism. This is not to assert that Blair was a Europeanist while Brown was an Atlanticist, or that Blair was 'pro' Europe and Brown was 'anti' (as we saw above, and following Naughtie 2002: 133, 142), not least because the labels themselves are highly problematic and politically charged. There were different 'Blairs' and 'Browns', depending on the time period and issue under consideration. Perhaps, therefore, Blair's Deputy Prime Minister John Prescott had it correct in his memoirs, that it was a case merely of Brown being 'more sceptical' than Blair on the euro (Prescott 2008: 303) – saying any more than that or generalizing over a longer period is fraught with problems. Prescott in fact says he himself was a 'sceptic' because he 'was worried about the establishment of a federal Europe' (Prescott 2008: 141), but so were both Blair and Brown and neither would class himself a sceptic, as we saw throughout this book. The labels are a real problem. To give a sense of the shifting sands over time, Sally Morgan said in interview that any government splits after 1997 could not necessarily have been predicted before New Labour came to office. 'Brown is not Eurosceptic.... Back in 1995, if you put the two of them in a room together they'd have both said one of the intentions of a New Labour government would be to sign up to the euro ... a joint agenda' (interview with Morgan).

However, Brown was particularly keen to 'affirm and to celebrate the historic partnership of shared purpose' between Britain and the US and to align himself with the spiritual father of the 'special relationship', Winston Churchill (Brown 2005i; Brown 2007b). He wistfully spoke of 'Britain's unique place in the new world' (Brown 2007c) and clearly set himself and the Labour government on a line he drew from Churchill to Obama (Brown 2008c). Blair was not averse to calling on Churchill, especially when in the US, and Brown had even fewer qualms: 'It is no secret that I am a lifelong admirer of America ... and I believe that our ties with America ... constitute our most important bilateral relationship' (Brown 2007c). When Brown celebrated the values Britain supposedly shares with America – 'the ties that bind us' – we get the impression that his warm sentiments simply *could not be expressed* in the same tone or language if he were talking about Britain's interest-based European connections and the pragmatic, hard-headed calculations out of which he formed British thinking on the single currency and the Lisbon Treaty (Brown 1999e; Brown 1999f; Brown 2000b; Brown 2002b; Brown 2002d;

Brown 2005i; Brown 2006d). Brown was a self-confessed fan of the
'special relationship' and believed 'no power on earth can drive us
apart' (Brown 2008a). He was committed not just to 'celebrating but
deepening' Anglo-American relations, on the commercial as well as
the political level (Brown 2003f). Brown's affection for the US and
its history prompted commentators such as Dyson to observe that
'Brown is at least as much of an Atlanticist as Blair, and perhaps
more instinctively cautious of Europe' (Dyson 2009b: 245). In short,
a values-based European discourse was a non-starter for Brown.
Could we ever have envisaged Brown telling the European Parliament (as he did tell the US Congress) 'it is never possible to come here
without having your faith in the future renewed' (Brown 2009a)? In
my opinion, those words *could not have been uttered* by Brown or any
other Prime Minister in Brussels or Strasbourg, because they are
part of a values-based not an interest-based discourse. Miliband has
added to this impression by arguing that: 'The US is the single most
important bilateral relationship. We are committed members of the
EU.' Britain, for Brown and Miliband, was locked in a values-based
relationship with the US but it was merely a run-of-the-mill, interest-
based *member* of the EU, 'an asset in economic terms' but not much
in the way of a shared sense of identity or destiny (Miliband 2007a).
Having said that, Miliband did confront Eurosceptics who nostal-
gically dream of a looser intergovernmental trading bloc with the
argument that the fragmentation of the single market 'would have
a devastating effect on the UK economy' (Miliband 2009a). This is
reminiscent of the 'crude' appeal prevalent in many of Blair's speeches
(see chapter 4) and goes to show that New Labour under Brown was,
on occasion, prepared to take the argument to the sceptics rather
than remaining silent on the issue of Europe.

A knock-on discontinuity is that Brown went further than Blair
in depicting the EU not as an end of British foreign policy but as the
means to the end of the creation of a global politico-economic order.
For instance, at the Lord Mayor's Banquet in 2007 Brown had it as
a positive that 'France and Germany and the European Union are
building stronger relationships with America'. Developing the later
Blair's ideas about the EU being too introspective and needing to be
fixed on 'competition across the world', Brown wanted to:

> work with others to propose a comprehensive agenda for Global
> Europe – a Europe that is outward looking, open, internationalist,
> able to effectively respond both through internal reform and external
> action to the economic, security and environmental imperatives of
> globalisation. (Brown 2007c)

Effectively, Brown wanted to impose on Europe 'a British model that
makes globalisation work for us' (Brown 2007a). Blair betrayed his

'EU working for Britain' agenda rather more subtly in the early years by talking of Britain being a 'leading' partner or player and a 'bridge' across the Atlantic while still paying lip service to the EU's regional successes and achievements. Brown, by contrast, seemed intent on not wasting time massaging the egos of leading member states in the EU or its institutions but sought simply to hook the Union as tightly as he could into his vision of a future international society.

Brown's distinctive agenda also showed through in two linguistic variations from the Blair years. One was that Brown had a slightly different take on Blair's 'international community', calling it a 'new global society' (Brown 2007c). Brown's thinking on this had apparently been moulded both by his religious beliefs and upbringing and, from a theoretical perspective, by Liberal thinking on the 'cobweb model' of interdependence. This encouraged him to emphasize the everyday effects of globalization on the 'average person'. As Brown the new Prime Minister expressed it:

> the defining image of the 21st [century – *sic*] is a web of connections – a world where we can rightly now talk not just of the wealth of nations but the wealth of networks. The web cannot be controlled in the end by any single force or any single leader. And what happens within it cannot be predicted from day to day. (Brown 2007c)

For Brown, greater connectedness could be harmful because its effects could be capricious. In this potentially intrusive and dangerous world, states retained a key role in protecting their citizens from some of its more deleterious effects. The ends might have been the same as Blair's, but Brown's was a more personally informed reading of globalization and interdependence. So with the other linguistic reworking Brown gave Blair, this time of his 'bridge' concept. As we have seen above, Brown was like Blair in seeing a unique, Churchillian role for Britain in the global political economy. Brown innovated on this model in two ways. The first was to construct Britain as a pivot in the international system by implicitly calling up its role in the three circles with talk of 'our membership of the European Union ... and the Commonwealth, and through our commitment to NATO and the UN', a series of partnerships Brown saw as 'mutually reinforcing' (Brown 2007c). Brown had long been convinced that 'British ideas can and will play a pivotal role' (Brown 2003e). A revised three-circles model it might have been and that seems to have been the goal because, when we add the US relationship, Brown seems to have been mapping *four* circles, taking in both nation states and the leading international organizations. The second way was to label this refreshed vision a 'hub', as in: 'Just as London has become a global hub linking commerce, ideas and people from all over the world, so too our enduring values and our network of alliances, can help secure the changes we need' (Brown 2007c). Blair had used this term in June 2000 when he suggested that 'Britain can become the European hub of the emerging global economy' (Blair 2000d). It seems, though, that the Brown team was even more wedded to the concept. For example, the Foreign Secretary worked the 'hub' theme in his July 2007 speech on foreign policy when he argued the case for Britain developing into a 'global hub' across the board, in economic, ideational, cultural, scientific and political terms (Miliband 2007a).

All in all then, the shift from Blair to Brown did not produce a radical overhaul of British foreign policy thinking. With the Blairite Miliband installed as Foreign Secretary, and the new Prime Minister and Chancellor concentrating on putting together a 'new deal' to help the global economy through the credit crisis, putting the case for the EU as Blair had set out to in 1997 was low on the government's 'to do' list. If anything, the case for seeing the EU as an 'end' of British foreign policy as the government did in 1997 had receded because the emphasis during the economic downturn was on global solutions to the credit crisis. Brown was able to secure a certain degree of consensus behind his EU reform agenda by setting it in the context of the reform of international financial institutions more generally. Different European nations also reacted with a series of their own national measures. With Britain cast in the role, with the US, of saviour of the international financial system, the time was hardly ripe for selling what would have been perceived as an unappealing account of Britain's contemporary strategic challenges on the world stage. It might have appeared retrograde; it would surely have been politically controversial; and it would certainly have gone against the manifest need to involve the US centrally in the reform process. It will be fascinating to see what policy and linguistic alterations are put in place to manage Britain's place in Europe under Prime Minister David Cameron and Foreign Secretary William Hague (for a study of some early trends see Daddow 2011). Whether the public will notice the shift, or care about it, are different matters altogether.

Coding scheme

Identities	Interests	History
National	*Economics*	*Individuals/parties*
Brit-/ain-/ish	Prosperity	Labour
Empire	Single market	Conservative
Imperial	Trade	Attlee
Commonwealth	Invest-/or-/ment	Bevin
Genius	Job	Churchill
Lead	Employ	Major
Heart-/ed		Thatcher
Engage	*Influence*	Monnet
Outward	Bridge	Schuman
Part-/ner	Pivot-/al	
Centre	Highway	*Britain and Europe*
European Union/EU	Special (relationship)	Miss
Europe	Alliance	Opportunity-/ies
Island	America/US	ECSC
Independent-/ce		EEC
Interdependent-/ce	*Security*	Opt (out)
Globalis-/e-/ation	Peace	Isolat-/e-/ion
Destiny	War	Ambivalent/ce
(Re-)new	Free	Indecision
Modern		Vacillate-/ion
		Misjudge
Personal/opponents		Hesitate-/ion
Pro		Hang (back)
Common (sense)		Alienate-/ion
Confident-/ce		
Open		*Uses*
Eurosceptic		The past
Anti		Lesson
Closed		Teach
Brussels		Learn
Superstate		Repeat
Federal		Mistake
Sovereign-/ty		Progress
Myth		Escape
Patriot-/ic-/ism		Guide
		Forgive

Appendix 2

A coded speech

This example of a coded speech is Tony Blair's at the Lord Mayor's Banquet, 10 November 1997 (Blair 1997g). Coded words (see appendix 1) appear here in bold.

Lord Mayor, Late Lord Mayor, Your Grace, Lord High Chancellor, Your Excellencies, Lords, Aldermen, Sheriffs, Ladies and Gentlemen.

It is a great pleasure for Cherie and me to be with you this evening. May I first of all congratulate you, Lord mayor, on your taking up this great office. Serving the City of London is a great national cause, which I wholeheartedly support.

My own case to you tonight is simple. **Britain** is once again a great place to be. It has new optimism, **confidence** and self-assurance about its future. What it needs now is to turn that spirit into a clear definition of national purpose, not just what we want for **Britain** in itself, but the direction of the nation and how it deals with the outside world.

The key goals of national purpose under this Government are these.

To run a well-managed economy with low inflation and tough rules on public finances; where having got stability for the long-term in place we focus policy on using the creative talent of all our people to build a true enterprise economy for the 21st century. We compete on brains not brawn.

To make a quantum leap in education, with high quality schools and universities open to all.

To put our hospitals and welfare system on a sure footing for today's society (not the hand to mouth existence we live now).

To tackle crime and its underlying causes of a social underclass set apart from society's mainstream.

To reform our Constitution to end the era of big centralised government.

And to allow **Britain's** standing in the world to grow and prosper.

These objectives are clear, right and achievable. They define our national purpose. They mean a politics no longer scarred by the irrelevant ideological battles of much of the 20th century. Most of the old left/right tags today are nothing but obstacles to good thinking. We have to concentrate on the things that really matter – what I call the big picture – not the periphery.

255

The goal of our foreign policy – tonight's subject – is clear. We cannot in these post-**Empire** days be a super-power in a military sense. But we can make the British presence in the world felt. With our historic alliances, we can be **pivotal**. We can be powerful in our **influence** – a nation to whom others listen. Why? Because we run **Britain** well and are successful ourselves. Because we have the right strategic alliances the world over. And because we are **engaged, open** and intelligent in how we use them.

And we can do this by using the strengths of our **history** to build our future. People sometimes misunderstand my emphasis on **modernity**. Of course I want **Britain** to be a **modern** forward-looking country. I also do believe we allow an old-fashioned image of Britain occasionally to obscure the **new** fashions of **Britain** to our detriment.

But I value and honour our **history** enormously. Who could stand at the Cenotaph yesterday and not feel both moved and proud?

I want us to make sense of our **history**. There is a lot of rubbish talked about the **Empire**. In my view, we should not either be apologising for it or wringing our hands about it. It is a fact of our **history**. It was, in many ways, a most extraordinary achievement and it has left us with some very valuable connections – in the **Commonwealth**, in the English language. So let us use them and be thankful we have them.

There are other strengths. We have the institutions: strong armed forces, a world-respected Diplomatic Service, international companies, the City, the **British** Council, the World Service, our **global** charities and NGOs. We have the technology and inventiveness. Most important, we have the people: entrepreneurs, creative talent in every field, world-renowned scientists, a dynamic multi-cultural, multi-ethnic society.

We also enjoy a unique set of relationships through the Security Council, NATO, the G8, **Europe** and the **Commonwealth**, not to mention our close **alliance** with **America**. We hold the Presidency of the **European Union** and the G8 next year, and are hosting the second Asia–Europe Meeting.

By virtue of our geography, our **history** and the strengths of our people, **Britain** is a **global** player.

As an **island** nation, **Britain** looks **outward** naturally. The **British** are inveterate travellers. We are the second biggest outward **investors**, and the second biggest recipients of inward **investment**, behind the **US** in both cases.

Our task has to be to shape these strengths and give them definition within a foreign policy that is clear and stated.

Tonight I will do so. I will set out, briefly but plainly, the 'guiding light' principles of a **modern British** foreign policy.

First. Consistent with our national **interest**, we must end the **isolation** of the last 20 years and be a **leading partner** in **Europe**. Of course, if **Europe** embarks on a path that is wrong or repugnant to **British interests**, we would have to stay apart. But subject to that, there is no place for misguided little Englander sentiment. The world is moving closer together. The **EU** will continue to develop. Look at South **America**, with Mercosur and the Andean Pact countries. North Asia and ASEAN. Or the **US** and NAFTA.

Britain is part of **Europe**. It must play its **full part** in **leading** it. Not because there is no alternative. There is: we could go. But because it is in **British national interests** to stay. And as we are staying – let us do so with effect.

Then we can change **Europe** where it needs changing. Reform of the CAP. Enlargement. Driving through the **single market**. Greater flexibility in the **EU** economy. Making a single currency work. A successful single currency would be good for the **EU**. Our own position will be judged on a hard-headed assessment of the economic benefits. They must be clear and unambiguous. But it will affect us in or out. And **influence** not impotence must be our objective in shaping how it works.

Europe wants us there as a **leading player**. **Britain** may need to be part of **Europe** but **Europe** needs **Britain** to be part of it. For four centuries, our destiny has been to help shape **Europe**. Let it be so again.

Second principle: Strong in **Europe** and strong with the **US**. There is no choice between the two. Stronger with one means stronger with the other.

Our aim should be to deepen our relationship with the **US** at all levels. We are the **bridge** between the **US** and **Europe**. Let us use it.

When **Britain** and **America** work together on the international scene, there is little we can't achieve.

We must never forget the historic and continuing **US** role in defending the political and economic freedoms we take for granted. Leaving all sentiment aside, they are a force for good in the world. They can always be relied on when the chips are down. The same should always be true of **Britain**.

We face another critical test of international resolve today. Saddam Hussein is once more defying the clearly expressed will of the United Nations by refusing to allow UN inspectors to fulfil their task of ensuring Iraq has no remaining weapons of mass destruction. It is vital for all of us that they be allowed to complete their work with no suggestion of discrimination against our **US** allies. Only then can the question of relaxing sanctions arise.

This Government's determination to stand firm against a still dangerous dictator is unshakeable. We want to see a diplomatic solution and will work with others to achieve this in the next few days. But Saddam should not take as a sign of weakness the international community's desire to find a peaceful way forward if possible. He has made this fatal miscalculation before. For his sake, I hope he will not make it again.

Third principle: we need strong defence, not just to defend our country, but for **British influence** abroad. Today, whether in Bosnia or the UN peace-keeping forces, or in any of the negotiations on disarmament and the reduction of weapons of mass destruction, sound defence is sound foreign policy. It is an instrument of **influence**. We must of course always look for efficiency in money spent on defence. But we must not reduce our capability to exercise a role on the international stage.

Fourth principle. We use power and **influence** for a purpose: for the values and aims we believe in. **Britain** must be a key player on major transnational issues: the environment, drugs, terrorism, crime, human rights and development. Human rights may sometimes seem an abstraction in the comfort of the West, but when they are ignored human misery and political instability all too easily follow. The same is true if we ignore the ethical dimension of the trade in arms.

Again, we are well placed to push forward international action through our position in all the major international groupings, not least the **Commonwealth**.

Environment and crime will be major themes of our **EU** presidency. Next year's Birmingham Summit will have international crime as one of the two or three critical issues on its agenda. Development was a preoccupation of the recent **Commonwealth** Summit.

Fifth, Britain must reinforce its position as a champion of free trade throughout the world. We are, above all, a trading nation, **open** to the world and ready to compete on a level playing field with all comers. We must also be champions of free **investment**, inward and outward. No-one gains in the end from protectionism.

Which brings me back to the starting point: national purpose. Foreign policy should not be seen as some self-contained part of government in a box marked 'abroad' or 'foreigners'. It should complement and reflect our domestic goals. It should be part of our mission of national **renewal**.

In the end I am, simply, a **patriot**. I believe in **Britain**. But it is an enlightened **patriotism**. **Patriotism** based not on narrow chauvinism but on the right values and principles. I believe in **Britain** because, at its best, it does stand for the right values and can give something to the world.

Tonight I have set out the guiding light principles of a modern **British** foreign policy. Properly followed, they do allow **Britain** to escape from the legacy of the **past** and shape an exciting future for ourselves.

A **new confidence** in **Britain** is not about style – though don't ignore the impact on the outside world of presenting a modern, professional face. It is of course about substance. It's about knowing where we are going. That's what gives us the **confidence**. We do. And with the right blend of intelligence and determination, we will get there.

Bibliography

Not long after Brown succeeded Blair in June 2007 the government overhauled its key websites, including the Downing Street, Treasury and Foreign Office portals. As a result of first Blair and then Brown being consigned to the 'history' sections of the relevant websites, the URLs for the speeches and statements were in a constant state of flux. This meant that midway through the research for this book many URLs for speeches and statements altered. I have included the URL and date of last access. The original speeches should all still be accessible through the archive section of the Downing Street website, now overseen by the National Archives.

Adams, S. (2008) 'EU flag and anthem revived by MEPs', *Daily Telegraph*, 12 September, www.telegraph.co.uk/news/worldnews/europe/2823052/EU-flag-and-anthem-revived-by-MEPs.html, last accessed 19 November 2009

Anderson, B. (2006) *Imagined Communities*, 2nd edn. London: Verso

Anderson, P. (2004) 'A flag of convenience? Discourse and motivations of the London-based Eurosceptic press', in R. Harmsen and M. Spiering (eds), *Euroscepticism: Party Politics, National Identity and European Integration*. Amsterdam and New York: Rodopi, pp. 151–70

Anderson, W., Coppola, R. and Schwarzman, J. (2007) *The Darjeeling Limited*, dir. Wes Anderson. Twentieth Century Fox

Aspinwall, M. (2004) *Rethinking Britain and Europe: Plurality Elections, Party Management and British Policy on European Integration*. Manchester and New York: Manchester University Press

Austin, J. L. (1975) *How To Do Things With Words*, 2nd edn, eds J. O. Urmson and Marina Sbisà. Cambridge, MA: Harvard University Press

Bache, I. and Jordan, A. (2006) 'Britain in Europe and Europe in Britain', in I. Bache and A. Jordan (eds), *The Europeanization of British Politics*. Basingstoke: Palgrave Macmillan, pp. 3–16

Bale, T. (1999) 'The logic of no alternative? Political scientists, historians and the politics of Labour's past', *British Journal of Politics and International Relations*, 1(2), pp. 192–204

BBC (1997) 'Emu timetable: a single European currency by 2002?', http://news.bbc.co.uk/1/business/11178.stm, last accessed 1 September 2010

BBC (2000) 'Dunkirk spirit: do we still have it?', 1 June, http://news.bbc.co.uk/1/hi/special_report/1999/02/99/e-cyclopedia/771944.stm, last accessed 9 September 2008

BBC (2005) *Timeshift*, last broadcast 31 May

BBC (2007) *The Blair Years*, part 1, last broadcast 18 November 2007

BBC (2009) 'Elections 2009', http://news.bbc.co.uk/1/shared/bsp/hi/elections-/local_council/09/html/region_99999.stm, last accessed 27 June 2009

Beck, P. J. (2003) 'The relevance of the "irrelevant": football as a missing dimension in the study of British relations with Germany', *International Affairs*, 79(2), pp. 389–411

Beckett, F. (2007) *Gordon Brown: Past, Present and Future*. London: Haus Books

Benn, T. (1987) *Out of the Wilderness: Diaries 1963–67*. London: Hutchinson

Benoit, B. (1997) *Social-Nationalism: An Anatomy of French Euroscepticism*. Aldershot: Ashgate

Berrington, H. and Hague, R. (1998) 'Europe, Thatcher and traditionalism: opinion, rebellion and the Maastricht Treaty in the backbench Conservative Party, 1992–1994', *West European Politics*, 21(1), pp. 44–71

Bevir, M. (2005) *New Labour: A Critique*. London and New York: Routledge

Bird, C. (2008) 'Strategic communication and behaviour change: lessons from domestic policy', in FCO, *Engagement: Public Diplomacy in a Globalised World*, July, www.fco.gov.uk/en/about-the-fco/publications/publications/pd-publication/behaviour-change, last accessed 30 April 2009

Blair, T. (1996) *New Britain: My Vision of a Young Country*. London: Fourth Estate Limited

Blair, T. (1997a) 'We'll see off Euro dragons', *Sun*, 22 April, p. 13

Blair, T. (1997b) Speech outside Downing Street, 2 May, www.number10.gov.uk/Page8073.asp, last accessed 1 September 2005

Blair, T. (1997c) Speech in Paris, 27 May, www.number10.gov.uk/Page1022, last accessed 1 September 2005

Blair, T. (1997d) Speech by Blair during Clinton's official visit to London, 29 May, www.number10.gov.uk/Page1025, last accessed 1 September 2005

Blair, T. (1997e) Speech at the Council of Europe summit, 10 October, www.number10.gov.uk/Page1062, last accessed 1 September 2005

Blair, T. (1997f) Speech at the Commonwealth Business Forum, 22 October, www.number10.gov.uk/Page1065, last accessed 1 September 2005

Blair, T. (1997g) Speech at the Lord Mayor's Banquet, 10 November, www.number10.gov.uk/Page1070, last accessed 1 September 2005

Blair, T. (1997h) Speech at the CBI conference, 11 November, www.number10.gov.uk/Page1072, last accessed 1 September 2005

Blair, T. (1997i) Speech at the British/Indian Golden Jubilee Banquet, 13 November, www.number10.gov.uk/Page1073, last accessed 1 September 2005

Blair, T. (1997j) Speech on the British Presidency, 6 December, www.number10.gov.uk/Page1087, last accessed 1 September 2005

Blair, T. (1998a) Speech, 'New Britain in the modern world', 9 January, www.number10.gov.uk/Page1148, last accessed 1 September 2005

Blair, T. (1998b) Speech, 'Change: a modern Britain in a modern Europe', 20 January, www.number10.gov.uk/Page1150, last accessed 2 September 2005

Blair, T. (1998c) Speech at the US State Department, 6 February, www.number10.gov.uk/Page1155, last accessed 2 September 2005

Blair, T. (1998d) Speech at the French National Assembly, 24 March, www.number10.gov.uk/Page1160, last accessed 2 September 2005

Blair, T. (1998e) Speech at the Irish Parliament, 26 November, www.number10.gov.uk/Page8069, last accessed 2 September 2005

Blair, T. (1998f) Speech on foreign affairs, 15 December, www.number10.gov.uk/Page1168, last accessed 2 September 2005

Blair, T. (1999a) Euro statement, 23 February, www.number10.gov.uk/Page1275, last accessed 6 September 2005

Blair, T. (1999b) Speech at the NATO fiftieth anniversary conference, 8 March, www.number-10.gov.uk/output/Page1286, last accessed 6 September 2005

Blair, T. (1999c) Statement on the European Council, Berlin, 29 March, www.number-10.gov.uk/output/Page1296, last accessed 6 September 2005

Blair, T. (1999d) 'Doctrine of the international community', Economic Club, Chicago, 22 April, www.number-10.gov.uk/output/Page1297, last accessed 6 September 2005

Blair, T. (1999e) 'New challenge for Europe', 20 May, www.number10.gov.uk/Page1334, 20 May, last accessed 7 September 2005

Blair, T. (1999f) Speech on Britain in Europe, 14 October, www.number10.gov.uk/Page1461, last accessed 7 September 2005

Blair, T. (2000a) Speech at the World Economic Forum, 18 January, www.number10.gov.uk/Page1508, last accessed 7 September 2005

Blair, T. (2000b) Speech, 'Committed to Europe: reforming Europe', 23 February, www.number10.gov.uk/Page1510, last accessed 7 September 2005

Blair, T. (2000c) Speech at the Scottish Parliament, 9 March, www.number10.gov.uk/Page1522, last accessed 7 September 2005

Blair, T. (2000d) Speech at the Global Borrowers and Investors Forum conference, 22 June, www.number10.gov.uk/Page1528, last accessed 7 September 2005

Blair, T. (2000e) Speech at the Global Ethics Foundation, Tübigen University, 30 June, www.number10.gov.uk/Page1529, last accessed 7 September 2005

Blair, T. (2000f) Speech at the Polish Stock Exchange, 6 October, www.number10.gov.uk/Page3384, last accessed 7 September 2005

Blair, T. (2000g) Speech at the University of Northumbria, 3 November, www.number10.gov.uk/Page1533, last accessed 7 September 2005

Blair, T. (2000h) Speech at the Lord Mayor's Banquet, 13 November, www.number10.gov.uk/Page1535, last accessed 7 September 2005

Blair, T. (2001a) Speech at the Canadian Parliament, 23 February, www.number10.gov.uk/Page1582, last accessed 9 September 2005

Blair, T. (2001b) Speech, Sao Paolo, 30 August, www.number10.gov.uk/Page1593, last accessed 9 September 2005

Blair, T. (2001c) Speech at the Lord Mayor's Banquet, 12 November, www.number10.gov.uk/Page1661, last accessed 9 September 2005

Blair, T. (2001d) Speech at the European Research Institute, 23 November, www.number10.gov.uk/Page1673, last accessed 9 September 2005

Blair, T. (2002a) Statement at the European Council, 18 March, www.number10.gov.uk/Page1705, last accessed 15 September 2005

Blair, T. (2002b) Speech at the Labour Party conference, 1 October, reproduced in *Guardian* online, www.guardian.co.uk/politics/2002/oct/01/labourconference.labour14 (part 1) and www.guardian.co.uk/politics/2002/oct/01/labourconference.labour15 (part 2), last accessed 14 November 2008

Blair, T. (2002c) Speech at the Lord Mayor's Banquet, 11 November, www.number10.gov.uk/Page1731, last accessed 15 September 2005

Blair, T. (2002d) 'A clear course for Europe', 28 November, www.number10.gov.uk/Page1739, last accessed 15 September 2005

Blair, T. (2003a) New Year's message, 1 January, www.number10.gov.uk/Page1747, last accessed 15 September 2005

Blair, T. (2003b) Speech at the Foreign Office conference, 7 January, www.number10.gov.uk/Page1765, last accessed 15 September 2005

Blair, T. (2003c) Speech on Europe, Warsaw, 30 May, www.number10.gov.uk/Page3787, last accessed 15 September 2005

Blair, T. (2003d) Statement on the European Council, 23 June, www.number10.gov.uk/Page4000, last accessed 15 September 2005

Blair, T. (2003e) Speech at the US Congress, 18 July, www.number10.gov.uk/Page4220, last accessed 15 September 2005

Blair, T. (2003f) Speech, Tokyo, 21 July, www.number10.gov.uk/Page4235, last accessed 7 June 2006

Blair, T. (2003g) Speech at the Lord Mayor's Banquet, 11 November, www.number10.gov.uk/Page4803, last accessed 15 September 2005

Blair, T. (2003h) Speech at the CBI conference, 17 November, www.number10.gov.uk/Page4851, last accessed 15 September 2005

Blair, T. (2004a) Statement to Parliament on the EU White Paper and the EU Constitution, 20 April, www.number10.gov.uk/Page5669, last accessed 15 September 2005

Blair, T. (2004b) Statement to Parliament on the EU Constitutional Treaty, 21 June, www.number10.gov.uk/Page5993, last accessed 15 September 2005

Blair, T. (2004c) Speech at the Lord Mayor's Banquet, 15 November, www.number10.gov.uk/Page6583, last accessed 15 September 2005

Blair, T. (2005a) Statement to Parliament on the European Council, 24 March, www.number10.gov.uk/Page7397, last accessed 15 September 2005

Blair, T. (2005b) Speech at the EU Parliament, 23 June, www.number10.gov.uk/Page7714, last accessed 30 April 2009

Blair, T. (2006a) Speech on the future of Europe, 2 February, www.number10.gov.uk/Page9003, last accessed 30 April 2009

Blair, T. (2006b) Speech on foreign policy 1, 21 March, www.number10.gov.uk/Page9224, last accessed 30 April 2009

Blair, T. (2006c) Speech on foreign policy 2, 27 March, www.number10.gov.uk/Page9245, last accessed 7 May 2009

Blair, T. (2006d) Speech at the CBI annual dinner, 16 May, www.number10.gov.uk/Page9470, last accessed 30 April 2009

Blair, T. (2006e) Speech on foreign policy 3, 26 May, www.number10.gov.uk/Page9549, last accessed 30 April 2009

Blair, T. (2006f) Speech at News Corps, 30 July, www.number10.gov.uk/Page9937, last accessed 30 April 2009

Blair, T. (2006g) Speech at the CBI conference, 27 November, www.number10.gov.uk/Page10496, last accessed 30 April 2009

Blair, T. (2006h) Speech at the Lord Mayor's Banquet, 30 November, www.number10.gov.uk/Page10409, last accessed 30 April 2009

Blair, T. (2010) *Tony Blair: A Journey*. London: Hutchinson

Blunkett, D. (2006) *The Blunkett Tapes*. London: Bloomsbury

Bogdanor, V. (2005) 'Footfalls echoing in the memory. Britain and Europe: the historical perspective', *International Affairs*, 81(4), pp. 689–701

Booker, C. (1996) *The Castle of Lies: Why Britain Must Get Out of Europe*. London: Duckworth

Booker, C. (2001) 'Britain and Europe: the culture of deceit', Bruges Group, paper no. 42, www.brugesgroup.com/mediacentre/index.live?article=91, last accessed 15 April 2009

Boulton, A. (2008) *Tony's Ten Years: Memories of the Blair Administration*. London, New York, Sydney and Toronto: Simon and Schuster

Bower, T. (2007) *Gordon Brown: Prime Minister*. London: HarperCollins

Broad, M. and Daddow, O. (2010) 'Half remembered quotations from mostly forgotten speeches: the limits of Labour's European discourse', *British Journal of Politics and International Relations*, 12(2), pp. 205–22

Brown, G. (1997a) Speech, 'Exploiting the British genius – the key to long-term economic success', 20 May, www.hm-treasury.gov.uk/speech_chex_200597.htm, last accessed 4 July 2006

Brown, G. (1997b) Speech at the Mansion House, 12 June, www.hm-treasury. gov.uk/speech_chex_120697.htm, last accessed 4 July 2006

Brown, G. (1997c) Speech at the Royal Institute of International Affairs, 17 July, www.hm-treasury.gov.uk/speech_chex_170797.htm, last accessed 4 July 2006

Brown, G. (1997d) Statement on Economic and Monetary Union, 27 October, www.hm-treasury.gov.uk/speech_chex_271097.htm, last accessed 4 July 2006

Brown, G. (1997e) Speech at the CBI conference, 10 November, www.hm-treasury.gov.uk/speech_chex_101197.htm, last accessed 4 July 2006

Brown, G. (1998a) Speech at the CBI President's Dinner, 22 April, www.hm-treasury.gov.uk/speech_chex_220498.htm, last accessed 4 July 2006

Brown, G. (1998b) Speech at the Lord Mayor's Banquet, 11 June, www.hm-treasury.gov.uk/speech_chex_110698.htm, last accessed 4 July 2006

Brown, G. (1998c) Speech at the News International conference, 17 July, www. hm-treasury.gov.uk/speech_chex_170798.htm, last accessed 4 July 2006

Brown, G. (1998d) Speech, 'New global structures for the new global age', 30 September, www.hm-treasury.gov.uk/speech_chex_300998.htm, last accessed 4 July 2006

Brown, G. (1998e) Speech at the annual meetings of the IMF and World Bank, 6 October, www.hm-treasury.gov.uk/speech_chex_051098.htm, last accessed 4 July 2006

Brown, G. (1998f) Speech at the CBI conference, 2 November, www.hm-treasury. gov.uk/speech_chex_021198.htm, last accessed 4 July 2006

Brown, G. (1999a) Speech at the Smith Institute, 15 April, www.hm-treasury. gov.uk/speech_chex_150499.htm, last accessed 4 July 2006

Brown, G. (1999b) Speech at the TUC conference on Economic and Monetary Union, 13 May, www.hm-treasury.gov.uk/speech_chex_130599.htm, last accessed 4 July 2006

Brown, G. (1999c) Speech at the CBI annual dinner, 18 May, www.hm-treasury. gov.uk/speech_chex_180599.htm, last accessed 4 July 2006

Brown, G. (1999d) Speech at the Mansion House, 10 June, www.hm-treasury. gov.uk/speech_chex_100699.htm, last accessed 4 July 2006

Brown, G. (1999e) Speech at the UK–US Enterprise conference, 2 July, www. hm-treasury.gov.uk/speech_chex_020799.htm, last accessed 4 July 2006

Brown, G. (1999f) Speech at the Council for Foreign Relations, 16 September, www.hm-treasury.gov.uk/speech_chex_160999.htm, last accessed 4 July 2006

Brown, G. (1999g) Mais Lecture, 19 October, www.hm-treasury.gov.uk/speech_ chex_191099.htm, last accessed 4 July 2006

Brown, G. (1999h) Speech at the CBI conference, 1 November, www.hm-treasury.gov.uk/speech_chex_011199.htm, last accessed 4 July 2006

Brown, G. (2000a) Speech, 'Britain and the knowledge economy', 16 February, www.hm-treasury.gov.uk/speech_chex_160200.htm, last accessed 4 July 2006

Brown, G. (2000b) Speech at the British American Chamber of Commerce, 22 February, www.hm-treasury.gov.uk/speech_chex_220200.htm, last accessed 4 July 2006

Brown, G. (2000c) Speech at the British Chamber of Commerce conference, 5 April, www.hm-treasury.gov.uk/speech_chex_050400.htm, last accessed 4 July 2006

Brown, G. (2000d) James Meade Memorial Lecture, 8 May, www.hm-treasury. gov.uk/speech_chex_080500.htm, last accessed 4 July 2006

Brown, G. (2000e) Speech at the Royal Economic Society, 13 July, http://archive.
treasury.gov.uk/press/2000/p90_00.html, last accessed 4 July 2006

Brown, G. (2000f) Speech, 'Civic society in modern Britain', 20 July, www.hm-
treasury.gov.uk/speech_chex_200700.htm, last accessed 4 July 2006

Brown, G. (2000g) Speech at the TUC congress, 12 September, www.hm-
treasury.gov.uk/speech_chex_120900.htm, last accessed 4 July 2006

Brown, G. (2001a) Speech at the Mansion House, 20 June, www.hm-treasury.
gov.uk/speech_chex_200601.htm, last accessed 4 July 2006

Brown, G. (2001b) Speech, 'Britain, Europe and America – the challenge of
globalisation', 26 July, www.hm-treasury.gov.uk/speech_chex_260701.htm,
last accessed 4 July 2006

Brown, G. (2001c) Speech at the CBI annual conference dinner, 5 November,
www.hm-treasury.gov.uk/speech_chex_051101.htm, last accessed 4 July
2006

Brown, G. (2001d) Speech at the Institute of Directors, 15 November, www.hm-
treasury.gov.uk/press_25_01.htm, last accessed 4 July 2006

Brown, G. (2001e) Speech at the Press Club, 17 December, www.hm-treasury.
gov.uk/press_146_01.htm, last accessed 4 July 2006

Brown, G. (2002a) Speech at the TGWU conference, 28 March, www.hm-
treasury.gov.uk/speech_chex_280302.htm, last accessed 4 July 2006

Brown, G. (2002b) Speech at British American Business Inc., 19 April, www.
hm-treasury.gov.uk/speech_chex_190402.htm, last accessed 4 July 2006

Brown, G. (2002c) Speech at the Mansion House, 26 June, www.hm-treasury.
gov.uk/speech_chex_260602.htm, last accessed 4 July 2006

Brown, G. (2002d) Speech at the CBI conference, 25 November, www.hm-
treasury.gov.uk/speech_chex_260602.htm, last accessed 4 July 2006

Brown, G. (2003a) Speech on corporate social responsibility, Chatham House,
22 January, www.hm-treasury.gov.uk/speech_chx_220103.htm, last accessed
4 July 2006

Brown, G. (2003b) Speech at the CBI annual dinner, 20 May, www.hm-treasury.
gov.uk/speech_chx_200503.htm, last accessed 4 July 2006

Brown, G. (2003c) Statement by the Chancellor of the Exchequer on UK
membership of the single currency, *Hansard*, 9 June, cols 407–15

Brown, G. (2003d) Speech at the Global Borrowers and Investors Forum, 17
June, www.hm-treasury.gov.uk/speech_chx_170603.htm, last accessed 4
July 2006

Brown, G. (2003e) Speech at the Lord Mayor's Banquet, 18 June, www.hm-
treasury.gov.uk/speech_chx_180603.htm, last accessed 4 July 2006

Brown, G. (2003f) Speech at the CBI conference, 18 November, www.hm-
treasury.gov.uk/speech_chx_181103.htm, last accessed 4 July 2006

Brown, G. (2003g) Speech at the Wall Street Journal CEO summit, 24
November, www.hm-treasury.gov.uk/speech_chx_241103.htm, last accessed
4 July 2006

Brown, G. (2004a) Speech at the conference 'Making globalisation work for us
all – the challenge of delivering monetary consensus', 16 February, www.hm-
treasury.gov.uk/speech_chex_160204.htm, last accessed 4 July 2006

Brown, G. (2004b) Remarks at the opening of the Lehman Brothers' European
headquarters, London, 5 April, www.hm-treasury.gov.uk/speech_chx_241103.
htm, last accessed 4 July 2006

Brown, G. (2004c) Speech at the Institute of Directors' annual convention, 28
April, www.hm-treasury.gov.uk/speech_chex_280404.htm, last accessed 4
July 2006

Brown, G. (2004d) Speech at the CBI conference on competitiveness in Europe post-enlargement, 12 May, www.hm-treasury.gov.uk/speech_chex_120504. htm, last accessed 4 July 2006

Brown, G. (2004e) Speech at the launch of UK Business Week, 8 June, www. hm-treasury.gov.uk/speech_chex_080604.htm, last accessed 4 July 2006

Brown, G. (2004f) Speech at the Mansion House, 16 June, www.hm-treasury. gov.uk/speech_chex_160604.htm, last accessed 4 July 2006

Brown, G. (2004g) British Council Annual Lecture, 7 July, www.hm-treasury. gov.uk/speech_chex_070704.htm, last accessed 4 July 2006

Brown, G. (2004h) Speech at the CBI conference, 9 November, www.hm-treasury.gov.uk/speech_chex_091104.htm, last accessed 4 July 2006

Brown, G. (2005a) Speech at the DfID/UNDP seminar, Lancaster House, 26 January, www.hm-treasury.gov.uk/speech_chex_260105.htm, last accessed 4 July 2006

Brown, G. (2005b) Speech at Advancing Enterprise 2005, 4 February, www.hm-treasury.gov.uk/press_15_05.htm, last accessed 30 August 2006

Brown, G. (2005c) Speech at the Academy of Social Science, Beijing, 21 February, www.hm-treasury.gov.uk/press_15_05.htm, last accessed 4 July 2006

Brown, G. (2005d) Video speech to the Science and Innovation Conference, Manchester, 21 February, www.hm-treasury.gov.uk/speech_chex_210205.htm, last accessed 4 July 2006

Brown, G. (2005e) Speech at the CBI annual dinner, 18 May, www.hm-treasury. gov.uk/speech_chex_180505.htm, last accessed 4 July 2006

Brown, G. (2005f) Speech at the Institute of Directors, 24 November, www.hm-treasury.gov.uk/speech_chex_241105.htm, last accessed 30 August 2006

Brown, G. (2005g) Speech at the CBI annual conference, 28 November, www. hm-treasury.gov.uk/speech_chex_281105.htm, last accessed 4 July

Brown, G. (2005h) Hugo Young Memorial Lecture, Chatham House, 13 December, www.hm-treasury.gov.uk/speech_chex_131205.htm, last accessed 4 July

Brown, G. (2005i) Speech at New York University, 15 December, www.hm-treasury.gov.uk/speech_chex_151205.htm, last accessed 4 July

Brown, G. (2006a) Speech at the Fabian New Year conference, 14 January, www. hm-treasury.gov.uk/speech_chex_140106.htm, last accessed 11 May 2009

Brown, G. (2006b) Speech at the CBI President's dinner, 5 June, www.hm-treasury.gov.uk/speech_chex_050606.htm, last accessed 11 May 2009

Brown, G. (2006c) Speech at the Mansion House, 21 June, www.hm-treasury. gov.uk/speech_chex_210606.htm, last accessed 11 May 2009

Brown, G. (2006d) Speech to the CBI, 28 November, www.hm-treasury.gov.uk/ speech_chex_281106.htm, last accessed 11 May 2009

Brown, G. (2007a) Speech at the CBI annual dinner, 15 May, www.hm-treasury. gov.uk/speech_chex_150507.htm, last accessed 11 May 2009

Brown, G. (2007b) Press conference with the US President at Camp David, 30 July, www.number10.gov.uk/Page12765, last accessed 30 April 2009

Brown, G. (2007c) Speech at the Lord Mayor's Banquet, 12 November, www. number10.gov.uk/Page13736, last accessed 30 April 2009

Brown, G. (2008a) Keynote foreign policy speech, John F. Kennedy Presidential Library, 18 April, www.number10.gov.uk/Page15303, last accessed 30 April 2009

Brown, G. (2008b) Speech at the Institute of Directors, 30 April, www. number10.gov.uk/Page15419, last accessed 30 April 2009

Brown, G. (2008c) Speech at the Lord Mayor's Banquet, 10 November, www. number10.gov.uk/Page17419, last accessed 30 April 2009

Brown, G. (2009a) Speech at the US Congress, 4 March, www.number10.gov.uk/ Page18506, last accessed 30 April 2009

Brown, G. (2009b) Speech at the CBI conference, 23 November, www.number10.
    gov.uk/Page21433, last accessed 23 November 2009
Bruges Group (undated a) 'About the Bruges Group', www.brugesgroup.com/
    about/index.live, last accessed 8 January 2009
Bruges Group (undated b) 'Dinner in the presence of Baroness Thatcher', www.
    brugesgroup.com/mediacentre/releases.live?article=14035, last accessed 8
    January 2009
BSA (2007) 'Question: do you think Britain's long-term policy should be...',
    www.britsocat.com/BodySecure.aspx?control=BritsocatMarginals&addsupe
    rmap=LBECPOLICY, last accessed 8 August 2008
Budge, I., McKay, D., Bartle, J. and Newton, K. (2007) *The New British Politics*,
    4th edn. Harlow: Pearson Education Limited
Bulmer, S. (2008) 'New Labour, new European policy? Blair, Brown and
    utilitarian supranationalism', *Parliamentary Affairs*, 61(4), pp. 597–620
Bulmer, S. and Burch, M. (2006) 'Central government', in I. Bache and A.
    Jordan (eds), *The Europeanization of British Politics*. Basingstoke: Palgrave
    Macmillan, pp. 37–51
Cabrera, M. A. (2005) *Postsocial History: An Introduction*, trans. M. McMahon.
    Lanham, MD: Lexington Books
Campbell, A. (2007) *The Blair Years: Extracts from the Alastair Campbell
    Diaries*. London: Hutchinson
Cannadine, D. (1988) 'The past in the present', in L. M. Smith (ed.), *The Making
    of Britain: Echoes of Greatness*. Basingstoke: Macmillan Education, pp. 9–20
Casey, T. (2009) 'Introduction: how to assess the Blair legacy?', in T. Casey
    (ed.), *The Blair Legacy: Politics, Policy, Governance, and Foreign Affairs*.
    Basingstoke and New York: Palgrave Macmillan, pp. 1–19
Castle, B. (1984) *The Castle Diaries 1964–70*. London: Weidenfeld and Nicolson
Castle, S. (1996) 'Tory left fights back in Major's "beef war"', *Independent*, 26
    May, www.independent.co.uk/news/tory-left-fights-back-in-majors-beef-war-
    1349173.html, last accessed 1 June 2009
Černý, D. (2009) 'Entropa', background notes, www.vlada.cz/assets/media-
    centrum/aktualne/entropa_1__1.pdf, last accessed 15 January 2009
Chalaby, J. K. (2003) 'Transnational television in Europe: affluence without
    influence', in M. Bond (ed.), *Europe, Parliament and the Media*. London:
    Federal Trust for Education and Research, pp. 13–30
Chapman, J. (2009) 'Labour "sellout" to give EU flag same status as Union
    Jack', *Mail* online, 19 November, www.dailymail.co.uk/news/article-397537/
    Labour-sellout-EU-flag-status-Union-Jack.html, last accessed 19 November
    2009
Charteris-Black, J. (2006) *Politicians and Rhetoric: The Persuasive Power of
    Metaphor*. London and New York: Palgrave Macmillan
Checkel, J. T. and Katzenstein, P. J. (2009) 'The politicization of European
    identity', in J. T. Checkel and P. J. Katzenstein (eds), *European Identity*.
    Cambridge: Cambridge University Press, pp. 1–25
Chilton, P. (2004) *Analysing Political Discourse: Theory and Practice*. London
    and New York: Routledge
Church, C. H. (2004) 'Swiss Euroscepticism: local variations on wider themes',
    in R. Harmsen and M. Spiering (eds), *Euroscepticism: Party Politics,
    National Identity and European Integration*. Amsterdam and New York:
    Rodopi, pp. 269–90
Churchill, W. (1948) Speech at the Conservative Party conference, in the official
    proceedings of Conservative Party conference, Bodleian Library Special
    Collections, shelf mark NUA 2/1/56, pp. 149–56

Churchill Centre (undated) 'Quotations and stories', www.winstonchurchill.org/
i4a/pages/index.cfm?pageid=388, last accessed 4 August 2008
CIB (2008a) 'Join the Campaign for an Independent Britain', www.eurofaq.
freeuk.com/services/, last accessed 23 September 2008
CIB (2008b) 'United we're stronger', www.eurofaq.freeuk.com/cib/index.html,
last accessed 23 September 2008
Citrin, J. and Sides, J. (2008) 'Immigration and the imagined community in
Europe and the United States', *Political Studies*, 56(1), pp. 33–56
Colley, L. (2005) *Britons: Forging the Nation 1707–1837*. New Haven, CT: Yale
University Press
Cook, R. (2003) *The Point of Departure*. London: Simon and Schuster
Coupland, P. (2006) *Britannia, Europe and Christendom: British Christians
and European Integration*. Basingstoke: Palgrave Macmillan
Crolley, L. and Hand, D. (2002) *Football, Europe and the Press*. London and
Portland, OR: Frank Cass
Crossman, R. (1976) *The Diaries of a Cabinet Minister: Vol. II, Lord President of
the Council and Leader of the House of Commons, 1966–68*. London: Hamish
Hamilton/Jonathan Cape
Crossman, R. (1977) *The Diaries of a Cabinet Minister: Vol. I, Minister of
Housing, 1964–66*. London: Hamish Hamilton/Jonathan Cape
Crowson, N. J. (2007) *The Conservative Party and European Integration Since
1945: At the Heart of Europe?* Abingdon and New York: Routledge
Cull, N. J. (2008) 'Public diplomacy: seven lessons for its future from its past', in
FCO, *Engagement: Public Diplomacy in a Globalised World*, July, www.fco.
gov.uk/en/about-the-fco/publications/publications/pd-publication/7-lessons,
last accessed 30 April 2009
Daddow, O. J. (2002) 'Facing the future: history in the writing of British
military doctrine', *Defence Studies*, 2(1), pp. 157–64
Daddow, O. J. (2003) 'The construction of British military doctrine in the 1980s
and 1990s', *Defence Studies*, 3(3), pp. 103–13
Daddow, O. J. (2004a) *Britain and Europe Since 1945: Historiographical Perspec-
tives on Integration*. Manchester and New York: Manchester University Press
Daddow, O. J. (2004b) 'Economics in the historiography of Britain's applications
to join the EEC in the 1960s', in R. Perron (ed.), *The Stability of Europe. The
Common Market: Towards European Integration of Industrial and Financial
Markets? (1958–1968)*. Paris: Presses de l'Université de Paris-Sorbonne,
pp. 81–97
Daddow, O. (2006) 'Euroscepticism and the culture of the discipline of history',
Review of International Studies, 32(2), pp. 309–28
Daddow, O. (2008) 'Exploding history: Hayden White on disciplinization',
Rethinking History, 12(1), pp. 41–58
Daddow, O. (2009) '"Tony's war"? Blair, Kosovo and the interventionist impulse
in British foreign policy', *International Affairs*, 85(3), pp. 547–60
Daddow, O. (2010) 'The UK, "Europe" and the 2009 European Parliament elec-
tions', in R. Harmsen and J. Schild (eds), *Debating Europe: The 2009 European
Parliament Elections and Beyond*. Baden-Baden: Nomos, forthcoming.
Daddow, O. (2011) 'Conclusion', in O. Daddow and J. Gaskarth (eds), *British
Foreign Policy: The New Labour Years*. Basingstoke: Palgrave Macmillan,
forthcoming
Daddow, O. and Gaskarth, J. (eds) (2011) *British Foreign Policy: The New
Labour Years*. Basingstoke: Palgrave Macmillan
Dad's Army Appreciation Society (2009a) Frontpage, www.dadsarmy.co.uk/
frontpage.html, last accessed 23 April 2009

Dad's Army Appreciation Society (2009b) 'What is Dad's Army?', www.dadsarmy.co.uk/whatisdad%27sarmy.html, last accessed 23 April 2009

Dad's Army Appreciation Society (2009c) 'Song lyrics', www.dadsarmy.co.uk/songlyrics.html, last accessed 23 April 2009

Daniels, P. (1998) 'From hostility to "constructive engagement": the Europeanisation of the Labour Party', *West European Politics*, 21(1), pp. 72–96

Darling, A. (2008a) Speech at the Brookings Institute, 11 April, www.hm-treasury.gov.uk/speech_chex_110408. htm, last accessed 11 May 2009

Darling, A. (2008b) Speech at the CBI annual dinner, 20 May, www.hm-treasury.gov.uk/speech_chex_200508.htm, last accessed 11 May 2009

Deighton, A. (2002) 'The past in the present: British imperial memories and the European question', in J.-W. Müller (ed.), *Memory and Power in Post-War Europe*. Cambridge: Cambridge University Press, pp. 100–20

Deighton, A. (2005) 'The foreign policy of British Prime Minister Tony Blair: radical or retrograde?', Centre for British Studies, Humboldt University, Berlin, 11 July, www.gbz.hu-berlin.de/publications/working-papers/downloads/pdf/WPS_Deighton_Blair.pdf, last accessed 3 March 2009

Diez, T. (1999) 'Speaking "Europe": the politics of integration discourse', *Journal of European Public Policy*, 6(4), pp. 598–613

Donnelly, B. (2005) 'The Euro and British politics', Federal Trust, European policy brief no. 15, September, www.fedtrust.co.uk/admin/uploads/PolicyBrief15.pdf, last accessed 3 April 2007

Dyson, S. B. (2009a) *The Blair Identity: Leadership and Foreign Policy*. Manchester and New York: Manchester University Press

Dyson, S. B. (2009b) 'What difference did he make? Tony Blair and British foreign policy from 1997–2007', in T. Casey (ed.), *The Blair Legacy: Politics, Policy, Governance, and Foreign Affairs*. Basingstoke and New York: Palgrave Macmillan, pp. 235–46

Ellison, J. (2000) *Threatening Europe: Britain and the Creation of the European Community, 1955–58*. Basingstoke: Macmillan

Epstein, C. (2008) *The Power of Words in International Relations: Birth of an Anti-whaling Discourse*. Cambridge, MA, and London: MIT Press

Eurobarometer (2007a) 'Standard Eurobarometer 67, spring, National Report: United Kingdom', http://ec.europa.eu/public_opinion/archives/eb/eb67/eb67_uk_nat.pdf, last accessed 8 August 2008

Eurobarometer (2007b) 'Standard Eurobarometer 68, autumn, Executive Summary, UK', http://ec.europa.eu/public_opinion/archives/eb/eb68/eb68_uk_exec.pdf, last accessed 7 May 2009

Eurobarometer (2007c) 'Attitudes towards the EU in the United Kingdom', Eurobarometer no. 203, http://ec.europa.eu/public_opinion/flash/fl203_en.pdf, last accessed 8 August 2008

Eurobarometer (2009) 'Public opinion analysis – flash Eurobarometer reports', May, http://ec.europa.eu/public_opinion/archives/flash_arch_en.htm, last accessed 7 May 2009

Europa (undated) 'The history of the European Union', http://europa.eu/abc/history/1945-1959/index_en.htm, last accessed 6 April 2009

European Council (1983) 'Solemn Declaration on European Union', Stuttgart, 19 June, *Bulletin of the European Communities*, 6/1983, http://aei.pitt.edu/1788/01/stuttgart_declaration_1983.pdf, last accessed 29 August 2008

Fairclough, N. (2000) *New Labour, New Language?* London: Routledge

Fairclough, N. (2009) 'The discourse of New Labour: critical discourse analysis', in M. Wetherell, S. Taylor and S. J. Yates (eds), *Discourse as Data: A Guide for Analysis*. London, Thousand Oaks, CA, and New Delhi: Sage, pp. 229–66

Fielding, S. (2003) *The Labour Party: Continuity and Change in the Making of 'New' Labour*. Basingstoke and New York: Palgrave Macmillan

Finnemore, M. and Sikkink, K. (1998) 'International norm dynamics and political change', *International Organization*, 52(4), pp. 887–917

Flint, C. (2009) 'Caroline Flint: resignation letter in full', www.telegraph.co.uk/news/newstopics/politics/5454526/Caroline-Flint-resignation-letter-in-full.html, last accessed 6 June 2009

Flood, C. (1995) 'French Euroscepticism and the politics of indifference', in H. Drake (ed.), *French Relations with the European Union*. London and New York: Routledge, pp. 42–63

Forster, A. (2002) *Euroscepticism in Contemporary British Politics: Opposition to Europe in the British Conservative and Labour Parties Since 1945*. London and New York: Routledge

Forster, A. and Blair, A. (2002) *The Making of Britain's European Foreign Policy*. Harlow: Pearson

Fowler, R. (1992) *Language in the News: Discourse and Ideology in the Press*. London: Routledge

Fowler, R. (2006) *Fowler: My Autobiography*. London: Pan Books

Frankel, J. (1968) *The Making of Foreign Policy: An Analysis of Decision Making*. Oxford: Oxford University Press

French Presidency of the Council of the European Union (2008) *Work Programme, 1 July – 31 December 2008*, www.ue2008.fr/webdav/site/PFUE/shared/ProgrammePFUE/Programme_EN.pdf, last accessed 4 August 2008

Gamble, A. (2003) *Between Europe and America: The Future of British Politics*. Basingstoke: Palgrave Macmillan

Garton Ash, T. (2001) 'The gamble of engagement', in M. Rosenbaum (ed.), *Britain and Europe: The Choices We Face*. Oxford: Oxford University Press, pp. 39–45

Garton Ash, T. (2007) 'Brown must learn the lessons from Blair's three big mistakes', *Guardian*, 10 May, www.guardian.co.uk/commentisfree/story/0,,2076177,00.html, last accessed 11 May 2007

Geddes, A. (2006) 'Political parties and party politics', in I. Bache and A. Jordan (eds), *The Europeanization of British Politics*. Basingstoke: Palgrave Macmillan, pp. 119–34

Gerrard, S. (2006) *Gerrard: My Autobiography*, London, Toronto, Sydney, Auckland and Johannesburg: Bantam Press

Graziano, A. M. and Raulin, M. L. (2007) *Research Methods: A Process of Inquiry*, 6th edn. Boston, MA, New York and London: Pearson

Hain, P. (2002a) 'Against Europe', speech at the Labour Party conference, 29 September, emailed to author by Peter Hain's parliamentary office, 31 July 2006

Hain, P. (2002b) 'Europe and the left', speech at the Labour Party conference, Independent fringe, 30 September, emailed to author by Peter Hain's parliamentary office, 31 July 2006

Hain, P. (2003a) 'Progressive Europeanism', speech at the Institute of Public Policy Research, 22 May, emailed to author by Peter Hain's parliamentary office, 31 July 2006

Hain, P. (2003b) 'The future of Europe', speech at the TUC congress, Trade Unions for Europe fringe, emailed to author by Peter Hain's parliamentary office, 31 July 2006

Haines, J. (1977) *The Politics of Power*. London: Jonathan Cape

Hannay, D. (2004) '1985–90, David Hannay', in A. Menon (ed.), *Britain and European Integration: Views from Within*. Oxford: Blackwell Publishing in association with Political Quarterly, pp. 19–21

Hari, J. (2004) 'The referendum will give pro-Europeans the chance to nail the Murdoch lies', *Independent*, 21 April, www.independent.co.uk/opinion/ commentators/johann-hari/the-referendum-will-give-proeuropeans-the-chance-to-nail-the-murdoch-lies-560676.html, last accessed 25 February 2009

Harmsen, R. and Spiering, M. (2004) 'Introduction: Euroscepticism and the evolution of European political debate', in R. Harmsen and M. Spiering (eds), *Euroscepticism: Party Politics, National Identity and European Integration*. Amsterdam and New York: Rodopi, pp. 13–35

Harris, R. (2007) *The Ghost*. London: Hutchinson

Haseler, S. (1996) *The English Tribe: Identity, Nation and Europe*. Basingstoke: Macmillan

Haseler, S. (2001) 'The case for a federal future', in I. Taylor, A. Mitchell, S. Haseler and G. Denton, *Federal Britain in a Federal Europe?* London: Federal Trust for Education and Research, pp. 51–96

Haskins, L. (2001) 'The benefits to business', in M. Rosenbaum (ed.), *Britain and Europe: The Choices We Face*. Oxford: Oxford University Press, pp. 49–56

Hay, C., Smith, N. J. and Watson, M. (2006) 'Beyond prospective accountancy: reassessing the case for British membership of the single currency comparatively', *British Journal of Politics and International Relations*, 8(1), pp. 101–21

Heclo, H. and Wildavsky, A. (1974) *The Private Government of Public Money: Community and Policy Inside British Politics*. Basingstoke: Macmillan

Henderson, D. (1998) 'The British Presidency of the EU and British European policy', discussion paper no. C7, Centre for European Integration Studies, Rheinische Friedrich Wilhelms-Universität Bonn

Hines, N. and Charter, D. (2009) 'Hoax EU sculpture by David Cerny sparks diplomatic spat', *Times* online, www.timesonline.co.uk/tol/news/world/europe/ article5517736.ece, last accessed 27 April 2009

HM Treasury (undated) 'EMU studies on membership of the single currency', http://webarchive.nationalarchives.gov.uk/+/http://www.hm-treasury.gov. uk/euro_assess03_studindex.htm, last accessed 3 September 2010

Holmes, M. (2002) 'Introduction', in M. Holmes (ed.), *The Eurosceptical Reader 2*. Basingstoke: Palgrave, pp. 1–4

Holmes, M. (undated) 'Bruges revisited', Bruges Group working paper no. 34, www.brugesgroup.com/mediacentre/index.live?article=92, last accessed 8 January 2009

Hopkin, J. and Wincott, D. (2006) 'New Labour, economic reform and the European social model', *British Journal of Politics and International Relations*, 8(1), pp. 50–68

Horolets, A. (2002) 'Uses of history in the Polish "European debate"', paper presented at the workshop on Interdisciplinary Comparative Cultural Politics, Ann Arbor, 5–10 May

Hoskinson.net (undated) Keyword analysis tool, http://seokeywordanalysis.com/ seotools/, last accessed 8 June 2006

Howard, M. and Paret, P. (eds and trans.) (1976) Carl von Clausewitz, *On War*. Princeton, NJ: Princeton University Press

Howarth, D. (1995) 'Discourse theory', in D. Marsh and G. Stoker (eds), *Theory and Methods in Political Science*. Basingstoke: Macmillan, pp. 115–33

Hughes, G. (2009) *Harold Wilson's Cold War: The Labour Government and East–West Politics, 1964–70*. London: Royal Historical Society/Boydell Press

Hughes, K. and Smith, E. (1998) 'New Labour – new Europe?', *International Affairs*, 74(1), pp. 93–104

Hutchison, D. (2009) 'The European Union and the press', in A. Charles (ed.),

Media in the Enlarged Europe: Politics, Policy and Industry. Bristol and Chicago, IL: Intellect/Chicago University Press, pp. 53–60

Hyman, P. (2005) *1 out of 10: From Downing Street Vision to Classroom Reality.* London: Vintage

Independent (2005) 'Once again, Mr Blair plays a different tune at home', http://findarticles.com/p/articles/mi_qn4158/is_20051222/ai_n15943698, last accessed 29 August 2008

Ipsos-MORI (2008) 'Political monitor, May', www.ipsos-mori.com/_assets/pdfs/may-2008-top-political.pdf, last accessed 7 August 2008

Jäger, S. (2006) 'Discourse and knowledge: theoretical and methodological aspects of a critical discourse and dispositive analysis', in R. Wodak and M. Meyer (eds), *Methods of Critical Discourse Analysis.* London, Thousand Oaks, CA, and New Delhi: Sage, pp. 32–62

James, S. and Opperman, K. (2009) 'Britain and the European Union', in T. Casey (ed.), *The Blair Legacy: Politics, Policy, Governance, and Foreign Affairs.* Basingstoke and New York: Palgrave Macmillan, pp. 285–98

Jay, D. (1980) *Change and Fortune: A Political Record.* London: Hutchinson

Jefferys, K. (1999) *Anthony Crosland: A New Biography.* London: Richard Cohen

Jenkins, K., ed. (1997) *The Postmodern History Reader.* London: Routledge

Jenkins, R. (1990) 'Foreword', in R. Mayne and J. Pinder, *Federal Union: The Pioneers.* Basingstoke: Macmillan, p. 8

Jenkins, S. (2007) *Thatcher and Sons: A Revolution in Three Acts.* London and New York: Penguin

Jones, B., Kavanagh, D., Moran, M. and Norton, P. (2007) *Politics UK*, 6th edn. Harlow: Pearson Education

Jones, D. M. and Smith, M. L. R. (2006) 'The commentariat and discourse failure: language and atrocity in cool Britannia', *International Affairs*, 82(6), pp. 1077–100

Jones, N. (1996) *Soundbites and Spin Doctors: How Politicians Manipulate the Media – and Vice Versa.* London: Indigo

Jones, N. (2000) *Sultans of Spin: The Media and the New Labour Government.* London: Orion

Jordan, A. (2006) 'Environmental policy', in I. Bache and A. Jordan (eds), *The Europeanization of British Politics.* Basingstoke: Palgrave Macmillan, pp. 231–47

Kaiser, W. (1996) *Using Europe, Abusing the Europeans: Britain and European Integration 1945–63.* Basingstoke: Macmillan

Kaiser, W. (2004) '"What alternative is open to us?": Britain', in W. Kaiser and J. Elvert (eds), *European Union Enlargement: A Comparative History.* New York and Abingdon: Routledge, pp. 9–30

Kampfner, J. (2004) *Blair's Wars.* London: Free Press

Kennedy, G. A. (trans.) (1991) Aristotle, *On Rhetoric: A Theory of Civic Discourse.* Oxford and New York: Oxford University Press

Kimber, R. (2008a) 'Results and analysis: general election 1 May 1997', www.psr.keele.ac.uk/area/uk/ge97/results.htm, last accessed 7 August 2008

Kimber, R. (2008b) 'Results and analysis: general election 7 June 2001', www.psr.keele.ac.uk/area/uk/e01/results.htm, last accessed 7 August 2008

Kimber R. (2008c) 'Results and analysis: general election 5 May 2005', www.psr.keele.ac.uk/area/uk/ge05/results.htm, last accessed 7 August 2008

Kimber, R. (2008d) 'Results and analysis: general election 5 July 1945', www.psr.keele.ac.uk/area/uk/ge45/results.htm, last accessed 7 August 2008

Kimber, R. (2008e) 'Turnout in general elections', www.psr.keele.ac.uk/area/uk/turnout.htm, last accessed 7 August 2008

Kimber, R. (2008f) 'UK members of the European Parliament 1999–2004', www.psr.keele.ac.uk/area/uk/meps.htm, last accessed 7 August 2008

Kimber, R. (2010) 'General election', www.politicsresources.net/area/uk/ge10/ ge10php, last accessed 1 September 2010

Kopecký, P. and Mudde, C. (2002) 'The two sides of Euroscepticism: party positions on European integration in East Central Europe', *European Union Politics*, 3(3), pp. 297–326

Kumar, K. (2003) *The Making of English National Identity*. Cambridge: Cambridge University Press

Labour Party (1997) 'Because Britain deserves better', general election manifesto, www.politicsresources.net/area/uk/man/lab97.htm, last accessed 19 November 2009

Langdridge, D. (2004) *Introduction to Research Methods and Data Analysis in Psychology*. Harlow: Pearson Education

Laughland, J. (1997) *The Tainted Source: The Undemocratic Origins of the European Idea*. London: Little, Brown

Lawrence, P. (2005) *Nationalism: History and Theory*. Harlow: Pearson Education

Leonard, D. and Leonard, M. (eds) (2002) *The Pro-European Reader*. Basingstoke: Palgrave

Lipinska, M. (2008) 'The Maastricht convergence criteria and optimal monetary policy for the EMU accession countries', European Central Bank working paper series no. 896, May, www.ecb.int/pub/pdf/scpwps/ecbwp896.pdf, last accessed 27 August 2008

Littlejohn, R. (2003) 'How dare Tony Blair call *us* unpatriotic', *Sun*, 3 June, p. 11

Lord, C. (2008) 'Two constitutionalisms? A comparison of British and French government attempts to justify the Constitutional Treaty', *Journal of European Public Policy*, 15(7), pp. 1001–18

Ludlow, P. (2002) 'Us or them? The meaning of Europe in British political discourse', in M. Malmborg and B. Stråth (eds), *The Meaning of Europe*. Oxford and New York: Berg, pp. 101–24

Macmillan, H. (1961) Address on the UK's application for membership to the European Communities, 31 July, www.ena.lu/, last accessed 3 March 2009

MacMillan, M. (2009) *The Uses and Abuses of History*. London: Profile Books

MacShane, D. (2006) Extract from Jean Monnet Annual Lecture, Hull University, 3 November, http://denismacshane-international.blogspot.com/2006_10_01_ archive.html, last accessed 11 May 2009

Malmborg, M. (2002) 'The dual appeal of "Europe" in Italy', in M. Malmborg, and B. Stråth (eds), *The Meaning of Europe*. Oxford and New York: Berg, pp. 51–75

Malmborg, M. and Stråth, B. (2002) 'Introduction: the national meanings of Europe', in M. Malmborg and B. Stråth (eds), *The Meaning of Europe*. Oxford and New York: Berg, pp. 1–25

Mandelson, P. (2002) *The Blair Revolution Revisited*. London: Politico's

Marquand, D. (1999) *The Progressive Dilemma: From Lloyd George to Blair*, 2nd edn. London: Phoenix Giant

McAllister, I. and Studlar, D. T. (2000) 'Conservative Euroscepticism and the Referendum Party in the 1997 British general election', *Party Politics*, 6(3), pp. 359–71

McInnes, C. J. (2002) *Spectator-Sport War: The West and Contemporary Conflict*. Boulder, CO: Lynne Rienner

Menéndez-Alarcón, A.V. (2004) *The Cultural Realm of European Integration: Social Representations in France, Spain, and the United Kingdom*. London and Westport, CT: Praeger

Menon, A. (2003) 'Britain and the Convention on the Future of Europe', *International Affairs*, 79(5), pp. 963–78

Menon, A. (2004) 'Conclusions: coping with change', in A. Menon (ed.), *Britain and European Integration: Views from Within*. Oxford: Blackwell Publishing in association with Political Quarterly, pp. 39–46

Meyer, C. (2006) *DC Confidential*. London: Phoenix

Miliband, D. (2007a) Speech, 'New diplomacy: challenges for foreign policy', 18 July, http:www.fco.gov.uk/en/newsroom/latest-news/?view=Speech&id=1892864, last accessed 30 April 2009

Miliband, D. (2007b) Wilberforce Lecture, 'Foundations of freedom: the promise of the new multilateralism', 21 November, http:www.fco.gov.uk/en/newsroom/latest-news/?view=Speech&id=9505008, last accessed 30 April 2009

Miliband, D. (2009a) Speech at the debate 'EU fit for purpose in a post 2009 global age', London School of Economics, 9 March, http:www.fco.gov.uk/en/newsroom/latest-news/?view=Speech&id=14672130, last accessed 30 April 2009

Miliband, D. (2009b) Speech at the Mansion House, 'Power dispersed, responsibility shared: Britain's role in building coalitions for change', 22 April, http:www.fco.gov.uk/en/newsroom/latest-news/?view=Speech&id=16747240, last accessed 30 April 2009

Milliken, J. (1999) 'The study of discourse in international relations', *European Journal of International Relations*, 5(2), pp. 225–54

Milward, A. S. (1992) *The European Rescue of the Nation-State*. London: Routledge

Morgan, D. (2003) 'Media coverage of the European Union', in M. Bond (ed.), *Europe, Parliament and the Media*. London: Federal Trust for Education and Research, pp. 35–54

Morgan, K. O. (1989) *Labour People: Leaders and Lieutenants: Hardie to Kinnock*. Oxford: Oxford University Press

Mullin, C. (2009) *A View from the Foothills: The Diaries of Chris Mullin*, ed. R. Winstone. London: Profile Books

Murakami, H. (2008) *What I Talk About When I Talk About Running*. London: Harvill Secker

National Policy Institute (2009) 'EU threat to the Union Jack and the national anthem', 19 November, www.nationalpolicyinstitute.org/2009/11/19/eu-threat-to-the-union-jack-and-national-anthem, last accessed 19 November 2009

NATO (1997) 'Founding Act on Mutual Relations, Cooperation and Security between NATO and the Russian Federation', Paris, 27 May, www.nato.int/docu/basictxt/fndact-a.htm, last accessed 10 April 2009

Naughtie, J. (2002) *The Rivals: Blair and Brown: The Intimate Story of a Political Marriage*. London: Fourth Estate

Nelson, T. E., Oxley, Z. M. and Clawson, R. A. (1997) 'Towards a psychology of framing effects', *Political Behaviour*, 19(3), pp. 221–46

Neuendorf, K. A. (2002) *The Content Analysis Guidebook*. London and Thousand Oaks, CA: Sage

Niblett, R. (2007) 'Choosing between America and Europe: a new context for British foreign policy', *International Affairs*, 83(4), pp. 627–41

Oborne, P. (1999) *Alastair Campbell: New Labour and the Rise of the Media Class*. London: Aurum Press

O'Donnell, C. M. and Whitman, R. G. (2007) 'European policy under Gordon Brown: perspectives on a future Prime Minister', *International Affairs*, 83(1), pp. 253–72

Opperman, K. (2008) 'Salience and sanctions: a principal-agent analysis of domestic win-sets in two-level games – the case of British European policy under the Blair governments', *Cambridge Review of International Affairs*, 21(2), pp. 179–97

Pascoe-Watson, G. (2007) 'No to a United States of Europe', *Sun*, 23 September, www.thesun.co.uk/sol/homepage/news/eu_referendum/article269097.ece, last accessed 3 August 2008

Paxman, J. (1999) *The English: A Portrait of a People*. London: Penguin

Pennings, P., Keman, H. and Kleinnijenhuis, J. (2006) *Doing Research in Political Science: An Introduction to Comparative Methods and Statistics*, 2nd edn. London, Thousand Oaks, CA, and New Delhi: Sage

Peston, R. (2005) *Brown's Britain*. London: Short Books

Phythian, M. (2008) 'From Clinton to Bush: New Labour, the USA and the Iraq War', in P. Corthorn and J. Davis (eds), *The British Labour Party and the Wider World: Domestic Politics, Internationalism and Foreign Policy*. London and New York: Tauris Academic Studies, pp. 209–26

Pine, M. (2007) *Harold Wilson and Europe: Pursuing Britain's Membership of the European Community*. London and New York: Tauris Academic Studies

Powell, J. (2008) *Great Hatred, Little Room: Making Peace in Northern Ireland*. London: Bodley Head

Prescott, J. (2008) *Prezza. My Story: Pulling No Punches*. London: Headline Review

Price, L. (2005) *The Spin Doctor's Diary: Inside Number Ten With New Labour*. London: Hodder and Stoughton

Price, L. (2007–8) 'Biography', www.lanceprice.co.uk/biography.htm, last accessed 26 August 2008

Prodi, R. (2002) 'Britain, Europe and the world', speech at the Saïd Business School, Oxford, 29 April, www.europaworld.org/week80/theeutheuk3502.htm, last accessed 20 January 2009

Pynchon, T. (2007) *Against the Day*. London: Vintage Books

Rasmussen, M.V. (2003) 'The history of a lesson: Versailles, Munich and the social construction of the past', *Review of International Studies*, 29(4), pp. 499–519

Rawnsley, A. (2001) *Servants of the People: The Inside Story of New Labour*. London and New York: Penguin

Rentoul, J. (1997) *Tony Blair*. London: Warner Books

Reuters (2008) 'Eiffel Tower to turn blue for French EU Presidency', www.reuters.com/article/worldNews/idUSL2066543720080620, last accessed 4 August 2008

Ricento, T. (2003) 'The discursive construction of Americanism', *Discourse and Society*, 14(5), pp. 611–37

Riddell, P. (2001) 'Blair as Prime Minister', in A. Seldon (ed.), *The Blair Effect: The Blair Government 1997–2001*. London: Little, Brown, pp. 21–40

Riddell, P. (2005) *The Unfulfilled Prime Minister: Tony Blair's Quest for a Legacy*. London: Politico's

Riishøj, S. (2007) 'Europeanization and Euroscepticism: experiences from Poland and the Czech Republic', *Nationalities Papers*, 35(3), pp. 503–35

Risse, T., Engelmann-Martin, D., Knopf, J. and Roscher, K. (1999) 'To euro or not to euro? The EMU and identity politics in the European Union', *European Journal of International Relations*, 5(2), pp. 147–87

Robbins, K. (1998) 'Britain and Europe: devolution and foreign policy', *International Affairs*, 74(1), pp. 105–18

Routledge, P. (1998) *Gordon Brown: The Biography*. London, Sydney and New York: Pocket Books

Rubin, J. (2005) *Haruki Murakami and the Music of Words*. London: Vintage Books

Savigny, H. (2007) 'Focus groups and political marketing: science and democracy as axiomatic?', *British Journal of Politics and International Relations*, 9(1), pp. 122–37

Schnapper, P. (2011) *British Political Parties and National Identity: A Changing Discourse*. Cambridge: Scholars Publishing

Scott, D. (2004) *Off Whitehall: A View from Downing Street by Tony Blair's Adviser*. London and New York: I. B. Tauris

Seldon, A. (2005) *Blair*. London: Free Press

Seldon, A., with Snowdon, P. and Collings, D. (2007) *Blair Unbound*. London: Simon and Schuster

Sherrington, P. (2006) 'Confronting Europe: UK political parties and the EU 2000–2005', *British Journal of Politics and International Relations*, 8(1), pp. 69–78

Shore, P. (2002) 'Separate ways', in M. Holmes (ed.), *The Eurosceptical Reader 2*. Basingstoke: Palgrave, pp. 227–37

Short, C. (2005) *An Honourable Deception? New Labour, Iraq, and the Misuse of Power*. London: Free Press

Smith, J. (2005) 'A missed opportunity? New Labour's European policy 1997–2005', *International Affairs*, 81(4), pp. 703–21

Sopel, J. (1995) *Tony Blair: The Moderniser*. London: Michael Joseph

Southgate, B. (2005) *What Is History For?* London and New York: Routledge

Sowemimo, M. (1999) 'Evaluating the success of the Labour government's European policy', *Journal of European Integration*, 21(4), pp. 343–68

Spiering, M. (2004) 'British Euroscepticism', in R. Harmsen and M. Spiering (eds), *Euroscepticism: Party Politics, National Identity and European Integration*. Amsterdam and New York: Rodopi, pp. 127–49

Stephens, P. (1997) *Politics and the Pound: The Tories, the Economy and Europe*. London: Papermac

Stephens, P. (2004) *Tony Blair: The Making of a World Leader*. London: Viking

Sweeney, M. (2009) 'Lebedev's London Evening Standard takeover confirmed', *Guardian* online, www.guardian.co.uk/media/2009/jan/21/alexander-lebedev-london-evening-standard, 21 January

Sylvester, R. (2004) 'Euroscepticism encourages Britain's dark streak of racism, says minister', www.telegraph.co.uk/news/uknews/1468846/Euroscepticism-encourages-Britains-dark-streak-of-racism-says-minister.html, last accessed 22 October 2008

Taggart, P. and Szczerbiak, A. (2001) 'Parties, positions and Europe: Euroscepticism in the EU candidate states of Central and Eastern Europe', Sussex European Institute working paper no. 46, OERN working paper no. 2, www.sussex.ac.uk/sei/documents/wp46.pdf, last accessed February 2003

Taggart, P. and Szczerbiak, A. (2002) 'The party politics of Euroscepticism in EU member and candidate states', Sussex European Institute working paper no. 51, OERN working paper no. 6, www.sussex.ac.uk/sei/documents/wp51.pdf, last accessed February 2003

Taggart, P. and Szczerbiak, A. (2003) 'Theorising party-based Euroscepticism: problems of definition, measurement and causality', Sussex European Institute working paper no. 69, EPERN working paper no. 12, www.sussex.ac.uk/sei/documents/wp69.pdf, last accessed September 2008

Taggart, P. and Szczerbiak, A. (2004) *Opposing Europe? The Comparative Party Politics of Euroscepticism*. Oxford: Oxford University Press

Taylor, S. (2009) 'Locating and conducting discourse analytic research', in

M. Wetherell, S. Taylor and S. J. Yates, *Discourse as Data: A Guide for Analysis*. London, Thousand Oaks, CA, and New Delhi: Sage, pp. 5–48

Temperton, P. (2001) *The UK and the Euro*. Chichester and New York: John Wiley and Sons

Thatcher, M. (1988) Speech to the College of Europe, 20 September, www.margaretthatcher.org/speeches/displaydocument.asp?docid=107332, last accessed 6 January 2009

Thatcher, M. (2003) *Statecraft: Strategies for a Changing World*. London: HarperCollins

This England (undated) Fontpage, www.thisengland.co.uk/index2.htm, last accessed 22 September 2008

Titscher, S., Meyer, M., Wodak, R. and Vetter, E. (2007) *Methods of Text and Discourse Analysis*, trans. B. Jenner. Los Angeles, CA, and London: Sage

Tomlinson, J. (2008) 'History as political rhetoric', *Political Studies Review*, 6(3), pp. 297–307

Tonge, J. (2009) 'Conclusion: the legacy of Tony Blair', in T. Casey (ed.), *The Blair Legacy: Politics, Policy, Governance, and Foreign Affairs*. Basingstoke and New York: Palgrave Macmillan, pp. 299–310

Toye, R. (2008) 'The Churchill syndrome: reputational entrepreneurship and the rhetoric of foreign policy since 1945', *British Journal of Politics and International Relations*, 10(3), pp. 364–78

Toynbee, P. and Walker, D. (2001) *Did Things Get Better? An Audit of New Labour's Successes and Failures*. London and New York: Penguin

UKIP (2005) 'We want our country back', general election manifesto, www.ukip.org/media/pdf/UKIPa4manifesto2005.pdf, last accessed 18 August 2006

UN (2002) Security Council Resolution 1441, http://daccessdds.un.org/doc/UNDOC/GEN/N02/682/26/PDF/N0268226.pdf?OpenElement, last accessed 24 April 2009

Updike, J. (1991a) 'Rabbit redux', in *A Rabbit Omnibus*. London: Quality Paperbacks Direct, pp. 179–414

Updike, J. (1991b) 'Rabbit is rich', in *A Rabbit Omnibus*. London: Quality Paperbacks Direct, pp. 415–700

Vickers, R. (2003) *The Labour Party and the World, Vol. 1: The Evolution of Labour's Foreign Policy 1900–51*. Manchester and New York: Manchester University Press

Vital, D. (1971) *The Making of British Foreign Policy*. London: George Allen and Unwin

Wæver, O. (1996) 'Discourse analysis as foreign policy theory: the case of Germany and Europe', November, www.ciaonet.org/wps/wao1, last accessed 12 August 2008

Wall, S. (2008) *A Stranger in Europe: Britain and the EU from Thatcher to Blair*. Oxford and New York: Oxford University Press

Wallace, W. (1977) *The Foreign Policy Process in Britain*, 2nd edn. London: Royal Institute of International Affairs

Wallace, W. (2005) 'The collapse of British foreign policy', *International Affairs*, 82(1), pp. 56–68

Waltz, K. (1979) *Theory of International Politics*. London: McGraw-Hill; New York: Random House; Reading, MA: Addison-Wesley

Watt, N. (2005) '"This is 2005 not 1945" – Blair attacks UKIP over budget deal', *Guardian*, 21 December, www.guardian.co.uk/politics/2005/dec/21/uk.eu, last accessed 29 August 2008

Weldon, T. D. (1953) *The Vocabulary of Politics: An Enquiry into the Use and Abuse of Language in the Making of Political Theories*. London: Penguin

Welsh, I. (2008) *Crime*. London: Jonathan Cape

Wheatcroft, G. (2005) *The Strange Death of Tory England*. London and New York: Allen Lane

White, M. (1994) 'Blair defines the new Labour', www.guardian.co.uk/politics/1994/oct/05/labour.uk, last accessed 20 January 2009

Whitman, R. (2005) 'No and after: options for Europe', *International Affairs*, 81(4), pp. 673–87

Wigg, G. (1972) *George Wigg*. London: Michael Joseph

Williams, M. (1972) *Inside Number Ten*. London: Weidenfeld and Nicolson

Williams, P. (2004) 'Who's making UK foreign policy?', *International Affairs*, 80(5), pp. 909–29

Williams, P. D. (2005) *British Foreign Policy Under New Labour, 1997–2005*. Basingstoke: Palgrave Macmillan

Wilson, H. (1967) Statement by Harold Wilson to the House of Commons on the United Kingdom's application for membership to the EC, 2 May, www.ena.lu, last accessed 3 March 2009

Wodak, R. (2009) *The Discourse of Politics in Action: Politics as Usual*. Basingstoke and New York: Palgrave Macmillan

Wodak, R., de Cilia, R., Reisigl, M. and Liebhart, K. (2003) *The Discursive Construction of National Identity*, trans. A. Hirsch and R. Mitten. Edinburgh: Edinburgh University Press

Worcester, R. and Mortimore, R. (1999) *Explaining Labour's Landslide*. London: Politico's

Wring, D. (2005) *The Politics of Marketing the Labour Party*. Basingstoke and New York: Palgrave Macmillan

Young, H. (1998) *This Blessed Plot: Britain and Europe from Churchill to Blair*. London: Macmillan

Young, H. (2008) *The Hugo Young Papers: Thirty Years of British Politics – Off the Record*. London and New York: Allen Lane

Young, J. W. (2003) 'Technological cooperation in Wilson's strategy for EEC entry', in O. J. Daddow (ed.), *Harold Wilson and European Integration: Britain's Second Application to Join the EEC*. London and Portland, OR: Frank Cass, pp. 95–114

Interviews

Philip Collins (Blair's chief speechwriter 2005–7), 10 October 2008

David Hill (Labour Party director of communications 1991–97 and 2003–7), 26 January 2009

Nicholas Jones (journalist), 7 January 2009

Sally Morgan (Number 10's director of political and government relations from 2001), 7 January 2009

Jonathan Powell (Blair's Downing Street chief of staff, 1997–2007), 10 September 2008

John Sawers (foreign affairs private secretary to Tony Blair 1999–2001 and political director of the Foreign Office 2003–7), 26 January 2009

Index